Next page: Louis Artan,
The Sea at Blankenberge
(detail). 1871. Canvas,
83.5 x 122.3 cm.
Museum voor Schone
Kunsten, Ghent (Photo by
H. Maertens).

The

ow

Countries

Arts and Society in Flanders

and the Netherlands

A Yearbook

1995-96

Published by the

Flemish-Netherlands Foundation 'Stichting Ons Erfdeel'

Contents

The

Richness of Imagination

Children's Books in the Netherlands

Jean Dulieu, *Paulus the Wood Gnome* (Paulus de boskabouter).

Alice, Pinocchio and Remi had long been world-famous when Dik Trom, born in 1892, was still sitting calmly facing backwards on his Dutch mule. His father regarded Dik as *'a special child, and that's for sure'*, but defying the village policeman remains the greatest claim to fame of this national hero created by C.J. Kieviet. Top Naeff's *School Idylls* (Schoolidyllen, 1900) was equally unsuccessful in achieving international standing, in spite of the painful death of its protagonist Jet van Maerle. And while *Afke's Ten* (Afke's tiental, 1903), the gripping story of the life of a Frisian working-class family recorded by the socialist Nienke van Hichtum through the mouth of her housemaid, briefly made it to the international top ten of books with a strong emotional impact, the bravery and tenacity of J.B. Schuil's *The Katjangs* (De Katjangs, 1912) remained a purely national affair.

Were the characters and situations in these books too 'Dutch' for young readers in France, Germany or England? Or was the problem that Dutch publishers in the first half of the twentieth century were fully occupied importing literary treasures from abroad? After the Second World War the situation gradually began to change. Annie Schmidt's *Bob and Jilly* (Jip en Janneke) and Jean Dulieu's *Paulus the Wood Gnome* (Paulus de bos-kabouter) were not yet completely ready for a 'grand tour', but the *Children on the Oregon Trail* (De kinderkaravaan, 1949) and *Avalanche!* (Lawines razen, 1954) by An Rutgers van der Loeff, or Miep Diekmann's *The Haunted Island* (De boten van Brakkeput, 1956) attracted worldwide attention on the back of the emerging ideas of brotherhood between nations. They were soon joined by Dick Bruna's colourful little books and the imaginative tales of Paul Biegel.

In recent years Dutch authors and illustrators have become firmly established figures in the international literary trade. In the words of the travel guides, the modern Dutch children's book is *'different, witty, innovative, courageous and also literary'*. A climate change has taken place in the Netherlands which has created room for experiments with language, imagery and imagination. The ghost of moral edification appears to have been laid for ever by the revolution in form. Children nowadays are brought up on a diet of exciting images and inspired words.

Naturally not all Dutch children's books are renewing and successful, but compared to their adult brothers and sisters writers such as Paul Biegel, Guus Kuijer, Annie Schmidt and Jan Terlouw perform extremely well. Their books are published in more than ten languages and enjoy high print runs; Anke de Vries, Rindert Kromhout and Harrie Geelen are well-loved by readers in Spain, Italy and Sweden. Dutch children's literature, once an unknown lowland terrain, now attracts the attention of large numbers of foreigners who want to see all these fine things for themselves. Specially for them, I have put together a brief travel guide describing the main tourist attractions, streets, statues and monuments.

Two monuments

On the finest and largest square in the Netherlands, in the heart of Amsterdam, our national monument towers above us. Annie M.G. Schmidt, who died in May 1995, was the 'true Queen of the Netherlands' (see *The Low Countries* 1994-95: 18-24), the author of innumerable verses, stories, musicals and radio plays on which every Dutch boy and girl was brought up. Her brain produced *Minnie* (Minoes, 1970), the schoolteacher who is actually a cat, as well as *Otje* (1980), the girl who, all by herself, takes on the might of bureaucracy, and Pluk, the boy who helps animals and children in need with his red breakdown lorry *(Pluk van de Petteflet,* 1971).

Wicked tongues claim that it was Annie Schmidt who turned the Dutch into a nation of drug-users and telephone box vandals, but this seems to be an exaggeration of the power of the sparkling-fresh children's verses she wrote in the fifties:

Nuff! I won't do what they say!
Not one more 'how d'you do?'
Or 'yes Miss Green' and 'yes Mr Grey'
Don't want to say those things all day …
Not ever again, it's really true!
I'll put my nose up in the air –
I won't say anything back, so there!

(Translated by Bev Jackson)

Annie M.G. Schmidt, *Bob and Jilly* (Jip en Janneke), drawn by Fiep Westendorp.

Her protest was more in the way of a naughty game, more a dream of freedom than an incitement to anarchy. Her contrariness – seen more than anything as a breath of fresh air following the suppression of the war years – is still able to stimulate the imagination of children and adults today, forty years later. Kings who refuse to take their medicine, princes who keep asking for chocolate or wander the streets in their nightclothes, and Mr Sweet, who washes his feet in the aquarium every Saturday, all evoke dreams of freedom and hope.

It was not only Annie Schmidt's ideas that went against the established order, but also her language. It was traditional but at the same time revolutionary, related to the old nursery rhymes and yet still understandable. Unusual rhyming couplets dance through her work together with exuberant neologisms. Schmidt took the dreams and longings of children seriously, set her face against the restricting bonds of edification and took every opportunity to poke fun at authority. When she was presented with the Hans Christian Andersen Award by Astrid Lindgren in 1988, it became clear how closely related these two ladies were and her work was able to begin its onward march once more.

A broad boulevard leads from the Annie Schmidt monument to Dick Bruna Square. Here we see a monument in red, green and blue in which Mondrian, Miro and Matisse can all be recognised. These colours betray Bruna's childish pleasure in simplicity. Although the spontaneity of his colour range is contained to some extent by the carefully drawn contour lines, the lack of perspective gives his figures a universal recognisability. Miffy, Peggy Piglet, Boris and Barbara, all drawn with big round heads and fat little bodies, with short arms and legs, appeal to the reader's feelings of endearment. They are pictograms representing a world in which a child can feel safe.

Bruna likes working for children because he feels a bond with them, *'because they are so direct, so honest and critical'*. His work has been translated into a host of languages and has found its way to every corner of the world. It contains more than seventy titles of which around fifty are continuously in print. Many of the illustrations have been given a second existence on bags, babies' bibs, calendars, cups, building blocks or pullovers. In Japan his work is so popular that special Bruna shops have been set up. Dick Bruna is a pictorial artist first and a writer second, but it would be difficult to find anyone among the reading public of the world who has not come across his work.

Dick Bruna, *Miffy* (Nijntje) (© Mercis BV. 1988).

Four statues

These two monuments are flanked by statues of rather more recent date. On Bruna's right hand stands Max Velthuijs, an artist from the early 1960s and the creator of picture books such as *The Boy and the Fish* (De jongen en de vis, 1978) and *Frog in Love* (Kikker is verliefd, 1989) which have sold more than one hundred and fifty thousand copies worldwide. His coloration and deceptive simplicity show his kinship with the CoBrA group of artists. His 'paintings' have become more subtle through the years, less heavily lined, and have acquired a greater emotionality. Frog, duck, fox, pig, hare and ele-

Max Velthuijs, two pages
of *Frog in Love* (Kikker is
verliefd, 1989).

Kikker kan bijna niet meer lopen!
Voorzichtig ondersteunt Eend hem en ze neemt hem mee naar haar
huis. Daar verzorgt ze hem liefdevol en geeft hem warme soep.
'O Kikker,' zegt ze. 'Je had wel dood kunnen vallen!
Wees toch voorzichtig, want ik houd zoveel van je.'
Als Kikker dat hoort, gaat zijn hart nog sneller kloppen dan ooit
tevoren en zijn gezicht wordt donkergroen.
'Eendje, ik houd ook zoveel van jou,' stottert hij.

Vanaf die dag zijn ze altijd bij elkaar en ze voelen
zich heel gelukkig. Een kikker en een eend – groen en wit.
Liefde kent geen grenzen.

Wim Hofman, *The Raft*
(Het vlot, 1988).

phant think and act like human beings, wrestling with serious issues such as
solidarity and friendship.

On the left stands Wim Hofman, a companion in coloration, childishness
and non-conformist thinking, and strongly inspired by the nonsense of
Edward Lear. His stories are full of the sound of the sea and everything associated with it: birds, fish, wind and waves, shells, the sky, islands and loneliness. The soberness of his descriptions gives his language enormous
power. Hofman also occupies a special position as a pictorial artist. His
colourful paintings and his pen-drawings often have a strongly alienating
character. There are chests that walk, run, fall, stumble; coats that fly and
houses that fall down. But there is also a recognisable reality in his work.
The Raft (Het vlot, 1988), which was inspired by Huckleberry Finn, tells
about the time after the War when everyone, including children, had to build
a new life. *A Good Hiding and Other Stories* (Straf en andere verhalen,
1985) portrays the loneliness of children living an unprotected existence.
His somewhat sombre view of life is tempered by the possibilities of the
dream and the magic of his language. In everything he does Hofman betrays
his origins as an island-dweller. Anyone wishing to participate in his imaginary world will have to wander around on his island for a little while.

Annie Schmidt Square is enhanced by statues of Paul Biegel and Tonke
Dragt. Both are richly gifted with Anglo-Saxon humour, fairy-tale images
and exotic fantasies.

Paul Biegel is the most outspoken representative of the Dutch fantasy
story. His is a world inhabited by dwarves, princesses, witches, robbers and
talking animals; his stories are set in ruined castles, noisy inns, dark woods,

Paul Biegel and illustrator
Carl Hollander
(Photo Letterkundig
Museum, The Hague).

dreamy gardens and lonely beaches. Against this fairy-tale backdrop, Biegel
attempts to solve the riddle of human existence. In addition to sparkling
reworkings of classics from world literature he also appealed to the imagination with the adventures of *The Little Captain* (De kleine kapitein, 1970),
who *'with legs wide apart and eyes on the horizon'* guides his ship over the
wild seas. Love which moves mountains and the universal urge for freedom
were given their own form in ingeniously composed masterpieces such as
The King of the Copper Mountains (Het sleutelkruid, 1964), *The Gardens of
Dorr* (De tuinen van Dorr, 1969), *The Ginger Princess* (De rode prinses,
1987) and *Night Tales* (Nachtverhaal, 1992).

   The author and illustrator Tonke Dragt has a predilection for the link
between the visible and the invisible, the puzzling and the obvious. The
philosophical slant of her themes evokes associations with the work of
Tolkien and makes her books attractive to readers who like a story they can
get their teeth into. Her thick novels have an 'invented' historical character
(e.g. *Letter for the King* – De brief voor de koning, 1962) or take place in the
future (as in *The Towers of February* – De torens van februari, 1986 or *The
Eyes of Tigers* – Ogen van tijgers, 1982). *On the Other Side of the Door*
(Aan de andere kant van de deur, 1992) is the first part of what together with
The Road to the Cell (De weg naar de cel) is intended to become a *magnum
opus* on the relativity of time and space, on the dimensions of music and
beauty, on semblance and reality, but also on the finding of one's own identity in the chaos of life's events.

Solidarity with children

Along the boulevard linking the two squares we find Guus Kuijer and Joke
van Leeuwen, two writers who are rarely mentioned in the same breath, but
who are nonetheless extremely well matched.

   It is difficult to say what Guus Kuijer derives his greatest fame from, his
liberating manner of writing or his essay collection *The Despised Child* (Het

Tonke Dragt's drawing for the cover of her book *The Secret of the Seventh Road* (De Zevensprong, 1966).

Guus Kuijer, as seen by one of his readers (Photo Letterkundig Museum, The Hague)

geminachte kind, 1980), in which he lambasts adults for losing their childishness. As an admirer and pupil of Annie Schmidt he takes the side of the children for whom he writes, both in his choice of themes and in his language. Titles such as *Daisy's New Head* (Met de poppen gooien, 1975), *Grown-Ups Should Be Made into Soup* (Grote mensen daar kan je beter soep van koken, 1976), *On Your Head in the Rubbish Bin* (Op je kop in de prullenbak, 1977) and *A Head Full of Macaroni* (Een hoofd vol macaroni, 1979) suggest an attack on the established order, but Kuijer never does this in a programmatic way. He regards solidarity with children as being more important than any message, because *'a writer must not seek to edify (…). Writing and edification get in each other's way. How can you write if you are trying to edify? Literature is exploring the terrain, not pointing the way.'*

The highpoint of his work is *Scratches on the Table Top* (Krassen in het tafelblad, 1978), a small, tightly structured novel about Madelief's grandmother, the mother of her mother whom she never knew. Since she died, Grandpa has been very lonely and Madelief spends a lot of time with him. Through this contact she discovers that her grandmother was never happy. She would have preferred to travel rather than spend her whole life shut away in a small village and in a house which she kept clean to drive away the boredom. Kuijer unfolds this complex situation with humour, sobriety and commitment.

Joke van Leeuwen possesses a comparable wilfulness. Like Hofman and

The Tjong Khing's drawing for the cover of Guus Kuijer's *Duck by Duck* (Eend voor eend, 1983).

Dragt, she writes and draws; text and drawings enter into a true dialogue in her work. Both are based on associations, of one emotion with another, of the literal with the figurative. Words and images are of absolutely equal importance. They are products of the same pen, often created in a flowing transition so that her drawings, notes, splotches, arrows and diagrams form a gateway to the winding paths behind the words. *The Story of Bobble Who Wanted to Become Rich* (Het verhaal van Bobbel die in een bakfiets woonde en rijk wilde worden, 1987) bears witness to a view of the world in which everything is in a continuous state of motion and there are always more possibilities than you think:

'There wasn't a lot of room for three people in the tricycle-van. But there was always a different view from the windows because they were always on the move. They were always on the move because they wanted to go somewhere that they could leave again afterwards, or because they were being chased away from somewhere else, or because they wanted to use the lights in the van. These only worked if someone was pedalling the tricycle.'

(Translated by Lance Salway)

The Boulevard of Broken Dreams

Crossing the boulevard linking Schmidt and Bruna is the Boulevard of Broken Dreams. It was built later than the other boulevard and offers an even stronger mix of fantasy and reality. On the left-hand side we find Willem Wilmink and Toon Tellegen, on the right the Heymans sisters, Imme Dros and Els Pelgrom. These authors each have their own highly individual character; what they share is their devotion to the word and their care for form.

The writing of Willem Wilmink, like Annie Schmidt an admirer of the eighteenth-century children's poet Hieronymus van Alphen, is very firmly anchored in the world of the child. The inside of the child's soul, the emotions and fears of children, are explored in an outside world which is quite contemporary and which is subjected to a critical examination. His rhyming verse is highly suited to a musical interpretation, e.g. *That Happens to Everyone* (Dat overkomt iedereen wel, 1973) and *I Understand It* (Ik snap het, 1993). Together with Hans Dorrestijn, Karel Eykman, Ries Moonen and Fetze Pijlman he set up a writers' collective in the 1970s; for these writers poetry is not *'the most individual expression of the most individual emotion'* but is a form of emotional socialism, of protest against social injustice and of indignation at the suppression of children. In the same spirit they wrote television screenplays such as *De Stratemakeropzeeshow* (televised in the seventies) and the *J.J. de Bom-show, voorheen de kindervriend* (in the eighties), in which children were consoled and taboos were broken.

Willem Wilmink, drawn by Waldemar Post (Photo Letterkundig Museum, The Hague).

Toon Tellegen introduced a new note into the ways of the imagination. His ultra-short, enigmatic animal tales in *Not a Day Passed* (Er ging geen dag voorbij, 1984), *When Nobody Had Anything to Do* (Toen niemand iets te doen had, 1987), *Slowly, as Fast as They Could* (Langzaam, zo snel als zij konden, 1989) have a pronounced poetic and sometimes absurd character. His animals defy the laws of biology whilst at the same time remaining faithful to them. The nightingale sings his song and the toad puffs up as he should, but squirrels write letters or drink cups of tea with ants and elephants. The animals behave as people and animals at the same time. In a non-existent habitat of woodland, river, desert and mountains whose dimensions are impossible to determine, they occupy themselves with the remarkable activity known as life. They write letters, organise parties, sit in the sun, think their thoughts and hold more or less coherent conversations. There is a general atmosphere of contentment in which vague longings now and again raise their heads. Tellegen's literary wanderings are melancholy and poetic in tone, but not inaccessible. They are briefly beautiful, but you never know precisely how long they will keep it up and in which direction they will go.

On the right-hand side of the boulevard the sisters Margriet and Annemie Heymans demonstrate their special talents. Both are trained in the theory and practice of art. Both write and draw, individually and together. *The Princess in the Kitchen Garden* (De prinses in de moestuin, 1991) is to date the high-spot of their collaboration. It is a moving and remarkable picture story about loss and standing up for yourself, about love and being lost, about seeking and finding. Since Mummy died, Hanna and Lutje Matte have lived alone with their father in the big house with the garden. Because

Daddy is so sad, he buries himself in paperwork and Hanna has to take care of everything. This makes her so cross and unhappy that she hides in Mummy's kitchen garden; Lutje Matte compensates for his sadness by dreaming about Princess Rosa. Until one night a great storm brings these three lonely people together and they are able to make a new beginning. The left-hand pages were drawn and painted by Margriet, with Annemie doing the right-hand pages. All the illustrations, both coloured and black-and-white, portray the nightmares and uncertainties with which the characters in this story wrestle.

Not far away on this boulevard stands *Annelie in the Depths of the Night* (Annetje Lie in het holst van de Nacht, 1988) by Imme Dros, in some respects a forerunner to *The Princess in the Kitchen Garden.* Here again we are introduced to a fantastic dream world in which dream and reality are in conflict. Annelie's father takes her to stay with her grandmother. Annelie doesn't know why and begins to worry. Her grandmother sings horrible songs, songs about sunlight that goes down in the West and about a Giant with a Cat's Mouth. No-one will tell her where her mother is nor how long she has to stay with her grandmother. *'Just for a little while'* could be a very long time, because grandma is already busy knitting a winter pullover. In the depths of the night she meets the friendly moon, the Frock Woman, the Mouse King and the scary Snatchweed Harry, who tries to tempt her into the water. The story is at least as fascinating as the detailed and wonderful drawings of Margriet Heymans.

The Journeys of the Clever Man (De reizen van de slimme man, 1988) is written for older children. It combines a richness of narrative forms with an ability to empathise with adolescents. Niels moves from an upstairs flat in Amsterdam to a luxury villa in the wealthy village of Wassenaar. At the same time he travels back to the past, to the time when Mr Frank told him the stories of the Odyssey, stories which teem with adventure and quests. And finally there is a journey through the language, a quest to find the words which will enable Niels to express his feelings and learn to comprehend the confusing world around him.

A highpoint in Dutch children's literature, and one which is held up as a symbol of the climate change in Dutch children's and youth literature, is *Little Sophie and Lanky Flop* (Kleine Sofie en Lange Wapper, 1984) by Els Pelgrom. In 1985 this book, which is often referred to as a 'classic', received both the *Gouden Griffel* (Golden Pencil) award for the author of the best children's book and the *Gouden Penseel* (Golden Brush) award for illustrator The Tjong Khing. The basis of this richly illustrated book is the story of a mortally ill girl who is given free rein for her desires in her delirious dreams. Together with her favourite doll, her teddy bear and the tabby cat she goes off at night in search of *'what can be bought in life'*. As with Dante, this quest ends in a tableau of life in which poverty, injustice and hypocrisy engage in battle with friendship, love and security. It is a moving story which can be enjoyed by children and adults at various levels.

The Elephant Mountain (De Olifantsberg, 1985) and *The Party that Never Began* (Het onbegonnen feest, 1987) form a chapter apart in Pelgrom's oeuvre. They are fantasy stories in which a varied collection of animals expound their philosophy of life while gathered on an Italian mountainside. *'If you're thirsty, there is water',* says Flemish Jay, or *'People who fly see*

more'. While awaiting things to come, Marten, Squirrel, Ram and Toad form a tight-knit alliance in which there is a place for everyone's idiosyncrasies and needs.

Other breathtaking works include *The Winter when Time Was Frozen* (De kinderen van het Achtste Woud, 1977) and *The Acorn Eaters* (De eikelvreters, 1989), two books in which it is harsh reality which is recounted rather than the world of dreams. The first book sketches life on a farm in a remote corner of the Netherlands during the Second World War. The fate of the Jews and the permanent fear of the Nazi occupiers are particularly well-illustrated themes. The second book tells of the poverty and the harrowing contrast between rich and poor, power and powerlessness in southern Spain shortly after the Spanish Civil War. Both books offer a socially committed portrayal of historical moments in time.

The two great boulevards are linked by a fascinating network of small and large streets, woodland paths and leafy lanes where still more talent is burgeoning: Ienne Biemans, Sjoerd Kuyper, Wouter Klootwijk, Mensje van Keulen, Peter van Gestel, Veronica Hazelhoff, Hans Hagen, Rita Törnqvist, Lydia Rood, Simone Schell or Anne Vegter. This talent is characterised by its great involvement with the fantasies, emotions and reality of children, in combination with a wealth of images and narrative structures. For these authors, communication is more important than edification, and form more interesting than message; and on the basis of this view they play with words and images. Ted van Lieshout and Harrie Geelen have their own role in these games, experimenting not only with language and genres but also with

The Tjong Khing's drawing for the cover of Els Pelgrom's *Little Sophie and Lanky Flop* (Kleine Sofie en Lange Wapper, 1984).

visual techniques. But through all their expressiveness they display a great understanding for the child who has to grow up in a wicked outside world.

The change in the climate of Dutch children's literature has perhaps been best expressed by the critic, essayist and writer Jacq Vogelaar:

'What we read, and especially how we read, will have a lot to do with our first acquaintance with books; everyone can talk about this from their own experience ... There are authors who remain faithful to the world of children's books all their lives and who do not forget what it is like to be a child. If young and adult readers have so much in common, why is this not taken seriously? Beside the differences, there is a great deal of correspondence in the reading world of youth books and literature, including in a qualitative sense.'

His plea for children's literature not to be regarded any longer as an appendage to 'real' literature, but as a crucial part of it, will give a boost to publishers, authors, critics and academics who labour to turn out artistic and literary products of high quality for children.

JOKE LINDERS
Translated by Julian Ross.

FURTHER READING

LINDERS, JOKE and MARITA DE STERCK, *Nice to Meet You. A Companion to Dutch & Flemish Children's Literature.* Amsterdam / Antwerp, 1993.

Quite a lot of Dutch children's books have been translated into English. The following is only a selection of titles mentioned in the above article.

BIEGEL, PAUL, *The Little Captain.* London, 1971.

BIEGEL, PAUL, *The King of the Copper Mountains.* London, 1971.

BIEGEL, PAUL, *The Gardens of Dorr* (English version by Gillian Hume & Paul Biegel). London, 1975.

BRUNA, DICK, *Miffy.* London, 1991.

DRAGT, TONKE, *The Towers of February.* New York, date unknown.

DROS, IMME, *Annelie in the Depths of the Night* (Tr. Arnold & Erica Pomerans). London, 1991.

DROS, IMME, *The Journeys of the Clever Man* (Tr. Lance Salway). Woodchester / Perth, 1992.

HEYMANS, MARGRIET & ANNEMIE, *The Princess in the Kitchen Garden.* London, 1992.

HOFMAN, WIM, *A Good Hiding and Other Stories* (Tr. Lance Salway). Woodchester, 1991.

KUIJER, GUUS, *Daisy's New Head* (Tr. Patricia Crampton). Harmondsworth, 1980.

LEEUWEN, JOKE VAN, *The Story of Bobble Who Wanted to Become Rich* (Tr. Lance Salway). Woodchester, 1990.

LIESHOUT, TED VAN, *The Dearest Boy of the World* (Tr. Lance Salway). Woodchester, 1990.

PELGROM, ELS, *The Acorn Eaters* (Tr. Johanna H. & Johanna W. Prins). New York, 1994.

PELGROM, ELS, *The Winter when Time Was Frozen* (Tr. Marijke & Raphael Rudnik). New York, 1980.

PELGROM, ELS, *Little Sophie and Lanky Flop* (Tr. Arnold Pomerans). London, 1987.

SCHMIDT, ANNIE M.G., *Minnie* (Tr. Lance Salway). Woodchester, 1992.

VELTHUIJS, MAX, *Frog in Love* (Tr. Anthea Bell). Toronto, 1989.

he

Jerusalem of the West

Jews and Goyim in Antwerp

The first official document to mention the Jewish community in Antwerp, the 1261 will of Duke Henry III of Brabant, was concerned with the expulsion of the Jews from his lands. When his widow, Duchess Adelheid, consulted Thomas Aquinas about this matter, the famous theologian replied that it would be wrong to convert Jewish children by force, as this infringed the divine and natural rights of their fathers, but that it was perfectly all right to increase taxes on the Jews, since most of their money derived from usury. This double-edged advice would govern the relationship between the Antwerp authorities and the Jews for some considerable time; but even this uneasy and unfair arrangement was not to last. In 1348 the Jews of Antwerp and other major cities were accused of poisoning the wells and were harshly punished for this, many of them being *'hanged, burned at the stake, beaten to death or drowned'*, while in 1370 the Jews of Brussels were accused of stealing and desecrating the sacred host and were persecuted accordingly. Their synagogue was destroyed and a chapel commemorating the 'Miracle of the Holy Sacrament' built on the site; and the city's cathedral still contains the stained glass windows which showed the illiterate Christian faithful how the Jews stabbed the consecrated wafer, from which the Blood of Christ then began to flow.

After all this, it was almost 150 years before there was any further sign of Jewish life in the Antwerp area. However, the expulsion of the Jews from Spain and Portugal in 1492 and 1497 brought a new wave of immigration. These Sephardic Jews – merchants, scientists and, above all, diamond traders – arrived in the Low Countries at exactly the wrong moment, for they became caught up in the increasingly bitter strife between the Catholic authorities, religious and secular, and their Neo-Baptist and Calvinist enemies. It was only natural that many Jews, having already experienced the ruthless intolerance of the Roman Catholic Church, should share the feelings of the 'heretics'. Consequently, when the mainly Calvinist city of Antwerp was recaptured by the Spanish army in 1585, most of its Jews followed their fellow citizens into exile and joined the Jewish communities in Amsterdam and other northern cities. Of the few who stayed behind most were Marranos, Jews who pretended to have converted to Christianity but

The burning of Jews, as pictured in a fourteenth-century miniature from Tournai (Koninklijke Bibliotheek, Brussels).

still tried to observe the Jewish feasts in the utmost secrecy.

A long battle ensued between the intransigent Spanish authorities and the Inquisition on the one hand, and on the other the moderate city fathers of Antwerp, who sought to protect the Jews as useful contributors to the city's economy. As early as the seventeenth century, Archduke Leopold William tried to obtain the King's permission for the Jews to practise their faith openly, and even to build a synagogue. As one might expect, permission was refused and the informers of the Holy Inquisition redoubled their zeal in an attempt to flush out all the remaining Jews; as in most West European countries, Antwerp's Jews had to wait for the Enlightenment and the new attitude of toleration to be officially accepted as equal citizens and gradually win their religious freedom. In the Austrian Netherlands this emancipation was initiated and supported by the Emperor Joseph II who decreed in 1786 that the Jews should be treated in all respects as equal citizens, including the right to practise their religion and build their own places of worship. The reign of Napoleon saw the first attempt to organise and control the Jewish citizens of Belgium by means of a representative body of religious leaders in the so-called 'Consistoire'. At last the Jews had won the right to build synagogues and to participate in politics and in civic life, even if only fifty families were registered in Antwerp.

At the end of the nineteenth century there was a third wave of immigration, which was to turn Antwerp into the 'Jerusalem of the West'; these were East European Jews, Ashkenazim fleeing the pogroms between 1885 and 1905, who passed through the port of Antwerp in transit to the United States and Canada. A surprising number of them, however, settled in the city and developed its flourishing diamond trade and industry. A few figures: between 1880 and 1901 the Jewish community increased from 1,000 to 8,000; by 1913 this figure had already risen to 13,000 and by 1927 to 35,500; and between 1933 and 1940, largely due to the antisemitic policies of the Nazis in Germany and Austria, the Jewish population rose to 55,000.

Between 80 and 85% of them were involved in the diamond trade, the others being engaged in retailing and other service industries and in religious occupations. Not surprisingly, since its members ranged from ardent Zionists to equally staunch anti-Zionists, from atheists to the ultra-Orthodox, and from Communists to Conservatives, the Jewish community contained more rival organisations, from sports clubs to political parties, than the Flemish community around it. All the Flemish political parties (except, of course, for the Catholic party and later the small but vocal fascist groups) had active and often prominent Jewish members, among them the Conservative Louis Franck, the Flemish Nationalist Maarten Rudelsheim and the Socialist Sam Emmerik; during the Second World War this proved a significant factor for the survival of a large number of Jews. All the rival Jewish groups had their own newspapers and journals, in Yiddish, Hebrew, Dutch, French and a variety of Eastern European languages. Theirs was an overwhelmingly liberal and secular community; about 85% of the children attended non-Jewish schools and hence had many non-Jewish friends and acquaintances – a fact which would prove vitally important in the years to come. The people of Antwerp, from the Catholics to the large Flemish Nationalist organisations – and Antwerp had been a bastion of Flemish Nationalism since the end of the nineteenth century – were generally tolerant of the Jewish presence and even took part in demonstrations of solidarity with the oppressed Jewry of Nazi Germany. Genuine antisemitism was to be found, however, in certain relatively small fascist organisations which drew their inspiration from their German political friends.

On May 10, 1940, the German invasion of Belgium changed all this, although it was more than a year before ss Major Ehlers, head of the *Sicherheitsdienst,* dared to impose the wearing of the yellow Star of David; as he explained in several letters to an impatient Heinrich Himmler, he feared a possible hostile reaction by the non-Jewish population. We need not discuss the mechanism of the Holocaust – the division of the Jews into various categories and the installation of a *Judenrat,* a council of distinguished Jewish citizens whose task it was to organise what remained of Jewish education and social services and to provide a monthly list of those to be deported to the so-called work camps in the East. Two points, however, should be highlighted: first, of the more than 50,000 Jews trapped in occupied Belgium, only 42,000 were officially registered; and second, only 25,600 were deported to the death camps. Of the latter, a mere 1,244 returned. Some 25,000 Jews were either hidden or smuggled out of the country – the result of a remarkable collaboration between the elaborate network of Catholic institutions and the Communist-dominated Resistance. A

significant number of Jews, mostly political refugees from the Third Reich or Nazi-occupied Eastern Europe, were actively involved in the armed struggle and eventually even formed their own military unit within the national coalition of resistance groups. Despite their heroism, however, by the end of the Second World War the flourishing Jewish community in Antwerp had been virtually destroyed.

Yet as early as 1946 the survivors were already starting to rebuild the economic and social structure of Jewish life in the city. But the make-up of Antwerp's Jewish community had been radically changed by the huge influx of Orthodox, and especially Hassidic, families from Poland and Hungary. These Hassidic Jews, themselves divided into seven distinct sects, found employment in the diamond trade and succeeded in making Antwerp once again one of the world's leading diamond centres, while at the same time they established their own religious and social ghetto, almost as if they were recreating an Eastern European *shtetl* (Yiddish for 'small town') in the heart of a twentieth-century city. But it is more complicated than that: although the great majority of their children attend Jewish schools, and apart from the Diamond Exchange they have virtually no contact with the non-Jewish population, these Hassidim contribute some 5% of Belgium's GNP and provide employment for around 20,000 of their non-Jewish fellow citizens. These facts are essential to an understanding of the relationship between the Antwerp Jews and the racists of the Far Right. Although the Hassidim represent not more than 40% of the 15-18,000 Jews in Antwerp, their religious and economic influence appears to be much greater than their numbers would suggest; more so than is the case with their fellow Hassidim (and kinsmen) in Williamsburg, Bne Brak or Mea Shearim, who are much less involved with other Jews. Those of Antwerp's Jews who do not belong to the Hassidic and Orthodox communities consider themselves traditionalists. There is not a single Reform synagogue among the twenty-three temples in the city, but there are at least fifteen *Beith Midrash* (houses of prayer and study, mainly strict Orthodox or Hassidic). On Fridays and Saturdays all these places of worship are filled with Jewish men singing and praying loudly, while the women participate in the ceremonies from their separate galleries above and around the central area of the synagogue.

It is safe to say that, historically, the relationship between the Jewish community of Antwerp and their overwhelmingly non-Jewish, nominally 'Christian' (i.e. Roman Catholic) fellow citizens has largely been defined by *money*: to the extent that the Jews were economically useful to the city fathers and the local bourgeoisie, they were protected from the Inquisition and the Spanish authorities. After their emancipation at the end of the eighteenth century their influential position in civic society, and consequently their safety, increased with their financial and economic power, especially in the flourishing diamond industry and trade. They currently enjoy total religious freedom and maintain excellent relations with the authorities and the major political parties.

Since about 1980, however, two new factors have emerged which might in the long run threaten the almost idyllic situation in the 'Jerusalem of the West', as the orthodox Jews call Antwerp. The first of these is the gradual decline of the diamond business worldwide and the increasing ascendancy of the Indian dealers, against whose low production costs (read: wages) the traditional Antwerp houses cannot possibly compete. As a result, almost half the diamond trade is no longer controlled by the Jews, who have thus become more vulnerable economically. The second factor is even more alarming: because of a number of economic, political and ethnic developments, the extreme right-wing Vlaams Blok (Flemish Bloc) party is now the largest political force in Antwerp. An amalgam of nationalistic separatists, outright fascists and militant xenophobes, the party has profited from the combination of economic decline and large-scale immigration by non-European workers and their families, mainly from Morocco and Turkey. Realising that popular animosity can much more easily be directed at the Moroccans and Turks than at the respectable and socially influential Jews, the Vlaams Blok leaders have refrained from any openly antisemitic comments; though some of their more zealous supporters in other cities have distributed leaflets promoting a country 'free of Arabs and Jews' alike. Of course, anyone who reads a Belgian newspaper is aware of the regular contacts between Vlaams Blok leaders and internationally notorious antisemites and neo-Nazis, and the participation of their youth organisation in neo-fascist summer camps and similar activities.

Their combination of open aggression against non-Europeans with a display of goodwill towards the Jews has confused and divided the Antwerp Jewish community. This is quite clear from the discussion pages of the Antwerp-based *Belgisch Israelitisch Weekblad* (Belgian Jewish Weekly), edited by Louis Davids. Whereas Mr Davids displays an attitude of guarded vigilance towards the Vlaams Blok and carefully avoids mentioning them in his paper, other Jewish community leaders such as the actively anti-fascist Senator Fred Erdman disagree and say so in no uncertain terms. The issue is: should the Jewish community lead the battle against the resurgence of fascism (Erdman) or ignore it as far as possible and hope it will go away (Davids)? As things stand now, it is legitimate to wonder whether we are witnessing a dangerous replay of the attitude adopted by many European

(Photo by Stephan Vanfleteren).

25

Jews in the thirties. If so, the current prolonged economic stagnation and the recession in the diamond trade could easily and rapidly erode the foundations of the present tolerant attitude to the Jews of Antwerp. While the present sizeable right-wing vote (around 25% in Antwerp) indicates a popular belief that the socio-economic crisis could be solved by deporting the non-European migrant labour force, who can guarantee that once the Jews have lost some of their grip on a major section of the city's employment opportunities they will not become the next target of the ultra-nationalists? And why should a party historically and internationally linked with antisemitism, and which denies that the Holocaust ever happened, hesitate to adopt such a strategy, once the Jews are no longer the socio-economic sacred cows they once were? There is an increasingly thin line between current anti-Moroccan racism and a new outburst of old-fashioned antisemitism; and this could be further eroded by a growing impatience with the policies of Israel, which the Antwerp Jewish community almost unquestioningly defends.

Despite popular belief, history never repeats itself; so the next wave of anti-Jewish intolerance will most probably not be comparable to past experiences. At present it looks as if any such occurrence can still be avoided; but the potential for it is definitely there, much more so than ten years ago. How the Antwerp community as a whole reacts to this very real threat will be crucial for its own survival as a centre of humanism and culture in a world which seems to be sliding into ever deeper ethical, political and social confusion.

LUDO ABICHT

FURTHER READING

ABICHT, LUDO, *De joden van Antwerpen*. Brussels, 1987.

BOK, WILLY, 'Considérations sur les estimations quantitatives de la population juive en Belgique', in: *La Vie Juive dans l'Europe Contemporaine*. Brussels, 1985.

BRACHFELD, SYLVAIN, *Uw Joodse buurman*. Antwerp, 1975.

Comité ter Verdediging van de rechten der Joden, *Het IIIde Rijk en de Joden. Eenige Documenten*. Antwerpen, 1933.

GERARD, JO, *Ces juifs qui firent la Belgique*. Bruxelles, 1990.

GUTWIRTH, JACQUES, *Vie juive traditionelle; Ethnologie d'une communauté hassidique*. Paris, 1980.

HELLER, CLARA, *Jaren van Angst. Het ware verhaal van Clara Heller*. Antwerp, 1992.

KLARSFELD, SERGE and MAXIME STEINBERG, *Die Endlösung der Judenfrage in Belgien*. New York, date unknown.

REISZ, MATTHEW, *Europe's Jewish Quarters*. London, 1991.

SCHMIDT, EPHRAÏM, *L'histoire des juifs à Anvers*. Antwerp, 1969.

STEINBERG, MAXIME, *L'étoile et le fusil. La traque des juifs*. Brussels, 1986, 2 vols.

STEINBERG, MAXIME, *De ogen van het monster. Volkerenmoord dag in dag uit*. Antwerp – Baarn, 1992.

STENGERS, J., *Les Juifs dans les Pays-Bas au Moyen-Age*. Brussels, 1950.

ULLMAN, S., *Histoire des Juifs en Belgique jusqu'au 18e siècle*. Antwerp, 1927.

ULLMAN, S., *Histoire des Juifs en Belgique jusqu'au 19e Siècle*. Antwerp, date unknown.

rom

'Red and Black' to 'Red and Blue'

Twenty-Five Years of Dutch Politics

The Netherlands in the post-war period: 1945-1965

A quarter of a century ago, no Dutch citizen could have imagined that a political alliance between social democrats and right-wing liberals would ever be possible in the Netherlands. Not only because such an alliance would not have had a majority in Parliament, but because the political strategy of both groups was to treat each other as the opposite ends of the left-right political spectrum and thus force the centre parties – the three confessional parties active at the time – to opt for either a right-of-centre (liberal) or a left-wing (social democrat) coalition partner.

This strategy was launched in the 1950s by the conservative-liberal VVD (People's Party for Freedom and Democracy – *Volkspartij voor Vrijheid en Democratie*) and enthusiastically embraced in the mid-sixties by the social democratic PvdA (Labour Party – *Partij van de Arbeid*). That the PvdA should have adopted this 'polarisation strategy' was in fact slightly paradoxical: on the one hand it forced the largest of the three confessional parties, the KVP (Catholic People's Party – *Katholieke Volkspartij*), into a long-term marriage with the political left, while on the other hand it was apparent that collaboration between the PvdA and the KVP was not what it had been and that the era of a more or less 'natural' alliance between these two parties was past. The polarisation was also a reaction by the PvdA to the social changes which began to manifest themselves in the Netherlands in the 1960s. To gain a clear picture of social and political developments over the last 25 years, however – including the creation in 1994 of a 'purple' (or, more accurately, a 'red and blue') coalition – it will first be necessary to understand a few important post-war developments in the Netherlands.

Dutch society had been shattered by the Second World War. For centuries, war and enemy occupation were problems which had passed it by, with the exception of the less than strikingly successful Napoleonic regime (1810-1813). Although a great deal of reflection and debate on issues of political and social reform took place in intellectual circles during the German Occupation, the majority of the population and their political representatives were more inclined to see the Occupation as a violation of

their history and as a terrible, but isolated, interlude. Above all, the people longed for a return to their pre-war calm and stability. The serious damage which had been done to a number of key commercial and industrial economic centres meant there was also a strong physical need for reconstruction. Quite simply, people had to roll up their sleeves and start putting things back to rights.

There were two complicating factors here. The first was that, while the Netherlands wished to return to the old order, its most important colony, Indonesia, did not. In the first five post-war years, accordingly, a great deal of attention, not to mention substantial financial and other resources, had to be devoted to this issue. Moreover, there was the fear of a sharp drop in prosperity in the Netherlands as a result of the loss of the Dutch East Indies – a concern which later proved unfounded. Its uncooperative attitude to decolonisation – even after 1950 – however, meant that the Netherlands lost a number of economic opportunities which an independent Indonesia would probably have offered under other circumstances.

The second complicating factor was that it was not really possible to proceed from the position in which the Netherlands had found itself in 1940. Not only would effort be needed to build economic recovery – with intensive state intervention – but there was also a general awareness that the still highly agricultural economy would have to embark on a radical industrialisation programme. Additionally, however, there was a genuine realisation that, measured in terms of the level and quality of social security and public services (in particular housing), the Netherlands lagged well behind its neighbours.

The country undeniably recovered at a rapid rate after 1945. Prosperity increased reasonably quickly and became relatively widespread in the population as a whole. Industry underwent major development and was more widely distributed across the country. Agriculture was not eclipsed by this development, but grew in parallel to industry. The same applied to trade, particularly once the German market had recovered and opened up to exports. Rising prosperity brought rapid urbanisation, leading not only to

Council offices and houses in Leeuwarden. These were designed by Abe Bonnema and built between 1972 and 1975.

the growth of existing towns, but also to increasing urbanisation of the formerly largely empty countryside. The general level of education of the population increased, and with it their physical and mental mobility. From the 1950s onwards public services also began to develop: not only education, but also housing and health care. At least as important was the start made in 1947 on the creation of an extensive and highly developed social security system to cushion the effects of unemployment, illness and disability, old age and the costs of health care. Finally, there was a broad consensus that the Netherlands needed to reappraise its position on the international stage; from being a self-satisfied country which cherished its neutrality, the Netherlands became a member of a range of international alliances such as the UN, NATO and the various European Communities, in which its enthusiasm and energy were for many years 'rewarded' with a disproportionate level of influence.

All these changes were supported and actively encouraged by an alliance of two political parties who were also each other's great rivals: the Catholic People's Party (KVP) and the social democratic PvdA. Although these two parties had little affection for one another, their interests and aspirations to some extent coincided: both had a desire to bring about social and economic recovery and modernisation in the country. They were less inclined to cling to pre-war political traditions and codes of conduct than the 'old' liberal party (VVD) and the Protestant confessional parties, the ARP (Anti-Revolutionary Party – *Anti-Revolutionaire Partij*) and CHU (Christian Historical Union – *Christelijke Historische Unie*). Until 1958 this alliance took the form of permanent collaboration in a government coalition between the 'black' KVP and the 'red' PvdA (the 'Roman-red' alliance). Thereafter the KVP became the governing party, with short interruptions, preferably in alliance with the liberals (VVD). The KVP's rivalry with the PvdA continued, however, along with a secret preference for social democracy – if not for collaboration, then in any event for its aspirations. The KVP wished to demonstrate that it was at least as concerned about social justice as the PvdA; and, with the PvdA in opposition, the KVP performed well – better, in fact, than the social democrats would probably have wished.

Almost unnoticed amidst all these developments, the socio-cultural nature of society was changing. A population which had formerly been compartmentalised along religious and social dividing lines gradually began to open up. The shared oppression of the German Occupation had in many cases brought people closer together, while at the same time the old order was being broken down in the cultural sphere – where more resources also became available. Writers such as Gerard van het Reve, Willem Frederik Hermans and Hugo Claus wrote a new language, while visual artists such as Karel Appel and Corneille and architects such as J.H. Van den Broek and J.B. Bakema created new 'images'. Later on, music and dance went through a similar revolutionary development. What in the past would have been handed down gradually as a cultural heritage penetrated the population in a highly accelerated tempo following the introduction of television.

Now that the turbulence which raged throughout Dutch society in the 1960s has settled again, it is evident that in several respects there have been radical, not to say revolutionary changes – though not in all sectors of life and society.

The most important changes have been in the pattern of daily life in what are, sociologically speaking, the smallest groups in society: the individual and the family. The publicist H.J.A. Hofland once appositely described this process as *'the decolonisation of daily life'*. Citizens began taking their own, individual line on issues of morality and social behaviour, no longer allowing their thoughts to be directed by social control or traditional institutions – in particular the Church. From a conformist society with a very strongly developed system of social divisions along ideological lines, the Netherlands developed in the space of twenty years into one of the most openly permissive societies in the world. A country where formerly nothing moved on a Sunday because of the mass attendance at the many and highly diverse Christian churches, began to secularise at a rapid rate. This did not so much signify the end of all religion and Christian belief as the 'privatisation' of religion. What had formerly been a highly organised society, structured in a system of tightly-knit unions, societies and political parties, underwent a process of individualisation. It is true that people today are still members of or sympathisers with many organisations, but they are less active and, in particular, switch their affections more frequently. The same applies to marriage and the family; supported by a new divorce law (1971), the number of divorces increased strongly until today one in every three marriages ends in divorce. As the experts have it: the Dutch citizen is still monogamous, but this has now become a 'serial' monogamy.

The Dutch had thus become convinced that the emancipation since the nineteenth century of the Catholic community, of orthodox Protestantism and of the labour movement – all striving against the dominant, free-thinking elite – was complete. They began to see themselves, in spite of all differences of origin and viewpoint, as belonging to a single, traditionally bourgeois and free society – to such an extent, in fact, that foreigners began to see the Dutch as one of the most cohesive societies in the world.

The completion of this emancipation process generated a certain amount of resistance to the established social and political elites and their alleged 'regent mentality'. The steamroller of criticism and resistance ran through parliament and town halls, schools and universities, farmer's organisations and trade unions. The call for democratisation was widespread and undeniably led to more democratic and egalitarian systems within all these institutions. More particularly, this democratisation led to a change in the position of women in society. In a country where by tradition married women, in particular, hardly ever went out to work – to just as limited an extent as in Ireland or Italy – they now began participating in paid employment, at least part-time. At the same time their position in political parties and interest groups also steadily strengthened. The 'second feminist wave' made deep inroads into Dutch society, partly because, in international terms, it represented a catching-up exercise.

Against this background it was not so much people's expectations of the

MOEDER IN HET GEZIN
EN NIET IN DE FABRIEK !

Postcard published by the Dutch Catholic Workers' Movement, c.1950. The caption reads: *'Mother at home, not at the factory!'* (Photo Katholiek Documentatiecentrum, Nijmegen).

political system as such which changed, as their behaviour at the ballot box. The abolition of compulsory voting (1970) led to a fall in the turnout at parliamentary elections from 95% to between 80 and 85%; participation in other elections fell even more sharply. Election results also became less predictable: voters changed their political allegiances more readily, albeit always within a limited 'bandwidth': the positions of the progressive parties (approximately 40%) and the more conservative groups (around 60%) have remained highly stable down to the present day, though preferences within the progressive and conservative blocs have fluctuated considerably.

One structural change did take place, however: the irresistible decline, in part due to secularisation, of the confessional parties of the centre, the KVP, ARP and CHU. Their membership fell from an average of around 50% of the total electorate between 1918 and 1967 to less than a third by the 1970s. In combination with a number of other factors, this acted as a strong incentive to collaboration; the result was a complete merger in 1980 to form the present CDA, or Christian Democratic Appeal (*Christen Democratisch Appel*). During the 1980s this new CDA appeared to enjoy reasonable success: electoral support stabilised and, partly due to the competence of its political leader Ruud Lubbers – who was also Prime Minister from 1982 to 1994 – the CDA attained a powerful position, which was certainly no less important than that held by the KVP in the first post-war decades.

What happened to the voters who had deserted the confessional parties? They were distributed among all the other parties, though with two striking consequences: first, election results became much less predictable than they had been up to 1967; and secondly, it has to be accepted that in the longer

Joop den Uyl (1919-1987)
(Photo by Vincent Menzel).

term the liberal parties have benefited to a relatively much greater extent than the PvdA and other parties of the left. The conservative-liberal VVD doubled its electorate between 1972 and 1994; the social-liberal D66 (Democrats 1966 – *Democraten 1966*) party which, as its name suggests, was set up in 1966, went through a more fluctuating development, but nonetheless grew into a party which in 1994 held 24 seats in the Lower House of Parliament (out of a total of 150). These two parties together formed what by 1994 had grown into the largest bloc in Dutch politics, with more than a third of all parliamentary seats (55 out of 150). Even if one is prepared to accept that D66 and VVD are slightly 'overrepresented' with these figures, the rise of liberal ideas in the Netherlands is still striking.

If this rise in liberalism was not so apparent at the end of the 1960s, the collapse of the confessional centre was. Reactions to this at parliamentary and party-leadership level were uncertain and ambivalent: confessional parties which avoided the PvdA and, in particular, D66 as much as possible; and conversely a PvdA which, as stated earlier, opted for radical polarisation against the confessional centre. Initially this approach appeared to have some success, in the form of the left-dominated cabinet under Prime Minister Den Uyl and the election victory of the PvdA in 1977. A second coalition led by Den Uyl failed to materialise, however, and the PvdA was condemned to many years in opposition, until it gave up its policy of polarisation towards the end of the eighties. The Dutch electorate had not been seduced by polarisation and supported the parties which rejected it. Society might have changed in many respects, but the political mores of the Dutch public remained solidly in favour of moderation, discussion and cooperation. The 1960s and their consequences had not so much brought about a political revolution (rather the reverse) as a silent revolution of daily existence and of the Church and social community. This revolution was made possible by growing prosperity and a protective welfare state, which fostered all kinds of spiritual and social relaxation in a free society where the limits of the possible and the permissible had been stretched. Until, that is, the economic tide turned.

The neo-conservative change of climate after 1980

At the end of the 1970s the welfare state was rocked twice in quick succession by two energy crises which were themselves the result of successive world dollar crises. The greatly reduced economic growth was no longer capable of sustaining the larger growth in private incomes and in collective spending on social security and public services. One of the first consequences was a substantial rise in unemployment, which proved to be unstoppable. This in turn placed severe pressure on social security spending: the burden of spending rose to new heights and the government's budget deficit climbed dramatically. This fostered a climate of neo-conservative intervention, albeit, as always in the Netherlands, in a moderate form. Not only was the government forced to embark on drastic austerity programmes, but concepts such as 'privatisation' and 'deregulation' also began to come into fashion, along with general, though sometimes ill-founded, criticism of 'the government' as itself a social problem.

In addition, the dark side of the permissive society, which initially had seemed to be no more than a means of liberation from paternalism, was becoming more and more apparent. Drug addiction and the associated explosive increase in crime began to be a source of serious concern. There was a sharp decline in willingness to pay taxes and social security contributions, quite apart from the fact that people were adopting a more critical and calculating stance to government and legislation in general. While many critics now saw the government as a problem, therefore, citizens and interest groups also became just as much of a thorn in the government's side. Interest groups launched vehement and often effective protest campaigns, more and more frequently seeking recourse to the courts. This in turn led to an unmistakeable hardening in a society which was becoming less 'civilised'.

This hardening was also apparent in the attitudes of the Dutch public to ethnic minorities in the Netherlands, whose numbers had grown quite substantially since 1970. Initially these were mainly immigrants from the former Dutch colony of Surinam who no longer wished to remain there following that country's independence in 1975, together with Turks and Moroccans who had come to the Netherlands as 'guest workers'. When the latter did not return to their homelands as intended, however, their numbers increased considerably through family formation and reunification. This process appeared to be more or less at an end by 1990, but then (as in the whole of Europe) a flood of asylum seekers began to appear, swelling the numbers of foreigners who were already residing in the Netherlands illegally.

Overall the total number of immigrants was and is limited (less than 10%), but in older districts of the major cities they now constitute a majority. These people, including the second generation, also face disproportionately high levels of unemployment, partly due to poor mastery of Dutch and

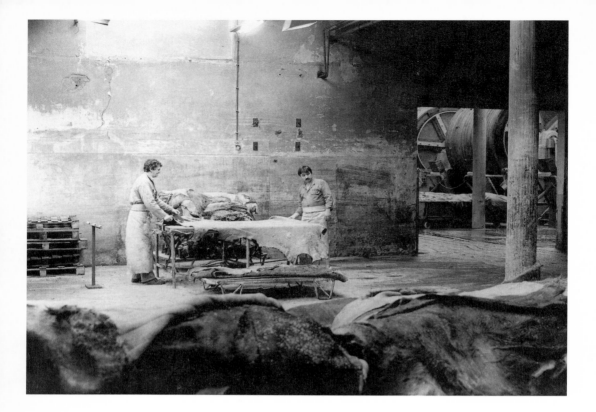

Immigrant workers in the Netherlands are usually not very high up the social ladder (Photo by Marian van Veen-Van Rijk).

inadequate education, but also as a result of discrimination in the labour market. The multicultural society had arrived, but in a far from cohesive way. A society which had already lost its old feeling of security and steadily rising prosperity began to see this multicultural society as more of a threat than a social and cultural enrichment.

Against this background, the effects of globalisation and Europeanisation could be felt all around. The acceleration of European integration was initially seen as a blessing: the Netherlands had after all displayed strongly federalistic ambitions since the 1950s. And yet in the Netherlands, too, the Treaty of Maastricht appeared to create more problems than opportunities. To some extent this was because problems were attributed to Brussels (e.g. bureaucracy), an apportionment of blame which was largely unjust. Additionally, people began to question the point of further integration and its effects on national interests. Europeanisation would in any event mean a loss of political democracy and constitutional sovereignty.

The trend towards globalisation, the total removal from national control of capital, information and investment, came as a severe blow to the highly socialised and regulated Netherlands. Not only did unemployment rise while the level of social benefits fell, but 'permanent jobs' for people with a reasonable level of education began to become less certain, in a repeat of the earlier and larger-scale development which had occurred in the United States. Diplomas, even at the highest level, no longer offered (or offer) young people the assurance of a secure existence. Older people sometimes have the greatest difficulty in keeping up with modern developments (particularly the increase in computerisation). The Netherlands has not only become a *semi-sovereign state* thanks to the European Union; as a result of globalisation it is also having to come to terms with the fact that it has become a *semi-sovereign society*.

Feelings of uncertainty and insecurity – in employment, on the street and even in one's own home, and also with regard to politics – are also fuelled by the realisation (highly developed in the Netherlands) that the natural environment is becoming more and more polluted, overloaded and exhausted. Nonetheless, it is proving difficult in a democratic society to adapt the individual and collective way of life to the new ecological dangers. Ecological needs constantly come up against (economic) resistance and powerlessness to introduce change and renewal. For many people, the ecological crisis has made a serious dent in their belief in progress – a belief which for so long dominated the political and social culture.

All these are problems and uncertainties for which traditional political ideas – either in Europe or in the Netherlands – are virtually incapable of providing coherent answers. Political parties are searching in a fairly dense ideological fog for new answers both to recurring issues (unemployment) and new problems (globalisation and ecological issues). In the Netherlands the parties ideologically associated with the post-war welfare state, namely the PvdA and the CDA, have borne the brunt of the criticism.

That welfare state has become 'too expensive' and 'too unwieldy' and has proved incapable of providing the promised security and protection when times are hard. Until the end of the 1980s many citizens were prepared to believe that, if precisely those two parties would work together again, things would return to normal. Hadn't the economy recovered and hadn't employment risen sharply? The wish became reality in 1989: the Christian Democrat Ruud Lubbers and the new social democrat leader Wim Kok

Ruud Lubbers (top) and Wim Kok (bottom), drawn by Waldemar Post for *de Volkskrant* in 1989 (Photo Stichting Atlas van Stolk, Rotterdam).

were to join forces in a new coalition. This coalition, it was confidently predicted, would be capable of setting about its task effectively, supported by a two-thirds parliamentary majority. What could possibly go wrong?

Everything, as it turned out. Although the coalition lasted the full four years, its course was anything but smooth. The allure which the Den Uyl cabinet had once had was missing completely between 1989 and 1994. In addition, the economic recession bit deeply and it became apparent how far the Dutch state was still living beyond its means. The Lubbers-Kok cabinet, which had started with such high expectations, was itself forced to introduce major austerity programmes and was left no choice but to contemplate a radical shake-up of the Netherlands' most valued social protection system, namely invalidity benefits. More generally, any political system naturally loses legitimacy if it is forced constantly to talk about nothing but money and retrenchment rather than renewal and reform.

Ruud Lubbers (1939-)
(Photo by Bert Verhoeff).

Support for the government coalition began to crumble rapidly and drastically. Initially the PvdA suffered worst, as a result of the understandable feelings of disappointment and criticism. However, when from 1993 onwards ministers and MPs belonging to the CDA increasingly began to clash with each other and the leaders of the parliamentary party began to distance themselves from their own Prime Minister (Lubbers was a member of the CDA), the decline of the Christian Democrats was also assured. In the last six months before the 1994 general election this decline became a dramatic slide.

On 3 May 1994 an event took place which had never before occurred since the introduction of universal suffrage in the Netherlands: the parties in the CDA-PvdA coalition lost so many seats that they saw a two-thirds majority in parliament shrivel away to a parliamentary minority, losing 32 seats out of 103. The PvdA suffered a dramatic loss of 12 seats, though this was still better than expected on the basis of the opinion polls. The CDA lost 20 seats, around 40% of its support, a catastrophic result which made the CDA even smaller than the PvdA in parliament. Contrasting with this was the 'march of the liberals' already referred to, and the rise of the small parties. If the 1960s were characterised by a youth revolution, it was now the turn of the elderly to revolt: two new parties for the elderly achieved a total of seven parliamentary seats. Undoubtedly an historic election result, then: but which history?

'Purple' coalition: intermezzo or new era?

Soon after 3 May 1994 a number of things became clear: racist parties such as the CD (Centre Democrats – *Centrum Democraten*) were and still are not a significant political force in the Netherlands. Liberal ideas were clearly in favour – but would that be a permanent phenomenon? The Christian democrats entered a deep existential crisis. The social democrats breathed a sigh of relief, but are still today facing a serious crisis of confidence in the large cities and among the young. The PvdA leader and Prime Minister, Wim Kok, had avoided a disaster for his party with his election campaign, but that was all.

The start of the period of cabinet formation – always a complicated and

Wim Kok (1938-)
(Photo by Fotobureau
Thuring B.V.).

Hans van Mierlo (1931-)
(Photo by Bert Verhoeff).

lengthy process in the Netherlands, if an entertaining one for the interested observer – quickly revealed one important fact. There would be no chance of forming a normal majority coalition without the left-wing liberal D66 party. This raised D66 and its successful leader Hans van Mierlo to a position of power which hitherto only the Christian Democrats had known. Van Mierlo's preference was clear and decisive, and he stuck to it firmly, notwithstanding an initial breakdown in the negotiations: a coalition between D66, VVD and PvdA. Since the PvdA, with 37 seats, was the largest of the three (D66 24 seats, VVD 31), it could supply the Prime Minister. Suffering a severe loss at the elections and still managing to supply the premier: it seemed a handsome consolation prize.

Cabinet formation became a long, complex process, because both the PvdA and the VVD initially wanted to govern together with the CDA – but then without each other. For the VVD, a continuation of its period in opposition was an attractive option. The CDA wanted either to go into opposition (to lick its wounds) or to work with the VVD, preferably in a minority combination. The CDA was plagued by uncertainty, however, and was saddled with a successor to party leader Ruud Lubbers, Elco Brinkman, who had been severely damaged by the elections. No one saw any future with Brinkman, not even the CDA. His only support came from his colleagues in the parliamentary party, and this lack of support increased when a thorough and open investigation by the CDA into its election debacle heavily criticised both the leader and the parliamentary party. They were accused of being technocrats, who had too little conviction and too little heart for the confessional and social beliefs of the party.

After a surprising intervention by the Queen in July, Wim Kok was charged with the task of forming a cabinet following the earlier failures, and he decided that nothing could be achieved with the CDA. He was also aware of the stubbornness of Van Mierlo and D66. After the historic elections came the historic switch by Kok to the conservative-liberal VVD, the old arch-enemy. At the end of August the resultant 'purple' cabinet consisting of social democrats, left-wing liberals and conservative-liberals took office with Kok as Prime Minister and with a government programme with clear liberal features and another radical programme of economies and tax cuts. The social security system was spared further cutbacks, at least for the time being. This government programme, even though it was written by Kok himself, was a perfect illustration of how weak the PvdA had become since the elections.

The cabinet is referred to as 'purple', suggesting a fusion of the 'red' of the left and the 'blue' of the liberal right. It is anything but a fusion, however: the VVD and, in particular, the PvdA, are too far apart for that. It would be more accurate to talk of a 'red and blue' coalition, in which the colours remain visibly standing next to each other.

An historic election and an historic coalition, then: for the first time since 1918 without a single confessional party in it. But is this an historical intermezzo – however striking and spectacular in itself – like the first confessional cabinet (1887-1891) or the left-wing Den Uyl cabinet, both of which were followed by more traditional combinations? Or is the Netherlands currently undergoing an historic change on the road towards a new political map? We would do well to be cautious with our opinions.

It is significant that the new coalition was forced on the parties by the electorate rather than being a conscious aim of the parties and their leaders, with the exception of D66 – though it gives them a pleasant feeling to have finally banished the Christian Democrats to the opposition for practically the first time in three-quarters of a century.

Seen in the light of some of its most important political tasks, this coalition has arrived too early. The reconstruction of the welfare state and the renewal of the economic production apparatus would have been activities more natural to the parties which built them up after the Second World War, namely the CDA and the PvdA. Only then would the way be open for a coalition in which the CDA and other confessional parties would stand for the preservation of traditional values and the non-confessional parties (now united in 'red and blue') for further secularisation and socio-cultural renewal. A further problem is that the balance of power shifts when it comes to ecological policies: the CDA and VVD are closest on these issues, ranged against the PvdA, D66 and the small left-wing groups – supported, surprisingly, by the small confessional parties, which often adopt radical standpoints on environmental issues.

The first test of the new coalition's popularity came with the provincial elections in March 1995. They turned out very badly for the CDA and PVDA; the former was unable to recover the ground it had lost, while the latter sank to its lowest point ever. D66, the architect of the 'purple' coalition, lost much of what it had gained in the national elections. To everyone's surprise it was the VVD, which had taken such risks in cooperating with the coalition, which gained most, doing particularly well in the cities. The triumph of the conservative-liberals was undeniably helped by the behaviour of Frits Bolkestein, the only political leader in the coalition who had not become a member of the government in 1994 but remained in the Second Chamber. This enabled him to support the Cabinet, while at the same time maintaining his distance from it. By so doing he was able, more effectively than the CDA, to cast his party in the role of a quasi-opposition, and this led to sizeable gains in the provincial elections, which always provide an opportunity for voters to express their dissatisfaction with the government. At the same time, however, Bolkestein – who knows how to appeal both to the intellectual middle classes and to the traditional, more lower-class, conservative voters – has done something to advance the recovery of liberalism following its temporary stagnation in the eighties.

The question is, though, whether the liberal victory of March 1995 has done anything to improve the stability of the 'purple' coalition; the 'blue' element was considerably better at getting through to the voters than the 'red', despite the personal popularity of the social democrat Prime Minister, Wim Kok. The results of the 1994 general election suggested that the PVDA was on its way back after the low point of the early nineties; a year later its situation proved to be just as grave as before. The prospects are not bright; not for Dutch social democracy, but not for the 'red-blue' coalition either.

Frits Bolkestein (1933-)
(Photo by Bert Verhoeff).

JOOP TH.J. VAN DEN BERG
March 1995
Translated by Julian Ross.

Dutch

Highest

Drugs and Drugs Policy in the Netherlands

'What's the price of "Dark Maroc" and how much is "Superskunk"?' The Netherlands is the only country where hashish and marijuana are on the menu and where questions like this are perfectly normal. It has been going on for almost twenty-five years now, and the Dutch population of over fifteen million has not become addicted *en masse*.

It all began in the early seventies. Amsterdam, along with San Francisco, was declared by the hippy movement to be the magic centre of the world. Here as elsewhere young people in the alternative scene were experimenting with drugs. At that time drugs had not yet become the problem they are today. Heroin was beginning to be used more widely, and was bought mainly by migrants from the former colony of Surinam. But the prophets of the hippy movement preached the virtues of the hard drug LSD and the soft drugs hashish and marijuana.

Everyone in this Amsterdam scene knew of a secret address, but drugs were being taken more and more openly without the police or the authorities doing anything about it. *Mellow Yellow* became one of the first coffee shops in the Netherlands where customers could buy their hashish and marijuana in small plastic bags. When it became clear that no hard drugs were being sold and that the customers were not causing a nuisance, the police left the place alone. Better in the open than in the underworld, was the argument. So more such coffee shops opened and a drugs policy developed in practice which by the mid-seventies became official: the Dutch 'policy of toleration'.

A distinction was made between soft and hard drugs. The use and sale of small quantities of soft drugs was tolerated in order to keep young people away from the growing hard drugs scene. Heroin was now becoming a problem and the authorities did not want hash smokers to be forced to turn to heroin dealers for supplies. Moreover, soft drugs were not associated with any addiction problems.

Help was aimed primarily at heroin users, and this quickly led to the second component in Dutch drugs policy: 'Harm limitation'. If you cannot force addicts to kick the habit, because all too often they get hooked again, you can at least try to keep them as healthy as possible and stop them getting involved in crime; this was the philosophy. So users of hard drugs were left alone, but no dealing was allowed.

Both primary and secondary schools provide information on the effects and dangers of drugs and alcohol. The Drugs and Alcohol Centres have special information leaflets which are available not only in schools but also in discos. The Drugs Advice Centre in Amsterdam targets its information and prevention activities mainly on hard-to-reach groups such as the young homeless, those attending raves and people experimenting with new substances such as toadstools and other plant-based drugs.

For the outside world Amsterdam and its hashish-selling coffee shops became 'the Las Vegas of drugs', and the Netherlands was the butt of many jokes. The Netherlands itself regarded its policy as pragmatic: not ideological or dogmatic, but business-like and down to earth, in the true Dutch spirit. Ignoring the criticism, the Netherlands continued to develop this policy: every addict who asked for help was eligible for methadone, a substitute for heroin. The Netherlands also took the lead in providing clean needles, well before the AIDS epidemic. A million clean needles are now distributed every year in Amsterdam alone.

By the end of the eighties this approach was beginning to attract international interest. It was true that the heroin addicts were also using other drugs such as cocaine and pills, but their numbers were hardly increasing at all. This was in sharp contrast to all other European countries, where there was an explosive increase in the numbers of deaths from drug overdoses and, later, AIDS.

For years the number of heroin addicts has fluctuated around twenty thousand. Even in Switzerland, with half the population, the number is higher at twenty-five thousand. There is even some 'greying' among the junkie population in the Netherlands, since their average age has been rising for years and is now 34 in Amsterdam. Because of such results the Dutch drugs policy has been copied in a number of countries, including Switzerland, the Czech Republic and parts of Germany.

But just when the Netherlands was no longer seen as a laughing stock on account of its drugs policy, cracks began to emerge in the foundations: the unexpected rise of the home-grown marijuana known as 'Netherweed', a proliferation of coffee shops, organised crime and the Ecstacy craze.

The rise of Netherweed has coincided with a revival in the use of soft drugs in Europe. A few gurus of the sixties soft drugs scene imported carefully selected hemp seeds from the United States and began improving the plant to turn it into a super variety. The result, according to insiders, was the best marijuana in the world, identified by a hint of red amongst the green.

Netherweed, upgraded 'Skunk' and 'Superskunk', is grown in attics, sheds, glasshouses and fields. This is in fact an archetypal Dutch activity: sowing, cultivating and harvesting. And making money, of course. At first it was restricted to a small circle, but in the early nineties there was a sudden breakthrough. Tens of thousands of small 'home growers' produced their own stock of this marijuana in a more or less professional way, and many of them tried to make a bit on the side by selling to coffee shops.

Dutch marijuana has already captured over half the domestic market. Some coffee shops, such as *Home Grown Fantasy* in the heart of Amsterdam, now sell only Netherweed. Others offer a whole range of home-grown

HOLLAND

products such as 'Skunk B', 'Northern Light' and 'Green Spirit' in addition to hashish.

Developments have been so rapid that the judicial authorities and the police, both in the Netherlands and abroad, fear that the Netherlands will become a major exporter of marijuana, just as Morocco and Lebanon are of hashish. Since the mid-eighties Dutch criminal organisations have worked their way up to become the Colombians of the hashish trade in Europe. They have now also turned their attention to the home-grown product. *Soft Secrets,* a monthly for small marijuana growers, has already complained that big nurseries are taking over the domestic market, driving out the home growers and those for whom it is a hobby. Netherweed nurseries have now been discovered in England, Germany and Belgium.

In the Netherlands the nurseries are everywhere, even in working-class areas of Amsterdam. In the shop window of an old building in West

Amsterdam the unsuspecting passer-by can see some cooker hoods and other equipment that suggest a firm of electrical fitters. It is a small shop with a large counter. Behind the shop is a room containing bags of fertiliser. Behind that is a small office, with a bookcase full of files against one wall.

The equipment business is officially registered with the Chamber of Commerce, but there is more to it. With his index finger the proprietor pushes aside a bookcase that turns out to be a door. It is a defence against the police and 'rippers', the dread of every entrepreneur in 'the trade'. No one is surprised any more when marijuana growers are robbed of hemp plants and equipment, and legitimate greenhouse growers are increasingly the victims. The largest agricultural insurer in Europe, Hagelunie, estimates that grow lights worth millions are stolen each year from market gardens. These expensive lamps are used for growing hemp.

Behind the bookcase is a glaringly lit 'cuttings room' measuring at least fifty square metres. It looks like a laboratory. The temperature is kept at close to 25 degrees; the humidity is carefully controlled and the growth of the plants is artificially regulated with grow lights. The mother plants are numbered and then cuttings are taken from them. The plants with the highest level of tetrahydrocannabinol (THC), the active ingredient in weed, are used for further breeding. 'Good Skunk', 'Superskunk' or one of the other miracle varieties from the Netherlands contains 25 to 35% THC. The strongest foreign marijuana has no more than 12%.

The grower waxes lyrical when pointing out some of his 'finest mothers'. Nearby is the incubator, a space measuring ten square metres where the cuttings from the mother plants grow and root. After that these clones are ready for sale. The grower earns at least fifteen thousand guilders (c. $ 10,000 / £ 6,000) a month. He is an example of the shady Netherweed entrepreneur trying to find his way between home growing as a hobby and large-scale criminal production.

According to figures issued by the Ministry of Health there are almost six hundred thousand cannabis users in the Netherlands. Old hands say there are more than a million. Researchers and aid organisations confirm that use is on the increase.

Despite the rising demand, and drug tourism from all over Europe, the Dutch market is too small to support the many coffee shops which opened their doors in the eighties in the hope of profiting from the toleration of small-scale dealing. Moreover, the new generation of cannabis users are demanding customers and want a shop that suits their lifestyle, which is another reason for a substantial increase in the number of shops. A chain like *Bulldog,* whose flagship is the shop in the former police station on Leidseplein in Amsterdam, does not attract the same type of people as the little 'brown shop' round the corner in an inner city neighbourhood. The trendy coffee shop with cappuccino and cakes does not fulfil the same function as the 'hardrock shop' or the growing number of centres for young people from ethnic minorities.

Some shops, such as *The Grasshopper,* sell their goods from behind a counter with a thick glass screen to prevent robberies. There the desired number of grams is weighed on a balance. The customer makes his choice from the sixteen varieties by pressing a button, which causes a light to go on in a built-in display case. Prices range from seven guilders for a gram of

'Thai Grass' to seventeen for 'Holland Highest'. This is an example of the Dutch business instinct, because in this way the ban on advertising is not broken: the customer himself asks to see the goods by pressing the button. This is not the only rule the shops have to obey: they must not sell to minors; hard drugs and alcohol are taboo; and they must not cause a nuisance.

In addition, they may carry only a limited stock. For years the coffee shops have been able to operate because of the rule applied by the judicial authorities that a person may have up to thirty grams of soft drugs in his possession without running the risk of being prosecuted. The Netherlands has between fifteen hundred and two thousand hash / coffee shops. In recent years quite a few have closed, partly as a result of a tougher line being taken to prevent them causing a nuisance or attracting criminals, partly through competition. Some proprietors who could barely keep their heads above water because of the sheer number of coffee shops were all too ready to listen to 'business' proposals from 'good' friends or 'smart' clients. In such cases the disappointing turnover was boosted by profits from the sale of stolen goods and other shady activities.

In an effort to prevent this, the Ministry of Justice and the local authorities are trying to reduce the number of coffee shops substantially. In part this is to be achieved by making them subject to the same regulations as a shop or bar. This will give the coffee shops a more official status, but it will be easier to combat crime and any nuisance they may cause. If they do not observe the rules, they will lose their licences. The bona fide proprietors are trying to dissociate themselves from the excesses and inconvenience that have brought discredit on the whole sector. In 1994 the Amsterdam coffee shop proprietor Reijer Elzinga founded the Association of Cannabis Retailers. It says that the shops ought to be able to hold a larger stock than thirty grams, and there is some support in Parliament for this.

In recent years the Netherlands has run into more and more problems because of the contradictions in the policy of toleration: everyone is allowed to buy and use hashish and marijuana but the seller is allowed to hold hardly any stock and is forced to obtain his supplies from illegal sources, including criminal organisations. The latter have become large and powerful as a result; their millions in illegal profits infiltrate the economy and corrupt society. The authorities have failed to find an adequate answer, despite increased efforts by crime squads and tougher legislation, and are not yet ready to move to legalisation.

The Octopus crime syndicate is one of the largest of these organisations. It owes its name to its many tentacles, both national and international, legitimate as well as in the underworld. It deals in cocaine and hashish and specialises in the laundering of drugs money; it has an estimated annual turnover of more than a hundred million guilders (c. $ 64 million / £38.5 million). In the Netherlands the Octopus Affair led to a number of sensational court cases in one of which, in January 1995, the Dutch ex-racing driver Charles Z. was sentenced to five years imprisonment by the Amsterdam Court for the large scale importation of cannabis resin from Morocco.

The view of Dutch drugs policy at street level is often rather different to that found in conference halls. While the council and aid organisations routinely demonstrate their approach to many foreign visitors, travellers on the

Amsterdam metro see something very different. On the platforms of some stations dozens of junkies hustle, freebase and deal. Particularly in bad weather, the Amsterdam metro has become the main meeting place for those known as 'street junkies'. For years there has been an unwritten law that the rear seats are the preserve of addicts, the homeless and other marginal figures.

The street scene shows that the addiction problem is far from being a question of just heroin. Three-quarters of the street junkies drink. Pills and cocaine also form part of their daily diet, and many have psychiatric problems. In the major cities they and other marginal groups form part of a street culture of muggings and dealing. Local residents put up with it as an unpleasant natural phenomenon, as long as they are not the victims.

In Amsterdam most of the nuisance and drug-related crime is caused by the over 1,200 street junkies, a fifth of the total number of addicts in the city. Some of them have been in trouble with the police over two hundred times. In Rotterdam 'Perron Nul' (Platform Zero), a refuge for junkies near the Central Station, was closed down at the end of 1994 because of the disturbances there; since then the street junkies have found shelter at St Paul's Church with its minister, Hans Visser. To keep out dealers and criminals a system of passes has been introduced for addicts.

Most heroin-users can manage with a job or social security benefit and special help if need be. The extensive methadone programmes play a very important part in this. Over seventy per cent of the addicts in Amsterdam receive methadone; in the Netherlands as a whole eleven thousand users receive it.

The question of heroin on prescription has been raised several times since the seventies, but is has always been rejected as impractical or undesirable. Nonetheless in recent years there has been increasing support among police commissioners, public prosecutors, politicians and the business community for free provision. All have warned against the growing disruption of the economy by the drugs trade. The new social democrat-liberal government which took office in 1994 also seems to be aware of the need for change, and is not opposed to local plans for hard drugs to be made available on a doctor's prescription.

And then there are the trendy drugs. Cocaine was 'in' during the eighties and became the drug of choice in fashionable business circles and clubs before being taken up by heroin addicts, disaffected youth and young criminals. In the late eighties amphetamine came back into fashion through the 'love drug' Ecstacy and the so-called rave culture, and Speed and LSD have also made comebacks.

In the Netherlands the Ecstacy craze was part of a subculture in which young people gathered in huge numbers at secret, last-minute parties in draughty sheds. The drug is no longer confined to raves, but that is still where most of the problems occur. The active element in Ecstacy is the banned MDMA (Methylene Dioxy Methyl Amphetamine), but more and more pills are available with MDEA, Speed, LSD or other substances which are stronger than Ecstacy. Experts disagree about the dangers of Ecstacy itself. However, there have been warnings about overdoses and about non-stop dancing while on pills, which can cause dehydration and heart failure.

Now that raves have become commercial and are held in well-insulated halls, things more often go wrong. Ministry of Health guidelines say that there must be a cooling-off area, an adequate supply of water and a First Aid team. Unlike hashish and marijuana, Ecstasy is regarded as a hard drug, but the parties at which it is taken by large numbers of people are organised under the supervision of the authorities, in the hope of keeping things under control. Its use is tolerated, but there are heavy penalties for producing or selling the drug. Organised crime, which has already done well out of marijuana, is benefitting greatly and for years has been Europe's biggest producer and exporter of Ecstacy and amphetamines.

Partly because of this, other countries still look at the Netherlands with some suspicion. But it has had more success than other countries with its drugs policy, and does not want to give it up. For years it has borne the burden resulting from the difference between that policy and those of its neighbours. Every day thousands of drugs tourists from surrounding countries cross the border to get hashish and marijuana, which are freely available there, and hard drugs, which are just as illegal as elsewhere but cheaper. In an attempt to reduce the nuisance caused by this tourism, drugs control at the borders has been tightened up.

It is not clear why the Germans are still coming to the Netherlands for hashish and marijuana. They can obtain it in their own cities along the border just as cheaply and almost as easily in clubs and on the street. Although hashish and marijuana are just as illegal as heroin and cocaine in German law, in the states along the border possession for personal use is increasingly tolerated. This relaxation does not, however, mean that selling is accepted. According to some this is why the more tolerant climate in Germany has led to an increase in soft drugs tourism to the Netherlands. *'They are allowed to use it over in Germany, but they have to come here to get it,'* says Reijer Elzinga, chairman of the Association of Cannabis Retailers.

FRANS BOSMAN AND KURT VAN ES
March 1995
Translated by John Rudge.

FURTHER READING

The Netherlands Institute for Alcohol and Drugs (NIAD) conducts research into drug use, assembles national and international data, and advises the Dutch Government. It has an extensive documentation centre.

P.O. Box 725 / 3500 AS Utrecht / The Netherlands.

tel. + 31 30 234 13 00 / fax + 31 30 231 63 62

Fifty

Years of Bob and Bobette

The 'cast' of *Bob and Bobette*. From the top: Bobette with her doll Molly, Bob, Aunt Agatha, Orville and Wilbur.

Flanders' most popular comic strip characters, Bob and Bobette (in Dutch: *Suske en Wiske*), are already fifty years old; but in all that time they have not aged a day. Several generations of children have grown up with their adventures. This makes *Bob and Bobette*, among other things, an interesting source for research into Flanders' postwar cultural history.

Bob and Bobette is of course first and foremost an entertainment product, to be found between the washing powder and the biscuits on the supermarket shelves. 400,000 copies are printed of each new book, and 3 million newspaper readers in Flanders and the Netherlands can follow the adventures of *Bob and Bobette* every day. More than 180 stories have so far been published. Roughly speaking, the chronological development of this comic strip can be divided into three main periods.

Willy Vandersteen (1913-1990), who in the thirties was a window-dresser, became acquainted with American comic strips through an American fashion magazine. At that time they surpassed European comic strips in both quality and quantity. The disappearance of the American comics during the Second World War left a vacuum in the Flemish press. So it was during the war that Vandersteen published his own first comic strips. Legend has it that the first depictions of Bobette and Aunt Agatha came into being in an air raid shelter in Antwerp with V1 and V2 bombs flying overhead. The story *Rikki and Bobette in Chocoslovakia* (Rikki en Wiske in Chocowakije) appeared in the newspaper *De Nieuwe Standaard* on Friday 30 March 1945, before the end of the war. Rikki, Bobette's older brother, had a quiff (just like Tintin), and they went on an adventurous journey to an East European country that had a secret police force called the 'Gestaco'. The story was very much of its time and reacted bitingly to the madness of war, a subject Vandersteen was often to touch upon.

In his second story the author made Rikki vanish and had Bobette meet Bob on the island of Amoras; they were to remain inseparable from then on. In his first stories Vandersteen drew them as squat but extremely supple figures who could twist themselves into unusual positions. Anatomical perfection was not for them, but they did have character, and were fun to look at.

Those first albums were full of local colour. In *The Reduction Beam (*De

sprietatoom, 1946) for example, Vandersteen gives us amusing Flemish scenes, such as the farmer's bedroom in the Kempen: the saint under a glass bell, the stoup, the salted ham, the painting of The Eye of God... All these interesting visual details disappeared in the sterile 1970 version by the Vandersteen studio; moreover, the smooth modern style of drawing is weak and totally without character.

Willy Vandersteen once said, about the first *Bob and Bobette* period: '*Impressions from my youth played a large part in my first creations. There's a part of my life in those first twenty-eight stories: they are the most spontaneous and take no account of technical or commercial concerns. But later on, when the whole business had expanded, other demands were made. The figures evolved over those thirty years. There is also a completely different humour in those first albums which does not appear in the later ones.*'

Differences between the 1946 and the 1971 edition of *The Reduction Beam* (De sprietatoom). The 1946 panel (1.) has more local colour and its language is racier. In 1946 the farmer's wife said '*Cornelius! The tax men! Put them taters away!*', while in 1971 her words read '*Cornelius, I think someone knocked at the door! Could that be the tax collector?*'.

Willy Vandersteen (1913-1990) (Photo by Bruno Vetters and Kris Venmans).

Close encounters of the third kind: a slightly more upper-class Orville, Bobette and Bob in *The Messengers from Mars* (De gezanten van Mars).

Breaking the rules of the comic strip in *The African Drummers* (De tamtam-kloppers): Orville knocks his opponent off the panel and the poor chap disappears behind one of the next panels.

This humour is a mixture of slapstick, absurdity and everyday popular humour (including a racist streak...). Vandersteen broke the rules of the comic strip on occasion, but always in an amusing way, as in *The African Drummers* (De tamtamkloppers, 1953).

Between 1948 and 1958, while he was writing and drawing new adventures for the newspaper, Vandersteen also produced eight *Bob and Bobette* stories for the weekly *Tintin / Kuifje*: among these were *The Spanish Ghost* (Het Spaanse spook) and *The Messengers from Mars* (De gezanten van Mars). Hergé, who was editor-in-chief of the weekly as well as author of the *Tintin* comic books, made Vandersteen tone down the popular elements: some characters were barred and others were adapted to a more sophisticated taste. These stories also had more structure and Vandersteen's drawing became more 'academic'. Pressure of work and lack of time even drove him to copy certain postures and settings from Hal Foster's *Prince Valiant*. But these stylistic differences between the newspaper comics and the stories for *Tintin / Kuifje* gradually disappeared.

The arrival of a new member of the clan, Wilbur, marked the moment of transition from the first to the second period. This second period began vigorously and full of promise. Vandersteen was writing superb stories, such as *The Circus Baron* (De circusbaron, 1954), and creating marvellous visual images like the horse on roller skates in *The Knight of the Streets* (De straatridder, 1955) and the pack of cards that comes to life in *The Dance of the*

Cards (De kaartendans, 1962). Because he was always publishing new stories, Vandersteen was up to his ears in work and came to rely more and more on assistants. *Bob and Bobette* was also exported to the Netherlands: from 1953 the Flemish text was adapted for the Dutch readership and after 1963 just one common version was printed in Standard Dutch. The characteristic Flemish elements were gradually eliminated.

The arrival of Wilbur, a rough Flemish version of an American superhero, had unexpected consequences. He made his first appearances dressed only in an animal skin, but, under pressure from a number of incensed readers, Vandersteen soon wrapped him up in normal civvies. At first, Wilbur and Orville lived with Aunt Agatha, but in 1954 they went to live on their own, which was not exactly a common occurrence in 1950s Flanders (this was, of course, avidly exploited by various sex parodies in the early eighties). Wilbur also presented Vandersteen with another problem: how do you bring a situation to an exciting and unexpected end in the presence of a superhuman muscle-man like this, who can get the better of anyone? That the heroes always win in the end goes without saying, but it is the way they achieve their triumph that can be interesting. That's why Vandersteen often tried to neutralise Wilbur by, for example, letting him sleep through a whole story...

Orville and Aunt Agatha emulating 007 in *The Carnival of the Apes* (De apekermis).

In addition to this, times had changed, and Vandersteen was well aware of it. The sixties may have been 'golden', but they also saw the bloodbaths in the Congo, Vietnam and the Middle East. A sizeable amount of Vandersteen's bitterness seeped through into his work. By the mid-sixties he was spicing his comics with cutting comments, more extreme than his former ironical swipes. In *The Carnival of the Apes* (De apekermis, 1965) the apes take over the running of the world, while the people, affected by meteor radiation, fail to see any difference; the politicians and generals are all replaced by apes and no one notices a thing ! Vandersteen once again hits hard, two stories later, in *Mad Meg* (De dulle Griet). This well-known character from Brueghel is brought to life to find out why people wage wars. The story ends on a sarcastic note with a crying Vietnamese girl under a barrage of bombs, followed by Bobette, who normally winks cheerfully at the reader, hiding her face in her hands. This is not a happy ending, and we are no longer able to laugh. The state of the world has become too serious and there seem to be no simple solutions, such as a comic strip would normally provide. Subsequent stories demonstrate a hard cynicism: Orville becomes successively a cold-hearted money-grabber and a hardbitten mercenary... These changes are also reflected in the clothing: Bob swaps his shorts (symbol of the child) for long trousers and Bobette often leaves her red-striped white dress hanging in the wardrobe. By the end of the sixties the original vividness had vanished completely and the stories weakened and became extremely middle-of-the-road.

In 1972, Willy Vandersteen, looking for new stimuli in other projects, handed over his most important brainchildren to Paul Geerts, who had been a member of the Vandersteen studio since 1968. While the name of Willy Vandersteen has always remained on the cover, the name of the actual author has only appeared on the title page for the last five years. Geerts' approach has been a great success both commercially and in terms of public appreciation, but some critics are less enthusiastic. It may be that older readers will no longer recognise 'their' *Bob and Bobette* in this contemporary approach, but it is today's young readers (7 to 13 years) that set the pace, and they prefer the recent books to the old Vandersteen comics.

There is a fair amount of veiled advertising in today's *Bob and Bobette* stories: Orville drives a clearly identifiable Suzuki jeep. The (Dutch) mar-

The last panels from *Mad Meg* (De dulle Griet): Our heroes have just shown Mad Meg, Pieter Brueghel's embodiment of war, the error of her ways. They are about to return home in the pouring rain. Meanwhile, it is raining bombs in Vietnam, right to the bitter end.

ket-orientation is also apparent in the Dutch characterisation of what were once thoroughly Flemish figures: the heroes no longer fly Sabena but KLM and Bob plays football not with the Red Devils (the Belgian national team) but with Orange, their Dutch equivalent.

Vandersteen's spiritual testament dictates that dangerous, meaning commercially risky, subjects like religion, racism, sex and drugs may not be mentioned. Even so, Geerts has been able to sidestep some of these prohibitions: in *The Sharp Scorpion* (De scherpe schorpioen, 1992), Bobette is cared for affectionately after an accident by a family of Moroccan immigrants. Geerts' personality is most conspicuous in a book he produced in his spare time and which was never published in a newspaper beforehand. *The Jewel in the Lotus* (De parel in de lotusbloem, 1987) begins with the basic feelings of Western man, who is then overwhelmed by reports of war, famine, terror and more. In this New Age, Paul Geerts seeks the remedy in Oriental wisdom and has Bobette call a Buddhist monk 'vicar'.

The characters in *Bob and Bobette* are not tied to time and space: while everything is changing around them (cars, furniture, etc.), they remain the same age, but this age is hard to estimate. Nor are they real children: they never have to go to school and they drive a wide variety of vehicles without a driving licence; on the other hand they sometimes behave in a genuinely childish way (e.g. Bobette's legendary close bond with her doll Molly).

A deck of cards shuffling on the dancefloor in *The Dance of the Cards* (De kaartendans).

SUSKE EN WISKE SLUIPEN DE NAR NA DIE ZICH NAAR DE ZAAL BEGEEFT WAAR SCHOPPEN EN KLAVEREN LUSTIG DANSEN.

Aunt Agatha and Orville occasionally behave like, but are most certainly not, parents. The reason for a false family like this is, of course, that real parents would never allow their children to become involved in such adventures and would prefer to put the emphasis on their performance at school. *Bob and Bobette* are like mini-adults with childlike aspects. Nor do the characters have real human emotions: Aunt Agatha will remain forever in love with that bully Orville, but they will never marry. That much is laid down in Vandersteen's spiritual testament.

Classic comics like this do not pretend to portray reality, rather they create a world entirely their own, which does not necessarily work according to normal logic. Even so, a cultural product like a comic is never totally divorced from its context. To take one example, in earlier days Vandersteen would take a swipe at taxation, as regularly as clockwork. The precise message is not always unequivocal. There are plenty of ambiguities and contradictions in these stories. In 1975, when the green political movement in Flanders was in its infancy, Geerts denounced the degeneration of the environment in *The Chubby Shad* (De mollige meivis) while only ten years later he produced a book with the dreadfully ambiguous Orwellian title of *The Jolly Millirem* (De mooie millirem), in which it is stated that radioactivity itself is not dangerous, only those who use it !

One of the keys to the success of these stories, apart from the popular humour, is the familiarity of the ingredients used. In *Bob and Bobette* one would have no trouble in tracing elements from fairy tales, folklore, myths, legends, bible stories, paintings, novels, plays, films and other comics. History and current affairs are also an almost inexhaustible source of inspiration. In this respect the time machine was a useful invention, allowing the characters to travel through time. But they are never historical stories, since the past is only used as a sort of fairy-tale backdrop. *Bob and Bobette* experience their own adventures in a 'past time'. They do not venture to change history, even fictitiously. The historical setting is there to provide the stories with variation or to shed a historical light on contemporary issues.

Its timeless, achronological structure and its internal contradictions and evolutions make the world of *Bob and Bobette* fairly complex and by no means unambiguous, however simplistic a single story may seem. This complexity is probably not consciously intended by the creators, since both Vandersteen and Geerts claim to think up their stories quite spontaneously. In any case, they have no time to reflect too long on individual questions: two rows have to appear in the paper every day. They tell stories in their own way, with their personal view of life playing its part, and their outlook is not so different from what the average Belgian or Dutchman thinks and feels.

PASCAL LEFEVRE
Translated by Gregory Ball.

n

Motion

Animated Film in Flanders

Raoul Servais, *Harpya*
(1979).

Raoul Servais, *Taxandria*
(1994).

Raoul Servais: the father of Flemish animated film

In 1979, the then 51-year-old Flemish animated film maker Raoul Servais
was awarded the Golden Palm at the Cannes Film Festival for his film
Harpya. Many years would pass before we heard of him again. For more
than fifteen years he had been working on his long cherished dream: the feature-length animated film *Taxandria* which he completed in 1994. For bud-
getary reasons, however, this European co-production became a film with
real actors instead of the animated film Servais had in mind. The decors are
nonetheless of exceptional quality. They were executed following the 'ser-
vaisgraphic process' at his own Anitrick animated film studio in Ghent.
    Servais, a self-taught artist, began modestly with *Harbour Lights* (Haven-
lichten, 1959) and went on to create *The False Note* (De valse noot, 1963),

Chromophobia (1966), *To Speak or Not To Speak* (1970), *Operation X-70* (1970), *Pegasus* (1973) and *The Song of Halewijn* (Het lied van Halewijn, 1975) among others. His eleven films have received fifty awards at festivals all over the world. Moreover, his international reputation resulted in him being chosen as successor to the famous British animated film maker John Halas as president of the International Association of Animated Film Makers in Cannes in 1985.

Raoul Servais' importance to animated film in Flanders extends beyond his unequalled reputation as a filmmaker. The fact that he has trained dozens of creative and competent young filmmakers over the years is of equal importance. This work began in 1961 when Servais, as a lecturer at the Royal Academy for the Fine Arts in Ghent, set up the Department of Animated Film. Servais evidently knew how to pass on his artistic vision and passion, his sense of professionalism and last but not least his perseverance and drive to numerous students under him. This quickly led to the creation of a type of animated film which, while exploring many different fields, tried to move away from the all-dominating norms of the Walt Disney productions. The artistic creativeness of style and concept which was to characterise their work has led to them becoming known as 'the Ghent school of animated film makers'. Thanks to Servais' stimulating influence, this Department of Animated Film grew to become one of the largest in Europe. International recognition was not long in following.

The Ghent school

Shortly after completing his studies in animated film at the Academy, Paul Demeyer received the Hollywood Student Academy Award, the Student's Oscar, for his cartoon *The Muse* while at the California Institute of Arts in 1977. In 1979, he created the 13-part cartoon series *The Wonder Shop* for Belgian television (BRTN), in cooperation with other former fellow students.

The international acclaim they received for this series was such that in

Paul Demeyer, *The Wonder Shop* (De wonderwinkel, 1979).

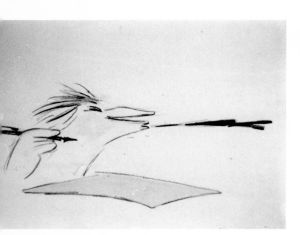

Paul Demeyer, *The Muse* (1977).

1983 one of these former students, Dirk de Paepe, then working for the PEN film studio in Ghent, was commissioned to create the cartoon that would introduce Blake Edwards' *The Curse of the Pink Panther*. The international success of *The Wonder Shop* also resulted in a second commission by the BRTN, this time for the first full-length Flemish animated film, *John the Fearless* (Jan zonder Vrees, 1985). Once again Dirk de Paepe was in charge of operations at the PEN film studio in Ghent and was assisted in the project by many former students of Raoul Servais.

John the Fearless is based on a well-known Flemish folk tale. It is the story of a young Antwerp boy from a poor background who takes up the fight against social injustice and poverty in the Middle Ages. Thanks to his extraordinary strength, he always succeeds in defeating his opponents. He is finally knighted. More important than this not so original plot, however, is the film's artistic design, the inspiration for which was drawn from the old Flemish masters such as Hieronymus Bosch, Brueghel and Jules de Bruycker. The style of drawing, the use of colour and especially the beautiful decors all contribute towards making the film uniquely 'Flemish'.

As a result of competition from Japan and the financial difficulties of one of PEN's most important contractors in France, the studio where these large animated film projects had been carried out was forced to close in 1987. Nevertheless, the training of competent film makers at the Ghent Academy continued. One of the latest talents is An Vrombaut, who after her studies in Ghent went on to work at studios in London, where she completed her studies at the Royal College of Art. In 1993 she completed *Little Wolf*, which was to become the discovery of the year at the renowned Annecy Festival in France and which took the prize for best first film. What is striking about

An Vrombaut, *Little Wolf* (1993).

Dirk de Paepe, *John the Fearless* (Jan zonder Vrees, 1985).

this children's cartoon in which the traditional roles of evil wolf and little innocent lamb are inverted is that the humour mainly lies in the exceptionally lively rhythm of the animation itself. This filmmaker of the Ghent school is now working on a TV series called *64 Zoo Lane,* a 14-part cartoon currently being made in London.

Another TV series, which will also be created by former students of Raoul Servais, is *Eb & Flo.* In charge here are Annemie Degryse as producer, Stefaan Vermeulen as director and Jeroen Jonckheere as chief animator. Vermeulen and Jonckheere have already demonstrated their talents in *Going Home on the Morning Train* (1992) and *Female Trouble* (1991). Their series on the tender and dotty adventures of an old maid and her inseparable cat, which runs to fifty-two episodes of six minutes each, is the first major Flemish production to be created thanks to the support of the European Union's media project Cartoon.

In stark contrast with the Ghent school's current achievements are such purely commercial productions as the *Bob and Bobette* (Suske and Wiske) series, based on the comic-strips by Flanders' most famous comic-strip artist Willy Vandersteen. Because of its poor artistic quality, the 30-part series *The Mad Musketeers* (De dolle musketiers, 1990) went practically unnoticed both at home and abroad. Belgium, be it in the French-speaking or in the Dutch-speaking part, has a remarkable tradition of comic-strip artists, but, with the exception of the work by French-speaking artist Picha, few have provided material exciting enough for animated film.

The talent and drive of Frits Standaert

The many former students of Servais who make up the internationally famous Ghent school of animated film makers have no trouble finding work doing commercial productions for studios in Brussels. They are doing well abroad too, in countries like Luxembourg, Great Britain, France and even the United States where the most talented of Servais' former students, Oscar

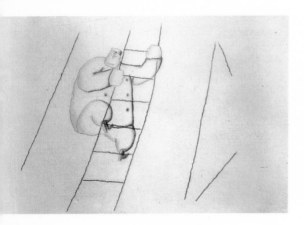

Frits Standaert, *Jailbirds* (1989).

Frits Standaert, *Wundermilch* (1991).

winner Paul Demeyer, is presently working. Because of the lack of prospects and funding at home, however, they are usually obliged to forget about purely creative work. This explains why artistic animated film in Flanders is usually developed and propagated in the film schools.

The animated film maker Frits Standaert is an exception to this state of affairs. As a student in Ghent he produced *Jailbirds,* of which he was able to make a professional 35 mm copy in 1989 with the help of the Horlait-Dapsens Foundation. This 5-minute long cartoon relates the grotesque story of a prisoner on a lonely rocky island where release literally turns into a nightmare. Full of panic and anxiety, he tries everything he can to resist his amnesty. For, unlike his guard, he is never bored. So violent is his desperate reaction to release that he becomes entangled in his chains during his sleep and involuntarily strangles himself. Because of this, his guard's life loses all meaning. Discouraged, he leaves the island pulling with him the lines of the image as if they were those of his very life. This means his end as a cartoon character and of course the end of this ingenious cartoon.

His *Wundermilch* (1991) is a seemingly naïve cartoon about a cow called Rosamunde who, because of the exceptionally vital qualities of her milk, ends up being an enormous commercial success. Her owner and the whole of society benefit from her, but eventually Rosamunde is milked dry. Standaert produced this 3.5-minute long off-beat advertising film on an extremely low budget. *Wundermilch* inspired him to create a 13-part series *(Rosamunde)* which he hopes to sell to television.

Frits Standaert was given another opportunity of creating on a professional level with *Kiss the Moon* (1993). This film is a gentle satire on the human urge to succeed. Unhappy with their egalitarian existence, Earth's inhabitants go in search of a more beautiful planet. They spare nothing in their attempts to reach the nearest planet first and have no qualms whatsoever about destroying each other in doing so. But all their various attempts are in vain. One by one the desperadoes fall to their destruction. In the end we learn that the planet they desired so much was exactly the same as the one they had been living on for centuries.

Frits Standaert, *Kiss the Moon* (1993).

Jacques Lemaire, *Axis Mundi* (1993).

Kiss the Moon is beautifully made. The artistic originality with which the characters and decors have been drawn, the perfect rhythm of the sequences and the exceptionally well-timed sound effects and musical accents are all outstanding. In short, the sober play of colour-pencil lines on tracing paper found in *Jailbirds,* the colour drawings of *Wundermilch* with their deliberate element of caricature and the highly competent cel animation of *Kiss the Moon* all illustrate the range of skills and techniques the young artist had mastered. It is little wonder that his films have been shown at all the main festivals and have been bought by most TV stations throughout Europe.

The Animation Art of Jacques Lemaire

The work of Jacques Lemaire is of a completely different nature. As painter and animator he belongs to what is known in the USA as Animation Art. His animated films are a logical extension of his own development in the plastic arts. As an artist he was initially influenced by movements such as Pop Art, New Realism and Minimal Art, but from 1972 onwards he started to develop his own language of signs, based on archetypical forms to which he ascribed metaphysical connotations. The basic elements of Lemaire's language of image consist of the primary colours red, yellow and blue, elementary forms like the cross, the square and the circle and the basic duality between horizontal and vertical lines. He combines these graphic components with the natural elements earth, air, fire and water. Lemaire's interest in light and movement led him to animated film: the ideal means for developing his archetypical forms and signs in one continuous movement.

In 1984, he painted his own personal vision in *Cosmogony* (Kosmogonie), an animated film which caused him considerable difficulty because of his lack of training in animated film techniques. Lemaire nevertheless achieved his aim: the film, a continuous harmonious flow of forms, lines and colours, was acclaimed as highly innovative at a number of festivals. As far as technique is concerned, this film maker / painter works according to the oldest methods. His hundreds of drawings are filmed drawing by drawing, and transformed during projection into a wonderful and well-executed flow of images, with an original soundtrack built on percussion.

Lemaire's latest film *Axis Mundi* was to follow in 1993. It is a synthesis of his artistic changes and developments during the 1980s. The tree of life is central to the film, an axial constant which mediates between heaven and earth while at the same time transforming itself into figurative as well as abstract symbols. At the beginning and the end of *Axis Mundi,* real-life images of the tree are shown. Lemaire leads the viewer from the visible material world via a finely syncopated movement of photographic and pictorial forms and signs into an invisible world of energy. Even more than in Cosmogony, the musical structure, in this case the *Stabat Mater* by Pergolesi, determines the changes, the build up and the rhythm of his pictorial language. The silences that accompany the live images of the tree provide the contrast.

At the moment, this unique Flemish representative of animation art is working on a third film, *Omega,* which is based on the theme of 'the eternal present' and will form the third of his triptych of films.

An Oscar for Nicole van Goethem

The work of Nicole van Goethem is quite different again. She studied at the Antwerp Academy for Fine Arts and first made a name for herself with her drawings, cartoons and posters. From 1974 on she worked as a decor and colour specialist on several animated film projects such as *Tarzoon* (1974) and *The Missing Link* (1980), both by the French-speaking Belgian comic-strip artist Picha, as well as on the first Flemish animated feature film, *John the Fearless.*

Her first film, *A Greek Tragedy* (Een Griekse tragedie, 1985), received no less than four first prizes at the prestigious animated film festival at Annecy in France. In 1987, she was presented with the highest film award of all for this 6-minute-long film, the much-coveted Oscar.

Contrary to what the title might suggest, this story about the last days of a temple in Athens is full of spicy and original inventiveness and naughty and ironic detail and never fails to surprise the viewer. Three Caryatids (columns in the form of women with long drapery) in a Greek temple have been resisting the effects of erosion, archaeologists and tourists for centuries. One day they decide they have had enough. One by one they become interested in life and decide to leave. The story of how these three Caryatids finally, with great difficulty, succeed in escaping is magnificently portrayed. The original way in which the three women are characterised, the timing and the pictorial quality of the soft pastel colours are, along with its cheerfully provocative, lively tone, the basic ingredients that made this film such a popular success.

Encouraged by this unexpected success, Van Goethem completed her second film *Full of Grace* (Vol van Gratie) two years later, in 1987. It is a somewhat naughty satire on three nuns who end up buying a number of 'candles' in a sex shop. Back at the convent chapel they discover that the 'candles' only give off thick black smoke. Unhappy about their purchase,

Rudi Mertens, *Dog Eat Dog* (1993).

Nicole van Goethem, *A Greek Tragedy* (Een Griekse tragedie, 1985).

the sisters return to the sex shop to speak to the manager. Having learned how the 'candles' should be used, they follow his instructions and end up in a state of ecstasy they had never experienced before.

This film, which has been considered by some to be rather provocative, makes remarkable use of richly coloured decor both in the red light area and in the church. Once again the animation is full of slap-stick humour and the characters are brilliantly portrayed. At the moment, Nicole van Goethem is working on *Living Apart Together.* We are all looking forward to seeing this third production of hers. As a filmmaker, she is slightly provocative and anarchic by nature and this gives her contributions to animated film in Flanders a particular 'adult' character.

Films issued by the Belgian Centre for Animated Film

Alongside the Centre for the Study of Animated Film in Ghent, which has been promoting the work of the Dept. of Animated Film at the Academy since 1971, and the Raoul Servais Foundation which since 1989 has been archiving and promoting the pioneer work of Raoul Servais and his co-workers, the Belgian Centre for Animated Film produces and distributes work by qualified animators.

Since it was founded in 1976, this Centre has been playing a leading role in the field. It has been able to help many talented young animators, thanks in part to the support of the Ministry for Culture of the Flemish Community. And here again international recognition soon followed. The brilliant film *The Country House* (Het landhuis), created by the late Josette Janssens and produced by the Centre for Animated Film, won the first prize at the Ottawa Festival in 1982. This little masterpiece is part of the first series of films produced by the Centre. During 1984, a second series was issued which included such remarkable films as *Cosmogony* (Jacques Lemaire), *Same Player* ... (Stef Viaene), *Cubic* (Kubiek, by Pierre Leterme) and *Oleander's Spring Birds* (De lentevogels van Oleander, by Suzanne Maes). These films were not only shown at all the festivals, they also received numerous awards. Artistic animated film in Flanders was, despite its lack of funding, at its zenith. However, the bankruptcy of PEN Film in 1987 also meant some hard years for the Centre. In 1989 it had to move to Brussels, where it was given a new lease of life under the inspiring leadership of Robert Vrielynck and producer Ivan D'hont. Thanks to the Centre, since then Frits Standaert and Jacques Lemaire have been able to create *Wundermilch* and *Kiss the Moon* and *Axis Mundi* respectively. The Centre also released the exceptionally well-made *Big Bad Little Willy* (1992) by Danny van Roy, a well-directed and unconventional story about Santa Claus in Flintstone style, as well as the remarkable *Dog Eat Dog* (1993) by Rudi Mertens. Both filmmakers studied at the Animation Department of the College for Communication Media in Brussels. *Dog Eat Dog,* the Centre's latest production, is a tribute to the Dutch graphic artist M.C. Escher (1898-1972), famous for his two-dimensional representations of complex geometric forms. Escher's work is both the object of Mertens' study and his source of inspiration. He has developed his own Escherian models, using as his point of departure three dogs who are biting each other's tails in never-ending violent embrace.

Characters emerge from the film's phenomenal decor in a spiralling movement only to be reabsorbed by the same decor. *Dog Eat Dog* has been masterfully drawn and is pictorially impressive, with its rhythm derived from original music of Jan Goovaerts. This film truly reflects its creator's talent.

In order to make animated film known to a larger audience, the Centre for Animated Film now runs exhibitions on the history of film and of animated film in particular. Its *Animation Machine,* a remarkable exhibition of the private collection of pre-cinema equipment belonging to Robert Vrielynck which has since toured the Japanese cities of Hiroshima, Tokyo and Osaka, is yet another means of putting Flemish animated film into the spotlight.

Prospects for the future

Six years ago, the European Community began to worry about the flood of junk cartoons from the USA and Japan being shown on European screens. PEN Film was certainly not the only studio that had to throw in the towel when confronted with these cheap poor-quality products. In order to stem this tide, the European Union set up the 'Media Program Cartoon' a few years ago and since then has been granting financial aid to all worthwhile European projects. This initiative has not been without result. The demand for quality is on the increase among many TV producers and stations. This is particularly the case in Great Britain and France and even in Germany, where until recently there has been little interest in animated film. Thanks to the efforts of Channel 4, for example, British animated film has now attained a level of quality unknown in the past. Unfortunately, however, there is no Channel 4 in Flanders. Quite to the contrary, neither the national radio and television station BRTN nor the commercial TV station VTM have shown any interest either in children's films or in adult films. Moreover since the setting up of a fund for film production following the new decree on film of 1 January 1994, the genre of short films to which most animated films belong has been seriously threatened. In the meantime, the so-called 'de-taxation scheme' which made the distribution of Flemish short films financially interesting for distributors and cinema owners has been scrapped. Confronting this growing problem is the unique artistic character of Flemish animated film. In the long term it is in precisely this area that Flemish film has the capacity to prove itself internationally.

WIM DE POORTER
Translated by Peter Flynn.

Marc

Mulders, Heir to Tradition

Marc Mulders, *Crack L.A. No. II.* 1989. Canvas, 130 x 240 cm. Museum voor Religieuze Kunst, Uden.

A persistent myth that arose during the Romantic period would have us believe that the genuine artist creates in the same way as God, out of nothing. For the last two centuries originality has been considered the prime criterion by which it was thought the worth of an oeuvre could be judged. Though the Romantic cult of genius has now been put into perspective by postmodernism, this has still had hardly any effect on the common belief that new work that resembles familiar work is by definition less significant than work that lays down its own set of standards.

The extent to which the Romantic view of total creativity is based on a myth can be confirmed by every museum visitor. Even when a series of successive works shows changes, it is a gradual process, variations on models that change just as slowly or rapidly as man himself. T.S. Eliot was right in saying that originality is nothing other than deviation from tradition.

Marc Mulders,
Ecce Homo. 1989. Canvas,
170 x 280 cm. Collection
J. des Bouvries.

Rembrandt H. van Rijn,
*The Anatomy Lesson of
Doctor Deyman*. 1656.
Canvas, 100 x 134 cm.
Rijksmuseum, Amsterdam.

In this sense the old is always retained in the new. Artists reach out towards each other across a chasm many centuries wide; Eliot meets Donne, Stravinsky greets Pergolesi, Francis Bacon revives a Velasquez motif. The repetition of a theme or motif can be considered as a tribute that endorses the tradition. But at the same time there are variations that are evidence of character and individuality.

In 1989 the Dutch painter Marc Mulders (1958-) painted his large canvas called *Ecce Homo*. The image is dominated by a man's dead body with its feet towards the spectator, its head slightly raised and the abdomen cut open. Anyone familiar with art history will recognise at a glance the central motif from Rembrandt's *The Anatomy Lesson of Doctor Deyman*. Those who have read their art history books even more thoroughly will know in addition that Rembrandt based his composition on that of Mantegna's famous painting of *The Burial of Christ*.

This reference, confirmed by one of the photo-collages Mulders himself describes as a sort of preliminary study, is more than a gratuitous display of erudition or a manifestation of the postmodernist realisation that everything is bound to repeat itself. There is no noncommittal eclecticism here, nor irony; each allusion to the art-historical past is part of an overall view.

The tribute to Mantegna and Rembrandt that can be descried in *Ecce Homo* may be considered as a testimony. Mulders feels himself to be indebted not only to pictorial tradition, but also to the ideas embedded in that tradition. The way he refers to these two paintings in his work shows that the affinity between them is based on a shared concern for suffering. It's true that Mantegna was preoccupied with the passion of the god become man and Rembrandt with the destiny of man as a mortal individual, but in both cases what we see is a manifestation of the body in its most vulnerable and tragic state. In this respect Mulders conforms to the essence of all Western art, which experienced peaks not only among the realistic painters of the sixteenth and seventeenth centuries but also in the work of the Greek trage-dians and Shakespeare, in Picasso's *Guernica* and Eliot's *The Waste Land.*

There is, however, more than the theme of suffering. In his variations on Mantegna and Rembrandt's central idea, Mulders demonstrates that his involvement with his predecessors is at least as much one of form as of content. After Cézanne, anything else would be difficult. Since art was revolutionised a century ago, we know that a painting is, in the first instance, a question of form and that it is the form that determines the content rather

Marc Mulders, *Lilies No. VIII.* 1994. Canvas, 100 x 100 cm. Collection T. Sas.

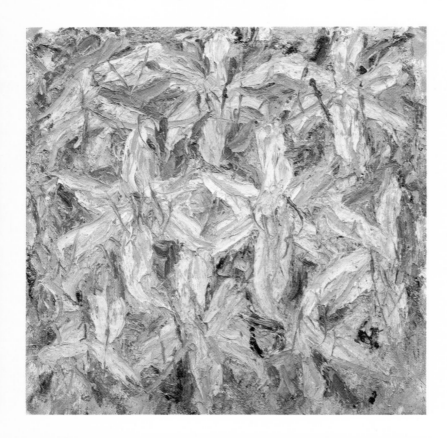

Marc Mulders,
*Five Skinned Rabbits
No. v.* 1993. Canvas,
100 x 100 cm. Private
Collection.

than the other way round. Concentrating on the work of Mulders: in the making of the painting the suffering body undergoes a transformation into paint. But at the same time the material with which the artist is working undergoes a process by which means it in its turn becomes a body. Mulders himself once made a telling observation on this when he described the relationship between model and image: '*Painting from a piece of meat in my left hand, the meat became soaked in oil and splashes of paint and became paint, the paint on the canvas became meat.*' And: '*The paint behaves like a muscle, exposed and contracting.*'

From close up, Mulders' paintings look like tanned hides covered in scars, or the gnarled bark of a tree. The canvas is covered in scratches and scoring, traces of the knife that appears to have tattooed the paint into it. The likeness to a tanned skin suggests a form of life that continues in the coagulated end product. The term still-life takes on a new meaning here: life is stopped still, like a single frame from a film. The dynamics of Mulders' flower pieces and portrayals of dead wild animals confirm this impression; they also show how much he differs from the seventeenth-century detail painters with whom he shares this choice of subject. The life-dynamic that also appears to continue into the process of decomposition is given shape on canvas in the series that Mulders paints: roses, dead rabbits and deer are, in a series of works, followed in a process of transformation which still carries on even in death.

Mulders is not so much concerned with a result achieved in the academic

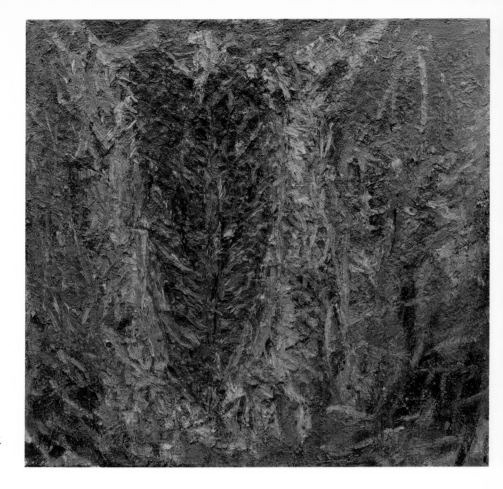

Marc Mulders, *Deer No. II.*
1993. Canvas, 120 x 120
cm. Private Collection.

manner, but in work in which the action, the gesture and the process can still
be seen, even when the painting has come to be hung in a museum or gallery.
He has never made a secret of his affinity with action painters like Jackson
Pollock or impulsively working artists like Van Gogh, the godfather of all
Expressionists.

Paintings may have developed out of gesture, but in the end they are
seen as fixed images. Even Mulders has in this respect spoken of the fundamental difference between near and far: he who stands close to the painting
discerns the action, while he who takes a step backward sees the performance.

A well-executed painting always provides a point, at a greater or lesser
distance, where the two perspectives coincide. In a bad painting the combination of gesture and image produces something unreal: the pose. This
makes itself felt as soon as quotations and symbols are no longer absorbed
organically into the whole. In this sense Mulders adheres to the organic
principle of coherence over fragmentation, despite his dynamic being
inspired by Expressionism. He is by no means a postmodernist. This is
understandable considering his loyalty to tradition, his ideological / philosophical streak and his aversion to the conceptual art that takes little account

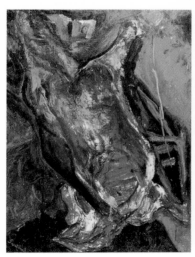

Chaim Soutine,
Slaughtered Ox. 1925.
Canvas, 140 x 82 cm.
Albright-Knox Art Gallery,
Buffalo (NY).

Rembrandt H. van Rijn,
Slaughtered Ox. 1655.
Panel, 94 x 69 cm.
Musée du Louvre, Paris.

FURTHER READING

Marc Mulders (Catalogue
n° 757, Stedelijk Museum
Amsterdam). Amsterdam,
1991.
Marc Mulders (Catalogue,
De Pont Foundation for
Contemporary Art).
Tilburg, 1993.

of craft. Mulders' conception of painting as an organic process of transformation and transcendence implies a preference for those artists who know how to depict flesh in all its materiality and in addition to invest it with a spiritual value. This applies first and foremost to Rembrandt. It is not only his *Anatomical Lesson* that was of great significance in the development of his artistry. The depiction of the slaughtered ox, which can be seen in the Louvre, is also a painting that guides and clarifies. Rembrandt did not restrict himself to depicting a dead animal as accurately as possible, but allowed himself to be inspired by the looseness and rawness of the flayed flesh in applying the paint as loosely and rawly as possible to the canvas. It is no surprise that it was precisely this painting that the Naturalist writers Zola and Huysmans put forward as a progressive work of art that anticipated their modernist views. Nor is it surprising that Chaim Soutine, the Post-Impressionist so admired by Mulders, should have repeated this motif numerous times.

There is, naturally, a common thread to be descried that links Rembrandt's *Anatomical Lesson* and *Slaughtered Ox,* through the work of Soutine, to that of Mulders. Two notions flow organically one into the other, the attention devoted to suffering as an existential theme and, as far as the paint and canvas are concerned, compassion for this suffering. Mulders' appreciation of predecessors such as Grünewald, Dürer and Goya is based on the same premise.

The influence of Francis Bacon on Mulders deserves separate consideration. There is, at first sight, a substantial correspondence between Mulders' so-called 'walls of flesh' from the late eighties and the depictions of deformed bodies that form part of Bacon's most famous works. The colour combinations (red, pink, white, grey and black) and the choice of subject by themselves force a comparison. But there are still great differences, however pronounced the affinity may be and however strongly the young Mulders was influenced by Bacon. In terms of form there is a totally different handling of paint. Mulders is in the habit of painting 'wet-into-wet', which results in his canvasses being covered with thick layers and looking like the slopes of a volcano covered in solidifying lava. Bacon was an artist who knew how to paint 'sparsely', as Mulders put it, not without a hint of jealousy.

But there are numerous differences in terms of content too. Bacon's mutilated, deformed bodies appear in a grotesque context. Mulders' ever-recurring subjects – the suffering or dead Christ, sometimes contrasted with the structure of a church that has become an institute for the fossilised, and the cadavers of slaughtered animals, flesh in its most naked state – reflect the tragedy of the one great history of suffering, whether it takes substantial form in the fate of man or of beast. Bacon diminishes the human state, whereas Mulders remains a committed humanist to the very depths of his being.

JAAP GOEDEGEBUURE
Translated by Gregory Ball.

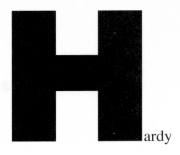

Hardy

Perennials of Dutch and Flemish Poetry

We've said it before and we'll say it again: Dutch poetry, whether from Flanders or the Netherlands, has a stronger claim to international appreciation than Dutch-language prose. In this field, at least, the small Dutch language area would be great. In Guido Gezelle, Herman Gorter, J. H. Leopold, Paul van Ostaijen, Martinus Nijhoff and Gerrit Achterberg it possesses home-grown poets who would be world-famous if they had written in English. But alas! You hear that quite often; and it may well be true, too.

Nevertheless, the Dutch and Flemings, like other people, have poems – and these are some of them – which everybody knows, or ought to know. Poems which are in every anthology and from which everybody can quote at least one line – usually the first line or the last, and almost always with something of the proverb about it. Poems which everyone should carry in their heads, for use in times of trouble or of joy. Or just because they're so beautiful.

Jan Sanders van Hemessen, *Poetry and the Poet.* c. 1550. Panel, 159 x 189 cm. Mauritshuis, The Hague.

Karel van de Woestijne (1878-1929)
Overture

My father's house, where the days passed more slowly,
was quiet, for within the garden's shade it lay
and in the over-arching leaves' tranquillity.
– I was a child, measured life by my mother's stray
laughter, who was not merry, and the regularity
of twilights round the trees, the desultory
years round the placid life of the unstirring day.

And I was happy in the shadow of this life
which walked beside my dreams like a good father...
– The days had given me the strange delight
of knowing how each evening a flock of birds would hover
in the gentle skies of summer, which suffuse
the souls of lowly men with blessed ease
when twilight falls and paints in its own evening hues
the heavy-tranquil fruit upon the peaceful trees.

...Then softly you became part of my life, and we
were like two meagre flowers in the evening of the day.
And I loved you. And though since then I may
have loved many women, with assurance or entreaty,
you I did love; for I saw your child's eyes glow
at leaning blossoms in the gardens, and your face
look on my solitary thoughts and deeds with solace
in my father's house, where the days passed so slow...

From *My Parents' House* (Het Vaderhuis, 1903)
Translated by Tanis Guest.

P.C. Boutens (1870-1943)
Good Death

Good Death whose clear pure piping
Penetrates life grown still,
Drawing smiles of understanding
From the young and beautiful,

For whom the wise and children
Gladly leave their books and play,
At whom only pinched old men
Shiver with cold dismay, –

I count each day bleak and empty
That lacks your beckoning horn;
For to me ever strange and lovely
Is this land of new wine and corn;

For not once did I ever drink here
The water that makes the soul young
But there'd ring out from somewhere near
The air of your distant song.

All the beauty of earth's giving
Leads to you with every breath,
And only then is life living
When it moves us even to death.

From *Voices* (Stemmen, 1907)
Translated by Tanis Guest.

J.H. Leopold (1865-1925)

Oh when I dead shall, dead shall be
come then and whisper, whisper tenderly,
my pale eyes shall I open to thee
and no wonder will in me be.

And no wonder will in me be –
in this love death will only be
a sleeping, sleeping quietly,
a waiting for thee, a waiting for thee.

From *Poems* (Verzen, 1912)
Translated by P.J. de Kanter (in 'The Valley of Irdîn', Amsterdam, 1957).

Richard Minne (1891-1965)
Days Poor and Rich (IV)

The world's a flute which has mouthpieces by the score.
And each plays his own tune. It makes a sad refrain
in which I cannot hear my own sound any more.
And you? Maybe you too have tapped at many a pane,
and been like me sent packing, sad and sore.

And yet: I dreamed, and hoped; and paid the penalty.
I saw the Alps, and Flanders, and Strassburg on the Rhine.
I loved. I often banged my drum for all to see.
I browsed through books of wisdom old and fine.
I searched with hands and feet – if that can be.

And at the end? – I have, inalienable and lasting,
the solace of my own true song, when I sit quietly
on the high bank and play a tune at evening,
not for all time and space, but for the moment only.
Then I've gained one more happy day. That's no small thing.

From *Open House* (In den Zoeten Inval, 1926)
Translated by Tanis Guest.

Paul van Ostaijen (1896-1928)
Recitative

For Gaston Burssens

Under the moon the long river slides by
Above the long river the moon mournfully slides
Under the moon on the long river the canoe slides to the sea

By tall reedbeds
by low meadows
the canoe slides to the sea
with the sliding moon the canoe slides to the sea
Companions then to the sea the canoe the moon and the man
Why do the moon and the man two together slide submissively to the sea

From *Poems* (Gedichten, 1928)
Translated by Tanis Guest.

Willem Elsschot (1882-1960)
The Marriage

When he once noticed how the mists of time
were dimming his wife's eyes and snuffing out their glow,
had worn and marked her face and touched her hair with snow,
he turned away from her and regret gnawed at him.

He was beside himself, he cursed and tore his hair,
measured her with his gaze but could desire no more,
he saw the supreme sin become a hellish chore
as she looked up at him with a dying beast's despair.

But die she did not, though his mouth with dreadful stealth
sucked the marrow from her bones, which yet still held her straight.
She dared no longer speak, to question or bemoan her fate,
and trembled where she stood, but lived and kept her health.

He thought: I'll strike her dead and burn the house above her.
I must get my stiffened feet clean of this mould,
run through the fire, splash through the water cold
to find a different country and another lover.

But kill he did not; for between dream and deed
are laws that bar the way, and problems stark and plain,
and melancholy too, which no-one can explain,
which comes at evening time when it is sleep you need.

And so the years went by. The children, now full-grown,
would see the man whom they called Father sitting
beside the fire, silent and unmoving,
with a desolate and a dreadful face, alone.

From *Yesterday's Poems* (Verzen van vroeger, 1934)
Translated by Tanis Guest.

H. Marsman (1899-1940)
Thinking of Holland

Thinking of Holland
I see broad rivers
languidly winding
through endless fen,
lines of incredibly
tenuous poplars
like giant plumes
on the polder's rim;
and sunk in tremendous
open expanses,
the farmsteads scattered
across the plain:
coppices, hamlets,
squat towers and churches
and elms composing
a rich domain.
Low leans the sky
and slowly the sun
in mist of mother
of pearl grows blurred,
and far and wide
the voice of the water,
of endless disaster,
is feared and heard.

From *Poetry* (Poëzie, 1938)
*Translated by James Brockway
(in 'The Literary Review',
V, 2, Teaneck (NJ), 1961-1962).*

Martinus Nijhoff (1894-1953)
The Bridge at Bommel

I went to look at the new bridge at Bommel.
I saw the bridge. Two facing banks there were,
which once seemed each of them to shun the other,
now neighbours once again. Lying there idle
for a while in the grass, after I'd drunk my tea,
my mind filled with the landscape all around –
let me from that infinity perceive a sound,
a voice filling my ears which spoke to me.

It was a woman. The boat that carried her
came downstream through the bridge, steady and calm.
She was alone on deck, stood at the tiller,

and what she sang, I heard then, was a psalm.
Oh, I thought, oh, that there went my mother.
Praise God, she sang, He'll keep you from all harm.

From *New Poems* (Nieuwe gedichten, 1934)
Translated by Tanis Guest.

J.C. Bloem (1887-1966)
Dapper Street

Nature is for the empty, the contented.
And then, what can we boast of in this land?
A hill with a few small villas set against it,
A patch of wood no bigger than your hand.

Give me instead the sombre city highroads,
The waterfront hemmed in between the quays.
Clouds that move across an attic window,
Were ever clouds more beautiful than these?

All things are riches to the unexpectant.
Life holds her wonders hidden from our sight,
Then suddenly reveals them to perfection.
I thought this over, walking through the sleet,
The city grime, one grey and drizzly morning,
Blissfully happy, drenched in Dapper Street.

From *Quiet though Sad* (1946)
Translated by James Brockway (in 'Lyrical Holland', Amsterdam, 1954).

P.N. van Eyck (1887-1954)
The Gardener and Death

A Persian nobleman speaks:

Early today, my gardener, terror-struck,
Rushed in and cried, 'Alas, my cursed luck!

I was at work, pruning the rosary;
I turned, and there stood Death and stared at me.

I was afraid and ran, in a cold sweat,
But saw him make the gesture of a threat.

Master, give me your horse, let me be gone!
Before nightfall I'll be in Ispahan.'

He fled. And I, before the day was dark,
Met Death a-strolling in the cedar park.

He said no word, waiting what I should say.
'What meant that threat you gave my man today?'

He smiled and said, 'That gesture meant no threat
To scare him, but surprise at finding yet

Him busy at his task at early dawn
Whom I must seize at night in Ispahan.'

From *Coming Hither* (Herwaarts, 1939)
Translated by A.J. Barnouw (in 'Lyrical Holland', Amsterdam, 1954).

Jan van Nijlen (1884-1965)
Notice to Travellers

Never get on the train without dreams in your luggage,
then you'll find decent lodging in any town or village.

Calmly and patiently sit by the open window;
you are a traveller and safely incognito.

Dredge from your past the fresh eyes of a child,
both cool and keen, excited and beguiled.

All you see growing in the dark spring fields you view,
you can be sure, was planted just for you.

Let the commercial travellers have their say
about the latest films; God smiles and waits his day.

Give every station-master a polite 'Hello';
without their signal not one train would ever go.

And if the train won't move, much to the detriment
of your desire and hopes, the hard-won cash you spent,

keep calm and open up your bag; draw on its store
and you will find you've wasted not an hour.

And if the train pulls in to some peculiar place
you'd never even heard of, not once in all your days,

then you have reached your goal; then you learn with surprise
what travel means for wanderers and the truly wise …

Above all, be not amazed when, past trees just like home,
a quite ordinary train transports you straight to Rome.

From *Secret Code* (Geheimschrift, 1934)
Translated by Tanis Guest.

M. Vasalis (1909 -)
The Idiot in the Bath

With shoulders hunched, eyes screwed tightly shut,
bent over the nurse's arm, unsightly and uncouth,
almost at a run, feet tangling in the mat,
week after week, the idiot takes his bath.

The clouds of vapour rising from the trough
of water calm him down: he's soothed by steam …
and with every stitch of clothing that comes off
he's drawn still deeper into an old, familiar dream.

He folds his skinny arms across his chest
as nurse eases him in until the water grips,
he sighs as if he was slaking his earliest thirst
and slowly a great joy dawns around his lips.

His worried face grows handsome, blank, at ease,
his slender feet stand up like palest flowers,
his long and pallid legs, where aging lowers,
rise out of the green water like the trunks of trees.

In all this green he is as one unborn,
he does not yet know that some fruits are but rind,
he has not lost the wisdom of the body
and does not need the wisdom of the mind.

And every time he's hauled out of his doze
and rubbed down with a brisk towel till he's dry,
then forced back into stiff, unyielding clothes,
he fights against it and will, for a moment, cry.

And every week it is his fate to be
reborn, wrenched from the water's womb, impaired,
and every week it is his destiny
to have remained once more an idiot, and scared.

From *Parkland and Deserts* (Parken en woestijnen, 1940)
Translated by James Brockway.

Leo Vroman (1915-)
For the Reader

Printed letters I will show You here
but of my warm lips no living speech
and from this text no hand will reappear.
What can I do? I find You out of reach.

Oh, could I comfort You, then I could cry.
Come, give Your hand this page, my skin;
soften the petrifying print that I am in
and speak the words I have tried living by.

I have written poems beyond recall,
am still a stranger where I think I live,
and whom I hurt I've nothing left to give
love, that is all.

It was love that often seemed to make
me fall asleep making my pencil write
the words that slept in this book's night
till now when You read them awake.

Behind this page would be my proper place
where I could be alive again
to look into Your reading face
and ache to see the ebbing of Your pain.

Do not arouse these words for naught;
their nudity would find themselves to blame,
so let Your gaze not reach their shame
unless love is Your driving thought.

Then, read this like a letter nearly
too late, relax, and after these delays
fear not its kisses when it says:
I love you dearly.

From *Poems, Early and Late*
(Gedichten, vroegere en latere, 1949)
Translated by Leo Vroman.

Jan Hanlo (1912-1969)
One Morning

For Mai

Half past four one April morning
I was walking and whistling the St Louis Blues
But I whistled it my way
And whistling I thought: may my whistling
be like the song of the great thrush
And what do you know, after a while my
whistling of the St Louis Blues
really *was* like the song of the great thrush:
Turdus viscivorus

From *The varnished – Het geverniste* (1952)
Translated by James S Holmes (in 'Dutch Interior. Postwar
Poetry of the Netherlands and Flanders', New York, 1984).

Lucebert (1924-1994)
I Try in Poetic Fashion

I try in poetic fashion
that is to say
simplicities luminous waters
to give expression to
the expanse of life at its fullest

if I had not been a man
like masses of men
but if I had been who I was
the stone or fluid angel
birth and decay would not have touched me
the road from forlornness to communion
the stones stones beasts beasts birds birds road
would not be so befouled
as it can be seen to be in my poems
that are snapshots of that road

in this age what was always called
beauty beauty has burnt her face
she no longer comforts man
she comforts the larvae the reptiles the rats
but she startles man
and strikes him with the awareness
of being a breadcrumb on the universe's skirt

no longer evil alone
the deathblow alone makes us rebellious or
meek
but also good
the embrace that leaves us fumbling in despair
at space

and so I sought out
language in her beauty
heard there she had nothing human left
but the speech defects of the shadow
but those of the earsplitting sunlight

From *Apocryphal – The Analphabetical Name*
(Apocrief – De Analphabetische naam, 1952).
Translated by James S Holmes (in 'Dutch Interior.
Postwar Poetry of the Netherlands and Flanders',
New York, 1984).

All poems selected by Anton Korteweg and Frits Niessen.
Introduction translated by Tanis Guest.

 an

Tinbergen, Economist and Visionary

Professor Jan Tinbergen, who was born in 1903 and died on 9 June 1994, was in some respects an extraordinary man and in others quite the reverse. His ideas and theories bore witness to exceptional gifts and very high moral standards. In his daily life he was modest, friendly and helpful; in this respect he was extraordinary in his ordinariness.

In 1969 Tinbergen was awarded the first-ever Nobel Prize for Economics for his work, jointly with the Norwegian Ragnar Frisch; this in itself indicates how great were his contributions in his own field. He received more than fifteen honorary doctorates and other honours, of which it may be said that he valued them only as expressions of esteem for his work and his ideas, not in any sense for his person.

Tinbergen's choice of subjects to work on was always governed by the desire to find solutions to concrete, pressing social problems. Chief among these were, in chronological order: in the 1930s, a practicable economic policy; after the Second World War, the fight against poverty, including in the Third World, and redistribution of income, particularly within a state; and, more recently, the necessity of establishing a world government.

Tinbergen received the Nobel Prize for the method he employed: econometrics. He set up a model using mathematical equations to reflect economic reality and then tried to ascertain how specific variables such as unemployment could be influenced by means of economic policies. The model used must, of course, approach as closely as possible to reality. The success of this method, which has been applied all over the world, is dependent in principle on the possibility of shaping the economic aspects of society. Tinbergen, with his background in physics, was thus a typical representative of what is known in the Netherlands as 'engineers' socialism': it would be possible to improve an undesirable situation by administrative means.

As we have said, Tinbergen's use of models has gained general acceptance; and in that respect his work has won a lasting place in everyday economic policy. His example has been followed with such enthusiasm that one can now speak of an overdose of mathematics and econometrics in the study of economics. The main question here concerns the usefulness of what is being written. Economic phenomena are social in nature, and therefore likely to contain all kinds of psychological components; human behaviour does not always submit to being captured in complicated mathematical formulae. Tinbergen himself did not consider the excessive use of mathematics to be a mark of progress. In any case, he was not the first economist to make use of mathematics. Walras and Edgeworth are two noted economists who did just that, and there have of course been many more. But Tinbergen was among the first to apply mathematics in models which embraced the whole economy; moreover, his specific purpose was to design economic policies for entire countries.

The introduction of quantitative methods in economics was not without its difficulties. From the beginning there were both supporters and opponents. The leading economist when Tinbergen first published his quantitative work was undoubtedly the Englishman John Maynard Keynes. In a discussion in *The Economic Journal* Keynes expressed a mainly negative view of Tinbergen's methodology. There is nothing to indicate that he found the latter's reply convincing. Keynes preferred to use his intuition; and the extent to which this is acceptable depends above all on that intuition being generally sound. Tinbergen clearly had more confidence in quantification; he argued in favour of it throughout his life.

After the war Tinbergen became director of the newly-established CPB (Central Planning Bureau). Here he was able to put into practice certain ideas he had already put forward in the Labour Plan published in 1935 by the SDAP (Social Democratic Labour Party) and the NVV (Dutch League of Trade Unions); he had been one of the driving forces behind this document. From 1945 until about 1955 Tinbergen was principally concerned with economic policy, as was to be expected in view of his position in the CPB.

His work over the next two decades was mainly in the field of aid to poor countries. He had been shocked by their unbelievable poverty and, typically, applied his talents to the search for solutions. He published a great deal on the necessity of providing more aid. He played a significant role at the United Nations in advisory and study committees, particularly on the subject of the amount of development aid that was needed.

Around 1975, when Tinbergen was already seventy-two years old, he began a series of publications on the distribution of income. As a student he had already been greatly affected by the severe poverty he had seen in Leiden when studying physics there in the 1920s. It was this that first led him to apply himself to the possibility of combatting the economic depression, and possible ways of influencing economic phenomena through government policies and thus eliminating poverty. Ever since the early fifties, Tinbergen had been arguing in print for an increase in aid to developing countries in order to combat the degrading poverty there. Here, too, he was driven by the urge to contribute to the solving of a social problem. In tackling this subject he followed two lines of economic thought. He first discussed the more or less technical problem of how development plans should be drawn up and implemented. No less important, however, is the economic motivation for increasing development aid. Ultimately this is based on the simple fact that £1, or $1, taken from the income of the rich and added to that of the poor reduces the well-being (what economists call 'welfare') of the former by less than it increases the welfare of the latter. Total (world) welfare is thus increased by the transfer. Those who argue in this way take a bird's eye view of the world and then consider how optimum welfare can be achieved for the world as a whole. It is a broad view, and a long view too, which takes the future into account; Tinbergen repeatedly drew attention to the fact that the poor will come knocking at the gates of the rich countries to obtain what they do not have in their own countries: a minimum standard of living. This phenomenon is already with us on a massive scale; with increasing ease of communication and ever faster and cheaper transport it will make itself felt to a much greater extent in the future.

Tinbergen based the need for a global redistribution of wealth on two arguments. The moral argument is actually a straightforward choice, based on the view that acute poverty is degrading and must therefore be combatted. The economic argument can also be stated in fairly simple terms. In terms of economic theory it rests on Gossen's First Law, that of diminishing marginal utility. In practical terms, this comes down to what we already said: that a pound taken from the rich and given to the poor reduces the welfare of the former by less than it increases that of the latter. This need not lead to an absolutely equal distribution of income, for the effort to earn money must also be rewarded. But – according to Tinbergen – the principle does lead to a marked levelling of income, both nationally and internationally.

In Tinbergen's view, differences in income have to be justified. In general he was in favour of (further) equalisation of income, both within and between countries. Large differences in income conflict with the objective of the greatest possible welfare within society. The market rewards labour according to its scarcity, not according to the effort involved. Scarcity and effort are far from being the same thing. Many human qualities or characteristics are to a significant extent either innate or acquired by education, often at society's expense. These require no special effort. All things considered, then, there are hardly any justifiable differences.

How to move from the present situation, with relatively large differences in income, to one with a more even distribution is, however, a different matter. Increased taxation is of course a possibility, but has the disadvantage of reducing the incentive for effort to a greater or lesser extent. Theoretically, this objection can be avoided by basing the increase in taxes on earning ability rather than on the earnings themselves. This ability tax is then a fixed amount which must be paid, the income achieved through that ability being free of further income tax. Effort is thus rewarded. The difficulty lies, of course, in the accurate assessment of each individual's ability. It is questionable whether this can be done with sufficient precision. When making a choice, it also has to be borne in mind that the present system of income tax is far from perfect.

Another method of reducing differences in income is to increase the supply of people with scarce abilities. This presupposes that the qualities necessary for an occupation can be learned, which is only partly true. Tinbergen sees this process as a race. On the one hand there is the technological development which requires ever more highly educated people and rewards them lavishly; this leads to increased differences in income. By increasing the supply of highly qualified workers this can be neutralised, or even overcompensated for, thus producing a levelling effect. On this reasoning, almost any expenditure on education is justified: not only does it increase the productivity of the work force, but the increased supply of highly qualified individuals also leads to greater equality of income, with a concomitant increase in total welfare. This argument can be taken still further. On a global view, the strength of the Western countries lies above all in their relative abundance of capital, both in the form of high-quality physical means of production (e.g. machines) and in a highly educated work force (human capital). If the West wishes to maintain its position it must therefore specialise in products which require a great deal of capital, including the above-mentioned human capital. From this viewpoint it would be difficult to justify any cuts in education, though it is still conceivable that virtually the same result could be achieved with less expenditure.

During the last years of his life Tinbergen repeatedly argued for the establishment of a world government. After all, in 1974 he had chaired the Club of Rome Committee which drew up the report *Reshaping the International Order*. A committed world federalist, he based his attitude on the theory of the best (or optimal) level of decision-making. This concerns the question of which decisions ought to be taken at which level; here Tinbergen opted for the principle of subsidiarity, which states that decisions should be taken at the lowest possible level. Here it is necessary to take account of the fact that certain decisions may have consequences for others not themselves involved in the decision-making process. Imagine two countries, A and C, with a river B running through both of them. When country A decides that so much water shall be discharged into river B that it leads to flooding in country C, then country A is in fact making decisions for country C. The latter has no voice in the decision and receives no compensation. In such a case economists speak of the existence of external effects. In this

Jan Tinbergen
(1903-1994)
(Photo by Paul van den Abeele).

instance the decision was taken at too low a level, because the principle of democracy demands that everyone should participate, directly or indirectly, in decisions which affect him or her.

As a result of the rapid developments in technology and communications, greatly increased international trade, and lastly the marked internationalisation or globalisation of trade and industry, the number of cross-border issues needing to be resolved in this way is steadily increasing. There is as yet no appropriate government framework for settling these issues. There are many international bodies and organisations; but in some cases they have no powers at all, while in others each member has the right of veto, with corresponding delay in decision-making.

Cross-border problems may be continent-wide or even global in scale. We have already seen an example of the first type: excessive discharge of water into international rivers. With regard to, for example, the Maas and the Rhine, this problem can best be resolved within the European Union. After the flooding in the Netherlands in early 1995 everyone suddenly started demanding just this. Examples of global problems are: pollution of the oceans, the greenhouse effect, the exhaustion of natural resources and the maintenance of peace. Tinbergen wanted to reshape the UN into a real government, with the same powers as those available to national governments. His ideas on this subject have often been regarded as utopian, but this is quite unjust. His analysis has a completely rational basis. Of course the powerful countries do not want to give up their position, but then they are putting might before right. Democracy itself is in conflict with this barbaric principle. It is true that there are many stumbling blocks on the way to a world government. They do not, however, invalidate the arguments in its favour.

Tinbergen's attitude is typical of his view of science. It must look beyond the illusions of the day and all subjective and irrational arguments. And always with the aim of assisting the politicians with rational analyses that are as objective as possible.

On a number of occasions Tinbergen spoke out against describing the Western economies as 'capitalist'. Capitalism is after all the situation in which the whole economic process is governed almost entirely by market forces, with a minimum of government action. However, this 'laisser faire' situation has not existed for a long time. From about the middle of the last century government has intervened more and more in economic life. Even in a 'capitalist' country like the United States more than a third of the national income is spent, directly or indirectly, by the government. In many European countries the figure is considerably higher. In Tinbergen's view the present Western economies could better be described using one of the following terms: 'mixed', 'on its way to democratic socialism', or 'on its way to optimality'.

A particular feature of the development of Western societies is that ownership of the means of production has remained to a significant extent in the hands of private individuals and companies. Their rights as owners have however become increasingly subject to restrictions, in the interest of the better functioning of society. Thus while ownership has remained in private hands the utilisation of the means of production has to a certain extent been socialised.

Tinbergen's lifelong objective, the solving of social problems and the elimination of contrasts, bred in him an abhorrence of absolutism. Brotherhood and toleration were among his most cherished values. Especially towards the end of his life, he often spoke of the danger of extremes and the desirability of avoiding them. He saw dangers in pure capitalism, with its dictatorship of the marketplace. Equally, he did not care for the absolutism which accompanied central economic planning in the Soviet Union and other states. Democratic socialism provided the middle way, and that was the road to take.

It is hard to say exactly what Tinbergen's attitude to planning was. In the 1930s he worked on the Labour Plan, which advocated a quite extensive degree of central control of the economy. Later he was a professor of development planning. However, there are many kinds of planning, from the general to the highly detailed and from the strictly imposed to the advisory. It is clear that Tinbergen was not averse to planning as such, for that was a consequence of the need to eliminate social evils. And naturally he never recommended planning in its most obsessive form. The planning he argued for was intended to convince others.

Tinbergen's friendly, modest nature did not prevent him adopting positions which can be labelled downright radical. In the last little book we wrote together, *The Future of Socialism* (De toekomst van de sociaal democratie, 1994), he continued to maintain that 25% of the world's income would ultimately need to be redistributed, a percentage that has currently been achieved in only a few modern states such as Sweden. His pacifism, too, indicates his willingness to adopt radical points of view.

Jan Tinbergen's scientific merits were enormous. Much of his pioneering work in the field of econometrics now forms part of the professional knowledge of almost every modern economist. That is an honour, but it is not the greatest honour that can be accorded an individual. That must by definition be moral in nature. And here, too, Jan Tinbergen was among the very great. His willingness to help, his unselfishness, his simplicity, the humanity which radiated from him, all these combined to make him a legendary figure even in his own lifetime.

JAN BERKOUWER
Translated by Tanis Guest.

FURTHER READING

TINBERGEN, JAN, *Economic Policy, Principles and Design.* Amsterdam, 1956.

TINBERGEN, JAN, *Income Distribution. Analysis and Policies.* Amsterdam, 1975.

TINBERGEN, JAN, *Production, Income and Welfare. The Search for an Optimum Social Order.* Brighton, 1985.

TINBERGEN JAN and D. FISCHER, *Welfare and Welfare.* Brighton, 1987.

TINBERGEN, JAN, *World Security and Equity.* Aldershot, 1990.

TINBERGEN, JAN and JAN BERKOUWER, *The Future of Socialism.* Rotterdam, 1994.

he

Delicacy of a Rain Forest

About the Poetry of Leo Vroman

Leo Vroman's collected poems (*Collected Poems 1946-1984* – Gedichten 1946-1984), published in one volume in 1985, amount to over 1,000 pages; but the collection is far removed from any notion of an ornate tombstone on a productive life. Four new volumes of original Dutch poetry have since seen the light, as well as 'Love, Greatly Enlarged', an English adaptation by Vroman of his lengthy narrative poem 'Liefde, sterk vergroot' (1981), linking his love for mankind and for his wife Tineke – to whom the poem is dedicated – with his research into the properties of proteins in the blood. In the Dutch volumes – *Fractal* (Fractaal, 1985), *Dear Indivisibility* (Dierbare ondeelbaarheid, 1989), *As I Was Still Alive* (Toen ik nog leefde, 1991) and *All Godforsaken Night* (De godganselijke nacht, 1993) – Vroman has rejuvenated his language and allowed it, more than ever before, to be cross-fertilised by science.

The early poems of Leo Vroman (1915-) already show a delight in playing with language as well as a strong biological point of view. From the very beginning, Vroman's poetical world teems with life, with the growth, changeability and decay of organisms. It's a mesmerising world, expressed in a language full of associations, neologisms and colloquialisms.

Vroman, who is a Jew, managed to make his escape from the Netherlands after the German invasion in May 1940, leaving behind his fiancée Tineke, whom he would not see again until seven years later. In Batavia (nowadays Jakarta) he completed his biological studies and developed his talents as a poet and illustrator. However, his freedom was short-lived; as the Japanese made their advance towards Indonesia, Vroman was drafted into the Dutch colonial army. It didn't take long before the Dutch resistance collapsed. Vroman was made a prisoner of war by the Japanese in March 1942 and held in various camps on the island of Java and in Japan. Some of his poems from this period show how severed he felt from life and the love of his life. In the gloomiest of them all, 'Night' ('Nacht'), God – still a familiar figure in Vroman's early poetry – is out of sight, but during the most silent nights God maybe still hears *'the sick rustling of my thoughts / that flap themselves to pieces outside on his pane.'* These poems are full of windows, blackened or staring windows, and walls.

After Vroman's release from the POW camp, he was first taken to Manilla, in September 1945, where he was officially discharged from the Dutch army. From Manilla he travelled to New York where his uncle convinced him that he shouldn't go back to Europe if he wanted to dedicate his life to research. It wasn't until September 1947 that Tineke came over to join him. They lived in New Brunswick before finally settling in Brooklyn NY where they raised a family. After Vroman's reunion with Tineke, his poems become more playful. Humour and self-mockery offer a light-hearted counterpoint in a poetry which explores the hidden reaches of life and death. In a poem entitled 'About People' ('Over mensen') Vroman states that he'd better shut up about butterflies, windows and water which inhabit his dreams and write *'a verse for people about people'*. People then are, in unique Vroman-style, described as *'those taller than tall animals / with nodes and twiggy branchings on their extremities / which become frowned and knotty from sheer misery. / We should adorn them with downy lids, / these nervetubers, seats of the intellects / which nourish the last tufts of their*

A self-portrait by Leo Vroman (1995).

furs / with a humus of their thoughts / fuming out of their uppermost walls.'

This haphazard translation may suggest Vroman's poetical subject matter but it doesn't do justice to his play with the Dutch language. In Vroman-idiom, many verbs and some nouns derived from verbs begin with the pre-fix *'ver-'*. Words with this prefix abound in the Dutch language, filling almost an entire volume of the comprehensive Dictionary of the Dutch Language (WNT; *Woordenboek der Nederlandsche Taal* – see *The Low Countries* 1994-95: 288-290). Usually these words indicate a process, a gradual development. One of Vroman's favourite words is *'vergaan':* to decay, but he doesn't need the WNT to come up with a host of *ver*-words of his own invention, like *'vertwijgsels'* (twiggy branchings), *'verfronzen'* and *'verknopen'* (to become frowned and knotty). This is just one of the techniques Vroman uses to create a poetical world of extreme liquidity. Neologisms like *'zenuw-knollen'* (nervetubers), smooth enjambements and a frequent use of synaes-thesia reinforce this impression of continuous motion. Unlike the work of experimental colleagues at the time, Vroman's poems still rhyme, but it's not a static kind of rhyme; it's more like a loosely draped garland, in tune with the changeable nature of Vroman's world. A prominent Dutch critic, Kees Fens, has clearly indicated how Vroman's rhyme differs from tradi-tional rhyme: *'(the rhyming words) don't both lose something in the process, they don't suavely melt together to shape a new meaning. In Vroman's poetry the rhyming words, precisely because of their rhyme, emphasise their uniqueness. Both remain singular; rhyme is used not to demonstrate conge-niality but as proof of strangeness.'*

Vroman breaks down the boundaries between humans and animals, ani-mate and inanimate, day and night, inside and outside and, ultimately, between himself and the world he wants to grasp in his loving embrace. Elements from one category seep into the other, transforming reality into a phantasmagorical universe. Often the poet represents himself while dream-ing, and then in his dream quirky things gradually dissolve all natural dimensions. Listen for instance to the first stanza of one of Vroman's English poems, 'Another Dream': *'Once I was caught in this dream: / I slept that my room was shrinking. / At the dead end of all thinking / I woke up with a scream.'* In the narration of this poem, the poet wakes up in someone else's grave, a recurrent theme in Vroman's poetry. In this case, it's a grave occu-pied by a girl whose organs *'(...) dreamily creep / like puppies, blind, vel-vety.'* The girl begs him to *'break this fat roof away!',* but all he can do for her is make her human again by communicating with her. In the end, the poet wakes up from his dream.

Another dreamlike event is depicted in the poem 'The Bird' ('De vogel') from *Going Sleepwalking* (Uit slaapwandelen, 1957). The poem begins with an idyllic country scene full of innocent, diminutive sweetness, when sud-denly the sky seems oppressive and a bird appears on the scene. The bird – which looks like a gentleman – is in a rather dejected mood. He tells how he has lost his birdlike qualities as a result of associating with people. He can-not fly any more and is therefore unable to join his father *'in his valley / under the seaweedtrees / where skypearls descend / at the long day's end.'* The poet tries to help the bird – which turns into a female – by throwing her into the sky, but she clasps him in an eerie embrace which leaves him cov-ered with feathers. The following morning the poet wakes up to a changed landscape and the extreme sense of solitude that results from a loss of illusions. It is as if the bird has taught us a lesson about the human condition, and we have become all the sadder and the wiser for it. In a poem written about thirty years later, 'With Other Eyes' ('Met andere ogen', in *Fractal*), another strange visitor arrives from the sky, who also changes into a woman. This visitor doesn't strike a tragic figure: he / she can fly, has even visited all the planets of the universe, but it's the earth which most enthralls him / her. Saturn was a *'gasfumeland'* and Mars a *'blooddesertfield'* but the planet Earth has taught this cosmic visitor human emotions: *'The delight of embarrassment, / red rims on the red roses / little children who pee and then blush (...)'* The mood of the poem is one of gratitude for being part of this dear, dear Earth.

This theme of Earth as his darling planet and his all-encompassing love for people (Tineke in particular) plays a considerable role in Vroman's poetry. Vroman reaches out to his readers, inviting them to be part of his everyday life. Vroman's readers know he has two daughters and that he likes to walk to Sheepshead Bay with Tineke. They know his feelings for America (*'Flesh land from which I live along'*) and for his small native country. But Vroman's poetry never becomes too homely and cozy. The limitations of time and space add a tragic note to the existence of people on this planet. They are threatened by various monsters: *'the monster Oblivion'* and the *'Voracious Monster Entropy'* but also by monsters of their own invention such as violence, murder and war. Since his volume *Curious* (Nieuwsgierig, 1980) Vroman has written a good number of anti-war poems, all without any connotation of propaganda. It's Vroman's unique voice that we recognise, an angry, pleading or desperate Vroman at that: *'well? what happens if the thunder / of these nukesick times / whitewhisks*

Leo Vroman, in his younger days, with a rather suspicious-looking experimental rat.

'Fortunately, my so-called remote controlled decapitating machine was harmless enough to make only a dent in a dead rat; so I never used it.' (Drawing by Leo Vroman, from *Warm, Red, Wet and Adorable* – Warm, rood, nat en lief, 1994).

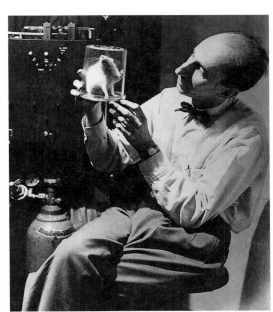

our flesh sweeping it asunder / without form, soul or eternity?' (from 'Ready' ('Klaar') in *Collected Poems 1946-1984).*

In 'Entropy's Last Convulsions' ('De laatste stuipen van de entropie') Vroman resists the belief that the only meaning of order would be chaos: *'That the power which makes creases in the mountains / and dimples in the cheeks / also should long for the end of all that / no I'll never be convinced.'* In this poem the dead are revived: their worms taken out, they walk the streets again, holding hands. Vroman himself would be the first to recognise that this fantasy is based on wishful thinking. A later poem, 'Beyond Progress' ('Voorbij de vooruitgang'), ends with the notion that there is no cure for life: *'today master tomorrow manure / there's no other way / but it's all right the way it is.'* Yet in Vroman's last four volumes the spectre of chaos is fought with new scientific ammunition. In *Fractal* Vroman uses a concept introduced by B.B. Mandelbrot in his book *The Fractal Geometry of Nature* (1983): 'fractal' is a number of dimensions which is not a complete number. A point doesn't need to have one, two or three dimensions but could as well occur in a dimension of 2.3 or 3.1. One of the consequences of this concept is that chaos changes into (a complex) order. The volume *Dear Indivisibility* owes a lot to this new discipline of 'chaotics', which investigates the orderly development of chaotic processes. Vroman stated in an interview: *'At the moment I see people as incomprehensible natural phenomena, terribly complicated, even mathematical.'* It's this sense of complexity that makes Vroman dismiss the idea that all of existence boils down to sheer chaos. Vroman's experience as a biochemist tells him that seeing things from a distance – the so-called 'perspective' – blurs finer distinctions. One of the conclusions in his most recent publication, *Warm, Red, Wet and Adorable* (Warm, rood, nat en lief, 1994), an autobiographical look at research into blood, is that the human body is infinitely complex, *'our last rain forest',* and should be treated with due respect.

Both time and space figure prominently in Vroman's poetical world, and increasingly so as he grows older. His volume *House and Yard* (Huis en tuin, 1979), illustrated by himself, consists of playful poems, distichs with a moral. One of the poems contains a dialogue between space and time: space schemes to swallow up time, but time is elusive and shies away from space's temptations. They will never mate. In 'Wrong time' ('Verkeerde tijd', in *Fractal)* the poet imagines himself outrunning time (which is likened to a cosmic horseman past his prime) and vanishing into space. This metaphorical representation of his death sums up a variety of emotions, from compassion, nostalgia and attachment to the earth to a feeling of doom. Since *Fractal* Vroman has written more poems of this nature, eschatological poems in which he imagines himself in a sort of flight through incredible spaces which interact with each other. The walls of his earliest poems, which started to crumble in the fifties, have really come down. In spite of the cosmic dimensions of these poems, it's still a very recognisable, utterly human and even vulnerable Vroman that emerges from them. Vroman's voice is unique in Dutch poetry. After reading a lot of his verse, you may feel like the poet in 'The Bird': your clothes show patches of Vroman-feathers and the landscape has been altered beyond recognition.

KEES SNOEK

FURTHER READING

DURLACHER, JESSICA, 'Leo Vroman, Dutch-American poet / biologist', *Dutch Heights,* September 1990, pp. 29-32.
KUIJPER, JAN et al. (ed.), *Het Vroman-effect. Over leven en werk van Leo Vroman.* The Hague, 1990.

TRANSLATIONS AND ENGLISH POETRY

Poems in English. Amsterdam, 1964.
Just One More World. Amsterdam, 1976.
Love, Greatly Enlarged (Tr. Leo Vroman). Merrick (NY), 1992.

The Bird

I was drinking tea on midmeadow.
The sun sparkled in the saucers.
Small birds crumbled their crumbs
and fluttered at me.

The wrought-iron table was warm,
and wobbled as I took a cookie.
The birdies said their tuts and teehees
and brushed their lips on my arm
(one-two) before hopping away.

The mushy ottoman on which I sat
made itself sweetly felt
but above my head was a blue as dense
as if I wore a skyhat
up to the distant, hardened city.
There the sky shone pale green.

Suddenly there was a difference,
and a bird, as large as a well-dressed man,
a conductor e.g., planted himself next to me.
His breath came in gasps, then there was silence again.

I put an arm around his neck
and noticed under his feathers the commotion
of veins and an indeterminate emotion
throbbing and streaming between breast and beak.

'Please sit down,' I said, 'and cheer up.'
But he could not make himself relax:
I had to put an arm around his legs
and bend him somewhat double.

I held out a cookie to him, but to no effect
and I asked: 'Is it because you are sad?'
He answered: 'I really have no idea.'
He sounded like a kazoo of ivory.

He stared at me uncertainly
like a peering reflection
and whispered:

'Because of too much mixing
with people, and also on account of my belly
I really lost it,

but I wish I could soar
in between the horizon
and the descending sky
to my Father, land in his valley
under the seaweedtrees
where skypearls descend
at the long day's end.
My beak-traits get besinewed
and my eyes frogfilmed
will sprout two fountains of tears
as I recall the virtuous beaks
of my father and my brother
and the arbor where I would seek
a quiet spot to read.
My Mother seemed to fear us;
a limp bird was Mother,
she was almost a pillowbosom.
On the other hand, my Father
was more a featherduster
but not home as often; rarely rather.
So our gazebo was all mine
and under its foliagegreen light
I would read, every day from nine
in the morning till late at night
I would read your drab would read
your drably enchanting books
full of your pedestrian greed
till I could no longer fly,
lost the power, or the need.
Here, feel this thigh.
I have hips now.

Yes, I am a female indeed.
When I flew it made me shy.
Now that I walk it does not satisfy
me either, for from this low point-of-view
people are just dusty beasts.
If you stand too close to their mouth,
evil spirits will sling out
and twist around your shoulders.
Where have the eyelashes gone
of the deer, the musing children?
What do people learn to think?
To stiffen, and then to shrink.'

Then the bird didn't say one more word.
I could pry and jerk, and squeeze

with a spoon, she wouldn't release
one more word, but again she started to wheeze.

So I clutched her neck, in fear,
and a soft and feverish thigh.
'Fly', I cried and threw her … no,
too heavy, she came down flowing,
sprawling with heat all over me.

I struggled from under her,
but large patches of feathers within
her already replaced my clothes
and my mouth was filled with her skin.
Once more I crawled toward her,
pulled her up by the wings
to a faltering trot,
but her eyes were withdrawn
her interest gone.
Throbbing and weak from the sprawl
she clasped me like a vault.

Morning returned
and found me alone.
A fleet of giant feathers drifted
on the ditches, shifted shifted.
Around me the field had been churned.

My God, what did I mean,
if all this never occurred?
What primordial bird have I seen?
Don't leave me alone
with this verse that is blown
in shreds over me.

From *Going Sleepwalking* (Uit slaapwandelen, 1957)

Space and Time

'Put anything you want in me'
said Space to Time, 'and you'll see.'

'See what! And where would I begin?'
'Why fret, and why not first come in?'

And so they squabble to this date,
hardly kiss and never mate.

MORAL

If Time is unable to,
who, dear readers, tell me who?

From *House and Yard* (Huis en tuin, 1979)

Wrong Time

Time, a little faster and I'll win.
He sweats already, galloping on
at my side, his antique weapon gone,
and sawdust blowing from his tattered skin,

and the stench worn off his hoofbeat hints
of chickenfeathers crushed upon
pillows full of shame-begone
kisses during lovebegin.

In the wake of his imagined face
I call out for a chance of turning
back to earth a lifetime later

without the same compressed embrace
of air from nude birds, torn kids burning
and that icepuke nuclear crater

From *Fractal* (Fractaal, 1985)

Route

The solemn stalling line of days
tells me I am sailing past
on their windless waterways'
widening avenue at last

onto the polished marble sea
under which the garbling deep
hides the voices born with me
that I awakened in my sleep

once echoed in its marble halls
to steep me but their inwardbound
choirs grew to waterfalls
their thunder melting in the ground

Now I shall fathom what it is
not ever once to search again
in story quarry and quatrain
for history as short as this

Half completed crownreports
crooked gourds of blood and wine
golden quills lolled by the tide

I shall go through empty courts
shall recall this all as mine
and shall be gone inside

From *Fractal* (Fractaal, 1985)

Honing the Silence

I recognise the cogs wear off my cogs
not as a mechanism going dead
but like the toothlessness of weary dogs
tired of biting others' gods and brides and bread

Oh yes they wear because I kick my brake
scaling them down to slipdiscs bless their hides
they scream so softly in their sleep when rubbing
sides
at every grinding curve I take

Soon I need no longer steer this cot
grown so light it sails without a puff
it can be laughed along by one dear tot
moonlight can polish it to dust and fluff

Shadows will stay with air behind them
still scratching symbols swirling off the ground
they will endure till morning to be found
by the sleeper who will never find them

From *Fractal* (Fractaal, 1985)

Cathedrals

We are cathedrals
dark with hallways
marked with doors
barring the halls
and fallen gargoyles
guarding the floors.
On the walls
are drawings of hallways
hung with coils
of unstrung foils
and always the choir
hides in the height
of its hollow night
its lore unsung
of doors flung wide
to something outside
in the sunlight

From *All Godforsaken Night* (De godganselijke nacht, 1993)

All Godforsaken Night

All damn night the top shelf full
of narrow vases and all the while
no smell of moldcorrupted tile
giants in the slumberpool

range dangling from the chimneystacks
the house prepares its minicracks

beyond: cracks among continents.
Under the crust one lavahand
gropes along the fissures and
finds another hand and vents

One more deep breath and then
China tilts over Japan

Relax my darling earth it's only me
trying to grasp your death instead of mine
to grope the soil of your uplifting mound

blind as a visionary
to the side-effects of own decline
grope for traces of myself I never found

feel the tremor, see the nightgulls far below
circle the cyclone as I am hurled

down

help me remember how to know
it's only me, it's not the world

From *All Godforsaken Night* (De godganselijke nacht, 1993)

All poems translated by Leo Vroman, except for 'The Bird'
(translated by Leo Vroman and Kees Snoek).

Resting

on Doubt

The editorial board of *The Low Countries* **invited Leo Vroman to write about his position as a Dutch-born poet / writer / biologist living in the United States. This is the text he sent us on 16 July 1994.**

If I knew anything, I would no longer do it. If I knew what follows death, I would probably never die or else not live to finish this sentence. But as I grow older and get closer to the dark, I begin to spew more and more messages in all aspects of my work: art, poetry, science, English and Dutch. I see myself as a child not only because in these few lines I have already used the word 'I' nine times (though including this last one is unfair), but also because I want to stay up. Imagine a kid at bed time: *'The cat is wearing my nightgown.'* *'Now she is dancing the polka.'* *'All the little aliens have come back and are watching.'* *'They want me and the cat to come with them when they take off in a minute.'* *'Will someone please open the window for them?'* You need a well-calculated increment of urgency until people react. Will I be depressed when, finally, some critic will write: *'Leo, go to bed!'?*

What message? Love, of course. Always love, ever since I started loving first animals, then people (mostly girls), then plants, and now, finally, earth with all of its mountains, lakes, oceans and idiots. How obviously lucky we are, not living on any one of the other planets in our solar system, or even on one of those thousands of other planets that support life but hopelessly far from our world, planets where all these unfortunately fingerless aliens are standing in line for water. And probably paying through the proboscis for it.

Further trying to avoid mentioning myself, let me generalise. Of course one wants to reach a maximum number of people with the message of love, or of Love or even LOVE.

1) *Art* is rather international. The knowledge that there is beauty on earth should help to lift people one step up out of their misery, especially if you can show that misery may be beautiful too so that it becomes self-rewarding. Sketches made in a prisoner-of-war camp, showing emaciated friends, the lack of furniture and of cameras, become documents that with additional help from wrinkles, dried-up remains of squashed bedbugs etc. gain the beauty of age and of distance in time.

More helpful, perhaps, is the art of breaking: draw a thing with a part broken or missing, and what is left gains the beauty of what unappreciated entity there once was. This is no joke. The beauty of wounded and of sick children can be overwhelming, and once witnessed remains a rich source of love so deep it hurts us back to health. No wonder there is a special joy in drawing for children. Flying sphinxes, deep-diving dogs, a longhaired elephant with a hand at the end of its trunk … anything that will make a child say 'Oh' or *'och'* will do.

But how international is art? We have shocked our neighbour, a well-educated recently immigrated Russian, when he asked to see some of our art books and we showed him one of Picasso's posters, beautifully reproduced. The 'distortions' horrified him, the abstracts were meaningless to him, and the pictures of nudes shocked him and his daughter. He retorted with a beautiful book of Russian treasures, some great, several Impressionist works unknown to us, and many romantic Russian statues of revealingly well-dressed women on their way to some sacrifice or other, none of whom would be welcome in our house either before or after their adventure. This was a few years ago. Now, the daughter is painting in previously unthinkable ways. Time, time. We may be able to reach farther to children with fairy tales not too unrealistically illustrated, or not illustrated at all: I think most of us have been disappointed by illustrations unless they were, even to adults, of lasting beauty. The warmth of telling sleepy kids that no, there are no wolves under the bed, there is no Snow Queen out to get you, and yes, even an Emperor can be stupid. But now we are drifting into speech.

2) *Language* in the form of poetry (for example) seems very direct, but wait till you start translating it. Why translate from the Dutch? Well, Dutch is great, but English is larger. For those of you who do not read Dutch, I cannot explain the difference between the two in words of one of the two. I mean that would be like trying to describe the difference between the taste of a tomato and a doughnut in terms of the taste of the doughnut only: and after tasting each, who needs an explanation?

Drawing by Leo Vroman (1994).

A nice example of the cultural gap between the two – no, it is not a macroscopic gap, it is more a porosity formed by countless tiny gaps through which a meaning may sink away. Take for example the sentence: *'He cut his pancake into four pieces with his teaspoon and stuck one piece in his mouth.'* Translated into Dutch, that would be: *'Hij sneed zijn pannekoek in vieren met zijn theelepeltje en stak een stuk in zijn mond.'* A normal action

in the United States becomes an insanely time-consuming and then dangerous action in Dutch. In prose, an explanatory note would be tolerable. But a
poem like:

He took his teaspoon and cut
his thick pancake in four,
then he ate each piece but
asked for seven more

bad enough as it is, would be further ruined by the two needed footnotes.

Many poems are full of locally, ethnically normal expressions that seem
highly original when translated. Who knows how many literary awards have
been handed out on the basis of such fruitful misunderstandings. Of my first
efforts in writing poems in English (using a fat rhyming dictionary, a the-
saurus, a fat Webster, and an even fatter and misplaced self-confidence), six
were accepted and published by Poetry Magazine in 1950, and many much
later ones were refused. Those early ones were thought more fresh and original. When I re-read them, I discovered that I had used wrong words, even
words that I thought existed but never did until then. Our love of quaintness,
and of broken language, may be like our love for other broken things, revealing what could have been.

Having slipped into the use of self-reference again, let me tell you how
wonderful it is to be obscure as a poet in this country. A good friend of ours,
Stanley Barkan, has published my 'Liefde, Sterk Vergroot' with my own re-
writing of it, 'Love, Greatly Enlarged'. He has made me read poetry in public, once in a park at night, a few times in corners of bookstores with audiences of about ten, sometimes four people. Each time after such a meeting
of minds I became deeper involved in anything else. Here, my poetry is not
obscure but I am. Sure, we know some poets: Adrienne Rich, Josef Brodsky,
Allen Ginsberg. Do they form a family or community? We never visit any,
and very very rarely call any of them. I don't even know if there is the kind
of talk among poets here that exists in other families or in the family of
Dutch poets, such as *'did you know that A and B broke up?'* We, my wife
Tineke and I, don't know whether or not we are part of that Dutch family.
We are surrounded by obscurity.

Of course there is charm in obscurity as there is in the dark and in the
dense jungles of our world and of our minds. The miracle of our ability to
understand each other is eclipsed only by the greater miracle of not understanding – as long as it feeds wonder. We can listen for hours to a mocking-
bird, or even to a bunch of crows, possibly because we do not understand
them. If we understood they were always talking about food, sex, and priv-
ileged space, we would wish them to shut up. But now we are slipping into
the world of science.

3) *Science,* especially 'hard', number-hungry science, can be quite international. Superficially, you might think it is because it has no message and
therefore cannot be misunderstood. If I say that I found that blood plasma
deposits a sequence of proteins onto glass, I do not think I am saying anything that would offend the Torah, Allah, Buddha, or the Queen of England.
(The Queen of the Netherlands is too wise to be offended by anything.)

Things change when I decide to append a message, like: *'You should learn to love a drop of blood more passionately than any body containing it.'* This leads to the conclusion that I love the total contents of an insane dictator more than I love the city of New York, or that I love anybody more than I do anyway. This would offend the dictator's slaves as much as it would offend common logic. It may offend most scientists as well: they believe in cold rather than warm reason. Objectivity is thought of as the gateway to universal understanding. If you have three cows and you sell one, how many do you have left? According to a professor I had half a century ago in Utrecht, an uneducated farm boy could not solve that problem because it was an impossibility: nobody with only three cows would sell one. Abstract numbers may not be universally understood. Neither are abstracted gestures. A scientist I met had an image engraved to send into outer space, to assure aliens of our friendliness. It showed a man, a woman and a child, I think, perhaps to show off our fertility. The man held one hand up, the palm facing the alien. Why, I asked. To show we are unarmed, he said. What, I asked, if these aliens have a five-tentacle weapon from the palm of which a deadly ray can be shot, and probably will? Well, it's too late now. Included with the disc, fortunately or not, were recorded numbers that only an intelligent organism, say the kind that could have designed this rocket to begin with, can put together. Tough. After all, what can you say to prove that you can talk?

There are certainly some differences in the ways scientists are regarded and awarded in different countries. In this country, scientists appear to be respected and suspected, but rarely inspected, because what a researcher does is, almost by definition, beyond the understanding of other people, including those who seem to be close colleagues. One lives (I have lived for almost fifty years) on grants that are awarded if your work sounds promising enough to those most likely to understand some of it. But the award will cover no more than five, and usually no more than three years. Raising a couple of children that way is as easy as living in a desert and migrating with the kids where you have reasons to expect water. Whether or not your children will look up to you depends on the ability to avoid collapsing. Scientists will therefore tend to sound more and more optimistic the worse their data look. And yet, I think dishonesty remains rare. Some famous and less famous people are each other's enemies of course; nothing special.

I don't know how things are exactly in the Low Countries: I have been away too long. At least for a while, there was a different attitude. For example: we were asked to try and put an outline of a liberal arts education together for a university in the Netherlands. Tineke did most of the work. When we came to that city, her first question was: what kind of job should the equivalent of a degree in liberal arts give access to? Job?! was the answer, we were not thinking in terms of any jobs, just in terms of education (but things change).

Here, college and university students will take any job if needed to pay for their education sooner or later. In summer, ask any waiter or waitress in a restaurant if they are doing this work full-time. The answer is always interesting. I found it is rarely *'I want to do basic research'*, though. The word 'basic' itself means less basic here than it does in the Netherlands: any research that does not immediately lead to industry and money is called basic. I got an award for basic research without knowing the basics that my work is based on. But now I am getting into the need to be awarded or even to be understood or just to be needed.

4) *Please, need me!* Obviously I am back to using 'I' again, but with a good excuse this time: I cannot talk for anyone else when my opinions under discussion are based on my own experience or the other way around.

A good poetry review, a good review of exhibited drawings, or a good review of a scientific grant application, all give me the same sense of having done something right, of course, but that to me means just a warmth of being understood. All three areas, in both countries, are closely related fields of experimentation, answering these questions: if I do this, will you be more understanding and thereby happier with the world you are living in? Will you do the same to make others happier? And have we together contributed something helpful to the universe, lasting even after the earth is destroyed?

LEO VROMAN

Domestic

Bliss and Excruciating Pain

The Life and Art of Rik Wouters

Rik Wouters (1882-1916) died of cancer eighty years ago at the age of thirty-four. Though the pain of his tumour sometimes drove this Flemish painter / sculptor to the edge of insanity, his suffering is scarcely noticeable in his mostly cheerful work. The bright colours of his best paintings are a tribute to his domestic happiness with his wife Nel.

One of Wouters' last paintings, dating from the spring of 1916, is called *Woman Ironing*. He was barely able to finish the work because the cancer had affected his eyesight. Despite the headache which racked him, he was here returning to a theme which had previously inspired him to do some quick colour sketches. Ironing must have been a fascinating activity for Rik Wouters. One has to remember that this was at the beginning of this century, when people were still using irons without a flex. Perhaps he was trying to capture the atmosphere of those quiet moments at the table or ironing board when the iron glided over the smaller pieces of cloth and they were folded by the free hand, and when the body inclined with the slow swinging movements. In his quick colour sketches Rik Wouters tried to evoke the hissing of the hot iron on the wet linen and the slight steam which pricked the nostrils, as well as many other familiar sounds and operations associated with the daily household chores. It was as if he was raking together fragments of domestic contentment, the value of which everyone failed to grasp, just as birds pick up little crumbs of bread in their beaks and carry them off to their nests as treasures.

One of the mysteries which surrounds Wouters' work is just how he succeeded in depicting a carefree picture of domestic happiness while from 1913 on his headaches were becoming more and more unbearable. He painted his wife absorbed in a book, combing her hair, at her toilet or at the washtub, sewing in front of the window, seen from behind putting on a jacket, reading in bed and sipping coffee. Some of those sketches are simply called *Female Attitudes,* as if he was searching for the indefinable in the inner being of his wife Nel.

Few would have expected that – of all things – it would be the intimacy of the snug nest that Rik Wouters would make the central theme of his short career. Of his youth, Rik wrote that he was a bad lot. One fine day, as a

Rik Wouters, *Woman Ironing*. 1916. Canvas, 107 x 123 cm. Koninklijk Museum voor Schone Kunsten, Antwerp.

twelve-year-old lad, he was expelled from school. And this young scapegrace was even unable to make a go of things in his father's furniture workshop in Mechelen. Then, another fine day, he left, wandering around for a few days with a rifle and, according to Theo Blickx, the money out of the till. When Rik was no longer content to cut wood and at the age of fifteen announced that he wanted to be an artist, Wouters senior entrusted the same Theo Blickx, an artist from Mechelen, with the task of giving Rik a strict apprenticeship. Above all, Rik learnt modelling and drawing from life. He went on to follow courses at the Royal Academy of Fine Arts in Brussels. After his military service (in the University Company so that he did not need to interrupt his studies at the Academy), he got to know the sculptor Léon Thumilaire, who lived in a room opposite the Academy above the café *La Rose du Midi.* And it was there that Rik Wouters met his friends Anne-Pierre de Kat, Edgard Tytgat and Jean Brusselmans and made the acquaintance of the French-speaking Hélène Duerinckx, usually called Nel by her friends.

The two fell in love and Nel moved in with Rik, who was renting a studio in a run-down house in Brussels. Not everyone was happy about the romance. For example, the friendship with painter / sculptor Ferdinand Schirren cooled off for a while. Nel had previously sat for Schirren and he was unable to accept that she was now the exclusive model of young

Wouters. It was probably from Schirren that Wouters learnt that painting in oil did not always mean laboriously applying coats of thick paint, as did Auguste Oleffe, the paternalistic mentor of the young Brabantine painters who opted for colour rather than a dark, grey naturalism. After an impressionistic period, in 1905 Ferdinand Schirren began to show how an interesting transparency could be achieved by thinning with turpentine.

Theo Blickx – like Schirren – was envious of the happiness of the two lovebirds and refused to be a witness when the couple married in 1905. As one cannot live on bliss alone, after barely two weeks Rik and Nel moved to his parents' home in Mechelen. The young couple did not want to accept charity, so Rik went back to work in his father's furniture workshop. However, predictably enough, living with the Wouters family caused friction. After the umpteenth quarrel with Wouters senior, the couple moved into two dingy, rented rooms in Sint-Joost-ten-Node. Nel was laid low with tuberculosis, while Rik worked away at his *Reverie,* a sculpture which won him joint second prize with Marcel Wolfers in the Godecharle competition. But life in the town did nothing to improve Nell's health and the couple went to live in Bosvoorde on the edge of the Zoniënwoud woods. Gradually Rik won some recognition as a sculptor and in August 1907 he received a state grant of 500 francs.

Yet the ties with the group which later came to be known as the Brabantine Fauvists had not been severed entirely. The Flemish writer Herman Teirlinck wrote in his *Collected Works* (Verzameld werk): *'In Linkebeek I was immediately admitted into a group of painters who have settled there. Among them were Ferdinand Schirren, Rik Wouters, Charles Dehoy, Willem Paerels, Edgard Tytgat and Louis Thévenet. Quite detached from any sort of academicism, these hotheads put their faith in a sunny impressionism in which forms and light indulged one another and left behind colours of a poignant refinement.'* Rik Wouters was also a regular participant when these Brabantine painters forgathered at the brewer François van Haelen's.

Nel sat for just about all the most important sculptures. But her role was not limited to modelling. She was a partner in Wouters' journey of exploration and she acted as a foil for the various shifts in his career. At that time, Ensor – who was also a friend of the art patron François van Haelen – was Rik's paradigm when he painted. It was not only Ensor's subdued light in atmospheric interiors and free brush technique which appealed to him; Wouters was also fascinated by the typical Ensorian use of colour (see *The Low Countries* 1994-95: 156-167), the silver-grey and the pink mother-of-pearl tints. Nel thought that development dangerous: *'At the start of his career, those silver-greys put him on the wrong path for a long time. Later he explained that this had been his way of having to learn to see clearly. And then he stopped dreaming of silver-grey and pink mother-of-pearl tones, dangerous dreams which he had to suppress with all his might.'*

An Etcher's Interior, which dates from 1908, is certainly one of Wouters' strongest early paintings. Though the paint was applied thinly, the work nevertheless reproduces the material of the glass bottles and the zinc etching bath. With that still life, Wouters was looking to give expression to his new passion: he spent his evenings preparing copper and zinc plates and engraving.

Rik Wouters, *Reverie.* 1907. Bronze, 193 x 50 cm. Koninklijk Museum voor Schone Kunsten, Antwerp.

Rik Wouters, *An Etcher's Interior*. 1908. Canvas, 80 x 80 cm. Collection Dr Cabolet, Brussels.

There followed another important stimulus for Wouters' painting, namely his friendship with Simon Lévy which began in 1909. Lévy was able to share his admiration for Cézanne with Wouters, who knew Cézanne's work only from reproductions. And Cézanne helped Wouters to resist the misleading lure of Ensor's fantasies. From Cézanne he learned to work according to nature, to be honest and to develop a personal style. And, like Cézanne, Wouters began to build up volume using colour strokes. Wouters became a sculptor of colour; a cheekbone became a pure red stroke of colour and he made the shadow around the eyes green. The academic light-dark effect which he had learned made way for the use of light, pure colours. He never coloured in flat surfaces, but built his composition up with vaguely indicated spots of colour.

In 1912 the critics accused Wouters of plagiarising Cézanne. Quite wrongly, for Wouters painted much more thinly, allowed the canvas to play a part by leaving bits unpainted and had a more pronounced, clearer coloration. His was not at all the *'belle peinture'* with the saturated colours people in Paris were accustomed to, but a gracefulness and volatility to which Flanders was no longer accustomed.

Was it the sight of Cézanne's work at the salon of La Libre Esthétique

which invited the – totally misplaced – criticism of Wouters as an epigone? It is true that Wouters went to Paris that year, accompanied by Lévy and several other artists, to look at Cézanne's work. Despite his interest in Cézanne and Van Gogh (*'Every work by that fellow is the eye of a bird of prey'*, Wouters said), Ensor was still Rik Wouters' shining example. This was emphasised several times in a correspondence studded with enthusiastic *'godverdommes'* (meaning it was 'damned good'). It is odd that the critics apparently made no comparisons with Matisse, though several of Wouters'

Rik Wouters, *The Red Curtains.* 1913. Canvas, 100 x 81 cm. Collection P. Vermeylen, Brussels.

works do have something of that artist. *The Red Curtains* (1913), for example, is pure Matisse: the attention to the decorativeness of the curtains, the explicit use of red and the open window in the background. That attention to decorative motifs and the predominance of powerful, bright red was already apparent in *Lilacs,* which dates from the productive year of 1912. Some of Wouters' paintings also have something in common with those of Matisse because of the brilliant intensity of the transparent paint. Indirectly the art critics did of course make a connection between Matisse and Wouters by grouping him together with painters such as Schirren, Paerels, Thévenet and Brusselmans in a Brabantine Fauvist movement – this by analogy with the Parisian painters Derain, De Vlaminck, Van Dongen, who were dubbed 'Fauvists' by the art critic Vauxelles in 1905 because of their daring use of unmixed colours. But in neither case was there any real movement or trend to speak of, because there was no clear-cut programme.

That Wouters could afford to travel to Paris in 1912 was due to the contract he signed with the Galerie Giroux in Brussels. Wouters was able to indulge himself as an artist because of the credit arranged by Giroux at the paint shop. He produced more than sixty paintings that year. The downside, however, was the fact that Wouters did not see much of the monthly allowance of 200 francs which Giroux had promised.

That same year saw the casting of *Crazy Girl*, a sculpture he had begun in 1910 after seeing a ballet performance by Isadora Duncan at la Monnaie theatre. Wouters, who wanted to freeze the magic of the graceful American

Rik Wouters, *Crazy Girl.*
1912. Bronze, 195 x 120 x
135 cm. Middelheim
Museum, Antwerp.

Rik Wouters, *Rik with a Black Eye-Patch.* 1915. Canvas, 102 x 85 cm. Koninklijk Museum voor Schone Kunsten, Antwerp.

dancer – dotingly known as 'Isadorable' in Parisian art circles – in a sculpture, ended up making a very different work. In the studio, an attic measuring four metres by seven, Nel could not evoke the image of the dancer: *'I was furious with Isadora, I ranted and raged against the tyranny of that dancer. I threw my body forward like a whip but suddenly Rik, delirious with joy, shouted: "At last, that's the movement I wanted!"'*

A characteristic of Rik Wouters' sculpture is that his figures have a faceted skin instead of a cool, smooth contour. That increases the vitality of his sculptures, which give the impression of having been reclaimed from the

Rik Wouters, *Domestic Cares.* 1913. Original plaster, 227 x 79 x 79 cm. Koninklijke Musea voor Schone Kunsten van België, Brussels.

inertia of clay. *Crazy Girl,* also known as *Foolish Violence,* vibrates with exuberant life. Along with *Reverie* (1911) and *Domestic Cares* (1913), it is one of Wouters' strongest sculptures. It is, however, difficult to share the view of his friend, the art critic Ary Delen, that Rik Wouters achieved *'the most perfect plastic beauty'* in his sculptures. Wouters' paintings, on which he concentrated his efforts after achieving a high point in sculpture with *Crazy Girl,* certainly rate more highly.

Paul Colin was probably right when he wrote in his book *Belgian Painting since 1830* (La Peinture Belge depuis 1830, 1930) that Wouters gave up sculpture because the execution and finishing were so time consuming. Wouters wrote in a letter to his friend Simon Lévy in 1912: *'Don't waste time, you are never old enough to paint.'* It is tempting to reinterpret that statement and to see it in the light of Wouters' death four years later. And yet, even in 1911, Wouters was complaining of a headache which prevented him from working. In 1913 he wrote to Lévy: *'But every morning when I get up I am afraid. Always that head, goddamn it!'* When Rik Wouters was called up on the outbreak of war in August 1914, he wrote in October that he did not feel ill, but was still suffering from spasms of neuralgia. Wouters, who deserted shortly afterwards but returned to his regiment, was interned as a prisoner of war in the Amersfoort camp after the fall of Antwerp. Later he was transferred to Zeist, where he was able to continue painting. But by now the pain had become unbearable. Nel wrote: *'It was painful to see him, poor old Rik with his woefully distorted mouth. We are paralysed with fear. Nothing helps Rik's pain, the camp doctor has given him a supply of aspirin and other medicines. I have decided that Rik should consult a civilian doctor.'* Rik Wouters' *via dolorosa* led through various doctors' surgeries and operating theatres. Five days after an operation in October 1915, Nel wrote: *'It really was terrible. A sharp red wound ran from his temple under his eye, down the side of his nose and ended in the middle of his still swollen upper lip. In his throat, a long incision closed with big stitches. His cheek was sunken and his eye drooped because part of his upper jawbone had been removed. Half of his palate had also been taken away and filled up with gauze.'*

It is remarkable that despite his suffering, Wouters, who was given permission to settle in Amsterdam with Nel in 1915, still painted so many cheerful paintings. Seventeen days after that difficult operation in October 1915, he painted his now famous last self-portrait, *Rik with a Black Eye-Patch.* Even this work, which is reminiscent of Van Gogh with his bandaged ear, is still painted with a distinctly *'glorious'* palette, as Jan Walravens pointed out in his book *Contemporary Paintings in Belgium* (Peintures Contemporaines en Belgique, 1916).

Wouters' style had developed very little since he started concentrating on painting in 1912. Yet in his late works a structured composition breaks through more and more often. The teeming strokes of colour on the canvas, previously scattered over the ground like rays of sun through foliage, are now more evenly positioned. But the linen still breathes, just as the colour and texture of the paper still play a part in an aquarelle. However, red becomes less dominant in his later works, while the earlier pastel tints reappear. *'When he was just beginning to paint, he was always enraptured by those pink and grey mother-of-pearl tones and in his last works he once again vividly expressed how much he adored those tones'*, Nel Wouters wrote. She remains the main theme in Rik's late works.

But despite his perseverance Rik's condition did not improve, and at the Huis Antoon van Leeuwenhoek, the 'House of Cancer', the doctor diagnosed a highly malignant tumour of the maxillary sinus. Radium treatment was tried, but to no avail. Again Rik clung to his painting. In April 1916 he was determined to go to the exhibition of his work at the Stedelijk Museum in Amsterdam. There *'blood splattered from his nose and mouth. He was taken home and lay on the bed, shivering with fever. One crisis followed another and Rik's despair bordered on insanity. But every crisis was followed by an improvement'*, Nel recorded later. After a third operation in April 1916, all hope was abandoned: Henri Wouters died on 11 July 1916.

ERIC BRACKE
Translated by Alison Mouthaan-Gwillim.

Rik Wouters, *Nude in a Cane Chair.* 1915. Canvas, 130 x 122 cm. Collection G. van Geluwe, Brussels.

Crossing

the Borders

Contemporary Theatre in the Low Countries

Anyone who tries to make sense of the connections between Flemish and Dutch culture, between Belgium and the Netherlands, between Flanders and Wallonia, is likely to get into a tangle. It's a tangle of languages, regions and communities, of national and federal borders which can be incomprehensible – and not just for foreigners. Too many historical or social demarcations, too many boundaries to take into account. *The Belgian Labyrinth* (Het Belgische labyrinth, 1989), an essay by the Flemish poet and journalist Geert van Istendael, attempted to clarify the complex cultural and constitutional connections which turn Flanders and Wallonia into Belgium. But Flanders' relationship with the Netherlands, Dutch language and culture adds even more passages to that labyrinth, the tiny triangle making up the Low Countries. Politicians try to draw boundaries as sharply and distinctly as possible, whether through jurisdiction or other means. But artists have always exploited the fertility and productivity of the triangle. For them, the labyrinth is a system of open cultural and national identity, of international barriers made invisible and of fundamental importance to their work. Though this chaos may fill the politician with anxiety, it is just what attracts the artist.

The artist doesn't generally recognise borders, though often the contours which he or she draws across different art forms, nationalities and time can be seen as an ever-changing border of sorts. This was true of Jacques Brel – a French-speaking Belgian who called himself a Fleming, who sang songs about Flanders in Dutch, about Amsterdam in French – just as it's true of Maatschappij Discordia (a Dutch theatre group whose greatest popularity is probably in Flanders and Brussels); for Franz Marijnen, Ivo van Hove, Sam Bogaerts and others (Flemish directors who bring the house down in the Netherlands); for Gerardjan Rijnders, artistic director of Toneelgroep Amsterdam, the Low Countries' largest producing company which contrary to Dutch tradition engages Dutch and Flemish directors and actors in one ensemble.

The melting-pot of language, culture and identity has actually become a model for a number of theatre-makers. The work of Jan Fabre, Jan Lauwers (Needcompany), of choreographers Wim Vandekeybus (Ultima Vez) and

Anne Teresa de Keersmaeker (Rosas) are leading international examples. At least two producing organisations – Kaaitheater in Brussels and, until its closure in 1991, Mickery in Amsterdam – engaged in international coproduction as second nature. Dutch-language theatre has also demonstrated its internationalism in its eclectic choice of writers and texts and its use of translation to build wide-ranging repertoires. There are also important international festivals: the Holland Festival, Kaaitheaterfestival, Kunsten-FESTIVAL des Arts, Springdance, Klapstuk and others, some of which have introduced the work of key figures like Robert Wilson, The Wooster Group, Pina Bausch, Jurgen Gosch and Steve Paxton. 'Internationalised' theatre faces an implicit political question about the value of cultural, national or linguistic borders in a Europe which simultaneously prepares itself for large-scale cultural co-operation and is unable to prevent bloody territorial conflicts.

Borders exist and do have to be respected, and if the theatrical landscape of the Low Countries could be drawn there would probably be six of them: first the political borders between Wallonia, Flanders and the Netherlands; second, the split between theatre of the head and theatre of the body; third, the difference between the theatrical centre and its margins; fourth, the divisions between theatre and other art forms; fifth, the border between the writer's desk and the stage; and sixth, between theatre for children and for adults.

Flanders, Wallonia and the Netherlands

It is instructive to trace and describe the actual regional and national borders which define the Low Countries. Bounded to the north and west by the sea, to the east by Germany and to the south by Belgium, the Kingdom of the Netherlands is a country of (predominantly) Dutch-speaking people and the real home of Dutch theatre culture; in the northern part of the Kingdom of Belgium, with the Netherlands as its northern border, the sea to the west and the so-called 'language border' to the south, lies Flanders: recognised in 1974 as a separate Dutch-speaking region, in 1980 as a separate Flemish cultural community and federal region. To the south of the language border, according to the Belgian constitution, lies the region of Wallonia – the Francophone part of Belgium. The coexistence of French and Dutch within national borders is of great importance to Flemish identity and its relationship with the Dutch.

Beneath the borders of Belgium and the Netherlands lies a much older map – the map of the Seventeen Provinces. In 1585, with the capture of Antwerp by the Spanish, past cultural unity came to an end and the Northern and Southern Netherlands was born. Taking refuge from occupying Spanish forces, Flemish artists, scientists and intellectuals migrated north, where they contributed heavily to the development of a bourgeois Dutch culture and a standard Dutch language. Flanders, decapitated, was left behind for a long, dark period of economic and cultural impoverishment. The Northern Netherlands' seventeenth century became its Golden Age: writers like Vondel, Hooft and Bredero produced a significant literary oeuvre. During successive domination by Spain, Austria, France and the Netherlands, the survival of language and literature in the South lay entirely in the hands of the Chambers of Rhetoric.

With Belgian independence in 1831, Flanders was faced with an almost impossible task: making up for 250 years of cultural deprivation in a completely 'gallicised' environment. Here the theatre played an important role in the formation and diffusion of Dutch in Flanders and its need for a liberated, distinct culture. But most of last century's dramatic and literary output, often springing from a need to educate an emerging Flemish people, does not stand the test of time. So a great deal of cultural 'energy' was expended in the struggle to develop the fledgling Flemish culture alongside the dominant French one. By the end of the last century Flemish cultural autonomy was a fact, and a new phase of cultural congruence between Flanders, the Netherlands and Wallonia began.

The mutual interest in each other's theatre, especially in the last few decades, is a good example of cultural border-crossing. It's hardly a surprising one either: the Flemish do, after all speak the same language as the Dutch, the difference between them little different from American and 'British' English, or the spoken language of Austria and Germany. Both communities have co-operated for years on texts in the same language and the Dutch Language Union promotes collaboration and joint initiatives. With an eye on European unity, the call for a co-ordinated foreign cultural policy has also strengthened recently.

Head and body

In the mid-eighties, Dutch theatres were invaded by hordes of young Flemish companies and artists looking for support – difficult to find in Flanders at that time – and audiences for their work. Some of which, like the work of Jan Decorte or Jan Fabre, was controversial; but Anne Teresa de Keersmaeker (see *The Low Countries* 1994-95: 59-62), Ivo van Hove, Sam Bogaerts, Luk Perceval and Lukas Vandervost found enthusiastic public loyalty. Dutch critics didn't seem to mind describing this invasion as *'the Flemish wave'*, suggesting inundation as well as vitality – a challenge to the order of the Dutch theatre. The 'head / body' metaphor was first used by the Dutch critic Robert Steijn in 1985 when he attempted to describe the renaissance of textual theatre:

'In the Netherlands the head has joined the struggle to create a new form of theatre. On stage the head is dominant: the rest of the body has been cut off and is completely denied. The disembodied head is amazed at the abundance of interpretations of reality and becomes ensnared in the web of its own associations. Gerardjan Rijnders, Maatschappij Discordia and Onafhankelijk Toneel are examples.
(…) In Flanders, Fabre, De Keersmaeker, Vanrunxt and, on the sidelines, Decorte have brought organic structure back to the stage after the bankruptcy of classical drama. (…) Just throw the body into the struggle. (…) Seeing a Flemish production is a complex experience in which head and heart attempt to resist the unapproachable world of the stage. In the body of the spectator irritations, incomprehension and false emotions rage together

in order to turn away from what is being presented on stage. But gradually the body surrenders and the spectator reaches a physical high. (…) The theatre has traded the impulse to exchange immediate reality for the creation of a new one. This is the temporary reality of the body, temporarily intact.'

These are interesting perceptions, but it would be a mistake to over-simplify the subtle and complex artistic qualities involved – never a straightforward contrast between the cerebral and physical, and certainly not to be seen as especially Dutch or Flemish in either case. Besides, many leading directors of Flemish 'physical' theatre have tackled major works from the mainstream repertoire. Ivo van Hove began as a maker of physically conceived, sometimes site-specific performances, but directed *Hamlet* in 1993.

Margin and centre

Theatrical landscapes, like real ones, always change. Sometimes the change is sudden, at other times hardly perceptible. In the Low Countries, a new landscape, atop the old one, is being created. It bears little similarity to its forebears, but this shouldn't surprise us. Few European theatre movements owe as little to their ancestry as that of the Dutch language. Their important historical playwrights – the medieval repertoire, Vondel, Hooft, Bredero, Langendijk, Heijermans, Buysse – are rarely performed, nor are the old acting traditions any longer studied. However there are some traditional links; these are mainly with the repertory theatres which, as in neighbouring countries, date from the eighteenth and nineteenth centuries and the urban, bourgeois theatre.

The position of repertory theatres differs profoundly in the theatre landscapes of the Netherlands and Flanders. In Flanders, they are now silent witnesses to the past and no longer (as in Germany) the incarnation of a theatrical ideal. The municipal theatres of Ghent (NTG – Nederlands Toneel Gent), Antwerp (KNS – Koninklijke Nederlandse Schouwburg) and Brussels (KVS – Koninklijke Vlaamse Schouwburg) have outlived their prestige and lost their overall educational and social function over the years. They survive as what geologists, referring to the flattened hills in the Flemish lowlands which were once ancient peaks, call *'hills of witness'* – custodians of a petrified past. The three established houses have not, except on a few occasions, been able to match or incorporate the dynamism of the Flemish theatre of the eighties.

In the Netherlands, municipal theatres in Rotterdam, Amsterdam and The Hague changed profoundly around 1985 and a contemporary notion of repertoire emerged. New companies appeared in The Hague (Het Nationaal Toneel) and Amsterdam (Toneelgroep Amsterdam), where often controversial directors like Gerardjan Rijnders, Sam Bogaerts and Jan Ritsema stole the scene. Toneelgroep Amsterdam staged striking, often high-risk, arrestingly directed interpretations of classical repertoire or new work in the main house, and included topical foreign work in their seasons.

Notably, the larger theatres in the Netherlands have become a focus for new approaches to writing, acting, directing and design. In short, they've led the way across the border separating the new style from the dominant theatre of naturalism. This brings it closer to the more innovative developments in the United States or Germany, distancing it from the main stage traditions of France, Britain, Spain or Italy. There are now hopes that the Flemish theatre establishment will begin to modernise: in Brussels' KVS, a new ensemble and repertoire is being formed under the leadership of Franz Marijnen; and the Ghent and Antwerp theatres both face new opportunities.

Artistic development often arises through the confrontation between margin and centre. On the periphery, the new, the unexpected, the unknown and the different come to life. In the Netherlands, margin and centre are less well defined because of the move into larger, better-subsidised structures by the key practitioners and representatives of the new. In Flanders the equivalent process may only just be starting, so that the fluidity of the margins and the petrified centre are far easier to detect. In truth, the most influential groups – some of them active in their own buildings, some not – sometimes occupy a midway point between margin and centre. Leading examples are the

KVS, 1993-1994, *King Lear* (William Shakespeare) (Photo by Leo van Velzen).

Toneelgroep Amsterdam, 1993-1994, *Richard III* (William Shakespeare) (Photo by Serge Ligtenberg).

De Tijd-Maatschappij Discordia, 1992-1993, *The Tyranny of Relief* (Fernando Pessoa) (Photo by Bert Nienhuis).

Hollandia, 1993-1994, *Lulu* (Frank Wedekind) (Photo by Ben van Duin).

Het Zuidelijk Toneel, 1993-1994, *Hamlet* (William Shakespeare) (Photo by Patrick G. Meis).

'untheatrical' theatre of Maatschappij Discordia, the site-specific work of Hollandia, the new expressionism of Nieuw West, the O'Neill cycle of Het Zuidelijk Toneel, the strident vision of Theu Boermans (working with the writer Schwab in De Trust) – all from the Netherlands.

A Maatschappij Discordia production is a rigorous dramaturgical interpretation of a work's social and psychological rhetoric. The performance analyses the ambiguities and concealments of the text; stage set and acting explore the textual complexity by means of a usually open set and multiple roles for the actors.

As well as works from the classical and the modern German repertoire, Hollandia also experiments with music theatre. Text and music are reduced to their essence and in no way illustrate each other. These musical experiments have also influenced the speaking of the text in the repertoire performances; here, too, the materiality of the text is allowed a large measure of autonomy, and this often strengthens its emotional impact.

The theatre work of Nieuw West, with author Rob Graaf, can best be described as 'expressionist'; works which are not bound by linearity and narrative psychology are performed in an emotionally amplified but somewhat formalised manner. Ivo van Hove of Het Zuidelijk Toneel alternates the classical with the modern repertoire (Shakespeare, O'Neill, Williams, Genet, Bond). He fills an increasingly open and suggestive setting with a physical style of acting which explores the emotional extremes of the characters without identifying with them. The outrageous is also to be found in the work of Theu Boermans and his company De Trust, which cannot be dissociated from the extreme works of Rainald Goetz and Werner Schwab. The central theme is that of 'violence', and mainly in the form of linguistic violence: language as ideology, as the instrument of power, with the characters drawn along like empty hulks in its wake.

In Flanders there is the performance research of Blauwe Maandag, the Musil and Maeterlinck repertoire of De Tijd, the radical cynicism of Jan Decorte and the theatre of political irony from Stan. The work of the latter group is akin to that of Maatschappij Discordia; here too there is an obsession with the immediate present in which the performance is taking place. In 1994 both Stan and Maatschappij Discordia performed Georg Büchner's *The Death of Danton* (Dantons Tod, 1835) as an invitation to reflect on politics, revolution and commitment in our own times. The basic elements of Stan's style – apart from political commitment – are irony, the stripped-down rhetoric of the texts and the pursuit of a synaesthesia of person, role and actor.

Unlike Stan, which works with young actors, the Blauwe Maandag Compagnie is a group of old hands. This company experiments in a wide variety of genres including naturalistic theatre, revue, the grotesque, theatre of the absurd, with an interesting form of performance theatre. This kind of theatre is constantly seeking confrontation, with modern as well as with classical works. Less extroverted is the work of Lukas Vandervost and De Tijd. Here the emphasis is on the disappearance of authentic language and the impossibility of capturing the inner world in words. De Tijd's explorations have led it to pay homage to the philosophically flavoured works of, among others, Robert Musil, Maurice Maeterlinck and H.M. Enzensberger.

In children's work, both communities excel: the new work of Stella Den Haag (The Netherlands) and Ghent's Oud Huis Stekelbees – now Victoria –

Stan, 1992-1993, *A Public Enemy* (after Henrik Ibsen) (Photo by Koen de Waal).

Blauwe Maandag Compagnie, 1990-1991, *Strange Interlude* (Eugene O'Neill) (Photo by Sonya Haas).

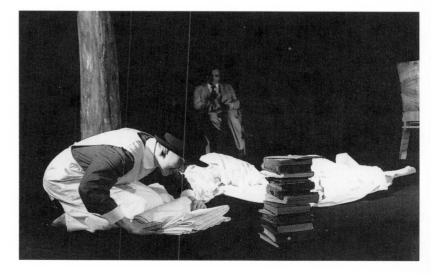

Rosas, 1990-1991, *Stella* (Photo by Herman Sorgeloos).

are examples. These groups have added something to theatre-making, built new and loyal audiences, infused their work with radical approaches to acting, writing and staging. They're driven by a genuine search for autonomy and new theatrical identity which, especially in recent years, looks again to the outside world but without recourse to naturalism.

In the no man's land between municipal theatres and the periphery, the ground has become fertile through the work, support and intervention of producing centres (mostly buildings or cultural centres without companies) like Toneelschuur Haarlem, Kaaitheater in Brussels (see *The Low Countries* 1994-95: 273-274) and Monty in Antwerp.

Theatre and other art forms

New theatre-makers have kept the borders with other art forms fluid and open. In fact the use and application of other media, especially video, has become something of a norm in dance and performance. Foreign influences, particularly The Wooster Group from New York, help to account for this. Although some interdisciplinary ideas and models date back to the first quarter of the century, the technique wasn't common in Flanders or the Netherlands until the seventies. It is striking how many visual artists feel attracted to the theatre and play an important role in it. As Janny Donker once wrote, *'wherever borders lose their sharpness, there is room for the appearance of the "unqualified"'*. A number of these *'unqualified'* have shifted the borders of Flemish theatre in the last decade, in particular Jan Fabre, Jan Lauwers and Guy Cassiers. They have no theatre training, but deploy techniques from dance, theatre, opera and music in their work. In the Netherlands, Orkater (formerly Hauser Orkater) and Onafhankelijk Toneel have incorporated music and the visual arts in their production or house styles.

In Flanders, there is also a firm connection between the worlds of theatre and dance. In the early eighties a new generation appeared – one which was neither an offshoot of seventies political theatre nor a conscious alternative to the playhouse stages. Simultaneously, the innovative, exciting work of young choreographers and dancers breaking loose from ballet, and the traditions offered by Maurice Béjart at his MUDRA school in Brussels, began to appear. Both groups of artists seem to be part of one and the same community, often hosted, presented or co-produced by the same centres or festivals. Some talk of a genuine hybrid in which it's difficult to tell theatre from dance. This is why Anne Teresa de Keersmaeker's 1990 dance piece *Stella* was easily selected for the Theatre Festival (the annual showcase for the most interesting Dutch-language productions from the previous season). So whether qualified or unqualified, this highly eclectic community of theatre and dance artists has been heavily supported by key Flemish centres like Monty (Antwerp), Stuc (Leuven), Vooruit (Ghent) and deSingel (Antwerp), just as critical writing and theatre publications such as *Etcetera* have become part of the new traditions of Flemish innovation.

Desk and stage

The Low Countries have neither national domestic repertoires nor staging traditions associated with them. The absence of a play-writing tradition has been a source of concern for theatres, even governments, for several decades – a problem which in 1971, the critic Ben Stroman accurately described as *'a deficiency.'*

But the absence of a tradition in stage texts for the theatre also means the absence of a border, and the absence of a dialogue across it – between old and new. Such a gap might have implied difficulties with purpose or role, but it seems instead to have stimulated a spontaneous search, amongst other repertoires especially, for alternative foundations for textual theatre. As the German critic Rischbieter expressed it, *'the rare, open character of the Dutch theatre, in the absence of a great domestic play-writing tradition, manages to make timely productions from the classical and modern repertoire for Dutch audiences, or to fill the gap with home-made scripts or collage productions.'*

As we've seen, bordercrossing into foreign repertoires is of great importance to Dutch-language theatre. But a headstrong dramatic literature has nonetheless recently appeared in both countries. There are of course, great and often-staged authors like Hugo Claus (author of the novel *The Sorrow of Belgium* – Het verdriet van België, 1983), whose texts are highly valued in the Netherlands and Flanders and have even been translated into English. But the strict division of territory which he and others represent, in which playwrights complete their plays in the isolation of their desks and hand the finished work to the director, is becoming rarer. This border too has been crossed: far more fluid relationships between writer and director – in fact new writing processes in which the author is involved in rehearsal or devising material and expected to reflect this in the writing – are now commonplace. Non-playwrights, whether actors, novelists, directors have frequently produced finished texts for the stage. Josse de Pauw (*Ward Comblez, Spanking the Maid* – De Meid Slaan) or Willy Thomas (*B = A In Bubbles*) are actors. Dutchmen Karst Woudstra (*A Black Pole* – Een zwarte Pool) and

Frans Strijards (*Coincidence, Incident* – Toeval, voorval) are both directors. The leading figure of this kind today is undoubtedly Gerardjan Rijnders, artistic director of Toneelgroep Amsterdam, who as director and author has built up an impressive consistently new and daring body of work.

The pattern of these 'new' writers and the traditions which they create or deny varies immensely. Karst Woudstra and Judith Herzberg (*Scratch* – Kras) write as analytical realists. Wanda Reisel (*On the Slopes of Vesuvius* – Op de hellingen van de Vesuvius) shows great poetic sensitivity. Using terms from visual arts genres, Robert Steijn describes the work of Frans Strijards as cubist, the oeuvre of Gerardjan Rijnders as surrealist, the writing of Rob de Graaf (of the Nieuw West company) as expressionist. Whether appropriate or not, these labels confirm that the texts of these and other writers go beyond the borders of psychological drama or the theatre of naturalism.

Montage pieces like Rijnders' *Titus. No Shakespeare* (Titus. Geen Shakespeare) go furthest in giving a new autonomy or freedom from meaning to language. In Flanders, texts by Willy Thomas or Paul Pourveur (*The Hunting of the Snark*) and Jan Decorte (*Colour is Everything* – Kleur is alles) do the same. *The Blacksmith's Child* (Het kind van de smid), by Josse de Pauw (see *The Low Countries* 1994-95: 275-276) and Peter van Kraaij or Arne Sierens' *The Drum Teacher* (De drumleraar) are inspired by storytelling traditions, coloured in poetic tones by De Pauw, given a tint of social sensitivity by Sierens. A large number of notable playwrights have begun to work for children's theatre in recent years: these include Pauline Mol, Ad de Bont, and Suzanne van Lohuizen (also popular in Germany). In fact one or two writers like Sierens and Thomas (*Mouchette* and *B = A in Bubbles* respectively) sometimes seem to produce their better pieces for children.

Most of the texts listed here have a limited performance history – produced once and sometimes in conjunction with, or even by, the author. Perhaps this is a consequence of the very intimate working process which brings these pieces to life. It goes without saying that second and subsequent productions are necessary.

Oud Huis Stekelbees, *B = A in Bubbles* (Willy Thomas) (Photo by Jan Simoen).

Speelteater, *Behind Glass* (Achter glas) (Photo by Peter Lorré).

Adult and children's theatre

Theatre for children and young people in the Low Countries experienced a great renewal in the seventies – pulled along in the same current of political theatre and its message of improved awareness and emancipation. The border between the innocent, fairy-tale world of children and the realistic adult one was disclosed as artificial, of middle-class construction.

The reaction against traditional make-believe theatre was radical. The content of productions had to be closer to the everyday world of children and young people. New topics and subjects appeared on the stage: parent-child conflicts, obedience and disobedience, criminality, discrimination, work and unemployment. Children became part of society and its important social themes. Another change in emphasis affecting theatre-makers was a move from theatre for children to theatre by children. This provided opportunities for the young to reach a point of view about the society in which they live. *'Meespeeltheater'* – literally, 'playing-along-with theatre' – was its most important expression.

Despite the impulse towards 'liberation' emitted by political theatre, children's work remained attached to a pedagogical mission – theatre as a vehicle for education. It wasn't until the eighties that children's theatre freed itself from the educational imperative to adopt its own artistic goals and objectives. (An important stage in this process was the Festival of Youth Theatre in Den Bosch, started in 1984 and held annually ever since). Pedagogy has turned to anti-pedagogy. Anti-pedagogues argue for a non-hierarchical attitude to the child – a fresh respect for the child's individuality. Free or open emotions, spontaneity, surprise and astonishment, fantasy and more associative ways of thinking are enjoying new currency and appreciation. New levels of artistic complexity, new aesthetics of design are apparent in the work of companies like Wederzijds, Stella Den Haag, Studio Peer, Teneeter, Mevrouw Smit (The Netherlands), Victoria (formerly Oud Huis Stekelbees), Eva Bal's Speelteater, Blauw Vier and Het Gevolg (Flanders). According to the critic Anita Twaalhoven *'realistic stories are being chosen less frequently, and there's a preference for classical themes and stories involving associative fantasy, with daring, painterly productions. Theatre for the young makes use of movement, dance, music and puppetry and is searching for new acting styles. And design is based on different styles from the visual arts.'*

The directors of young people's and children's theatre use the history of the drama and world repertoires as inspiration – the Greek classics, Shakespeare, Büchner, Chekhov, Ionesco, Beckett and Handke. Productions don't try to simplify or trivialise the contents or philosophy of such genres or texts, but to search them for the sensitivity or essence with which they can be communicated to the child. In a production for Teneeter Pauline Mol adapted Euripides' *Iphigenia in Aulis* into *Iphigenia. Child of a King* (Iphigenea Koningskind), approaching the well-known myth from the feelings of the child to be sacrificed. In the production directed by Liesbeth Colthof, the figure of Iphigenia was played by two actors, providing an image of her inner conflict. Willy Thomas' *B = A in Bubbles* was an adaptation of Handke's *Kaspar Hauser,* directed by Guy Cassiers for Oud Huis Stekelbees. The piece is concerned with the difficulties of communication between A and B: A eloquent and dominant; B mute and necessarily submissive. Once B learns to speak the result is laboured though funny and touching, helping close the gap between them. The production used a revolving see-saw, on which the characters communicated.

Even productions based on history or aspects of social reality avoid the need to represent or even respect reality. In *Hitler's Youth* (De jeugd van Hitler), presented by Wederzijds, Hitler was played by two actresses who de-emphasised their own individuality in a bid to create room for the creative imaginations of their young audience.

Some theatre made with young people has been startlingly radical: Jan Ritsema's *The Leave-Taking* (Het Heengaan), inspired by Rainer Maria Rilke's *Die Aufzeichnungen des Malte Laurids Brigge* (1910) and performed by a group of teenagers was theatrically daring and full of restrained eroticism. Lukas Vandervost staged Wedekinds' *Spring Awakenings* (Frühlings Erwachen, 1891) with young actors, and Guy Cassiers has worked with children and young people on several occasions. Their point of departure has always been the openness and authenticity of the perceptual world of the young – productions which question, and move, the borders of perception and performance for both director and audience.

It is the presence of these borders, and the tendency to cross and re-cross them, from which the constant tensions of cultural identity and place in Dutch and Flemish theatre arise. Identities are anything but constant or pre-given: in fact stable cultural identity is, if anything, undermined by theatre itself. If municipal theatres don't occupy the dominant position in the theatrical landscape of the Low Countries, this is hardly a drawback or even important. It is the turbulence of groups, styles, aesthetics, points of view, technical developments which, on the peripheries of the more traditional centre, encourages new traditions and initiatives to unfold.

ERWIN JANS AND GEERT OPSOMER
Translated by Neil Wallace.

FURTHER INFORMATION

The Netherlands Theatre Institute
Herengracht 166-168 / 1016 BP Amsterdam / The Netherlands
tel. +31 20 623 51 04 / fax +31 20 620 00 51

The Flemish Theatre Institute
Sainctelettesquare 19 / 1210 Brussels / Belgium
tel. +32 2 201 09 06 / fax +32 2 203 02 05

These institutes jointly publish the bilingual (English / French) journal *Carnet.*

This article is an adaptation of a text written at the request of the Netherlands and Flemish Theatre Institutes on the occasion of the 1993 Frankfurt Book Fair.

General of Beauty

The Work of Jan Fabre

If there was ever an artist who entered the performing arts in an unorthodox way, that artist is Jan Fabre (1958-). A native of Antwerp, Fabre had no theatrical training, but studied at the Academy of Fine Arts and at the Municipal Institute for Decorative Arts and Crafts in Antwerp. Yet his development was nevertheless organic: during his studies, between 1976 and 1980, he not only produced his first theatre texts and his first visual work, but also gave performances. These originated from his training as a window-dresser. From the beginning Fabre was an artist who strove for freedom: *'My ideal is always to have the illusion or feeling that I know or possess freedom.'* This is why, in his performances – which he first staged in a shop window – he literally forced his way to the fore.

New horizons

Fabre is an artist who continually explores his own limitations and attempts to push them back. His drawings are searches for space, and are therefore at least as important as his theatre work and choreography. The Dutch verb *'tekenen'*, 'to draw', is often used in the sense of 'to signify', thus also 'to give meaning to'; that Fabre is sensitive to this complex of meanings is evident from, for example, *The Bic-Art Room* (1981). Fabre shut himself in a room for seventy-two hours and drew on everything in the room, even his own body. Fabre himself said of this: *'I wanted to be a drawing machine which drew everything it thought and felt at the moment it was drawing.'* Like a prisoner who makes time tangible by marking off the days on the wall, and writing his own name over and over again because he is afraid of forgetting himself and thus disappearing. Other work by Fabre also deals with the disappearance of the self. There is a continual tension between that which is private and individual, and that which is spatial and collective.

The suggestion of the spatial in the drawings is reinforced by the material: Fabre uses mainly blue Bic ballpoints, conventional implements *par excellence*, to let fly on large canvasses and give expression to his own ideas, dreams, visions and experience. The blue ballpoint colour imparts a

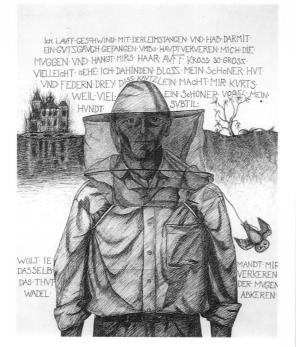

Jan Fabre, *Wolt iemandt mir dasselb verkeren das thut der mugen wadel abkeren...* 1990. Ballpoint on paper, 210 x 150 cm (Photo Troubleyn).

Jan Fabre, *Tivoli Castle.* 1990. Ballpoint on cloths (Photo Troubleyn).

gloss which appears to give depth to the flat surface. Fabre connects this with the *'blue hour'*, the moment at which night fades into day. It is a moment during which time and space appear to lose their conventional dimensions.

Desire for freedom

Fabre not only tests his limits, but also strives for freedom to achieve complete physical and spiritual expression. This clashes with the awareness of transience. While drawing, Fabre often lies naked on his work in order to maximise the physical and spiritual conveyance. Yet, at the same time, he chooses a transient way of working by using ballpoint ink, which begins to discolour even after a short time. Fabre is genuinely engaged with visual art, yet he also takes it to task. He remains an anarchist, as his self-portrait *Wolt iemandt mir dasselb verkeren das thut der mugen wadel abkeren...* from 1990 illustrates: he depicts himself not as an inspired romantic, but as a bee-tamer with a menacing look. Behind him, a fairytale castle burns and a tree grows bearing new ideas. The drawing is framed, but there is something odd about this: the frame is more like a small cupboard and above it is an aluminium 'canopy'. It looks more like a blueprint for a fairytale forest than a drawing intended for a museum. *'I want to see it hanging in a museum where it rains in'* states Fabre. He does not allow himself to be framed by a system in which good taste is guarded by the keepers of the imagination, museum directors and critics with a trendy taste. Fabre's irony proves that his visual work should not be seen as an interpretation of the avant-garde question *'what is art?'*, but rather as the product of an artist who is concerned to maximise the physical, aesthetic and spiritual conveyance of the imagination.

Tumultuous silence

In addition to the drawings in which he gives meaning to his complex imagination and physically creates what he calls *'the tumult of silence'*, Fabre has produced a number of 'sculptures' which illustrate the importance of silence, introspection, withdrawal and meditation in his work. Thus, as early as 1977, he designed *La Maison de J.F.*, small houses of copper and aluminium without a roof, so that the viewer was able to look inside. They are a symbol of the artist's compulsive desire for freedom, but at the same time they are a place to withdraw from life. The houses bear a quotation by Artaud which confirms this: *'Life shall happen; events shall take their course, human conflicts shall resolve themselves, and I shall not participate.'*

In 1990 he decorated the exterior of Tivoli Castle near Mechelen with large cloths bearing drawings in ballpoint-blue, which gave the castle the air of an introverted, still, fairytale world. At least as important was the reflection in the water which created a duality whereby fiction and reality kept each other in balance. Listening to the *'tumult of silence'* is very important in Fabre's work. The spectator's viewing is an intermediary phase, after which he loses himself in silence. Fabre demonstrated this clearly during Documenta IX in 1992 by placing on the wall, in each room of the museum, seven drinking glasses in blue ballpoint with his hand drawn round them. Thus the viewer could withdraw from the bustle of Documenta and listen, through the drinking glasses, to the unfamiliar and indefinable on the other side of the wall. There was also a work in glass and ballpoint representing Fabre's head, with two horns which listened antenna-like to the reality around them. The horns remind us of the feelers of insects; these, along with other animals, also feature strongly in Fabre's work.

Metamorphosis

Fabre attributes his fascination with animals to the nineteenth-century French entomologist Jean-Henri Fabre, whom he even calls his *'great-grandfather'*. Jean-Henri Fabre was the first person to look at the insect world from an anthropological point of view. We see the anthropomorphic quality in insects in Fabre's theatre and dance pieces and in his operas: the actors and dancers are sometimes armoured and resemble beetles.

Insects also feature strongly in his visual work: he draws them, mounts dead examples on his canvasses or gives them attributes. We are constantly struck by his fascination with their ability to metamorphose. The insects are in that respect beings which can 'split' real time and space and allude to a forgotten language; as Fabre says: *'The presence of animals, the fairytale elements and the dream feeling in my work all form an introduction to the understanding of a forgotten language. It is a language which we all carry within us, but suppress. It is a language which is closer to the essence of things and has an empathy with life. It has different arrangements concerning time and space.'*

Metamorphosis, in which Fabre appears to treat man and animals as equals, is represented in a more expressive way in his recent beautiful sculptures such as *Mur de la Montée des Anges* (1993), a dress made up of thousands of green, brown and blue jewel beetles.

Theatre

Thus we arrive, via animal metamorphosis, at Jan Fabre's theatre productions. Fabre is currently one of the most important contemporary creators of theatre, choreographers and operatic directors. His scenic construction, dramaturgical approach and direction of dancers, actors and singers show clearly that he is primarily a visual artist. *'For me drawing is the touchstone of every project I have carried out or am carrying out',* he claims. He calls animals, as well as actors and dancers, *'warriors of beauty'* who are fighting for a space and time other than the accepted ones. In his productions, animals as well as actors are engaged in the struggle between reality and imagination, order and chaos, simulation and authenticity. In *The Power of Theatrical Madness* (De macht der theaterlijke dwaasheden), a key production from 1984 in which the central theme is the lie of theatrical illusion, frogs are kissed and, as in a fairy tale, become heroes who must carry the little princesses until they are physically exhausted. The audience is thereby confronted with the limited physical capacities of the actors, and thus with reality. This issue is intensified by the confrontation between visual art and theatre, as the actors move against large white backcloths onto which are projected slides of paintings from the Renaissance to the beginning of the Modernist period. A double illusion is provided by the confrontation between theatrical action and the images on the backcloths, in which elements of theatre are clearly recognisable.

In this performance, which heralded an international breakthrough for Fabre (and which he took on a world tour), the physical reality of the actors secured him a place in theatre history. Fabre's favourite actress Els Deceukelier literally had to fight her way onto the stage because she did not answer the actor guarding the scene when he asked her what happened in 1876. Completely exhausted, she eventually screams *'Richard Wagner, "Ring des Nibelungen", Festspielhaus Bayreuth'*. Later in the performance the actors, running on the spot in a race they must continue until they drop, call out the titles of historical performances by, among others, Pina Bausch, Peter Brook and Bob Wilson. The first production to bring Fabre a wider audience was *Theatre Spelt with a k is a Tomcat* (Theater geschreven met een k is een kater) in 1980. This concluded his performance period, but at the same time integrated it by awakening in the audience the illusion of real time and action. The language of theatre was presented in three forms: parts of the text were written, in manuscript, on the back wall of the theatre. In a sort of marathon session, the actors worked themselves to exhaustion speaking the text. In addition, the author himself was present as a character on stage. One actor typed the text while another actor spoke it. The pace of the typing determined the pace of the performance.

Jan Fabre, *Mur de la Montée des Anges.* 1993. Jewel beetles, iron wire, 160 x 50 x 50 cm (Photo Troubleyn).

Jan Fabre, *The Power of Theatrical Madness* (De macht der theaterlijke dwaasheden, 1984) (Photo by Patrick T. Sellitto).

Reality and imagination also clash in the production which followed this in 1982, *This is Theatre like It Was to Be Expected and Foreseen* (Het is theater zoals te verwachten en te voorzien was). The production, which Fabre had rehearsed during a five-month 'quarantine', resulted in something diametrically opposed to conventional beliefs about acting. During an eight-hour performance actors performed, with the utmost precision, acts such as licking up yoghurt which had dripped from plastic bags onto the stage. In endlessly repeated movements, two actors walk up to each other, kiss each other on the cheek and return, walking backwards, to their place. Marc van Overmeir and Els Deceukelier, who were to become Fabre's principal actors, introduced themselves at the end of the performance as a '*gambler*' and a '*child-care worker*', because at that time Fabre still refused to speak of 'actors' and took pride in working with non-professionals. Thirteen years later, this has changed. Els Deceukelier and Marc van Overmeir have had an indelible influence on Fabre, and he reproduces these experiences in his recent texts *Forgery as It Really Is, Unforged (*Vervalsing zoals ze is, onvervalst, 1992) and *The Emperor of Loss* (De keizer van het verlies, 1994). In *This is Theatre like It Was to Be Expected and Foreseen* Van Overmeir and Deceukelier expressed two important elements in Fabre's theatre: the physical and repetition. Bare-chested, Marc van Overmeir walked on the spot for minutes at a time so that his physical exhaustion was clearly visible. Els Deceukelier and another actor dressed and undressed themselves continuously for half an hour.

Fabre uses this repetition to counter the speed of mediatised society. He wants to make tangible another dimension of time and space by 'splitting' time and space as we know it. In his theatre texts he sometimes does this by using recurring series of associative words. In theatre performances, chore-

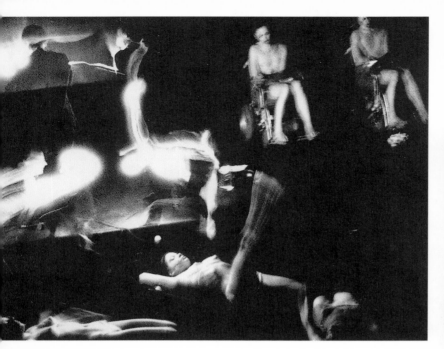

Jan Fabre, *Sweet Temptations* (1991) (Photo by J.G. Rittenberg).

Jan Fabre, *She Was and She Is, Even* (Zij was en zij is, zelfs, 1991) (Photo by J.P. Stoop).

ography and operas he uses the repetition – sometimes endless – of movements and actions, and recurring silence.

Twins

Fabre sends his actors on stage like a general sending his warriors into battle. These warriors of beauty battle against the simulacrum, the deceptive beauty of society which we like to see on stage so that we can lose ourselves in it. *The Interview that Dies (*Het Interview dat sterft, 1975) is a sharp criticism of this false ideal of beauty and the media. The piece is a confrontation between a director, a journalist, a beauty specialist and another journalist who is her client. Here, too, the accepted dimension of time is destroyed: through the silences incorporated by the actors, the twenty-minute text is extended to four hours.

Symmetry is a fundamental characteristic of Fabre's theatre, dance and opera. Often this has to do with opposing elements which, at the same time, reflect each other. In that sense Fabre's theatre is above all visual because it does not provide psychological explanations, but deals with actors and dancers moving through space and 'splitting' it. This also happens when the text is spoken in a certain rhythm, thereby distorting time. In his theatrical productions symmetry is often represented by twins.

Sweet Temptations, a text from 1978 staged in 1991, is a key production in Fabre's oeuvre. There is a direct clash between order and chaos, reason and emotion, reality and imagination. The text is full of ironic allusions to previous productions. We hear fragments of reality as stage-managed by the media, which are destroyed in the acting. Above all, there are the twins

Gerard and Elias, philosophers inspired by Stephen Hawking who keep raising fundamental objections but are in wheelchairs and fall victim to the 'sweet temptations'.

Monologues

After this feast of chaos, anti-psychology and collectivity, Fabre returned to the order and psychology of his favourite actors in his theatrical monologues *She Was and She Is, Even* (Zij was en zij is, zelfs, 1975), *Who Shall Speak of my Thought* (Wie spreekt mijn gedachte, 1980), *Forgery as It Really Is, Unforged* (1992) and *The Emperor of Loss* (1994). The last two texts were dedicated to the actors and the first two – solo pieces – were performed by Els Deceukelier and Marc van Overmeir respectively. In *She Was and She Is, Even*, the solo performance which had its premiere in 1991, Fabre brings on the bride like a machine, to be looked at by the audience, as voyeurs. But there are various elements which prevent this: the idyllic vision of Els Deceukelier in bridal dress is spoiled by the fact that she is smoking a pipe. Also, bird spiders crawl about in the illuminated space between her and the audience. Again we have a duality, in the form of the 'other side'. In *She Was and She Is, Even* the actress asks, as in the story of Snow White, who is the fairest in the land but, with her back to the audience, she can only answer herself: *'It is the other side / the past / I know it.'* The other side is known only to her, while the audience so much wants to see it, even if she were only to turn round and show them the other side of the bride.

The 'other side' is also the central theme of *Who Shall Speak of my Thought,* which had its premiere in 1992. This is a monologue, interpreted by Marc van Overmeir, who is also, as an actor, a wounded rabbit with an axe in its head, someone obsessively listening to the *'tumultuous silence'*. The actor's obsession with keeping sounds together evokes Fabre's drinking glasses for eavesdropping at Documenta in 1992. The actor is listening primarily to 'the other side' in himself: the flowing of his blood and the beating of his heart, led by Fabre who administers electrical pulses at regular intervals.

Jan Fabre, *Who Shall Speak of my Thought* (Wie spreekt mijn gedachte, 1992) (Photo by J.P. Stoop).

Dance

The three choreographies produced by Jan Fabre to date are too frequently interpreted as preliminary studies for his opera trilogy, because they were repeatedly presented as a new part of the opera *The Minds of Helena Troubleyn*. *The Dance Sections* (De Danssecties, 1987) was incorporated as choreography in the first part of the trilogy *Das Glas im Kopf wird vom Glas* (1990), and the same thing happened with *The Sound of One Hand Clapping* (1990), which preceded *Silent Screams, Difficult Dreams* (1992). November 1993 saw the premiere of the choreography *Da un'altra faccia del tempo*, in which Fabre manipulated the language of classical dance by slowing or repeating movements, and providing occasional ironic commentary. In this, his ideas relating to space and time and the function of the dancers are realised in an aesthetic manner which is often astounding. The dancers cre-

123

ate inner space because they move like atoms within the universe of Fabre's choreography. Unlike classical ballet dancers, they are not anonymous or sexless, but are present as vulnerable individuals, particularly when the female dancers are wearing only lingerie. They are often brought into the discipline of collective dance, as a way of creating beauty. The personal element of the dancers is particularly emphasised when their nakedness is contrasted with moments when they wear armour and look like insects, as in *The Dance Sections* and *The Sound of One Hand Clapping*. Both these pieces are also characterised by strict symmetry, in particular through the presence of Els Deceukelier. In *The Dance Sections* she is high up on the back wall with her naked back to the audience, and in *The Sound of One Hand Clapping* she is in the foreground, seated at a miniature piano and looking provocatively at the audience.

Jan Fabre, *Silent Screams, Difficult Dreams* (1992) (Photo Troubleyn).

Opera trilogy

As regards content, Fabre's choreography is of course incorporated in the opera trilogy *The Minds of Helena Troubleyn*, about a woman who lives in her own world of imagination and dreams. The Pole Eugeniusz Knapik wrote the music, which is at once consonant and dissonant. The composition of sounds is, like Fabre's text, both open and hermetic, and the activity on stage characterises but does not interpret.

In the first part of the trilogy, *Das Glas im Kopf wird vom Glas*, we meet the main characters. *'Il Ragazzo con la luna e le stelle sulla testa'* ('the boy with the moon and stars on his head'), represents the anarchy of nature and is always accompanied by an owl. He is the poet who dreams and creates the world in which Helena (based on a woman who lived completely in her own

Jan Fabre, *The Sound of One Hand Clapping* (1990) (Photo by D. Mentzos).

Jan Fabre, *Das Glas im Kopf wird vom Glas* (1990) (Photo Carl de Keyzer).

FURTHER READING

The Power of Theatrical Madness (Photos by Robert Mapplethorpe). London 1986.
The Dance Sections (Photos by Helmut Newton). Ghent, 1990.
Fabre's Book of Insects. Ghent, 1990.
Jan Fabre. Texts on his Theatre Work. Brussels / Frankfurt, 1993.

fantasy and who fascinated Fabre) lives. He throws scissors into the air which remain suspended like stars above the heads of the singers, dancers and actors as a symbol of the splitting of space and time. *Il Ragazzo* advises Helena, stands by her and observes her bizarre fantasies. Helena invents Fressia, personified on stage by Els Deceukelier. Fressia is protected by the armoured, dancing guards of fantasy. When she cuts Helena's hair at the end of the performance, this is an allusion to the end of the trilogy, when Helena and the world of the imagination come to grief.

In the second part of the trilogy, *Silent Screams, Difficult Dreams,* Helena's power is at its strongest. She manipulates all the characters by giving them a place in her imagination because they are fascinated by her and her creation Fressia. Three women are led into her world where there is no longer any distinction between individuals. It seems like a world between day and night, translated into the ballpoint-blue of the scenery. The only person to escape Helena's control is *Il Ragazzo*, who rises in the background and, with an owl perched on his shoulder, juggles with scissors. The audience, like the characters, cannot grasp what is happening because the actors are engaged in strange rituals such as the careful picking up and putting down of an object that remains invisible. Helena triumphs in this world, reaching for invisible insects. She firmly rejects the warning of *Il Ragazzo*, who announces that the secret of death must be sought in life itself, by drawing the other characters' attention to the owl on his shoulder and encouraging them to fantasise about it. Thus she smugly holds on to her own wisdom. When the characters, through their imagination, are confronted with their own past, Helena promises to make the past disappear. Initially she appears to be winning when the past, symbolised by a pile of white plates, smashes to pieces. But at the end *Il Ragazzo*, who has observed this, comes to announce the end of Helena's dream world.

The parts of the trilogy seen so far are especially interesting as the synthesis of Fabre's versatility. Yet the impression they give is a static one; and this highlights the fact that Fabre is above all a visual artist who takes the spectator's breath away and draws him into the deep blue of his universe.

PAUL DEMETS
Translated by Yvette Mead.

125

Step

by Step

The Story of the Nederlands Dans Theater

In 1959 business manager Carel Birnie, ballet master Benjamin Harkarvy and fourteen prominent dancers of what was then the Nederlands Ballet decided to leave and set up their own company: the Nederlands Dans Theater. Their decision followed a series of conflicts with the director of the Nederlands Ballet, Sonia Gaskell. Those conflicts were largely due to Gaskell's chaotic leadership, the absence of work schedules and the lack of a permanent and competent ballet master. There were no prospects of financial support for the new company; it had no premises of its own, and could be certain that its performances would not be enthusiastically received by the circle of prominent Dutch dance critics, who were unquestioning supporters of Gaskell.

But what the 'rebels' *did* have was artistic vision, huge dance talent, boundless energy, inventiveness, a sense of unity and faith in their own abilities. There was no hierarchy within the Nederlands Dans Theater. Everyone was a soloist and worked initially for the same, very meagre, salary. In the early years the repertoire consisted of works by the thoroughly professional Harkarvy, and by Rudi van Dantzig, Hans van Manen and Job Sanders – who were proving to be young, self-willed and interesting creators of dance – supplemented by the familiar fireworks of *pas de deux* from the classical repertoire.

Audiences reacted enthusiastically to the quality of performances and dancers, and there were favourable reviews in the independent press both at home and abroad. When after two years of struggle, and despite performances and much success – abroad as well as at home –, there was still no prospect of financial support and debts were growing, the decision had to be taken to disband the company. The farewell performance had already taken place when the Hague City Council granted a substantial subsidy. Now the company's artistic direction could be more clearly delineated. The traditional, classical *pas de deux* disappeared from the programmes and dance innovators from America could be enticed to the Netherlands, among them Anna Sokolov, John Butler and Glen Tetley. These added important works to the repertoire, such as *Rooms* (Sokolov), *Pierrot Lunaire* (Tetley) and *Carmina Burana* (Butler). With their arrival audiences and dancers alike were confronted with modern dance techniques developed in America. As a result the Nederlands Dans Theater (soon referred to simply by its initials, NDT) developed into a company free of the awkward dichotomy between classical and modern dance which still beset other companies, and the female dancers danced just as easily in bare feet or sneakers as on points.

From the beginning the NDT's repertoire was largely shaped by the choreography of Hans van Manen who was the company's artistic director from 1961 to 1970, first with Benjamin Harkarvy and then for a short period with Glen Tetley. During this period Van Manen created twenty-two ballets of which *Metaphors* (Metaforen, 1965), *Five Sketches* (Vijf schetsen, 1966) and *Squares* (1969) are still performed, although only the last of these is performed by the NDT itself. Benjamin Harkarvy and Job Sanders also made important contributions with *Madrigalesco* (1963), *Grand pas Espagnole* (1962), *Recital for Cello and Eight Dancers* (1964) and *The Rag-and-Bone Man* (De voddenraper, 1963), *Pop Beat* (1965) and *Impressions* (Impressies, 1967) by Sanders. The dancer Jaap Flier proved to be also an intriguing choreographer with his *Thanatos* (1962), *Interview* (1964) and *New Adventures* (Nouvelles aventures, 1968). The most remarkable dancers of the period were Willy de la Bye, Marian Sarstädt, Alexandra Radius, Martinette Janmaat, Käthy Gosschalk, Han Ebbelaar, Jaap Flier, Gerard Lemaitre and Charles Czarny.

The NDT's big international breakthrough came in 1963 when it was invited to perform at the important Theatre Festival in Paris, where the audience included many foreign theatre directors and critics. On the strength of the NDT's success at this Paris Festival, one director invited the NDT to give a series of performances in his own theatre: the Empire Theatre in Sunderland, near Newcastle. All the important London critics attended, undeterred by the long journey from the capital. The reviews were fabulous: '*NDT has the most varied repertoire of modern ballet in the world*', '*A revelation – there is no company like them*' (A.V. Cotton in *The Daily Telegraph*), '*They were wonderful. Their repertoire, their spirit, their style are wonderful*' (Clive Barnes in *Dance and Dancers*) and '*Most lively ballet company in Europe*'. One of the consequences of the NDT's British performances was that Dame Marie Rambert decided to follow their example and transform her company into a modern company with its foundation in classical dance. From 1963 the NDT had the world at its feet. The many performances abroad which followed were not only valuable from the point of view of professional contacts and artistic recognition and appreciation. The financial rewards negotiated by Carel Birnie were also important because they enabled the company to undertake projects which could not have been financed by the regular subsidies. Thus the NDT was able to acquire the badly needed office space above its scenery warehouse, and a work complex which was the subject of a long article in the English publication *Dance and Dancers* in 1963.

NDT was a company which did not shun artistic or commercial risks and the commitment of those involved enabled it to steer clear of or overcome catastrophes. Nevertheless, at the end of the 1960s difficulties arose within the company: in spite of the many new ballets, many dancers felt that they were stagnating, and left the NDT in search of new challenges. In addition, there were increasing clashes between the egos of the inspired and inspiring

Jaap Flier, *New Adventures* (Nouvelles aventures, 1968) (Photo by Anthony Crickmay).

Glen Tetley and Hans van Manen, *Mutations* (1970) (Photo by Anthony Crickmay).

trio Van Manen, Harkarvy and Birnie. Harkarvy was the first to leave. Glen Tetley stepped into his shoes, but this collaboration was short-lived. By 1970 neither Hans van Manen nor Tetley were connected with the NDT.

The final straw of artistic and commercial discord proved to be the ballet *Mutations* (1970), a joint work by Hans van Manen and Glen Tetley. The innovative elements in the work – the choreography which defied theatrical convention, the use of film, and especially the costume design and nude scenes – made *Mutations* a worldwide box-office success; with the result that the programmers almost forgot that the NDT also had other important ballets in its repertoire. Dancer / choreographer Jaap Flier tried to save the company from its internal crisis by offering to take on the artistic directorship. However, it soon became apparent that he had too little personal authority and his ideas became so avant-garde that the majority of the dancers could not identify with them. A new generation of American and Australian dance-makers such as Cliff Keuter, Don Asker, Louis Falco and Jennifer Muller enabled the NDT to continue to present a successful image to the outside world. Yet Carel Birnie, as alert and enthusiastic as ever, saw his company descending into an artistic vacuum. A combination of increasingly acrimonious conflicts between dancers and artistic director and serious differences of opinion on business matters led, in 1973, to the departure of Jaap Flier.

For two seasons the company had no artistic director: Carel Birnie acted as general director, supported by an artistic committee. The problems were not solved until guest choreographer Jiri Kylian and the dancer Hans Knill were appointed artistic directors. Peace then returned, to a certain extent.

Kylian had already rehearsed five ballets with the NDT, including *Stoolgame* (1974) and *The Engulfed Cathedral* (La Cathédrale Engloutie, 1975). He proved to be a great inspiration to the dancers, and to provide the secure footing which was so necessary; he emerged as a natural leader. After two seasons Hans Knill withdrew from the artistic directorship and became the company's producer. Under Kylian's influence the NDT entered a new era of success in its rich history. His ballets, with their surprising momentum, virtuosity, flexibility and richness of inventive movement, propelled the company to new artistic heights. The NDT's reputation in the dance world was such that dancers from all over the world tried to join it. Thus a new generation of dancers replaced the Dutch dancers who had been with the company from the beginning. Now it was Jean Solan, Arlette van Boven, Roslyn Anderson, Sabine Kupferberg, Alida Chase, Joke Zijlstra, Gerald Tibbs, Glenn Eddy and Nils Christe who shone in the repertoire. After the arrival of Kylian that repertoire consisted almost entirely of his own works. It seemed that there was no room for other styles. All Van Manen's ballets – in fact the entire pre-1975 repertoire – disappeared. Much criticism followed, particularly in the Netherlands, but this was overborne by the quality of Kylian's choreography and the new inspiration he was able to give to the dancers. The NDT's performance at the Spoleto Festival in America in 1978, with the première of Kylian's *Sinfonietta,* was a further milestone for the company. A minute and a half before the end of the performance the audience burst into tumultuous applause and could not be silenced. This phenomenal success encouraged the company to risk booking the City Dance Center in New York, at a time when there was strong competition from other companies performing in New York. The performance by the company from The Hague proved an overwhelming success. The critics vied with each other in singing their praises. Kylian became *'the wonder boy of European dance'* and *'a choreographic genius'* (Clive Barnes in *The New York Post).* The NDT was hailed as *'the most energetic, exciting and shining company appearing in New York'* (Walter Terry in *Wall Street Journal).* Not only the press was enthusiastic; there were large audiences at all performances. Three years later the success was repeated in the famous Metropolitan Opera House.

In the 1980s there was more scope within the repertoire for other important choreographers. William Forsythe, Mats Ek and Ohad Naharim provided a positive contrast to Kylian's work, and the return of Hans van Manen as house choreographer in 1988 was of major importance.

It is remarkable how Kylian and Van Manen constantly manage to exploit new facets of their artistry. Initially Kylian's choreography was remarkable for its constant, flowing movements and enormous energy. In the first half of the 1980s, however, he created ballets which were clearly inspired by the life and culture of the Aborigines. In *Nomads* (Nomaden, 1981), *Stamping Ground* (1983) and *Dreamtime* (1983), the outlandish animal language of movement reflects the bond with nature and the mystique of ancient rituals. After this Kylian created a series of works in which great theatricality was emphasised. Not all of these were successful, and some provoked the first plainly bad reviews abroad. *'European trash'* was Clive Barnes' destructive opinion from New York in 1986. This was a blow, but Kylian tapped new creative sources and created what came to be known as the black-and-white

Jiri Kylian, *Falling Angels*
(1989) (Photo by Hans
Gerritsen).

Jiri Kylian, *Whereabouts
Unknown* (1993) (Photo by
Dirk Buwalda).

ballets, because of the black costumes and harsh planes of bright white light.
These works included *Falling Angels* (1989), *No More Play* (1988) and
Small Death (Petite Mort, 1991). The movements which had previously
been so flowing and harmonious became sharper, more angular; the choreographic concept became more enigmatic. Hans van Manen's talent unfolded
more gradually. As always, there was a great clarity in his work, which was
free of even the smallest embellishment. With ever more minimal means, he
seems to approach the deepest essence of human relations ever more
closely. The duets *Two* (1990) and *Andante* (1991), and the subtle
Concertante (1994) are striking examples of this. The choreographic styles
of Kylian and Van Manen each show, in their own way, an inescapable link
with music and theatre, and each bears a strongly individual signature. Once
more there is a young generation of dancers, most from the home 'nursery'.
Fiona Lummis, Brigitte Martin, Nancy Euverink, Cora Kroese, Paul Lightfoot, Aryeh Weiner and Patrick Delcroix are now the stars. The NDT has
renewed itself in more ways than one. In 1977 the group took the initiative
of forming a second smaller company in order to provide dancers (often
recently graduated) with two years of training and practical experience, to

The auditorium of the
AT & T Danstheater.

equip them for affiliation to the main company, where soloist qualities are still required. After several years of experiment and learning from mistakes NDT2, as the group has been known for many years, has grown into a fully-fledged company of twelve to fourteen young dancers, whose membership is limited to two years. Initially the company developed under the inspiring leadership of Arlette van Boven, who has been succeeded by Gerald Tibbs; it still functions as the 'nursery' for NDT1, 80% of whose dancers are drawn from NDT2. Like the original company, NDT2 performs a great deal abroad. It also provides a showcase for young choreographers – both from within and outside the company – who are given the chance to display and develop their talents. Nils Christe, Nacho Duato, Ed Wubbe, Lionel Hoche, Philip Taylor and Paul Lightfoot, choreographers who have in the meantime made a name for themselves, produced their first works for NDT2, which was known first as *Springplank* (Springboard) and then *Junioren* (Juniors).

Since 1991 the NDT has has another string to its bow: the company for senior dancers, NDT3, consisting of four to six prominent dancers above 40 years of age. The composition of this group changes with each programme. The permanent members are Sabine Kupferberg and Gerard Lemaitre. Foreign interest in this group is also considerable. Choreographers such as Béjart, Mats Ek, Martha Clark and, of course, Kylian all create special works for NDT3.

Business manager Carel Birnie's wealth of ideas, tough determination and ingenuity ensured that in 1988, after years of negotiations, the NDT acquired its own theatre, the first and only theatre in the world built exclusively for dance: the AT & T Danstheater, designed by Rem Koolhaas (see *The Low Countries* 1994-95: 223-228). The building is a tremendous asset for The Hague itself. It has almost 1,000 seats, good sightlines and acous-

Jiri Kylian, *Kaguyahime* (1994) (Photo by Dirk Buwalda).

tics, its own restaurant, spacious theatrical proportions, well-equipped studios (also for the use of visiting companies), and TV and video recording facilities. At last, large dance companies from abroad are able to perform in The Hague.

In 1992 Carel Birnie was forced, for health reasons, to renounce his position as business manager, although he continued as director of 'his' theatre until April 1994. Michael de Roo succeeded Birnie (who died in March 1995) in both positions, Jiri Kylian is general artistic director, supported by Glenn Edgerton (leader of NDT1 from 1 September 1994), Gerald Tibbs (leader of NDT2) and Arlette van Boven (leader of NDT3). In Autumn 1994 in New York, after separate tours of the United States and Canada, the three NDT companies performed together for the first time. Once again, the critics were euphoric (although not about the full-length ballet *Kaguyahime*). The performances were acclaimed as an *'absolute knock-out'* and Kylian as *'one of the best choreographers in the world'* (Clive Barnes in *The New York Post)*. Although not all the works performed were received with equal enthusiasm, everyone agreed on one thing: the dancers were fantastic. But we have known that since 1959!

INE RIETSTAP
Translated by Yvette Mead.

The

Melody Makers

Contemporary Music in the Netherlands

Louis Andriessen (1939-)
(Photo by Marco Borggreve
/ Donemus).

The history of today's contemporary music in the Netherlands has its roots in the sixties, that turbulent decade which disposed of so many outdated standards and values. This fresh start was not unique to the Netherlands, nor to the world of music; but the way in which the up-and-coming generation of composers changed the Dutch musical scene once and for all was unparalleled in Europe. Not only was there a fierce debate as to the significance of contemporary music in society and concert programming, but organisations and ensembles were created to promote and play new music and to bring about a change of mentality in existing institutions.

The challenge this generation faced was to free itself from what was internationally regarded as modern music and to attract an audience with their own new musical language. Serialism, the twelve-tone technique which formed the basis for the most dominant avant-garde school of Western music after the Second World War, had clearly found little favour with audiences, and new music in the Netherlands also suffered the consequences of this. A number of Dutch composers sought to revive interest in contemporary music by producing works with a strong political commitment, one such being the opera *Reconstruction* (Reconstructie) about the freedom fighter Che Guevara (Holland Festival 1969) composed by a composers' collective made up of Louis Andriessen, Reinbert de Leeuw, Misha Mengelberg, Peter Schat and Jan van Vlijmen. At the same time some composers and musicians decided to bring their new music to where it was least expected, but where there was a large audience: namely the streets. The most important exponent of this strategy is the orchestra De Volharding (Perseverance). This orchestra, unconventionally composed of eleven wind instruments, one piano and a double bass, was set up in 1972 by Louis Andriessen, who also strongly influenced the direction the repertoire should take. Among the works performed by De Volharding in its early years were *Liberate the South* (Bevrijdt het Zuiden), composed by Huynh Minh Sieng and arranged in 1972 by Misha Mengelberg, arrangements of works by Hanns Eisler, Kurt Weill and Igor Stravinsky, and Andriessen's *Workers Union* (1975). Another composition by Andriessen, which though characteristic of the period was not written specifically for De Volharding, is

National Anthem (Volkslied, 1971) in which the tune of the Dutch national anthem, the *Wilhelmus,* is pulled apart and put together again as the socialist *International.*

De Volharding is still active and still organised as a strictly democratic 'cooperative association'. The development of its repertoire serves as a model of the evolution of political commitment in Dutch music. Even when the revolutionary spirit of the sixties had run its course, the desire to give music a new content remained undiminished. Composers from what became known as the Hague school (after the Royal Conservatory in The Hague where Kees van Baaren had been their mentor) made a point of composing music with a more and more complex but a *'natural respiration'*, as Diderik Wagenaar, a somewhat younger member of the Hague School, expressed it. It seems as if an attack was launched first on what was felt to be the serial composers' lack of social awareness, and subsequently on the weak points in their musical content. When all is said and done, a natural rhythmic progression cannot be said to have been a top priority of serialism. Without wishing to repudiate the achievements of the serialists, a number of Dutch composers wanted to continue the exploration of rhythm begun by for example Stravinsky, Janaçek and Messiaen. It goes without saying that the influence of jazz was also to play a part in this. And once again Louis Andriessen took the lead, with a composition inspired by the Boogie-woogie pianist Jimmy Yancey *(On Jimmy Yancey,* 1973), while more or less explicit references to jazz can likewise be heard in many works by his students and associates.

More than in any other European country, composers in the Netherlands have been influenced by jazz and improvised music. Not only have composers fallen under the spell of some of the big names in jazz, but a number of Dutch jazz musicians have switched to composing. The non-academic past of jazz saxophonist Theo Loevendie gave him the freedom to open up an entirely new perspective in a music world that was already remarkably unconventional. For a long time, however, he continued to draw a strict dividing line between improvisation and composition. It was not until 1991 that he wrote *Bang* (Bons)*,* a piece requiring solos by one or more improvising musicians, for one of the most outstanding contemporary music ensembles in the Netherlands, the Nieuw Ensemble. Trombone player Wolter Wierbos' performances were notable examples of the viability of this combination.

The combination of improvisation and composition has been pursued even more thoroughly by the double-bass player Maarten Altena, who like Loevendie began his career as a jazz musician, both as a member of various groups and as a solo performer. His own Maarten Altena Ensemble, to which Wolter Wierbos also belongs, is made up of nine musicians from very varied backgrounds, ranging from a classically trained Baroque musician to a jazz improvisor. The music that Altena writes for this ensemble is characterised by a singular rapport with the individual aptitude of the musicians and a subtly integrated use of improvisation. *Code,* composed in 1990 and available on a CD of that name, is an eloquent example. Guus Janssen is another prominent member of this movement so unique to the Netherlands. In his opera *Noach* (premiere June 1994, libretto in Dutch by Friso Haverkamp and sets by Karel Appel) he employs an ensemble of classically

Theo Loevendie (1930-)
(Photo by Marco Borggreve
/ Donemus).

trained singers and musicians, four harmonics singers from Tuvinskaya (a republic to the north of Mongolia), a classical string quartet and improvising musicians. In addition to composing, Janssen keeps his hand in as an improvisor in various ensembles. In improvisation he displays an inventiveness which borders on genius.

There is of course also room for loners like Misha Mengelberg, who as a free-jazz pianist and composer has always remained a Dadaist. He is a master of irony, who plays with his audience's listening conventions not only with his notes but by choosing far-out titles for his off-centre music. *With Polite Greetings from the Camel* (Met welbeleefde groet van de kameel, 1973) is one such title, as are *Sideboard* (Dressoir, 1977, commissioned by De Volharding) and *Hello Windyboys* (1968). Lack of meaning is of considerable significance in his music. Mengelberg, who made the LP *Last Date* with Eric Dolphy in 1964, went the opposite way to Theo Loevendie and Maarten Altena; after a short period as a composer he has concentrated more and more on improvisation. In the seventies he teamed up with composer / saxophonist Willem Breuker and percussionist Han Bennink and established the Instant Composers Pool, which still makes an important contribution both to composing and improvisation.

The clear and straightforward style pioneered by Louis Andriessen has largely been decisive for the standing of Dutch music abroad and has resulted in its substantial reputation. According to Andrew Clements in *The Guardian* of 24 June 1994 Andriessen is *'an individual voice in European music.'* The interest shown in his work in the United States resulted in his being invited to teach at Yale, and he has had a demonstrable influence on the work of New York composers like Michael Gordon. At the same time, young composers from a number of countries have been attracted by the Dutch musical scene to come and partake of the hospitality the Netherlands has always offered to artists and intellectuals from abroad. American, British, Greek and German students, to mention but a few, have come to the Netherlands to complete their study of composition, and to embark on their professional careers.

Maarten Altena (1943-)
(Photo by David Hanson
/ Donemus).

Guus Janssen (1951-)
(Photo by Frans
Schellekens).

Misha Mengelberg (1935-)
(Photo by Frans
Schellekens).

Tristan Keuris (1946-)
(Photo by Marco Borggreve
/ Donemus).

In addition to the music which draws on the oeuvre of Stravinsky and jazz, there is an important trend in contemporary Dutch music which emphasises a musical logic and comprehensibility that seems to be linked with the achievements of a more distant musical past. In the music of Tristan Keuris, for example, melody plays an important part, as do his indisputable talent for musical metaphor and his desire to master the composition of long works for large ensembles. He may not yet have tried his hand at an opera, but with his work for choir and orchestra *To Brooklyn Bridge* (1988), a musical evocation of the famous bridge in New York, he has a multimedia project to his name. The film made by the Dutch filmmaker Fred Van Dijk shows how sound and image can come together on the same imaginative level. *To Brooklyn Bridge* had its American premiere in March 1994; it was performed by the New York Virtuoso Singers conducted by Harold Rosenbaum.

Tristan Keuris is probably the Dutch composer most performed abroad; *Movements* (1981), for example, is played regularly by the Royal Concertgebouw Orchestra when it goes on tour. Another composer well-known abroad is Ton de Leeuw, whose music is coloured by his interest in Eastern philosophy.

Partly by taking over the Institute of Sonology's prestigious electronics studio a few years ago, the Royal Conservatory in The Hague gradually became an internationally recognised centre for electronic music. A comparatively independent 'Hague school' of electronic music gradually emerged, although it has never been known by that name. Jan Boerman has had an influence on the work of many composers from The Hague, while among the younger generation Kees Tazelaar must not be overlooked. The Royal Conservatory has long been one of the most important training grounds for composers in the Netherlands. As visiting professors at this conservatory both the American John Cage and the Englishman Brian Ferneyhough, to mention but two, have left their mark on the up-and-coming young composers.

Just as it was extremely difficult for young composers who came up shortly after the Second World War to determine their attitude towards pre-war modernism, so now those between thirty to thirty-five years of age have to deal with the question of how they can distinguish themselves from their forerunners, who made their reputations in the sixties and now hold key positions as teachers, conductors and conservatory directors. These men and women are responsible both for contemporary music in the Netherlands, and its role in music in general, and for the formation of a generation of musicians who have grown up in an entirely different ambience from themselves. Everything around us tells us that the days of protest are over, and the voice of contemporary music is no exception.

The young are reaping the benefits of what was achieved in the sixties, not only as regards increased freedom of musical content, but also the comprehensive infrastructure, on which the Dutch musical world has come to rest. Internationally acclaimed ensembles have sprung up which specialise in the performance of contemporary music and of course pay due attention to the home-grown product; there is the state-subsidised publishing house Donemus, unique in the world, whose task is the promotion of Dutch music; there is a growing number of venues open to contemporary music; works are commissioned; and all this receives financial support from central government. Although the composers are quick to say that more could be done, this provides a solid basis for those now setting out on their careers, even if the social and musical challenges facing them are still not entirely clear. While remarkably many composers who started off in the sixties have focussed especially on writing for opera, today's thirty-year-olds show an interest in, for example, experiments with rhythm (Martijn Padding), with the crossover between jazz and pop-influences (Rob Zuidam), anti-academism (Arthur Sauer) and neo-Romanticism (Joost Kleppe). So it might seem that not much new is happening in this postmodern period. Nevertheless, a debate has recently begun on a subject that would never have been an issue thirty years ago; namely, the true nature of the musical innovation which is an essential feature of contemporary Dutch music. The Dutch tendency to put things in pigeon-holes has led to the trailblazing music of the fundamentally undogmatic generation of the sixties and their direct successors being considered as symbolic of musical innovation. Composers like Ed de Boer and Reinhold Selen who embrace other aesthetic values question this, and rightly point out that an uncritical use of the term 'innovation' can lead to undeserved discrimination against their work. They are beginning to make themselves heard in the world of Dutch music. It is an illustration of the fact that there is something brewing in contemporary music in the Netherlands after all. And there always will be. The diversity of styles and characters guarantees the dynamic situation and ongoing debate that are essential to the vitality of modern music as a living art form.

JOHAN KOLSTEEG
Translated by Elizabeth Mollison.

For further information, it is best to contact Donemus, who publish an English-language magazine (*Keynotes*) and a series of LPs and CDs (*Composers' Voice*). In 1992 a *Composers' Voice Highlights* series was introduced.

Donemus
Publishing House and Library of Contemporary Dutch Music
Paulus Potterstraat 14
NL 1071 CZ Amsterdam
The Netherlands
tel. +31 20 676 44 36
fax +31 20 673 35 88

Distribution of the *Composers' Voice* series

For the USA:
Albany Music Distributors, Inc.
98 Wolf Road
Albany, NY 12205-0011
USA
tel. +1 518 453 2203
fax +1 518 453 2205

For the UK:
Impetus
P.O. Box 1324
London W5 2ZU
United Kingdom
tel. / fax +44 181 998 6411

Forward
into a New Era
The Story of the Royal Concertgebouw Orchestra

'The Royal Concertgebouw Orchestra is unique, in that few if any comparable orchestras in the international music world so excel in the performance both of music by Wagner, Bruckner, Mahler and Richard Strauss, composers who have always been and still are closely linked with the Orchestra's tradition, and of the masterpieces of twentieth-century and contemporary music. In Riccardo Chailly, the Royal Concertgebouw Orchestra has found a principal conductor whose qualities continue to develop and deepen in various areas of symphonic music and opera, and who has a clear personal commitment to living contemporary composers.'

Fine words, but they happen to be true. They come from the guide to the programme for the Royal Concertgebouw Orchestra's 1994-1995 season, which bears the signatures of two directors who have been making their mark on the daily life of the Netherlands' greatest orchestra for only a few years: Willem Wijnbergen, who is responsible for business management, and artistic director Jan Zekveld. Even Chailly is still a newcomer compared with the long service of his predecessors Kes, Mengelberg, Van Beinum and Haitink. He accepted the post of principal conductor in 1988 after the turbulent departure of Haitink, who went on to become musical director of Covent Garden Opera House in London. For the first time in the hundred-year history of the Concertgebouw Orchestra it had a non-Dutchman as principal conductor. This caused some raised eyebrows, particularly because up to then Chailly had been seen as a remarkable interpreter of contemporary music rather than as someone who would – or could – throw himself heart and soul into the traditional repertoire. However, to quote once again from the introduction mentioned above, his qualities are continuing to develop, and so the Orchestra has found itself in a new era. Its contribution to the Holland Festival in June 1995 (organised to commemorate the Liberation of the Netherlands in 1945) is significant in itself: a performance of Shostakovitch's Seventh Symphony, *Leningrad,* a concert with works by Rihm and Stockhausen and a programme organised around one of the Festival's main composers, Bernd Alois Zimmermann. The Orchestra is being pushed very consciously towards modern classical and contemporary music, but the artistic management will ensure that works from the

Romantic and late Romantic composers (Brahms, Bruckner, Mahler and Wagner) are not neglected, because these are precisely what is in demand from a significant segment of the record market and the international concert market.

In any case, 'renewal' is by no means an invention of the Orchestra's present administration. The former artistic director of the Royal Concertgebouw Orchestra, Professor Marius Flothuis, recalled some time ago that Arnold Schönberg performed his *Fünf Orchesterstücke* with the Concertgebouw Orchestra in 1914, the same year in which Claude Debussy gave the first performance of his *Marche écossaise, Prélude à l'apres-midi d'un faune* and two of the *Nocturnes* in Amsterdam. To this we should add that *Ein Heldenleben* by Richard Strauss is dedicated to Willem Mengelberg and the Concertgebouw Orchestra, and that Gustav Mahler found a tremendous advocate in Mengelberg (and himself took the podium in Amsterdam on several occasions, including a performance of his Third Symphony on 22 October 1903). All this shows quite clearly that the Orchestra and its artistic directors never degenerated into a fossilised institution, interested in nothing but classical tradition. However, the clear preference for contemporary music shown by its present principal conductor Riccardo Chailly, which meshes remarkably well with the activities of his record company Decca, is contributing towards an inexorable change in emphasis.

A few examples: early September 1994 saw the release of a CD which included all the new pieces recorded by Chailly and the Orchestra in the Concertgebouw's Great Hall (during its 107-year history this orchestra has made only one recording outside its own doors: Bruckner's Fifth Symphony, conducted by Eugen Jochum on 30 and 31 May 1964 in the former Abbey church in Ottobeuren). It contains complete renderings of Hindemith's *Kammermusik 1* and the *First Jazz Suite* by Shostakovitch, and also parts of works by Berio, Schnittke, Messiaen *(Turangalila Symphony,* which won an Edison in 1994), Schönberg and Zemlinsky. The title of this promotional compact disc is *21st Century Classics.*

The inclusion of the *Andante Moderato* from Mahler's Sixth Symphony may seem a little strange – the symphony dates from 1906! – but with just a little generosity this can be allowed, since Mahler's late Romantic work has the same atonal character as what was to come later. In fact Chailly is quite enthusiastic about Mahler: in Autumn 1994 the Concertgebouw Orchestra took the First Symphony on a very extensive tour of Italy, Japan and South America, and has since recorded it for Decca. Mahler's *Lied von der Erde* will follow later.

In the late summer of 1994 the same record company announced plans which point mainly in the direction of the 'twenty-first century': more Messiaen, Schönberg, Berg, Varese, Zemlinsky, and also Bartok and Stravinsky. The newspaper *de Volkskrant* wrote that *'the hand of the new artistic director of the Concertgebouw Orchestra, Jan Zekveld, can clearly be seen behind this change of direction. Very sensible, too, because Chailly cannot really compete in the international record market when it comes to Schumann, Brahms and Tchaikovsky'.* That may be true, but Chailly did simultaneously receive two golden CDs for what were clearly very successful recordings: one of his first recordings with the Concertgebouw Orchestra, namely *Pictures from an Exhibition* by Mussorgsky (1988)

Ricardo Chailly (1954-)
(Photo by Decca / Terry O'Neill).

139

together with Ravel's *Bolero* (1988), and his recording of *Carmina Burana* by Carl Orff with the Radio-Sinfonia Orchestra of Berlin (1986), both sold more than fifteen thousand copies. These commercial feats will have been warmly received both in Amsterdam and also at Decca in London.

The Concertgebouw Orchestra (it became 'Royal' in 1988) gave its first public performance on 3 November 1888, with Willem Kes as conductor. Kes introduced the 'modern' rules for concert audiences: latecomers were forbidden to enter the hall during the performance, and talkers were removed. The then unknown 24-year-old Dutchman Willem Mengelberg was brought in from Lucerne, and succeeded Kes in 1895. Under his leadership (1895-1945) the Concertgebouw Orchestra developed and acquired a world-wide reputation. Links were forged with composers and conductors such as Mahler, Richard Strauss, Richter, Debussy, Muck, Ravel, Monteux, Walter, Stravinsky, Schönberg, Pierné, Casella, Hindemith, Milhaud and many others.

After the war Eduard van Beinum, who had been appointed as second conductor in 1931, took the reins. Mengelberg had been barred from conducting because of his pro-German attitude during the Second World War, and he died in Switzerland shortly before the ban expired. He was an authoritarian and was often unapproachable, but even today is still world-famous as a brilliant conductor. Van Beinum had a very different character: he was well-loved both by audiences and also by the members of the orchestra, to whom he was the first among equals. He communicated his passion for the music of Bruckner and the French repertoire to both orchestra and audience. Van Beinum died in 1959 during a rehearsal, 'with his boots on', and although this was unexpected it had been known that he was suffering from a heart condition and on one occasion he had even had to cancel a foreign tour.

After a few years during which he shared the leadership of the Concertgebouw Orchestra with Eugen Jochum, Bernard Haitink, who came from the Radio Philharmonic Orchestra, took on the post of principal conductor in 1963. Haitink not only succeeded in continuing the musical tradition, he also made his own very personal mark on it. His performances of Bruckner, Mahler (whose symphony cycles were recorded in full for the first time by Philips), Richard Strauss, Debussy, Ravel, Brahms and Shostakovitch were proof of his great artistic versatility. The number of recordings and foreign tours rose steadily (1954 saw the first tour to the United States, followed by many more tours under Haitink). In 1988, after twenty-seven years as principal conductor, Haitink left for London. Plans to grant him an honour came to nothing, partly because the circumstances of his departure were far from ideal, and also because Haitink himself did not want one. He was not to return as a guest conductor until five years later, in 1993; he is now a regular visitor. Haitink has received numerous distinctions from other quarters: in 1991 he was awarded the prestigious Erasmus Prize and in 1990 an honorary doctorate from the University of Amsterdam. In 1979 Kyrill Kondrashin, formerly musical director of the Bolshoi Theatre and the Philharmonic Orchestra in Moscow, was appointed alongside Haitink as a full-time conductor. The cooperation with this great orchestral teacher was brought to a premature end by his sudden death in 1981. Aside from recordings, his name also lives on in the biennial Kondrashin competition named

Bernard Haitink (1929-)
(Photo by Michael Ward).

Willem Mengelberg (1871-1951) (Photo Philips Classics Productions).

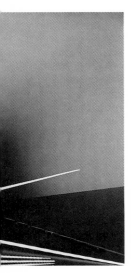

after him; one of the world's most important competitions for young conductors, this was established by the then artistic director of the Orchestra, H.J. van Royen. During the 1988-1989 season Chailly was appointed as principal conductor, having made a great impression at his first performance in 1985. In fact the orchestra had set its heart on Claudio Abbado as a successor for Haitink, but he had just accepted an appointment in Berlin as successor to Herbert von Karajan. Riccardo Chailly also continued as the musical director of the Bologna Opera until the spring of 1994. So far he has done relatively little work on opera with the Concertgebouw Orchestra, unlike Nikolaus Harnoncourt, who performed all three of Mozart's Da Ponte operas with the Orchestra and made recordings for the record company Teldec.

The Concertgebouw Orchestra has sometimes been accused of having shown too little interest in *Dutch* music. When Chailly made a recording of music by Johan Wagenaar very soon after his appointment, it appeared that he was countering this accusation. It was in any case not entirely fair, as was shown six years ago with the release of a cassette and four CDs of exclusively Dutch music. In these co-productions with NOS (the Dutch Broadcasting Programme Foundation), *Donemus* (Dutch Music Documentation Institute) and *Centrum Nederlandse Muziek* (Centre for Dutch Music), the in-house conductors Mengelberg, Van Beinum and Haitink, together with guest conductors including Kyrill Kondrashin, Eugen Jochum, George Szell, Hans Vonk and Lucas Vis, perform works by Julius Röntgen, Johan Wagenaar, Alphons Diepenbrock, Hans Henkemans, Jan van Gilse, Marius Flothuis, Otto Ketting, Willem Frederik Bon, Kees Olthuis, Willem Pijper, Hendrik Andriessen, Henk Badings, Willem van Otterloo, Ton de Leeuw, Robert Heppener, Rudolf Escher and Geert van Keulen. A very respectable list, though it must be said that the material was taken from tapes of original performances for radio, and that not a single one of these works was ever played directly for a recording.

The Royal Concertgebouw Orchestra is not only the best in the Netherlands in artistic terms (although it is now almost equalled by the Rotterdam Philharmonic Orchestra, which has become a serious competitor with Valery Gergiev as principal conductor), it is also the best-paid. Nevertheless, salaries are still far below those of orchestras of similar quality such as the Berlin Philharmonic and the Vienna Philharmonic. Before the Second World War the profession of orchestral musician was rated very poorly in the Netherlands. In the anniversary issue produced by the Concertgebouw Orchestra Association *What's it to do with you? Seventy-five years of conflicting interest* (Waar bemoei je je mee? 75 jaar belangenstrijd), Johan Giskes wrote: *'In those days* (1888, author) *the public saw members of the orchestra as craftsmen, driven by their artistic sensibilities to choose an extremely "impractical" type of work, and considered that precisely because of their artistic nature and the "awkwardness which almost always accompanies it", they had a more difficult life than ordinary tradesmen. The Concertgebouw Administration regarded the musicians in the orchestra as overgrown children, and that is how the orchestra's members were treated. They were supposed to be thankful that they could work, and although poorly paid it was at least a permanent job. Members of the orchestra who stepped out of line could be replaced at a moment's notice.'*

This rather strange situation actually persisted until 1952, because it was not until then that *Het Concertgebouw NV,* the company responsible for running the building, was separated from the Concertgebouw Orchestra. It is true that the *members* already had their own Association – just as the orchestras mentioned above in Berlin and Vienna also have their own groups to protect their interests – but the Orchestra itself still did not have its own administrative structure. This came in 1954 in the form of the *Stichting tot beheer van het Concertgebouworkest* (Foundation for the Administration of the Concertgebouw Orchestra), with its own administrative staff and management. It was only then that the 'child' of 1888 became an adult: *Het Concertgebouw NV* still only rents its famous Great Hall to the Orchestra, but over the years it has developed its own very ambitious artistic policy, full of famous orchestras and soloists. This has caused a spectacular increase in audience numbers at concerts, to 400,000 per year.

However, the Orchestra cannot do without its famous Great Hall; and *Het Concertgebouw NV* continues to attach a great deal of importance to the world-famous orchestra which is named after the building and is funded not only by the national and municipal governments, but also by millions of guilders in sponsorship from the Dutch business community. This sponsorship money is mainly intended to increase the Orchestra's prestige abroad, and to allow it to take part in important events. The 'Second Mahler Festival' in 1995 was one of these: in May of that year all Mahler's symphonic works were performed, some of them by the Royal Concertgebouw Orchestra (in memory of the first Mahler Festival seventy-five years ago, directed by Willem Mengelberg, who celebrated his own twenty-fifth anniversary as conductor on the same occasion). In May 1995 the Berlin Philharmonic, the Vienna Philharmonic and the Gustav Mahler Youth Orchestra also performed in the Amsterdam Concertgebouw building. As regards foreign tours planned for the 1995-1996 season, the programme includes another major tour of the United States in February 1996, with concerts in New York, Los Angeles, San Francisco and other cities; concerts during the Salzburg Festival in August 1996, conducted by Chailly, with a production of Schönberg's *Moses and Aaron* conducted by Pierre Boulez; two concerts in September 1996 during the London 'Proms'; and a trip to the Far East, also in September, with concerts in Tokyo and Hong Kong.

JAN RUBINSTEIN
Translated by Steve Judd.

SELECTIVE DISCOGRAPHY

The Royal Concertgebouw Orchestra + Ricardo Chailly:
Anton Bruckner:
Symphony No. 5, Decca, CD 433 819-2
Gustav Mahler:
Symphony No. 6 / Alexander von Zemlinsky: 6 Songs, Decca, 2 CDS 430 165-2
Modest Mussorgsky:
Pictures at an Exhibition / Maurice Ravel: Bolero / Claude Debussy: Danse; Sarabande, Decca, CD 417 611-2
Arnold Schönberg:
Chamber Symphony No. 1; 5 Orchesterstücke, op. 16 / Anton von Webern:
Im Sommerwind; Passacaglia. Decca, CD 436 467-2
21st Century Classics, Decca, CD 443 752-2

The Royal Concertgebouw Orchestra + Bernard Haitink:
Claude Debussy:
La Mer; Images: No. 2 Ibéria; Prélude à l'après-midi d'un faune, Philips, CD 416 444-2
Gustav Mahler:
Symphony No. 1, Philips, CD 426 067-2
Richard Strauss:
Ein Heldenleben / Edward Elgar: 'Enigma' Variations, Philips, CD 432 276-2

'Good

and Bad Have Been Reduced to the Same Thing'

The Poetry of Charles Ducal

Charles Ducal (1952-)
(Photo by Frank Toussaint).

The debut of the Flemish poet Charles Ducal (1952-), *The Marriage* (Het huwelijk, 1987), created quite a stir in poetry-reading circles, first and foremost because of its themes and the way they were treated. The cohabitation of man and woman in marriage was depicted as frustrating, deadening drudgery, a struggle bordering on murder and mayhem. What is more, the humiliating account seemed so autobiographical that there was a rather unfortunate mixture of literary appreciation and *succès de scandale*. This was a pity, since the poems, with their lapidary cynicism and multi-layered wealth of meaning, did not need such sensationalism.

The collection comprises four sections, plus opening and concluding poems. Each section from a different perspective expresses dissatisfaction with the state of matrimony, which is bound round with compromises, agreements and restrictions. The initial emphasis is on the contrast between deadly order and stasis on the one hand and the dream of adventure, passion and revolt on the other, and this is followed by fantasies of violence and murder; the third section introduces the other, dream woman, the woman who – as his own creation – fulfils the poet's longings. Accordingly she also embodies the forbidden world of imagination, and of poetry, the alternative to humdrum reality, an alternative charged with both pride and guilt, since it denies reality, even that of true married love.

The fourth section, 'Body to Body' ('Lijf aan lijf'), gives the themes concrete form in the sexual domain, which is permeated by absence, ossification and routine. Ultimately there is nothing left but solitary withdrawal into oneself, eroticism with one's own reflection, blasphemous deification of one's own ego, though marked by cynical self-mockery.

This description may make the collection appear rather banal and all too familiar. It is both those things, but at the same time it is much more. Everyday frustrations are subtly linked to archetypal images from the world of myth, or most commonly from religion. This gives the scenes depicted great depth, charging them as it were with our deepest spiritual impulses: guilt and atonement, nostalgia for the absolute, sin, the life instinct, inescapable loneliness. Great poetic force is generated by the clash between the lapidary tone and strict form on the one hand, and on the other the chaos of what is suppressed and yet evoked among the domestic anecdotes and mythical images. Expulsion from the earthly paradise, for example:

She dries my underwear, I feel no shame.
We live in a state that God must endorse,
Expulsion is only possible by accident.

Good and bad have been reduced to the same thing.
Sin's hung out to dry like a white wash.
The lines bend like weary snakes.
She sings. I finish my flowerbed.

The shocking quality of this poetry derives largely from the strict mastery of form. An extremely murky, deeply emotional world is evoked, but with no hint of pathos. Hatred, violence, cynicism and mockery are presented in an almost mumbling, monotonous way. The collection's theme and tone led the critics to link it directly with Willem Elsschot's famous poem, also entitled 'The Marriage' (see p. 71).

The same distanced tone predominates in *The Duke and I* (De hertog en ik, 1989). There are other similarities with the poet's debut. Like its predecessor it is a tightly constructed collection. Not an assembly of separate poems, but the elaboration of one central theme in various directions. It has a narrative-like quality: the successive scenes echo each other, enriching and imparting added resonance. Lines of motifs grow, we become familiar with the characters and the settings: a farm in a country village, a dark wood ... Just as in *The Marriage* we saw the imaginary space created from the house, the study, the bathroom, the garden, with the gloomy main characters in them. However, the structure of the collection does not follow the line of a course of action, but balances motifs, moments and perspectives against each other.

Put crudely, this collection deals with the juxtaposition of power and impotence, or the conflict between the law and the urge towards autonomy. At bottom, moreover, that is the same theme that dominated *The Marriage*.

In *The Duke and I* that underlying theme is developed in two different areas. The first section deals with the confrontation between father and son. The father is concretely depicted but is basically archetypal, and moreover sometimes acts like a god. Fear is the predominant emotion in the relationship. As in *The Marriage* the worlds of man and woman are sharply contrasted, here too the father is blown up into an inviolable, mythical figure. The son cannot help being small, powerless, afraid, petrified, but at the same time absolutely fascinated and filled with admiration and awe. However, elsewhere the father also appears as a protector, master of night and chaos: someone whose eyes not only *'see right through one'*, but who also controls the darkness. The price of the sense of safety (from the law, from God, from tradition) which the child derives from his father is fear, subservience, passivity and loss of self.

Here again everyday domestic incidents appear in a totally alienated, perverted light. For example, the traditional 'crossing oneself before bed' in the poem 'Evening Prayer' ('Avondgebed') becomes more of a punishment, a brand, a mutilation: *'We offered our heads. / He pressed his thumb in our*

Jan Massys, *Judith*. After 1543. Panel, 115 x 80.5 cm. Koninklijk Museum voor Schone Kunsten, Antwerp.

brains.' Now this is further complicated and broadened by the use of mythical, fairy-tale and religious motifs and imagery. For example, the three cycles in this section are called 'The God on the Mountain' ('De God op de berg'), 'The Parents of God' ('De ouders van God') and 'East of Eden' ('Ten oosten van Eden') respectively.

In an analogous way the second section explores the relations between an I and a fatal, inaccessibly powerful woman, who appears as Medusa, a witch, the Old-Testament Judith or the Muse. The I has no defence against this *'Belle Dame sans Merci'*. She too confronts him with his own smallness, impotence and guilt. Language and imagination, with which he tries to reach her, turn against him. Because that is precisely where she lives, that is where she is an image and a myth, stronger and greater than reality.

The last sequence in this section, 'The Hole in the Mirror' ('Het gat in de spiegel') makes it clear that more is involved than simple erotic fantasy or fatal infatuation. The ultimate desire is that dream and reality, literature and life, should coincide, but literature has usurped reality:

I want a room without imagination,
a woman who is what I read.
(...)

I want your disgrace, your little faults,
your beauty in human language.
But I fear that too much has been written,
that reality no longer exists.

Mother Tongue (Moedertaal, 1994) seems like the conclusion of a poetic triptych. After the various manifestations of woman and the father, the mother has now become central. However, just as in previous collections personal anecdotes were enriched and transcended by being grafted onto a layer of myths and archetypes, here the image of the very concrete mother constantly interacts with the problems of language and poethood. Just as the worlds of man and woman, child and father were previously presented as extreme opposites but unable to survive without each other, the same happens here with the worlds of mother and language. The world of the mother, that is the world in which everything has its natural place. Although the child understands little about it, things are true and as they should be. As in the epilogue poem 'Home' ('Thuis'):

In the milking shed the churn turned,
but without curdling,
a singing mother cranked the handle,
time was full,
and I thought: I'm home.

In that maternal world language is also natural, it is in the fullest sense of the word a 'mother tongue':

The word's made flesh. This is how it was:
I was lost, she hauled me in

by a thread that bound the whole world,
I clung to the mother tongue, I spoke blindly.

Familiar, physical, but also restrictive and blind, such is the world of the mother. She nourishes the poet, but he must escape her, in order to reach the world of consciousness, culture, language: a world which is no longer natural. *'To grow up and cast myself out, / to kill the love which moves you'*, as the mother puts it in the guise of a prophetess. The poet himself says:

no mother tongue, no breast in the mouth,
but instruments, grammar
and dictionary, to graft on an I,
loveless, high above the ground.

The collection describes that journey back and forth made by the poet, beginning with conception and ending with the dreamed-of return home; the pendulum movement between dependence and autonomy. On that journey we encounter virtually all the characters, figures and motifs from the first collection: the father, humiliating sexuality, woman as wife and *femme fatale*, the muse and poethood, god and death.

The field of force is now complete and hence far richer and more complex than in the previous collections: self-abandonment and dislike, fear and pride, impotence and self-determination, constantly conflict in changing combinations, inextricable and inescapable. 'Impasse', which is an idiosyncratic reworking of the poem of the same title by Martinus Nijhoff, neatly summarises this tangle. The poet is sitting in the bath, *'head clamped / in his knees, alone with himself'*, despondent and impotent. Precisely in that vulnerable situation the woman sees how *'naked and human'* he is *'beyond language'*, how he is as it were a defenceless and dependent foetus, in need of her maternal attention. *'This, she thought, if only he could capture this ...'*, but of course this is an impossibility, since that is the core of the impasse: regression to the phase of infantile dependence, the very denial of poetic potency. The poet's reaction is consequently inevitable: love and hatred. Hatred because the woman confronts him with failure and impotence; love because in the bath, as in the amniotic fluid, he can surrender to her nurturing care:

He did not see her, smelled his sweat,
looked at his member in the rising water.
The water was hotter than he could bear.
He hated. He loved the woman.

HUGO BREMS
Translated by Paul Vincent.

Compassionate

Her head hung over the basin,
defencelessly rounding her rump.
The moment seemed made for striking,
no struggle, a straight rabbit-punch.

He stroked lightly with teasing finger.
Her back tautened like skin on warm milk.
Desire hardened. He tried hard to will it.
She cooed: is it now? soft as silk.

Then he saw himself in the mirror,
too-large shirt, thin legs knotted like wood.
His eye filled with the glow of love's power.
He pinched her rump, in compassionate mood.

From *The Marriage* (Het huwelijk, 1987)
Translated by Tanis Guest.

The Duke and I (2)

Two men pulled a cart through the wood,
through the mud of light-shy roads,
serving a woman who divided
and ruled. Their joy, their bane, she stood

naked over them, whip clasped tight,
proud, and never any man's wife,
save in the sacrifice of a life
split in two. One man was me, the other the night

had sent: through me his fear ran amuck.
We pulled together, the duke led the way,
he knew the wood and all of its secrets.
She saw the difference. Struck.

From *The Duke and I* (De hertog en ik, 1989)
Translated by Paul Vincent.

Misunderstanding 3

My partner is a poet's wife,
although she'd had quite a different plan.
She'd thought of a father, a lover, a man.
He writes. That's *his* sole duty in life,

and rarely is more than his body in bed:
in its lonely desire it is pallid and thin.
He sometimes gets up, a new word's put in,
'beloved' is changed to 'slut' instead,

and he licks his lips, self-satisfied.
They never collaborate in schemes,
though now and then she mumbles in her dreams,
garbled talk that leaves one mystified.

From *The Marriage* (Het huwelijk, 1987)
Translated by Paul Vincent.

Impasse

The woman found her husband, the poet:
squatting in the bath, head clamped
in his knees, alone with himself,
the old flesh, the shrivelled author

of her happiness. She saw how bent,
how naked and human beyond language.
The warmth billowed, peace sang from the tap.
This, she thought, if only he could capture this …

He did not see her, smelled his sweat,
looked at his member in the rising water.
The water was hotter than he could bear.
He hated. He loved the woman.

From *Mother Tongue* (Moedertaal, 1994)
Translated by Paul Vincent.

Bob

van Reeth

and the Demands of Architecture

Precisely because he has always resisted originality, Bob van Reeth (1943-) is now one of today's most original architects. He does not fit into any school or movement, not even that of the traditionalists who reject all schools and trends. He was like that when still a student in the mid-sixties; he did not rebel against existing systems but went in search of the places where architecture could still be found in its freedom and necessity. He knew the fundamental strength of architecture from the brickyards of his native region, the banks of the Scheldt between Temse and Niel, and discovered its imaginative power in the sometimes bizarre outbuildings that proliferated behind conventional blocks of houses.

He was still a student at the St Luke Institute in Brussels when in 1965 he was responsible for the renovation of a jeweller's shop with accomodation on the Paardenmarkt in Antwerp. He left the skeleton as it was. It gave him an anchor in the street, the necessity that inspired his imagination. He showed the possibilities within the existing structure, both inside the flat

Bob van Reeth, *The renovated jeweller's shop on the Paardenmarkt in Antwerp (1965).*

and, most strikingly, in the shop front. With a nod to Brutalism, then enjoying its heyday, but at the same time defying it, he gave the raw concrete straight from the formwork crystalline shapes that contrasted sharply with the frameless tall glass display windows in which the jewellery and watches glistened. The free-standing framing of the unusually high door gave an additional emphasis to the access to the free space of the shop. The door handle was a huge watch. The mastery with which an unknown architect here handled the whole spectrum of architecture, from constructional ingenuity, programmatic tours de force and nods to prevailing fashion to contrasts of scale and even humour, came as a complete surprise and immediately brought Bob van Reeth to the forefront. It is indicative of his approach that he continued to work on this building; in 1994 a penthouse apartment was added under a semi-circular dome.

A little later, in 1966, Bob van Reeth showed that his mastery was not restricted to small-scale projects but was equally evident in a complex assignment involving business premises and living accomodation in an open meadow. The former offices of the publisher Walter Beckers in Kalmthout were converted and extended by Bob van Reeth, also over a number of years. The building had a clear structure which was used in playful way, as if here the unchanging and lasting elements of architecture had entered into an alliance with its changing and provisional manifestation.

But it was not these two early projects that determined the course of Bob van Reeth's turbulent career. They were no more than an overture indicating the level of his ambitions. His true manifesto was seen in the Botte house in Mechelen, built in 1969, and the conversion into his own home of a house in the Klein Begijnhof in the same city. The directness of the Botte house was challenging. This was no longer architecture in the normal sense of the word. A concrete skeleton outlined the structure, within which one could improvise to one's heart's content. No formal design had primacy. The final result was determined by a process of gradually taking possession of the structure and making it one's own, a process which by its nature had no end. Bob van Reeth approached the existing house in the Klein Begijnhof in the

Bob van Reeth, *The Botte house in Mechelen (1969-1971)*.

Bob van Reeth, *The new wing of the Onze Lieve Vrouwe College in Antwerp (1973-1978).*

same way. This design kissed goodbye to every conventional idea of a house. It was intended to restore freedom to the dwelling-place. Living in this kind of non-architecture becomes a real adventure, the discovering of an unknown world in and around oneself. This spontaneity in building, which referred to the 'all power to the imagination' idea of the late sixties, should not, however, be viewed simplistically and reduced to its superficial, somewhat chaotic appearance. Even in the earliest works the freedom of the architecture was already underpinned by a strong, geometrically controlled structure. This was a precondition for that freedom.

This was what his imitators, of whom there were many, failed to understand. On all sides triangular windows and other features from the Van Reeth repertoire began to appear; but the austere mastery behind the brilliant improvisation went unrecognised. The quirks and jokes were there, but not the disciplined expertise through which architecture rose above gratuitous playing with form to become the construction of a real world.

While the Van Reeth style flourished during the seventies, Van Reeth himself had moved on in his exploration of an appropriate architecture for the age. While the structural aspect became still more autonomous, increasing attention was paid to a more controlled form that would express this structure. With his taste for lapidary definitions, Van Reeth characterises his work as the building of ruins, what survives of the experience of a building and can be continually reinterpreted. In this minimalist statement one recognises the approach evident in the buildings already discussed. But in the subsequent evolution of his work structure and form were to become more and more closely related.

One project marks a turning point in this development, the first large building Bob van Reeth designed. At the Onze Lieve Vrouwe College (a secondary school) on the Rubenslei in Antwerp a worn-out classroom wing which had been added to the classical-style complex with its neo-Gothic church was to be replaced. Van Reeth made his new wing, for which the first design dates from 1973, a tribute to the classical architecture in which it was to be integrated. While in his early work the fragmentation and differentiation of the elements tested the unity of the structure to its limits, in the new approach the emphasis was on the clarity of the volume and the balance between the planes. But within the confines of these new requirements Van Reeth still could not resist playing games with the differentiation of the components. Facades were created with their own rhythm and articulation, alluding to a Palladian-style tranquillity. Inside, behind these facades, the constructional inventiveness and lively playfulness of interrelated spaces were given free rein, to an even greater extent than in the early work. Convention and law now vied with vitality and spontaneity. The tranquillity gained was not dead but full of tension.

The new wing of the Onze Lieve Vrouwe College no more belonged to any particular movement than the earlier work. But, just as the jeweller's shop on the Paardemarkt acknowledged Brutalism without being part of it, so this design was not insensitive to what was going on in the real world, not just in the world of architecture. The introduction into the work of a marked awareness of form was bound up with the rediscovery of the historical dimension of our culture and with awareness of the cultural dimension of architecture. Bob van Reeth has continued with the development that began here. He has been increasingly concerned with the ordering and control of chance, while ensuring that this ordering and control confirms chance as a vital principle rather than excluding it. His plans have been based less and less on repetitive or associative structures, tending instead towards the closed quality of geometrical figures with symmetrical development around a central axis. However, the geometry has never become absolute. It has remained a geometry of experience. The architecture, however autonomous it became, has never let go of the link with the reality of dwelling. This vital ambiguity is characteristic of all Bob van Reeth's work from this point on, and of the whole development of his oeuvre. This makes his work intriguing but unamenable to simple, fashionable interpretations.

After an unfortunate period in which for various reasons one project after another was not carried out, he had a new debut, as it were, in the mid-eighties. The impact was even greater than in the sixties. The Van Roosmalen

Bob van Reeth, *The café-restaurant at the Zuiderterras in Antwerp (1987-1991).*

house (1985) on the Scheldekaaien in Antwerp, with its explicit references to Adolf Loos' house for Josephine Baker, became a huge popular success. It enjoys the kind of national and international fame few works of architecture can claim. Van Reeth also designed a café-restaurant on the quays of the Scheldt at the Zuiderterras (1987) and a large office building, though the latter was never built. The Van Roosmalen house and the Zuiderterras café seem like a new profession of faith. Inspired by the maritime architecture of pleasure boats, the designs are stripped of all gravity. Architecture appears as a mobile, almost transparent phenomenon whose dynamics are restrained, as in a dance, by the geometry of the figures.

It would have been unlike Van Reeth, however, to care greatly about this success. While his lighter work was causing general amazement, he was building on sites in the centre of Antwerp that had lain empty for decades and creating an inconspicuous but carefully considered architecture that drew no attention to itself but ensured that the urban pattern would be restored in that vital location. At the same time inside the walls of the historic Averbode Abbey a new office building (1991) was under construction for the publishing company located there. It links up with the anonymous urban architecture of Antwerp and with an underground extension to the existing monastery library. In 1994 the publisher's offices won an award for 'best business premises'. These buildings not only reveal the range of possibilities in Bob van Reeth's architecture but also throw light on his approach, which is primarily concerned not with the originality of an oeuvre but with the question that each new assignment asks of architecture.

GEERT BEKAERT
Translated by John Rudge.

Bob van Reeth, *The underground extension to the library of the Averbode Abbey (1991)* (Photo by Lautwein & Ritzenhoff BFF).

utch

Colonial Architecture and Town Planning

History, Preservation and Present Use

The seventeenth century

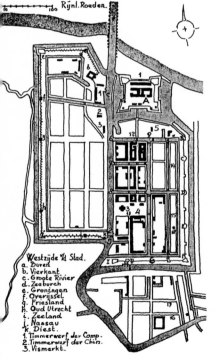

Indonesia: Plan of Batavia (now Jakarta), as it was in 1635, sixteen years after its foundation. The dominant direction (North-South) is accentuated by the canalised Ciliwung river (H.A. Breuning, *Het voormalige Batavia*. Amsterdam, 1954).

The newly formed Dutch Republic of the Seven United Provinces was the base from which in the seventeenth century trading posts were founded in what are now fifteen different countries in Asia, Africa and America. Today, there are still numerous tangible reminders of this colonial background in the form of street patterns and buildings. There are also names, such as New Zealand and Cape Horn, to evidence the fact that Dutch seamen filled in plenty of other blank spaces on the world map.

The old centres of such huge conurbations as New York, Recife, Cape Town and Jakarta still retain the structures of the seventeenth-century settlements known as New Amsterdam, Mauritsstad, Kaapstad (Cape Town) and Batavia. The last mentioned of these cities was the first to be founded, in 1619. It grew rapidly to become the largest European town in Asia, and was referred to as the 'Queen of the East', although it was in fact the riches offered by the Moluccas, then called the Spice Islands, which had led to the foundation of the United East India Company (VOC) in 1602.

Towns like Willemstad (on Curaçao, founded in 1634) and Paramaribo (Surinam, 1667), on the other hand, both of which were under the dominion of the West India Company (WIC), grew at a much slower pace. Even today, they still illustrate the difference between the compact type of town, enclosed by water and walls, and the more expansive, open layout with a fort to defend it at just one point. The same layout can be found in Cape Town, South Africa (VOC, 1666).

Willemstad still provides a living picture of what New Amsterdam must have looked like in 1664-1667, when it was captured by the British and renamed New York. Both towns were bounded by water on three sides, the fourth or landward side being protected by a wall; in New York the location of this is still recognisable in the name of Wall Street. In the same way, Broadway is the equivalent of Bredestraat, which is still the name of the main street of Willemstad in Curaçao. This street marks the division between the fort area and the original residential district. Willemstad's Fort Amsterdam still retains its Governor's Residence and Protestant church,

Brazil: Frans Post, *Rio São Francisco and Fort Maurice.* 1639. Canvas, 62 x 95 cm. Musée du Louvre, Paris.

structures which were once to be found in the old fort of New Amsterdam. In both cases the original town centre with its formal layout has acquired a less formally structured residential area across the water: Brooklyn (originally Breukelen) in New York and Otrabande (Farside) in Willemstad.

Malacca (Malaysia) and Colombo (Sri Lanka), by contrast, are not Dutch towns by origin. They were captured from the Portuguese, in 1641 and 1656 respectively, and it was not until they were rebuilt and extended that they acquired a distinctive Dutch character (Colombo still has Dutch street names like Keyser Street). Settlements were also captured from the Portuguese in the Gold Coast (now Ghana), one example being Elmina, with its enormous St George's Castle, which fell in 1637. Although the Dutch built new forts and adapted some of those already in existence, Elmina was the only place where any sort of town building occurred, and even there it was only on a very modest scale. The islands of Gorée (Senegal) and Mauritius (to the east of Madagascar) were both lost to the French, Gorée in 1677 and Mauritius in 1710. In 1654, the Dutch part of Brazil returned to Portuguese rule. Before that happened, however, the painter Frans Post had had time to produce a record of the area that is without parallel in the whole of the colonial world.

A large number of trading posts were also founded along the Indian coast, and the Dutch had a settlement in Taiwan up to 1661. But the most extraordinary of all the smaller settlements was undoubtedly that on the island of Deshima near Nagasaki. For more than two hundred years, from 1641 until Japan was effectively opened up in 1856, Deshima formed the sole contact between the Western world and this most mysterious of countries. Attempts are now being made to re-create the situation there as it was during the time of the Dutch. Deshima, a small island shaped like a segment of a circle, had

Ghana: The Castle of St George d'Elmina, seen from St Jago. The Portuguese core was rebuilt and enlarged after its reduction by the Dutch (from Brazil) in 1637. The place remained in Dutch hands until 1872. The houses on the foreground date from the early nineteenth century. One of them collapsed some ten years ago. (Photo by C.L. Temminck Groll, 1966).

a number of curving streets running parallel to each other, along which stood merchants' houses with their adjoining offices and warehouses. The Japanese authorities permitted the United East India Company's officials to live and work there – the only foreigners allowed to do so – but wished to prevent any permanent settlement. For this reason the Dutch were not allowed to take their wives to Deshima; and they were permitted to leave the island only once a year, to attend the Emperor at his Court.

As for the towns, they were not built to any sort of standard plan. Nonetheless, they shared a number of common characteristics. In the first place, all layouts show one dominant direction which is accentuated, where possible, by one or more canals. Secondly, the street plans are not rigid, in contrast to Roman, Spanish colonial and modern American towns, but follow the local topography. Lastly, the squares are usually fairly informal and the building plots in the towns are often some 20 to 25 feet wide, narrower than in most other towns.

There was (or is) generally either a 'Herenstraat' or a 'Herengracht' ('*Heer*' meaning a patrician gentleman and '*gracht*' being a canal) running in the dominant direction of the town, and most towns also had a 'Prinsenstraat' or 'Prinsengracht' of slightly less grandeur. Although the Stadholders, the Princes of Orange who were the chief magistrates of the former Dutch republic, did not play a prominent role in the East and West India Companies, many forts were named after them: Orange, Nassau and William all figure on the list. And it was in this way, too, that the island of Mauritius received its name as far back as 1598.

With the exception of a number of forts, there are not many seventeenth-century buildings still standing on the three continents referred to. The most remarkable of those which do survive is the Town Hall of Malacca, which was built before 1656. This building has now been restored and converted into a museum. In Surinam one can find the painstakingly preserved ruins of the oldest synagogue in the Western hemisphere, built in Jodensavanne in 1685. Its grounds contain an impressive cemetery.

Jakarta has its 'Portuguese Outer Church', a building with an extremely beautiful interior that was erected right at the end of the seventeenth century; despite its name, it is a Protestant church. It retained this function (present

Japan: Kawahara Keiga (?), *View of Deshima*. c.1850. Silk, 47.9 x 80.4 cm. Rijksmuseum voor Volkenkunde, Leiden.

name Gereja (church) Sion). The building is rectangular in shape, divided by two rows of columns into a wide central aisle and two narrower side aisles. It has a sober exterior, but inside a richly ornamented organ stands facing a finely carved pulpit by Hendrik Bruyn (1695). The same arrangement is often to be found in Lutheran and Mennonite churches in the Netherlands. Other Indonesian remnants of the seventeenth century are the fort church and other parts of Fort Rotterdam in Ujung Pandang (formerly Makassar).

The eighteenth century

The eighteenth century saw fewer new settlements, but a spreading of the influence already established in those territories still in the possession of the Dutch. Although one or two new towns were built, such as Philipsburg on St Martin and New Amsterdam in Guyana, it was rather a question of a great deal of building work going on in towns already in place. Fortunately, many important fruits of this labour have been preserved in towns all over the world. Most of these buildings are unreservedly considered by the local authorities as being of great historical value, and some of them are listed as protected buildings. Today, many of the large houses built by the Dutch are in use as museums or offices, housing either government departments or private organisations.

Curaçao, one of the islands of the Netherlands Antilles, is well-known for its striking town and country houses built during this period. It is also the home of the splendid Mikve Israel synagogue, built in 1732 and now the oldest synagogue in the western hemisphere that is still in use. The Beth Chayim Jewish cemetery contains a remarkable collection of sculpted tombstones. On St Eustatius, the fascinating ruins of the buildings erected during the island's golden age, which reached a peak at the time of the War of American Independence, have been preserved. Oranjestad, the island's small capital, is divided into an upper and lower part. In the upper town stands Fort Oranje, famous for the 'First Salute' to the flag of the United States of America in 1776, when that country's independence had not yet been recognised by the British. There are also a number of eighteenth-century government buildings and private houses, one of which is now a museum. In addition there are the preserved ruins of a church and a synagogue, both dating from the eighteenth century. The lower town consisted of a row of warehouses along the waterfront. Some of these are still standing, and foundations are visible over a distance of more than a kilometre.

At the heart of Paramaribo, capital of Surinam, lies the Square behind the seventeenth / eighteenth-century Fort Zeelandia. Here stands the former Governor's Residence, built of wood on brick and dating mainly from about 1770; it is now the Presidential Palace. There are also some fine eighteenth- and nineteenth-century buildings. The town's two principal streets lead off this square. The first is Gravenstraat, which still boasts a series of magnificent eighteenth-century houses. All except one are of wood and this row is probably unique in the Americas. Then there is Waterkant (Waterside) which runs along the Surinam River and has fine early nineteenth-century properties. These too, with one exception, are of wood and date from the period of reconstruction after a great fire in 1827. Fort New Amsterdam, an earthen

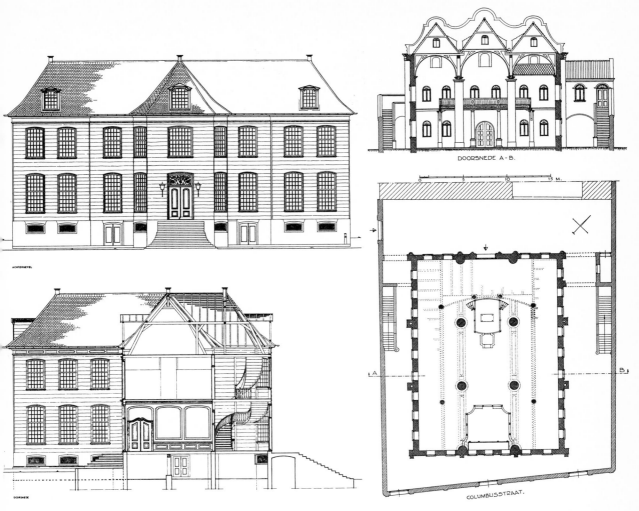

ACHTERGEVEL

DOORSNEDE A - B.

DOORSNEDE

COLUMBUSSTRAAT.

Surinam: Garden facade and cross section of an imposing wooden house (1774) in Paramaribo (Gravenstraat). Since its restoration in 1962, it has housed the Ministry of General Affairs. A few years ago the roof was damaged by fire (Survey by R. Krooshof in: C.L. Temminck Groll and A.R.H. Tjin A Djie, *De architectuur van Suriname 1667-1930*. Zutphen, 1973).

Curaçao, Netherlands Antilles: The Mikve Israel synagogue (1732) in Willemstad. It is the oldest synagogue in use in the Western hemisphere (Survey by H. van der Wal in: M.D. Ozinga, *De monu-menten van Curaçao in woord en beeld*. The Hague / Curaçao, 1959).

structure erected in 1747, was restored during the sixties and converted into a spacious open air museum, but has unfortunately now reverted to a state of neglect.

In Ghana, a number of forts were refurbished during this period. Some of these were – as mentioned above – already existing Portuguese trading forts captured in the first half of the seventeenth century. They include the oldest European structure to be built outside Europe since Roman times: the Castle of St George d'Elmina, begun in 1482. The buildings were modified and new forts were also built. Some of them are dilapidated, but others still fulfil a social function as the largest stone buildings in the locality. The whole

South Africa: Late eighteenth-century country house: *Bosch en Dal*

(Photo by C.L. Temminck Groll, 1991).

Indonesia: The former Batavia Town Hall (1705) in Jakarta (Picture postcard, 1985).

group, which also includes English and Danish forts, is on the Unesco World Heritage list. In South Africa, a large number of handsome town and country houses – later to become one of the country's distinctive features – were built, in line with the trend seen on Curaçao. Many of these houses are in excellent condition, thanks to the care of private owners or of Foundations charged with their upkeep.

The houses built in Asia (i.e. in Sri Lanka, Malaysia and Indonesia) were frequently of very large proportions. A number of cases are known in which houses were built to a width of 96 Amsterdam feet: 27 metres! The former Town Hall of Batavia dates from 1705. It has been restored and now houses a historical museum. Some of the old warehouses of the United East India Company fulfil the same purpose today. Apart from a large number of forts, Sri Lanka also boasts of several eighteenth-century Dutch churches still in use, an orphanage (restored to house a Dutch Period Museum) and a Dutch hospital. A particularly fine example of colonial town planning is the fortified town of Galle at the south-west tip of the island. This town, like the forts in Ghana, has been placed on the World Heritage List at the request of the local government authorities.

Among the outstanding topographical draughtsmen whose work has left us with detailed descriptions of the local configurations in the eighteent century, particular mention should be made of Johannes Rach, who worked first in South Africa before spending a long time in Java.

The nineteenth and twentieth centuries

After the end of the Napoleonic era, a wind of change swept through the Netherlands. The Republic became a Kingdom. The overseas settlements

Surinam: The wooden
Roman Catholic Cathedral
of St Peter and St Paul
(1883) in Paramaribo,

designed by F.J.L. Harmes
(Photo by H.J.F. de Roy
van Zuydewijn, 1974).

Sri Lanka: The Reformed
Church (1755) in Galle
(Photo by C.L. Temminck
Groll, 1993).

were no longer managed by the trading companies, but by the national government. Guyana, to the west of Surinam, South Africa, Sri Lanka, Malaysia and the posts in India were all lost to the British. The settlements in the Gold Coast followed by treaty in 1871. The territories still held by the Dutch were Surinam (which became independent in 1975) and the Netherlands Antilles in the West, and Indonesia in the East (held until the Second World War). The Indonesian archipelago was welded together in the nineteenth century to form one large, amalgamated country comprising a myriad of different cultures.

Government buildings in the classical style sprang up in many places in both East and West (the recently restored theatre in Jakarta, built around 1820, being a fine example), although they were generally much less 'grand' than those built in British-controlled territories. More distinctive, however, are the nineteenth-century churches strewn all over the world. Earlier than other nineteenth-century edifices, these churches and synagogues came to be regarded locally as buildings with a clear historical value worthy of preservation. There are two interesting extremes of style: the austere, highly classical domed Dutch Reformed Church in Jakarta (1839) and the spacious, airy neo-romanesque wooden Roman Catholic Cathedral in Paramaribo, dating back to 1883. Another remarkable building in the same town is the large national hospital (c.1850). This occupies an unusually deep plot on Gravenstraat, the old main street. It has a very modern design for its time: its wings with their broad balconies finished with fine cast-iron balustrades are set around what were then well laid-out gardens.

In the West, house-builders often tended to continue along the same paths that had been laid out in the eighteenth century, whilst the trend in the East

was more one of adapting to local traditions: many houses were built with just a single storey and with wide, shady verandas. Local building traditions there were, of course, often extremely rich and varied and became the subject of growing academic interest.

A serious interest also began to develop in the Hindhu and Buddhist antiquities in Indonesia, the most important of which date back to the seventh, eighth and ninth centuries. As early as the beginning of the twentieth century, Th. van Erp carried out an extremely conscientious initial restoration of the temple of Borobudur, working in accordance with principles stricter even than those applied in the Netherlands. In 1925, the magnificent country house of Reinier de Klerk, later Governor-General of the Netherlands East Indies, was restored and turned into the home of the National Archive, a function which this 1760 building fulfilled until recently for the Republic of Indonesia, as the country later became. Even at that time, there was a National Antiquities Department in operation and in 1931 (nine years earlier than in the Netherlands!), a bill was enacted to preserve buildings of outstanding historical value. The Monuments Act, which was updated a few years ago, was primarily conceived with the purpose of saving indigenous antiquities, but it was also utilised to preserve important Dutch buildings from the seventeenth and eighteenth centuries.

Around 1920, Indonesia became the breeding ground for a number of daring variations on contemporary Dutch architectural and town planning themes. Although the developments taking place in the Netherlands were a focus of international attention right from the outset, their Indonesian parallels (which were in many cases more lavish) remained relatively unknown. Since the capital, Batavia (now Jakarta), was poorly situated from a climatic viewpoint – certainly by European standards – for a considerable time the Dutch had been looking at sites farther inland. This led to the idea of moving the centre of government to Bandung, which was higher up and cooler,

Indonesia: The temple of Plaosan (Java, ninth century), restored in 1961 and protected in accordance with the 'Monuments Act' of 1931 (Photo by C.L. Temminck Groll, 1979).

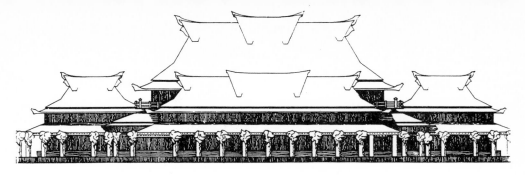

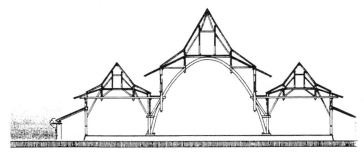

Indonesia: A design (original drawing) by the architect H. Maclaine Pont for one of the main halls of Bandung Technical High School (1920). The building is still in use (B.F. van Leerdam, *Henri Maclaine Pont: architect tussen twee werelden*. Delft, 1988).

and as a result many important buildings were constructed there between 1900 and 1940. These included the Technical High School (now the ITB), the Department of Public Works, several large hotels and commercial buildings, a social club and many fine houses. Both the layout of the town and its architecture were of a high standard. Various architects and town planners in Indonesia expended a great deal of their energy on the salient elements of regional traditions, which were then still very much alive. This is a period which is now receiving much attention from researchers.

In the West, commissions were more modest and contemporary trends had less impact. The building of the Shell Oil refinery on Curaçao, where Venezuelan oil was refined, led to a period of economic prosperity for the island from about 1920. The same thing happened on Aruba ten years later, thanks to Lago. However, the new-found wealth generated little exciting architecture (although there are some magnificent water towers and several new residential areas near Willemstad on Curacao which definitely deserve the epithet 'attractive'). In implementing new construction plans there was a tendency to draw on existing experience from 'Home' on the other side of the world; so that developments in the Netherlands Antilles followed those in Indonesia, on a smaller scale but more colourfully. In Indonesia white still predominated, while the Antilles had a tradition of using colour going back more than a century. After the Second World War and against the background of a burgeoning tourist industry, interest in various forms of conservation began to emerge. An active preservation society was founded on Curaçao in 1954, and the small island of St Eustatius followed in 1974 with its own Historical Foundation. In Surinam, a great deal of restoration work was carried out during the period from 1960 to 1975. Despite a large number of promising initiatives, however, legal framework for preservation is only now coming into being in a practicable way, both in the Antilles and in Surinam.

In general, despite wide divergences (Ghana and Surinam, for example, are facing enormous financial difficulties at present), the level of care for town structures and historic buildings dating back to the seventeenth and eighteenth centuries is reasonable to good. But as far as the nineteenth and twentieth centuries are concerned, research and preservation work are in many cases still in their infancy, except for Indonesia where much has already been done in this field.

It is of immense significance that, although the buildings concerned are of colonial origin, the local people and governments are prepared to regard them as being part and parcel of their own history and culture. And there is every reason for doing so. After all, if one compares eighteenth-century houses in Jakarta, Cape Town, Paramaribo and Willemstad, what strikes one is not just the similarities, but particularly the great differences.

There are, of course, similarities with the Netherlands. In town-planning terms this means the presence of canals wherever possible; and invariably there is the dominance of a single direction (Spanish-Colonial towns are based on a grid system). The theories of Simon Stevin (1548-1620) certainly had an influence. The churches are inspired by the clear forms developed by Jacob van Campen and his contemporaries in the mid-seventeenth century. In urban houses it is the comparitively narrow, tall properties topped with cornices or the so-called 'Dutch gables' which remind us of the Netherlands. They invariably have sash windows and entrances ornamented with pilasters; inside, the exceptionally steep staircases are a striking feature.

Country houses in the East often resemble those along the Dutch River Vecht but on a larger scale, while in Curaçao and South Africa, where they are always single-storied, they are more like the 'Havezaten' or large farmsteads of Drenthe and Overijssel. But, above all, every historic building is in the first place a reflection of the country in which it stands.

C.L. TEMMINCK GROLL
Translated by Tanis Guest.

FURTHER READING

It goes without saying that a great deal has been written on these topics. However, this type of information is frequently difficult to get hold of outside the Netherlands and the area to which it relates. For this reason, it would seem more expedient to contact the Netherlands Department for Conservation: P.O. Box 1001 / 3700 BA Zeist / The Netherlands (fax: +31 30 691 61 89).

# Flemish

and Dutch Brazil

The Story of a Missed Opportunity

Seldom has any political or religious conflict been so contrary to the economic and cultural interest of both sides as the Eighty Years' War (1568-1648), in which King Philip II of Spain and his successors tried to enforce the total obedience of their rebellious subjects in the Low Countries. Spain devoted vast amounts of the wealth derived from the Americas, as well as the proceeds from heavy taxation of its own Castillian subjects, to the reconquest of the southern, Flemish and Walloon, provinces of the Netherlands, but lost the northern provinces of Zeeland, Holland and Friesland. The tyrannical rule of the Spanish commander and Governor, the Duke of Alva, the mutinous and destructive behaviour of the Spanish troops, and above all the Spanish capture of Antwerp in 1585, drove many wealthy and well-connected merchants to flee to the North, where they settled in Middelburg, Rotterdam and – the largest number – Amsterdam.

From there they continued to trade with the Iberian peninsula; this was trading with the enemy, but it was a trade which was indispensable and extremely profitable to both parties. Nevertheless, Philip II embargoed or confiscated Dutch cargoes and shipping in Spanish and Portuguese ports, while suspect Flemish and Dutch merchants were expelled or penalised by extra taxation. In consequence some of them preferred to trade directly with the colonies, at first mainly the Portuguese territories in South East Asia, and they eventually established the United East India Company (VOC) in 1602. On the other hand, Philip II did provide an attractive alternative when in 1598 he granted autonomous government of the Netherlands to his daughter, the Archduchess Isabella, and her husband Archduke Albert. In 1609 the arch-ducal couple successfully agreed a Twelve-Year Truce with the rebels, and for a short time it seemed that a general reconciliation was in the making.

But with the execution of the Grand Pensionary of Holland, Oldenbarnevelt, the radical Reformed Church war party gained the upper hand; and in 1621 hostilities between North and South resumed. The founding in the same year of a West India Company (WIC) enabled the Dutch to attack increasing numbers of Spanish and Portuguese ships in the Atlantic, and in 1628 Piet Hein captured the Spanish silver fleet. The proceeds of this exploit financed a second great fleet which, after a short-lived siege of Bahia in 1624, carried out a second, more succesful, attack on Pernambuco in 1630. Between 1637 and 1644 it was under the governorship of John Maurice of Nassau; his administration was culturally brilliant but economically disastrous. However, this Dutch Brazil was lost in 1654; Portugal had become independent of Spain in 1640 and concluded a treaty with the United Provinces, from 1644 on the rebellious Brazilian colonists had gained the initiative, and in 1648 peace was finally agreed between the Dutch and the Spanish. The Southern Netherlands had returned to Spanish rule after the death of Archduke Albert in 1621 and were excluded from direct colonial trade for centuries by the closing of the Scheldt.

(Tr. Tanis Guest)

On 29 January 1615 Joris van Spilbergen's fleet was anchored in the Bay of St Vincent, close to the present-day Brazilian port of Santos, during a round-the-world voyage. A gang of seamen went ashore and set fire to a well-positioned, well-built sugar mill (*engenho*), its chapel *Nostra Senhora das Neves,* and the sugar cane plantation; however, they did first make sure that all oranges and lemons had been picked for their stores on board ship. They were well aware that the estate belonged to the Antwerp *'Schotsen'* family, descendants of the great merchant Erasmus Schetz. The following day Van Spilbergen's men also set fire to a small Portuguese ship which had just

arrived from Lisbon with a cargo of salt and oil as well as holy relics, cruci-
fixes, indulgences and other such 'trinkets'. However, they spared a trunk
full of fine books, prints and paintings which very probably came from
Antwerp and were intended for the local Jesuits with whom the Schetz family was in close contact.

The Dutch justified their shameless behaviour by claiming that the
Portuguese had been taunting them for more than two weeks. Moreover, the
Portuguese were highly uncooperative in the matter of ship's provisions and
in negotiations about the release of prisoners. The few Portuguese communications indicated that their king, or the governor, had forbidden them to
trade or communicate with the Dutch ships. This was not the first such incident. In 1599, after an unsuccessful trading expedition in the Rio de la Plata,
the captain of the *Zilveren Werelt,* Hendrik Ottsen, had also discovered that
he was not welcome in Bahia de Todos os Santos, the capital of Portuguese
America. He was even briefly imprisoned when ships from another Dutch
squadron under Broer and Hartmann bombarded the town and plundered the
surrounding area. In 1601, during his world voyage, Olivier van Noort lost
many men dead or captured after an unsuccessful landing in Rio de Janeiro.
Also in 1604, Paulus van Caarden's arrival in Bahia turned into a veritable
marauding expedition, the like of which had only previously been carried
out by English and French pirates. On the Dutch side, the white flag of peace
made way for the belligerent Orange flag on the coast of Brazil.

In 1621 the Dutch West India Company (WIC) was established with a relatively clear objective: the establishment of Calvinist communities on the
American continent. In practice, however, the company's urge for expansion went hand in hand with looting interests. The violence escalated, and in
1624 came the first – albeit short-lived – conquest of Bahia. Pernambuco
was occupied in 1630 and then came under the authority of the WIC for
almost a quarter of a century. Thus 'Dutch Brazil' came into being, replac-

*Dutch Ships Attacking
Pernambuco.* Coloured
engraving (1630) after an
etching by N.J. Visscher
(Photo Stichting Atlas van
Stolk, Rotterdam).

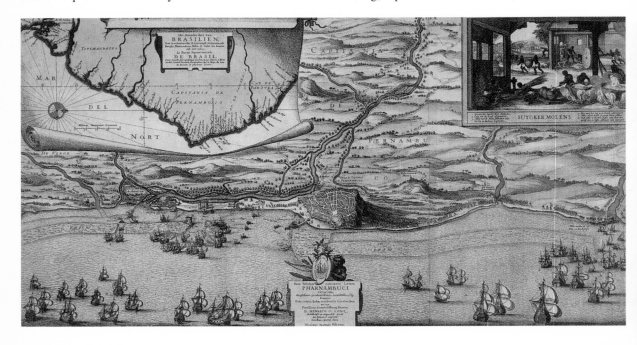

The *Engenho dos Erasmos* in São Vicente. This was the first Flemish sugar mill on Brazilian soil (Photo by Jorge Maruta).

ing the somewhat more obscure *Brasil dos Flamengos* (Flemish Brazil). For more than a century the latter had been an unusual experiment, not only in bilateral commercial and technological co-operation between Portugal and Flanders, the Netherlands in the broadest sense of the word with its many Italian, German and French merchants, but also in intercultural confrontation between the most diverse peoples. This embryonic Flemish Brazil, which needed no clear political profile of its own and was much more open culturally, never became as well-known as Dutch Brazil because it did not fit very well into a strongly patriotic, almost nationalist historiography. At best historiographers saw the Flemish presence on the coast of Brazil as a kind of 'fifth column', a development towards future Dutch conquest, although this conquest too can be regarded as an ill-judged substitute for peaceful trade which yielded more military prestige than real benefits. In any case the obstacles which would cause the failure of the WIC's attempt at colonisation were already visible several decades before 1630. The fact that the WIC nevertheless took the bit between its teeth was due either to recklessness or to the shortsighted self-interest of certain privateers.

In fact, there had been a considerable amount of knowledge and experience on Brazil for some time already. In 1505, shortly after Amerigo Vespucci's journey along the coasts of Brazil, his account was published in Antwerp in the *Mundus Novus,* and all manner of editions and reprints followed. In 1558 the German Hans Staden's account of captivity among the Brazilian Indians was published almost immediately in a Dutch translation in Antwerp. Everyone talked about Staden's experiences among the cannibals. The same year saw the publication of an Antwerp edition of the French cosmographer André Thévet's book on Brazil.

In the years that followed more precise scientific information about Brazil appeared in the botanical works of Carolus Clusius and in the atlasses of Abraham Ortelius and Cornelis Wytfliet. Picture books on costume and all manner of allegorical prints trivialised the reader's perception of the natives. Around 1600 several ships's journals were published, following the example of Jan Huyghen van Linschoten, the first Dutchman to publish his East India experiences in *Itinerario* in 1596. Hendrik Ottsen, Olivier van Noort and Joris van Spilbergen had all had Brazilian adventures. Meanwhile, the most scintillating book on Brazil, by Frenchman Jean de Léry, had also been translated into Dutch, despite the inquisitorial ban on this protestant author. A true forerunner of modern anthropology, this work was largely incorporated into Van Linschoten's *Itinerario* and was subsequently published separately in Amsterdam by Cornelis Claesz. One of the first treatises on tobacco also appeared in Amsterdam. Tobacco-smoking was a custom of the Brazilian Indians, and was recommended to seafarers. From this milieu came the most down-to-earth popular account of life in Brazil: *The Torch of Seamanship* (Toortse der Zeevaart, 1623) by the Middelburg captain Dirck Ruiters.

In the meantime the Jesuits had also begun to publish letters from Brazil, and in school plays they made their pupils play the parts of cannibals. The many tall stories related by Portuguese, German and Flemish sailors returning from Brazil were enthusiastically received in the strong oral culture of that time. In Antwerp as early as 1503, the German humanist Johan Kollauer learned wondrous facts from the Portuguese, which, according to him, rendered the old authoritative works worthless. Although Indians rarely came to the Netherlands – as they did to Portugal or even Normandy – there were always plenty of travellers with considerable experience of Brazil, such as the Portuguese humanist Aquiles Estaço or the Jesuit Fernão Cardim. There were also merchants such as Hans van Uffele, who brought back parrots, hummingbirds, armadilloes, plants and shells, or sketchbooks.

Correspondence was a source of more confidential and measured information. Probably the oldest surviving Dutch-language document in America, and one of the earliest European business letters from the New World, was written by an employee of the Antwerp merchant Erasmus Schetz. Writing in 1548, he reported to his master from São Vincente on the management of the sugar plantation the burning of which was mentioned above. His sober analysis of the current problems shows that the Flemish were already very familiar with overseas capitalistic exploitation. Indeed, from the second half of the fifteenth century several merchants from Bruges and Antwerp had established sugar plantations on Madeira, the Canary Islands and later also São Tomé. They had also farmed land on the islands of Terceira and Faial in the Azores, and traded along the coast of West Africa. Subsequently, other Flemings had gone with the Portuguese to Goa and other East Indian trading posts or, particularly after 1560, established new sugar plantations on the northeast coast of Brazil from Bahia to Pernambuco. Sugar cane grown in these locations yielded less water and more sugar when pressed than that grown in São Vicente, which lay too far south.

Thanks to these experiences, Brazil lost its character of total unpredictability and came to be seen as a paradisiacal and highly promising colonial province, even more so than Mexico or Peru. A considerable amount of information had become available about wind directions, safe bays and all the discomforts to be encountered. Around Rio de Janeiro cold rain and hailstorms might be expected to cut the seamen's fingers to the bone. Everywhere citrus fruits had to be gathered to protect the sailors from scurvy, so that they would still be able to handle the heavy rigging on the ships; ships which were built larger and larger as time went on. They had

Albert Eckhout, *Study of Two Brazilian Savanna Tortoises.* Paper on panel, 30.5 x 51 cm. Mauritshuis, The Hague.

Hunting and Fishing Tapuya Indians. 1687-1723. Wool, 350 x 285 cm (tapestry after a painting by Albert Eckhout). Rijksmuseum, Amsterdam.

learned from the Portuguese to answer the call of nature overboard then to immediately clean themselves with sea water, in order to prevent *bicho do cu,* a burning anal infection which could drive the sufferer to madness. Ashore they were warned against the many types of insect which spoiled instant enjoyment of the beautiful green landscape: the all-devouring ant (the 'king of Brazil'); the poisonous snakes (some of which could swallow a calf whole); the *carapatos* (a kind of leeches) and the insidious *bicho do pé,* an unsightly worm which eventually caused the toes to rot away.

Brazil nevertheless retained sufficient mystery to arouse the curiosity and imagination of both layman and scholar; it remained to some extent an exciting and adventurous *Terra Incognita.* There were birds which would sing continuously for as much as a quarter of an hour, and still be impossible to find. A skunk which could ruin clothing with a single spray. A magical region, completely parched and subject to the destructiveness of monstrous baboons. There were also natives with shining but intangible stones in their chins, which enabled them to work in the dark.

The contact with the many tribes of Brazilian Indians was in every sense a fascinating experience. The Brazilian Indians, unlike the Aztecs and Incas,

continued to be a challenge to the Europeans long after they had been discovered. They were not at all ashamed of their nakedness and the Dutch
often found human bones in their deserted huts. According to a gruesome
account by Dirck Ruiters, they made their children jump from tall trees in
order to select the strongest.

Apart from these *levantados* or eternal rebels there were, fortunately, also
coitados who in their total subservience to the Portuguese were only afraid
that they would not appear brave. The Portuguese made use of them by chas-
ing them with sticks towards the Dutch enemy, thus forcing them to shower
the bewildered Dutch with arrows. Yet Ruiters and other Dutchmen were
convinced that they could incite these Indians to revolt against the
Portuguese. Some even followed the example of the French and lived
among the Indians in order to learn their language and customs. The concept
of an alliance originated from Bartolomé de las Casas' popular pamphlet of
1552, through which the Dutch came to identify themselves with the Indian
victims of Spanish tyranny. This later proved to be a dangerous self-decep-
tion and the Dutch had a great deal to learn from the Portuguese regarding
the manipulation of the Indians; none of those involved in the conquest of
the Americas were as skilful in this respect as the Portuguese. On Schetz's
sugar plantation they had realised early on that the Indian workers were –
from a western point of view – unpredictable and unreliable, and black
African slaves were preferred.

The Flemish were already familiar with slavery and the slave trade, due
to their experiences in Portugal and on the coast of West Africa. It is very
questionable whether some of the objections to slavery on principle, as they
were set out in the common laws (*Costuymen*) of Antwerp for example,
were also put into practice. The humanist Clenardus bought three slaves in
Lisbon, and almost every Flemish merchant in the southern area had a black
slave. At the *Landjuweel* (a drama festival) in Antwerp in 1561, Melchior
Schetz even led the parade accompanied by a 'well-mannered' black slave.
Apart from their adaptability, black slaves were prized for their physical
strength, and could supposedly fell a tree better than the Norwegian strong-
men. The Dutch sympathised with the fate of the Africans because the
Portuguese treated them badly, and this led them to suppose that the
Africans could be completely won over to their side.

It is not surprising that the Portuguese were accused of every sin in the
book, in particular of sloth and dishonesty. Yet the relationship between the
Flemish and the Portuguese was very ambiguous. There were frequent references to friendship and preferential treatment. The captive captain Ottsen
was even permitted to walk freely in the street, was given a small daily
allowance, and could thus quietly plan his escape. The Portuguese valued
the skills of the Flemings, employing many of them and paying them well,
for example to search for precious metals in Brazil. There were many mixed
marriages, even with 'New Christians', and in addition to the specifically
Brazilian phenomenon of the half-breed or *mestizo,* there was also the
Portuguese-Fleming. In Rio de Janeiro a certain Pieter Tack – a Dutch
speaker – reported to Olivier van Noort's fleet. Tack is known from
Brazilian sources as Pedro Tacques, the founder of a famous family. There
were also the Lam-Leme family, the Becaudt-Bicudo family, Vanderborcht-
Campos and Lins-de Olanda.

Sugar cane.

Brazilian fairground attraction showing the infernal production chain in a sugar mill (Museu do Açúcar, Recife).

This inter-marriage was furthered not only by dynastic and political links, and cultural affinity, but, more importantly, by economic interests. A stimulating association had developed between the Netherlands, Portugal and the latter's overseas territories. The division of tasks within this association was interesting: the terms of trade constantly favoured the Netherlands. The Flemings acquired vital goods from South America such as salt, fruit and colonial raw materials, and in exchange exported finished products such as textiles, metalware, weapons and *objets d'art*. Moreover, they learned about shipbuilding and shipping routes from the Portuguese, and were therefore soon able to sail to the colonies themselves. They preferred to retain ports-of-call in Portugal, where they could stock up on vital citrus fruits and supplement their cargoes with wines and oil to be sold at a good profit in Brazil. Slavery was also a well-established part of this triangular trade. Flemish and Portuguese merchants enjoyed much greater freedom in their Brazilian trade than in the heavily regulated and protected Spanish-American trade via the *Casa de la Contratación* in Seville, or even the Dutch Company trade in the East Indies. They were thus able to take more initiatives and make more international connections. Thus, during the last decades of the sixteenth century, the Brazil trade, with its branches in the Baltic and the Mediterranean and on the coasts of Africa, became a thriving growth centre of international trade. Sugar became one of the most valued commodities in those troublesome years. It changed the diet and culture of the wealthy and even of the middle class profoundly. Merchants from Antwerp, Lisbon, Amsterdam and

169

Frans Post, *View of Olinda* (detail). Rijksmuseum, Amsterdam.

Venice were eager to invest in this treasure of sweetness and the number of sugar plantations in Pernambuco and Bahia rapidly increased. The wealthy towns of Salvador and Olinda became known for their 'glamour' – splendid attire and banquets in the Flemish-Burgundian style. According to Manuel Callado's pun, Olinda had become *'Olanda'* long before it was captured and destroyed by the Dutch in 1630.

Indeed many were envious of this decadent paradise, this Sodom and Gomorrah of new international capitalism. Not only did it feed the green-eyed monster, it also clashed with political interests, deep-rooted religious convictions and moral principles. The Portuguese-Flemish ships, richly laden with sugar, often fell prey to French and English privateers. Even skippers from Zeeland and Holland could not resist striking a blow. When Philip II became king of Portugal in 1580, this Flemish-Portuguese shipping was affected by embargoes and prohibitions on trade with the enemy. As a rule a blind eye was turned in the ports of Porto, Viana and Madeira, but in 1591 and again in 1618 an inquisitor was sent to Brazil and several Flemings and 'New Christians' were arrested. The States General came under increasing pressure from Calvinists and Radicals who, like Willem Usselincx, supported autonomous Dutch colonisation of America or at least the mobilisation of all seamen and ships under the Dutch flag. Immediately it became more difficult for the more internationally-minded merchants of the Amsterdam lobby (including many 'New Christians') to recover cargoes captured by the privateers. Many had meanwhile made their pile and could cloak their new wealth in a patriotic respectability. Gruesome incidents had already occurred during the Twelve-Year Truce, but when hostilities between Spain and the United Provinces resumed in 1621 the days of Flemish Brazil were numbered and all sides were forced to nail their colours to the mast. Portugal, which had regained its independence in 1640 under a new dynasty but was losing its hold on the East Indies, would not accept a Dutch Brazil. In 1654 the WIC finally had to beat a retreat from Brazil. The Netherlands, both North and South, had missed a fine opportunity to become a favoured partner of Portugal and help develop the Brazilian economy. Soon afterwards, in 1703, Britain stepped into their place under the Methuen Treaty and was able to finance some of her industrial development with Brazilian gold. *'Verzuymd Brasiel'* ('lost Brazil') was a direct consequence of the partition of the Northern and Southern Netherlands, and the mourning for it should in fact rather concern the 'first' *Brasil dos Flamengos* than the 'second' Dutch Brazil.

EDDY STOLS
Translated by Yvette Mead.

The

Seventeenth-Century Anglo-Dutch Wars:

Economic or Political Issues?

Bartholomeus van der Helst,
*The Celebration of the
Peace of Münster in the
Headquarters of the
St George's Guard,
Amsterdam.* 1648. Canvas,
232 x 547 cm.
Rijksmuseum, Amsterdam.

In 1648 the Dutch Republic signed the Peace of Münster with Spain, bringing to end a period of some eighty years of war. The main benefit of the treaty immediately became apparent, as economic activity in the Provinces of Holland and Zeeland entered a period of rapid growth following the recession and stagnation of the war years.[1] However, the Peace of Münster also had other consequences, not the least of which was the prestige which it lent to this small Republic as a state of some note within Europe; had the United Provinces, as the Republic was known, not succeeded in defeating mighty Spain? But it remained to be seen whether the Republic, great power and economic centre that it had become, would be able to continue to exist peacefully, as many desired.

The answer was not long in coming. Within thirty years of the signing of the Treaty, the United Provinces had fought three wars with England: from 1652 to 1654, between 1665 and 1667 and between 1672 and 1674. During the same period they were also involved in conflicts in the Sont region and between France and Spain, were at war with the Bishopric of Münster and, since 1672, had had to withstand the combined forces of France, Münster and Cologne, as well as England – a conflict in which the Provinces themselves became the core of an alliance with Spain, the German Emperor, Denmark and Brandenburg. And the end was not yet in sight.[2]

Interpretations

In general historical surveys the Anglo-Dutch wars have traditionally been characterised as trade wars or sea wars – in other words as economic conflicts. More specialised books and articles bring more detail to this general picture. In his book *Profit and Power*,[3] for example, Charles Wilson describes the first war as a purely economic affair. The English were not able to cope with the competition from Holland and Zeeland fishermen off the British coasts, nor that from Dutch traders and merchantmen. Envy led to English aggression and, in 1652, to war.[4] This aspect is discussed in more detail by J.I. Israel in his extensive and stimulating study of Dutch trade: *Dutch Primacy in World Trade, 1585-1740*.[5] The Dutch historian Pieter Geyl, however, adopts a totally different approach. The decisive factor for him was the action of the Stadholders of the House of Orange – Frederick Henry and William II. In his book *Orange and Stuart 1641-1672* (Oranje en Stuart 1641-1672), Geyl argues that both Princes were seeking to raise the status of their house. Frederick Henry allied himself with the English Royal House of Stuart by marrying his son William into that family. When civil war broke out in England in 1642 and continued, with some interruptions, until the 1650s, it was an obvious decision for the Prince of Orange to choose the side of Stuart against the English Parliament. The latter ultimately gained the upper hand, however, founded a new state – the Commonwealth – and, in its irritation over the help given by Orangists to the Stuart supporters, headed for war with the Republic.[6] The English historian J.R. Jones adopts an intermediate position which, while recognising economic causes underlying the war, attributes the conflict mainly to political factors. He argues that the Dutch had repeatedly derived benefit during talks with the English

Johannes Lingelbach, *The Naval Battle near Livorno in 1653* (detail). 1653. Panel, 114 x 216 cm. Rijksmuseum, Amsterdam.

from a tactic of delaying decisions. In 1651-1652, however, Parliament was no longer prepared to join in this game, making war unavoidable: *'The first war was not the direct result of deliberate English aggression, but followed from Dutch miscalculations based on underestimates of English determination and power.'*[7]

The result was a fierce war which went badly for the Dutch in the North Sea but which, as Israel points out, was less dramatic for them elsewhere in the world because of the superiority over the English which the Dutch derived from their tremendous trading potential.[8]

The views of the different authors show a greater consensus regarding the second war, which was fought after the restoration of the monarchy in England (1660). Wilson quotes his fellow countryman G.N. Clark, stating that this war was *'the clearest case in our history of a purely commercial war'.*[9] Others – including both Israel and Geyl – draw the same conclusion. The conflict was the result of a growing English rejection of the continuing Dutch supremacy throughout the world. The war was fought on a worldwide front: in Europe, in Africa – where it began – and in America.

Jones, however, points out that it was not only the merchants in Parliament who tried to persuade the new king, Charles II, to go to war, but also a politically motivated faction with James, Duke of York – later James II – as the driving force behind it. His aim was to revive British claims to sovereignty of the surrounding seas, so that the English would be able to demand taxes from foreign fishermen and merchantmen in order to provide financial reinforcement for an absolute monarchy.[10]

However, this war ran a different course from that which the aggressive English leaders had expected on the basis of their successes in the first war. While it was true that the Dutch fleet, though greatly strengthened, was not impregnable, the Dutch maritime potential worldwide still proved stronger than the English. At the Treaty of Breda in 1667, the English were even forced to make a number of economic concessions.

The third war was only five years in coming. During those five years, however, the shifts which took place in Anglo-Dutch relations were such that several authors prefer not to describe this as a trade war. In 1930 Johan E. Elias even concluded that the economic agreements contained in the 1667 Treaty made further economic confrontations superfluous. The English and the Dutch had reached agreement in the Treaty and were to develop into allies; the war of 1672-1674 was no more than an unfortunate intermezzo. This view was contested by Geyl, who maintained that political tension remained and that the 1672 conflict was therefore above all a political struggle, connected to the rise of French absolutism and the opportunism of Charles II of England who, with French support, wished to become independent of the English Parliament – and who hoped to make the Republic subordinate to himself through collaboration with his young cousin, William III of Orange; the latter, however, proved unwilling to be a party to this plan.[11] Wilson goes along with this to some extent. It is true, he writes, that rivalry remained between English and Dutch merchants, but the former saw that war had brought no solution and were less inclined to the conflict; this left only the political argument.[12]

Yet the economic factor did not disappear entirely. Jones and Israel point out that England was still trying in 1672 to break the Dutch commercial

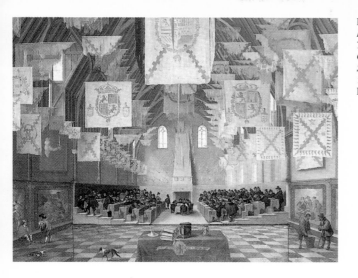

Dirck van Delen, *The Great Hall of the Binnenhof, The Hague, during the Great Assembly of the States General in 1651.* 1651. Panel, 52 x 66 cm. Rijksmuseum, Amsterdam.

hegemony and to conquer Dutch colonies. The chief aggressor now, however, was France, which was able to draw the English into its bid for political as well as economic advantage. When Charles II declared war on the Republic in March 1672, however, he cited both economic and political motives: conflicts concerning the East Indies and Surinam and failure to observe English sovereignty at sea. According to Jones, however, *'these commercial issues were pretexts. Once again the real reason for war was predatory greed – this time for power as well as wealth'*.[13] The behaviour of English merchants during the war confirms the correctness of this view. The English failed to win any battles in the North Sea, but lost large numbers of ships to Dutch privateers. The English merchants affected added to the pressure on Charles II to make peace in 1674. The heavily threatened Republic survived this attack, too, and retained its world-wide trade supremacy.[14]

This brief summary makes it clear enough that labelling the Anglo-Dutch wars as trade wars is at the very least open to discussion. The same applies if the wars are described as purely political conflicts. Can these wars in fact be explained on the basis of a single cause? Analysis of the background to the First Anglo-Dutch War can provide a first, tentative answer to this question.

Political developments [15]

Undoubtedly there were political factors underlying the First Anglo-Dutch War. In order to understand these factors, we have to go back to the 1630s. The Dutch Republic was still in a full state of conflict with Spain: its war policy, like its foreign policy, was determined by the States-General, in which each of the seven regional States Colleges had a delegation. These regional States Colleges were each sovereign within their own province. Their armies fought under the command of Frederick Henry of Orange, the highest nobleman in the Republic. In five provinces, he was also Stadholder, the highest official of the province, though subordinate to the States College.

England at that time was ruled by King Charles I, who governed with the advice of his Privy Council, and who only summoned Parliament when he deemed it necessary. This was primarily when he needed money. However, precisely because Parliament was seeking to influence the King's policy via its control on royal expenditure, the King convened it as infrequently as possible. After 1629 Charles ruled without a Parliament; but in 1640 his problems became so great that he was forced to summon the Upper and Lower Houses of Parliament on no less than two occasions.

War was raging throughout Western Europe. England was the only neutral power, a not unattractive position as it was approached from all sides with requests for support and was able to select the highest bidder. France and Spain, who were at war with each other from 1635 onwards, were particularly anxious to curry English favour; both countries had much to gain from a safe passage through the Channel, which was ruled by England. Towards 1639, Spain was in favour. The Spanish King, Philip IV, even talked with Charles about the possibility of a marriage between his son and Charles' eldest daughter. In these circumstances, Philip received English cooperation in ensuring the safe passage of a combined war and transport convoy to his domains in the Southern Netherlands. This was a direct threat to the Dutch Republic, which accordingly showed no hesitation in attacking – and defeating – the Spanish fleet in English waters.

Now that it was clear to the Dutch how dangerous a neutral England could be for them, they immediately sought diplomatic contact with King Charles in order to break his good relations with Philip IV. At first the King proved unwilling, but he changed his mind when the Spanish King, following revolts in Portugal and Catalonia, was no longer able to offer him any benefits, particularly money. And money was precisely what the English King needed to reduce his dependence on Parliament. Accordingly, he responded to the approaches of the Dutch. Ultimately this resulted not in a political treaty but in a marriage between William II of Orange and Charles' eldest daughter Mary, who had originally been intended for the Spanish crown prince (1641). This was a great victory for the Dutch, who had succeeded in driving a wedge between the Spanish and English rulers and between their lands.

Shortly after this, the conflicts between the English King and his Parliament led to the outbreak of the English Civil War. Both parties now sought support from the Dutch Republic, the King via the regular ambassador in The Hague, Parliament via its own delegate, Walter Strickland. The English were thus now the appellants. It was up to the Dutch to whom they were appealing to decide what stance they would adopt towards the two English camps.

Opinions in the Republic were not undivided. In the States-General the eastern provinces had little interest in English affairs and could therefore not be prodded into involvement in them. More important was the opinion of the maritime Province of Holland. Here, there were two factions in the States College with opposing views on foreign policy. One faction, led by the merchant cities of Amsterdam, Rotterdam and Dordrecht, had long been seeking an end to the damaging maritime war with Spain. They now wished to pursue a policy of active neutrality vis-à-vis England, in which contacts were maintained with both parties in order to influence developments in England as much as possible without themselves becoming involved in the

School of Anthony van Dyck, *Portrait of William II and Mary Stuart.* 1641.

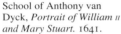

Canvas. Rijksmuseum, Amsterdam.

Daniel Mytens, *Portrait of Charles I.* 1631. Canvas. National Portrait Gallery, London.

British conflicts. The other Holland faction, spearheaded by the industrial towns of Leiden and Haarlem, was primarily interested in continuing the struggle against Philip IV which was causing such damage to the competitive position of the textile industry in the Southern Netherlands. Action by the States in England would only make the problem more difficult. This faction was therefore in favour of a policy of passive neutrality vis-à-vis the English, and this policy line was in fact passed by a majority in the States-General in November 1642. In spite of this Holland maintained direct contacts with the delegates of both English camps, and the Amsterdam faction continued to hammer away at the need for mediation.

The English Parliament, too, contained diverse factions.[16] The two extremes were marked by a war faction and a faction favouring peace, with an influential centre group between them. From the end of 1643 onwards, however, several members of this centre group became more radical and aligned themselves with the war faction. In spite of this turbulent situation, the Amsterdam faction managed to continue sending mediators from the States-General. When they arrived in England in 1644, however, they caused only embarrassment; neither of the two warring parties was in the mood for mediation, but at the same time no one wanted to offend the Dutch. Accordingly, Charles I in principle agreed with the offer from the States-General, while Parliament endlessly postponed its reaction. In 1645 the embassy returned to The Hague without having achieved any success; the only result was irritation. Both Charles and the English Parliament were irritated because the Dutch had proved willing only to provide mediation rather than actual support for the war effort. The Dutch States, for their part, were irritated because they felt they had been dealt with so undiplomatically by the English, particularly by Lords and Commons. This irritation was to be exacerbated in the late 1640s. In 1646 Charles fell into the hands of his opponents, bringing an end to the conflict. Trouble flared up again in 1648, however, when Parliament became even more radical; it sentenced the King to death, had him beheaded, established the Commonwealth (1649) – and caused new problems for the Dutch.

Religious factors

The desire of the English Parliament to avoid offending the Dutch of all people in their mediation efforts was primarily based on religious factors.[17] Like its forerunners in the 1620s, this Parliament contained a strong puritanical element. This was not restricted to a single faction, but was spread throughout the various groupings. The puritans saw England as the new Israel, the chosen people whose destiny was to lead the struggle against the Anti-Christ, which they equated with the strongly Catholic Spain. The Dutch were at the forefront of the peoples alongside whom this apocalyptic struggle had to be fought. Had they not fought against Philip IV and his predecessors for decades? Did they not share the English beliefs very closely? Had they not constantly shown hospitality to religious exiles? And did their trading successes, however irritating they might be for some English people, not bear witness to God's rich blessing of their actions? When the Civil War broke out, these ideas changed on one point. Charles I was now seen as the Anti-Christ on the grounds that he himself showed Roman Catholic leanings, was misled by his French Catholic wife Henrietta Maria and his papist advisers, and thus oppressed his subjects in their liberty and religious beliefs. From now on, the apocalyptic struggle would have to be fought out on British soil.

In this situation it was a natural step for the English Parliament to send the first delegate it accredited at a foreign court, to the Dutch Republic. Here he was to call for a *'more neere and straight league and union'* between the Republic and Parliament; Strickland set out this idea in more detail in a letter to the States-General in which he called for the formation of a confederation based on religious, economic and historical grounds.[18] Parliament continued to repeat this proposal, even while the war faction was gaining support and when, from 1643 onwards, it began working in closer cooperation with Scotland by signing the Solemn League and Covenant.

What was the position of the Dutch in all this? Here, too, there were ideas of a new Israel – though this was equated to the Northern Dutch in their struggle against Spain, with no role being accorded to England.[19] Politicians paid no attention to this; they received the English proposal for union with the same reserve with which they had approached political rapprochement. They had no wish to burn their fingers in the fire of English affairs, and thus refrained from responding to any suggestions. In 1645 the States of Utrecht even went so far as to request that Strickland, following a meeting, should not leave any copies of the Covenant with them, so as to remove any appearance of agreement.[20] The response of the church organisations was very different. The four *classes* of Zeeland expressed feelings of spiritual kinship with the English and Scottish puritans by urging them in letters written in 1643 to fight against the papist superstitions with all their might. When the States of Zeeland discovered this, they forbade the church elders to enter into any further correspondence on this subject.[21] The *Heren Staten* persisted in this attitude for many years. The irritated English puritans, however, concluded that the Dutch brothers were subordinating spiritual interests to material profit.

Dynastic causes[22]

In the same way that political factors were sometimes intertwined with religious issues, they occasionally also became entangled with dynastic interests, both on the part of the Orangists and the Stuarts. This is already apparent from the marriage treaty of 1641. Politically, the treaty brought an end to the collaboration between England and Spain. Its dynastic significance, however, was entirely different for Charles I and Frederick Henry of Orange. For the English King, it set the seal on a misalliance: after all, the House of Orange was of a much lower order in the hierarchy of royal families than the Stuarts. For Orange, the marriage held out the promise of an increase in status. Thus it was able to form the counterpart to the unionist plans of the English Parliament: a basis for close collaboration, but this time between the Royalists and the Republic, stimulated by Orange. Would this actually happen?

The question arose as early as 1642, when Queen Henrietta Maria personally brought Prince William's bride Mary to the Republic. The main purpose of her journey was to acquire funds, to buy munitions, and to obtain permission for English officers serving the Dutch States to go over to the Royalist army. She was counting heavily on the cooperation of a grateful Frederick Henry. Contrary to her expectations, however, he first left her in the cold for four months before providing any support in acquiring funding, and granted permission for only a few officers to leave. In a letter to Charles, the Queen wrote that the Prince appeared to be *'une personne malaysée à engager'*.[23] She was even more upset when Frederick Henry granted an audience to the Parliamentary delegate Strickland in January 1643. Shortly afterwards she left the Republic in a fury, taking with her a shipload of weapons. Strictly speaking this was contrary to the neutrality resolution of November 1642, but Frederick Henry managed to instill a degree of flexibility into those who criticised this action. Otherwise she would remain even longer in the Republic, *'doing a very great disservice to the country',* as he wrote.[24]

The fact that dynastic advantage did not cause the Prince of Orange to lose sight of the national interest of the Dutch States is also apparent from the following. When discussions took place in the Republic on mediation in England, he adopted the same standpoint as the Amsterdam faction in the States of Holland. He felt that such mediation should take place, but that it must not lead to the involvement of the Dutch States in the English conflicts. He was not in favour of passive neutrality.

Even clearer were his actions in 1644-1645 with respect to a plan for a second Stuart-Orange marriage. The proposal came from the circle surrounding Henrietta Maria, who was now looking after the affairs of the Stuarts from her mother-country France. It was a proposal filled with tempting conditions. Frederick Henry's eldest daughter was to marry the crown prince Charles: the Dutch Stadholder could not wish for anything more prestigious. The House of Orange would be expected to pay only a small dowry, but would have to join an offensive and defensive alliance with the Royalists and, according to a later proposal, participate in a maritime action against the English Parliament. However, Frederick Henry showed no desire whatsoever to cooperate, finally producing convincing evidence of his lack of commitment by putting forward a different bridegroom, the Elector of Brandenburg! The marriage took place in December 1646. Everything had taken place behind closed doors; the States had no knowledge of anything. The House of Orange had not subordinated the Republic to its own dynastic interests.

Things changed after Frederick Henry's death in 1647, however, when his 21-year-old son William II assumed his titles. The young prince still had little authority. Moreover, he was confronted with the Dutch-Spanish peace process, making it impossible for him to gain esteem through military exploits, as his father had done. Accordingly, he worked quietly towards a war policy, in opposition to the peace policy of the States-General. For England this meant that he did not take the neutrality resolution of 1642 seriously, not even after the States-General had renewed it on 6 November 1648.

William maintained contact with his brother-in-law Charles, later to become Charles II, who had left England, travelled to France via the Channel Islands and came to The Hague in 1648, followed by his father's Privy Council. The number of royal exiles in The Hague was to grow rapidly in subsequent years. Having the honour of being associated with the Stuart family, William was keen to offer support, he wrote to the young Charles. Accordingly, he encouraged the sale in the Republic of booty obtained by the Royalists, even though the States-General had forbidden this. In addition, he encouraged cooperation between the Stuarts and Scotland, an endeavour in which he expected cooperation from Dutch Calvinists. And more than once he became ensnared in attack plans of precisely the type which Frederick Henry had rejected during negotiations for a second marriage. Ultimately all these plans led to nothing, but they did cost William a great deal of money.

What the Prince hoped to achieve for himself through these actions is not entirely clear. He probably thought that in due course he would obtain the support of his in-laws in his bid to strengthen his position within the Republic. His sudden death in November 1650, however, precluded such an outcome. He had undoubtedly contributed to the fact that The Hague had become a Royalist stronghold – something which raised doubts in the English Parliament as to how genuine the Dutch neutrality really was.

Maritime issues[25]

Neutrality also played an important part in confrontations on the North Sea and in the English Channel, where the Republic fought against the Spaniards

and the inhabitants of the Southern Netherlands (Flanders) until shortly before the Peace of Münster. These same seas were also the scene of battles between Royalists and Parliamentarians in the English Civil War. All this led to the development of new rules of international law, or the application or tightening up of existing rules.

Jan van de Cappelle, *The Home Fleet Saluting the State Barge.* 1650. Panel, 64 x 92.5 cm. Rijksmuseum, Amsterdam.

From the end of the sixteenth century, the Dutch attempted to paralyse the shipping trade to and from the Flemish ports. Initially they did this through written bans on navigation, which also forbade the import of all goods. However, the development of international law led to the rule that such a ban should be realised by means of an effective blockade and that, except in the case of a siege, only the import of a limited number of goods – contraband – could be forbidden.[26] The difficulty lay in strictly enforcing the blockade.

The English, in particular, caused problems. Following Scottish examples, the Stuart kings James I and Charles I applied sovereign rights to the seas around England. These rights, so they claimed, stretched as far as the opposite coasts.[27] They therefore expected all passing ships to signal a greeting with flags and topsail, and began demanding money from the users of their *Mare Brittanicum,* in particular fishermen, in recognition of their sovereign power. Charles I even equipped a new war fleet for this purpose in the late 1630s, though this brought in little revenue. Opposing this English argument and the inconvenience it brought, the Dutch, who were major users of these waters, claimed that, apart from the coastal waters, the seas were nobody's property.

The inconvenience mounted when the English announced that they regarded their warships and the water around them as inviolable English territory. This stance assumed particular importance when England became the only neutral power in Western Europe after 1635. From that time on, all manner of warring countries attempted to sail in and out of Flanders in safety with their trading goods via Dover in convoys guarded by neutral English warships. This policy was successful, to the anger of the blockading

Dutch, who did not wish to come into conflict with the English and who could therefore do no more than stand and watch.

The advent of the English Civil War made the whole situation even more complicated. In June and October 1642 the English Parliament enacted ordinances banning voyages involving contraband goods to Royalist ports in Ireland. A similar ban followed in the same year for voyages into Newcastle and surrounding ports. In 1643 and 1644 the Lords and Commons extended these measures to cover all Royalist towns in Great Britain. These bans applied both to the English and to foreigners. Anyone infringing the bans would be arrested and tried before a new, central body in London, the High Court of Admiralty.[28]

For reasons which are unclear, Charles I did not issue any similar ordinances until July 1643. Ships and goods intercepted by his supporters were not tried in one location, but according to the old-fashioned, decentralised apparatus of admiralty courts, which had sittings in various port towns in England, Ireland and Jersey.[29]

The English found it difficult to implement these measures. Part of their fleet had remained loyal to the Crown, while the remainder had sided with Parliament. Both sides had insufficient ships to simultaneously fight their opponents, protect the trade of their own followers and prevent voyages to hostile ports. Accordingly, Parliament chartered armed merchantmen from private owners, in particular from the 'New Merchants' in London. These were merchants who did not belong to the large, monopolistic trading companies, but who had become rich as interlopers, traders who managed to operate commercially in specific areas in spite of a monopoly. They also obtained letters of marque from Parliament, which enabled them to act as privateers operating separately from the Parliamentary fleet. They made a great deal of profit from both chartering and their privateering activities. Charles, too, in addition to his war fleet, was supported by private merchantmen.

All these ordinances and actions by English ships had their effect on the Republic. Sometimes this was because the conflicting parties carried the fight into Dutch waters; usually, however, it was because Dutch skippers infringed the ordinances or were suspected of doing so, and were brought in by one of the two English sides, in spite of the Dutch States' neutrality. Most of the arrests were carried out by Parliament: five in 1643, twenty-nine in 1644, nineteen in 1645 and four in 1646. The fluctuation in these figures reflects the intensification and weakening of the conflict between Parliament and Charles I. Royalist arrests are more difficult to trace because of the decentralised system of admiralty courts. Sources reveal only four cases over the years in question, plus four Dutch ships which became ensnared in battles between the two English sides.

The lull in the Civil War in 1646 meant that the number of arrests in 1647 was also low: nine arrests by Parliament, two by Irish Royalists. When the conflict flared up again in 1648, however, the picture changed. Parliament won ground and drove its opponents to outlying parts of the British Isles and into the sea. Many sought support and shelter abroad. In line with its earlier ordinances, Parliament issued new bans on navigation: against Ireland in 1649 and against Scotland in 1650 – both of them Stuart kingdoms. In addition, a general ban on navigation was issued in 1650, affecting all trade goods – not just contraband – to and from the English settlements in America which had remained loyal to the Crown. Similar orders followed against foreign powers which provided help to the Royalists: against France in 1649, which led to the start of an undeclared war, and against Portugal in 1650. The Royalists, for their part, were forced to make more and more use of foreign ports – in France (Dunkirk) and Flanders – in order to bring in and try their prizes. This was banned in the Republic because of its official neutrality. Nonetheless, the Council of the later Charles II did sometimes function as a prize court thanks to the dubious support of William II.

Unavoidably, more and more Dutch ships were now taken. The numbers once again reflect the shifts in English power relations. In 1648 the Royalists confiscated fourteen Dutch vessels; in 1649 the figure was twenty-five, in 1650 eleven and in 1651 fourteen. Parliamentary ships, for their part, confiscated twelve Dutch vessels in 1648, twenty-two in 1649, fifty in 1650 and one hundred and twenty-six in 1651; in the first half of 1652 alone the figure was as high as one hundred and six. There was a clear turnaround in the years 1649-1650, when the triumphant Parliament began to expand its land-based sovereignty over the land to include the sea, continuing the former pretensions of the Stuarts.

The Dutch suffered greatly as a result of the English Civil War. On average, a fully laden ship was valued in London at £15,000 in this period. Some ships and / or cargoes were later released by the English, but they were seldom undamaged. As neutrals, the Dutch States felt an increasing irritation towards their neighbours across the sea. The latter, for their part, were indignant that precisely this neutral Republic took so little notice of their parliamentary ordinances, and provided both English camps – and thus the Stuarts too – with all manner of goods.

The ups and downs of trade

The battles at sea also had a trading aspect. On the one hand war damaged trade, while on the other hand it generated profit. For example, the English benefitted from the trade to and from Flanders, while on the Dutch side a great many arms suppliers profited from the English Civil War.

In the late sixteenth century the Hollanders and Zeelanders were not only the freight carriers of the world, but also built up inside their provinces the international stock of all manner of goods. According to most studies the economy of the western provinces of the Republic continued to flourish until the middle of the seventeenth century. Recently, J.I. Israel has added some further detail to this broad picture,[30] arguing that the war against Philip IV brought a serious economic setback for the Dutch in the years 1621-1647/8. Embargoes were promulgated in the Iberian kingdoms of Aragon, Castile and Portugal, which meant that subjects of the Republic were no longer permitted to transport the highly prized Spanish and American goods themselves. In addition, they suffered great damage on the high seas from the warships and privateers of Philip IV. However, the Spaniards were not capable of shipping their goods to the European markets themselves. As a result, the Dutch activities were taken over by the Hanseatics, with Hamburg as their leading city, and by the English. The former derived most benefit from this arrangement in the 1620s, with the English rising to supremacy after 1630.

Hanseatic ships brought goods from Spain directly to Hamburg, while the English transhipped many goods in Dover. The English pushed the Dutch out of the Mediterranean Sea entirely. In the Baltic, however, neither the Hanseatics nor the English managed to achieve this; although the volume of trade handled by the Dutch in the Baltic was smaller than before 1621, they did not lose their supremacy. The English also failed to push the Dutch out of the East Indies. In the West Indies, with Spanish support, they had more success. The rise of the English at the expense of the Dutch gave rise to optimism among English merchants, though they were also irritated when that rise to supremacy took place less quickly elsewhere, or failed to materialise altogether.[31]

A sudden change took place in 1647-1648, however, mainly under the influence of the Spanish-Dutch peace process. The misery caused by the English Civil War to the English themselves also played a role here.[32] Philip IV opened up his European and American ports to the Dutch once again. Dutch primacy in the Baltic grew at the expense of English trade. In Portugal, which had shaken off Philip's authority in an uprising in 1640, the Dutch managed to secure the whole of the important salt trade once again. In the Caribbean, they encouraged the growth in sugar production in the mainly Royalist English colonies by financial investment, and suddenly found themselves in control of the shipment of freight.

The recovery of the Republic was reflected in a rapid reduction in Dutch freight fees and insurance costs. And because bullion from Spain no longer had to be shipped via Dover but went directly to the Republic, the price of this commodity also fell. Dutch profits rose so rapidly, that it was soon possible to reduce interest rates on loans to, on average, half the levels charged in England.[33] In the face of this thriving economic activity, the surrounding countries, particularly England, were plunged into crisis. A new source of irritation had been created.

The build-up[34]

All the loose ends came together in the years 1651-1652. In England, the newly-formed Commonwealth had been striving since 1649 to achieve rapid recognition abroad, above all by the Republic. As early as 1649 the Commonwealth sent an embassy to The Hague for this purpose. This raised the old question of union once again, though this met with little response in the Republic. Significant in this were not only the strong Stuart coterie surrounding William II, but also the general Dutch distaste regarding the beheading of Charles I. The fact that the Republic was itself not a kingdom was irrelevant: the Dutch felt that a ruler whose power existed by the grace of God should not be executed.[35] As a result, the two states stood alongside each other without formal relations.

For the Provinces of Holland and Zeeland, in particular, this situation was unacceptable because of the damage it inflicted on their trading activities. On the death of William II in November 1650, therefore, both provinces immediately took steps to recognise the Commonwealth, which became effective on 29 January 1651. The Republic and Commonwealth could now at least discuss their problems together.

Even before that date, work had been going on in Westminster to set up an embassy in the Low Countries. Once again the instruction was to work towards *'a more strict and intimate alliance and union'* with the Dutch. Once again, reference was made to mutual affinity on a religious and economic level; and this time reference was also made to the fact that both states had freed themselves from royal tyranny. A majority of members of the Commons (forty-two, to be exact), apparently moderates, were prepared to go quite a long way here; this caused their twenty-nine more radical opponents to speak dismissively of an *'impotent haste to integrate with neighbouring states'*.[36]

Negotiations in The Hague went anything but smoothly, however. The English – represented by Lord Chief Justice Oliver St John and Strickland – were hampered by exiled Royalists, by the distaste on the part of the Dutch population for 'regicides', by their own arrogance as victors in the Civil War, and by their unfamiliarity with the complex administrative apparatus of the Republic. On arrival on 27 March 1651 they immediately demanded a general declaration of intent by the Republic, a somewhat bold approach. The Province of Holland, which was keen to cooperate at most, was able to convince all the other provinces to back this demand within a month – a rapid achievement given the sluggishness of the administration, but much too slow for the English. The latter now proposed entering into a confederation, which among other things would defend itself against its common enemies – i.e. the Stuarts and their protectors, the House of Orange – by expelling exiles and banning the supply of contraband goods. The Dutch made a number of amendments to the English proposals and countered them by submitting thirty-six articles of their own, dealing primarily with economic relations between the two states. The two sides continued to talk at cross purposes until the English suddenly departed on 2 July. This disappointed the Province of Holland so much that within three days the States College proposed sending an embassy to London in order to pick up the thread of the discussions once again. The Province thus accepted that the Republic would once again become the requesting rather than the requested party. It was to be December 1651, however, before the proposed embassy actually arrived in London.

In the autumn of the same year the English Parliament underwent a further radicalisation. In September 1651 the Royalists suffered a decisive defeat in a land battle near Worcester. Army officers now returned to Parliament and strengthened the radical element there. The Dutch ambassadors identified four factions in the English Parliament. Some, they wrote, wished to see an immediate break with the Republic for political reasons. A second group was seeking legally defensible means of paralysing Dutch trade without coming to a state of war. A third group hoped to be able to repay the Dutch for old defeats through reprisals. And a fourth faction, to which Oliver Cromwell belonged, was genuinely in favour of an alliance with the Republic, though the latter would immediately have to *'ruin the house of Stuart'*.[37]

This latter faction, which had undoubtedly been the driving force behind the mission of St John and Strickland in early 1651, was now outvoted by more radical members. It was primarily the New Merchants within the other factions who added to the existing legislation against overseas enemies of the Commonwealth; the Act of Navigation passed by the Commons on 19 October was prepared by them and their friends. This Act forbade free passage to foreigners except where they were carrying their own products. The aim was to stimulate British shipping, both for the benefit of trade and to foster the acquiring and maintenance of sovereignty at sea which, following the victories on land, a majority of the Parliament now wished to achieve.[38] This Act was thus part economic, part military in nature, and would undoubtedly have harmed the Dutch more than others. This danger became even greater when, before the end of the same year, letters of reprisal were granted to the heirs of a certain Pawlett empowering them to seek recourse for earlier damage caused by the Dutch.[39]

It was under these circumstances that the Dutch embassy had to hold their discussions with England from the end of 1651. The first aim was to have the measures relating to free passage of ships lifted before the interrupted negotiations could be reopened. Amsterdam stimulated these efforts in December 1651 by arranging through the States of Holland a ban by the States-General, forbidding merchants from sailing, in order to avoid the risk of a further deterioration in relations. These efforts were successful, and the Act of Navigation was barely enforced in the first half of the following year. With the same aim in mind, the States of Holland and Zeeland avoided issuing any hard statements against Parliament, banned the printing of defamatory writings and described a large war fleet, which had put to sea in the spring, not as offensive but as being *'purely for the defense and conservation of free shipping and commerce'*.[40]

Negotiations in Westminster, meanwhile, did not really get going until May. The Dutch were taken aback by the English view that the Republic had failed to take a stance in the previous year; the Dutch had thought that agreements on a political union had been reached to the satisfaction of St John and

Reconstructed model of the *Prins Willem,* built for the Dutch United East Indies Company. During the First Anglo-Dutch War it was converted to a warship and served as Admiral Witte de With's flag-ship (Rijksmuseum, Amsterdam).

Strickland. As a result, discussions began once more on the treatment of enemies of the other side, particularly the Stuarts, and on free passage at sea. Before these barriers had been removed, an incident took place off Dover between a Dutch and an English flotilla regarding the 'obligation' of the Dutch to lower the flag to the English in recognition of their sovereignty at sea. The talks were immediately broken off, and the English flatly refused to consider any new Dutch concessions. The ultimate political weapon – war – would have to resolve these issues.

Conclusion

Many issues – political, religious, dynastic, maritime and economic – had led to growing irritation between the Dutch and the English in the 1640s and early 1650s. All of these contributed directly to the First Anglo-Dutch War. At this stage, the economic factor did not stand out emphatically among these causes; it was only in the final run-up to the outbreak of hostilities that this factor began to predominate. The reason for this was that merchants held an important position in the radicalising English Parliament, while the Dutch, for their part, were primarily seeking to protect their trading interests during the negotiations with England. On the English side, however, the political element remained of equal importance, expressed in the commitment of the triumphant Parliament to achieving the *Dominium Maris,* a commitment which ultimately proved stronger than the puritanical urge towards union with the Republic. This latter urge continued to be cherished by a minority, however, and from 1653 onwards was to become a not insignificant factor in the achievement of peace between the two states.

This analysis of the causes leading up to the First Anglo-Dutch War shows with sharp clarity that this conflict cannot simply be labelled a trade war, nor yet a political conflict. The term 'sea war' says little in this context, because it can at best be applied to the area where the actual battles took place and says nothing about the causes leading up to the conflict. The First Anglo-Dutch War was a multi-faceted conflict, which does not lend itself to a monolithic explanation. In fact, this applies equally to the two subsequent wars as well; further research will be needed, however, in order to ascertain whether it is correct to describe the second war primarily as a trade war and the third as a mainly political conflict.

S. GROENVELD
Translated by Julian Ross.

NOTES

1. ISRAEL, J.I., *Dutch Primacy in World Trade 1585-1740.* Oxford, 1989, pp. 197-207.

2. For a summary of these international developments, see: GROENVELD, S. and G.J. SCHUTTE, *Delta. Nederlands verleden in vogelvlucht. Deel 2: De nieuwe tijd: 1500 tot 1813.* Leiden / Antwerp, 1992, pp. 226-242.

3. WILSON, CHARLES, *Profit and Power. A Study of England and the Dutch Wars.* London / New York / Toronto, 1957; The Hague / Boston / London, 1978.

4. WILSON, *Profit and Power,* pp. 1-60, pp. 145-148.

5. ISRAEL, *Dutch Primacy*, pp. 121-210.

6. GEYL, PIETER, *Oranje en Stuart 1641-1672.* Zeist / Arnhem / Antwerp, 1963², pp. 13-80.

7. JONES, J.R., *Britain and Europe in the Seventeenth Century.* London, 1966, pp. 38-49; pp. 48-49.

8. ISRAEL, *Dutch Primacy,* pp. 207-213.

9. WILSON, *Profit and Power,* p. 151; on the causes of this war: pp. 90-126.

10. JONES, *Britain and Europe,* pp. 55-60. Cf. JONES, J.R., *Country and Court. England 1658-1714.* London, 1978, pp. 98-99.

11. ELIAS, JOHAN E., *De Tweede Engelsche oorlog als Keerpunt in Onze Betrekkingen met Engeland.* The Hague, 1930. GEYL, PIETER, 'Economische verklaringen van politieke verhoudingen', in: *Kernproblemen van onze geschiedenis. Opstellen en voordrachten 1925-1936.* Utrecht, 1937, pp. 106-115. Idem, *Oranje en Stuart,* pp. 338-341.

12. WILSON, *Profit and Power,* pp. 154-158.

13. ISRAEL, *Dutch Primacy,* pp. 282-299. JONES, *Britain and Europe,* pp. 61-66. Idem, *Country and Court,* pp. 103-106.

14. ISRAEL, *Dutch Primacy,* pp. 297-299.

15. For a discussion of subsequent developments, see: GROENVELD, S., *Verlopend getij. De Nederlandse Republiek en de Engelse Burgeroorlog 1640-1646.* Dieren, 1984. Idem, 'The English Civil Wars as a Cause of the First Anglo-Dutch War, 1640-1652', *The Historical Journal,* 30 (1987), pp. 541-566.

16. For a discussion of relationships within Parliament during this revolutionary period, see: HEXTER, J.H., *The Reign of King Pym.* Cambridge (MA), 1968³. UNDERDOWN, D., *Pride's Purge. Politics in the Puritan Revolution.* Oxford, 1971. WORDEN, B., *The Rump Parliament 1648-1653.* Cambridge, 1974.

17. See: GROENVELD, S., '"Als by het huwelyck van man ende wyff". Puriteinse voorstellen voor een Nederlands-Engelse unie, 1642-1652', in: GROOTES, E.K. and J. DEN HAAN (ed.), *Geschiedenis, godsdienst, letterkunde, Opstellen aangeboden aan S.B.J. Zilverberg.* Roden, 1989, pp. 147-158. BRESLOW, M.A., *A Mirror of England. English puritan views of foreign nations, 1618-1640.* Cambridge (MA), 1970. HILL, C., 'The English Revolution and the Brotherhood of Man', in his *Puritanism and Revolution. Studies in Interpretation of the English Revolution of the Seventeenth Century.* London, 1958, pp. 123-152. MITZUKURI, G., *English-Holländische Unionsbestrebungen im Zeitalter Cromwells.* Tübingen, 1891.

18. Algemeen Rijksarchief (ARA), The Hague, Loketkas Staten-Generaal, 12576.51, 18 October 1642: Strickland to the States-General.

19. GROENHUIS, G., 'Calvinism and National Consciousness: The Dutch Republic as the New Israel', in: DUKE, A.C. and C.A. TAMSE (ed.), *Britain and the Netherlands VII: Church and State since the Reformation.* The Hague, 1981, pp. 118-133. Cf. Idem, *De Predikanten. De sociale positie van de gereformeerde predikanten in de Republiek der Verenigde Nederlanden voor ± 1700.* Groningen, 1977, pp. 77-107.

20. WORP, J.A. (ed.), *De briefwisseling van Constantijn Huygens.* (Vol. IV). The Hague, 1915, p. 219 (20/30 September 1645): Johan van Reede van Renswoude to Constantijn Huygens.

21. AITZEMA, L. VAN, *Saken van Staet en Oorlogh in, ende omtrent de Verenigde Nederlanden* (7 vols). The Hague, 1669-1672, II, pp. 928-932. KLUIVER, J.H., 'Zeeuwse Reacties op de Acte van Seclusie', *Bijdragen en Mededelingen betreffende de Geschiedenis der Nederlanden* (BMGN), 91 (1976), pp. 406-428. *Calendar of State Papers, Venetian Series 1643-1647.* London, 1926, pp. 85-86 (1 April 1644): Agostini from London to Venice.

22. For a discussion of this topic see: GEYL, *Oranje en Stuart,* pp. 13-80, The views posited here are contested on a number of essential points in: GROENVELD, S., 'Frederik Hendrik en de Stuarts, 1640-1647. Herziening van de opvattingen van Pieter Geyl', *Oranje-Nassau*

Museum Jaarboek 1987, pp. 7-28. Idem, 'Willem II en de Stuarts, 1647-1650', BMGN, 103 (1988), pp. 157-181. Idem, 'The House of Orange and the House of Stuart, 1639-1650: a revision', *The Historical Journal,* 34 (1991), pp. 955-972.

23. COMTE DE BAILLON C., (ed.), *Lettres inédites de Henriette-Marie de France, reine d'Angleterre.* Paris, 1884, pp. 21-24 (27 March 1642): Henriette Marie to Charles I.

24. District Archive of the West Frisian Municipalities in Hoorn, Resolutions of the States of Holland by Nicolaes Stellingwerff 115, 25 February 1643.

25. For a discussion, see *inter alia* Groenveld, *Verlopend getij,* pp. 135-219. Idem, 'English Civil Wars', passim.

26. JESSUP, P.C. and F. DEAK, *Neutrality. Its history, economics, and law. Vol. I: The Origins.* New York, 1935, pp. 30-81, pp. 105-117. OUDENDIJK, J.K., 'Blockaded seaports in the history of international law', *Tijdschrift voor Rechtsgeschiedenis,* 42 (1974), pp. 1-22.

27. For a discussion of the English pretensions, see: FULTON T.W., *The Sovereignty of the Sea.* Edinburgh / London, 1911. MULLER FZN., S., *Mare Clausum. Bijdrage tot de geschiedenis der rivaliteit van Engeland en Nederland in de zeventiende eeuw.* Amsterdam, 1872. OUDENDIJK, J.K., *Status and Extent of Adjacent Waters. A Historical Orientation.* Leiden, 1970.

28. FIRTH, C.H. and R.S. RAIT (ed.), *Acts and Ordinances of the Interregnum, 1642-1662.* (3 vols.). London, 1911, I, pp. 9-12, pp. 33-36, pp. 42-44, pp. 347-351.

29. LARKIN, J.F. (ed.), *Stuart Royal Proclamations. Vol. II: Royal Proclamations of King Charles I 1625-1646.* Oxford, 1983, pp. 825-826, pp. 932-935, pp. 961-965, pp. 1034-1036.

30. ISRAEL, *Dutch Primacy,* pp. 121-196. Idem, *The Dutch Republic and the Hispanic World 1606-1661.* Oxford, 1982. Cf. TAYLOR, H., 'Trade, Neutrality, and the "English Road", 1630-1648', *Economic History Review,* 2nd series 25 (1972), pp. 236-260. KEPLER, J.S., *The Exchange of Christendom. The International Entrepot at Dover 1622-1641.* Leicester, 1970.

31. See *inter alia:* MUN, THOMAS, *England's Treasure by Forraign Trade, Or, The Balance of our Forraign Trade is The Rule of our Treasure.* Published in: MCCULLOCH, J.R., (ed.), *Early English Tracts on Commerce.* Cambridge, 1954, pp. 115-209. Although this text appeared only in 1664, it was written between 1620 and 1630 and should be seen as a reflection of the relationships of that time. Cf. WILSON, *Profit and Power,* pp. 19-24.

32. ISRAEL, *Dutch Primacy,* pp. 197-207.

33. Cf. BARBOUR, VIOLET, 'Dutch and English merchant shipping in the seventeenth century', *Economic History Review,* 2 (1930), pp. 261-290.

34. See *inter alia:* GROENVELD, 'English Civil Wars', pp. 551-566.

35. GROSHEIDE, D., *Cromwell naar het oordeel van zijn Nederlandse tijdgenoten.* Amsterdam, 1951, pp. 5-34.

36. *Journals of the House of Commons.* Vol. VI, no location, undated, pp. 527-528, 535. *The Manuscripts of his grace the Duke of Portland, preserved in Welbeck Abbey.* Vol. I, London, 1891, pp. 556-558. WORDEN, *Rump Parliament,* pp. 237-262.

37. ARA, Loketkas Staten-Generaal 12589.62: secret letter of 10 February 1652 from the ambassadors to the States-General.

38. The text of this Act is contained in: FIRTH and RAIT (ed.), *Acts* II, pp. 559-562. Cf. FARNELL, J.E., 'The Navigation Act of 1651, The First Dutch War, and the London Merchant Community', *Economic History Review,* 2nd series, 16 (1963-1964), pp. 439-454. JUNGE, H.C., *Flottenpolitik und Revolution. Die Entstehung der englischen Seemacht während der Herrschaft Cromwells.* Stuttgart, 1980, pp. 156-157. On the New Merchants: BRENNER, R., 'The Civil War Politics of London's Merchants Community', *Past and Present,* 58 (1973), pp. 53-107.

39. Bodleian Library Oxford, Rawlinson Papers A 226, Orderbook of the Admiralty Committee 1651-1652, 27ro.

40. ARA, Resolutiën van de Staten van Holland 1652, 83, 97.

hrough

Foreign Eyes

Painters from the Low Countries

in Seventeenth-Century England

England has from the beginning been a nation of writers but it is only from
the early eighteenth century that we can claim to have produced a body of
native painters, responsible for providing the lion's share of the nation's pictures. With the exception of miniature painters practising a specialist art and
the occasional native of distinction such as William Dobson, John Michael
Wright and Francis Barlow, the history of painting in England during the
seventeenth century was very largely the creation of foreign artists, particularly from the Netherlands, both north and south, who either came on short
visits or for various reasons took up residence here. In the later sixteenth
century they were often refugees fleeing from war and religious persecution,
whereas a century later economic hardship sometimes prompted their emi-
gration to England. Portraiture, that essential accompaniment to the life of a
court, was very largely served by foreigners, primarily by Anthony van
Dyck and Daniel Mytens before the Civil War, and by Peter Lely and
Godfrey Kneller after the Restoration - with the result that our image of the
Stuart kings is very largely their creation. Although portraiture was the predominant activity of painting in seventeenth-century England, there were
other categories of subject-matter painted by the visiting artists from the
Low Countries and some of what they produced forms the subject of this
essay.

Although the hostile political situation between England and the Northern
Netherlands during the reign of Queen Elizabeth I continued under her successor James I, largely owing to maritime and mercantile rivalry, this did not
prevent the influx of Dutch as well as of Flemish artists, who served to
establish flourishing artistic and cultural ties between the countries. James I,
although he recognised the political need for painting, took little interest
in art, but his consort Anne of Denmark was a keen collector and patron,
who, it was reported, preferred pictures to people. Despite the King's lack
of interest, his reign witnessed the beginnings of the great tradition of
English collectors, of whom the most notable were the Earl of Arundel and
the Duke of Buckingham. These two noblemen were, for instance, responsible for attracting the young Van Dyck, anxious to establish himself away

from the shadow of Rubens, to England in 1620. Apart from painting a straightforward portrait of Arundel and a *portrait historié* of Buckingham and his wife as Venus and Adonis, as well as carrying out an unspecified commission for the King, Van Dyck produced, in his *The Continence of Scipio,* probably painted for Buckingham, the first major picture in England which was not a portrait. Arranged across a large surface with narrow depth and painted in his lively linear manner of this period, the Roman ruler, in an exemplum of generosity and continence, is seen after his conquest of New Carthage reuniting the beautiful female captive to her betrothed, Allucius, and handing over to her as a dowry the ransom gifts her parents had offered him. (Whether the three principals are to be identified as James I and Buckingham and his wife, as has been suggested, remains very much open to doubt.) With such a developing star in its midst, the English court must have grieved to see Van Dyck depart after only four months, ostensibly to travel for a period of eight months but in reality for an absence of eleven years.

In 1625 James was succeeded by his younger son Charles and there began one of the great eras of English patronage and collecting, not to be rivalled until the reign of George IV. Both Buckingham, at least for the three years before his assassination, and Arundel were still on hand to act as influential artistic advisers and exempla. In addition Sir Dudley Carleton, English ambassador at The Hague from 1616 to 1625 and again from 1626 to 1628 was to serve as a perceptive and highly effective 'talent-spotter'. He was responsible for introducing the painting of the strange still-life painter Jan Torrentius to the King, who in an enlightened act of patronage invited the painter to come to England to save him from a recently imposed twenty-year gaolsentence for membership of the outlawed Rosicrucian Society

Anthony van Dyck,
The Continence of Scipio.
1620-1621. Canvas,
183 x 232.5 cm.
The Governing Body,
Christ Church, Oxford.

and apparent blasphemy and immorality. Unfortunately Torrentius, inclined to melancholia, produced nothing for his English saviour and returned home.

Earlier Sir Dudley Carleton, with eventually more rewarding results, had spotted the talent of Gerrit van Honthorst immediately after his return from Rome and introduced his name and painting to Arundel, thus laying the groundwork for the artist's visit to England in 1628. There, in addition to a number of portraits, he produced his enormous picture of *Apollo and Diana,* possibly to hang at the end of the newly built Banqueting House in Whitehall, the ceiling of which was to be decorated by Rubens. Following the taste of the time, Mercury, in the guise of the Duke of Buckingham, leads a procession of the liberal arts to pay homage to Apollo and Diana, who, personated by Charles I and Henrietta Maria, are seated above in the clouds. With its allusions to the peace-loving enlightenment and sophistication of the Caroline court, it offered the first large-scale public representation of what was being created so memorably in the English capital.

A year later Honthorst was followed to London by Rubens, on a diplomatic mission which must also represent the most distinguished artistic event of the reign. During his nine months in England he painted portraits of Arundel, a *portrait historié* of the King and Queen in a composition of *St George and the Dragon* (H.M. The Queen), which, a contemporary reported, *'he has sent home into Flanders to remain there as a monument of his abode and employment here'*. During his stay he received the commission to decorate the ceiling of the Banqueting House, no doubt undertaking the necessary preparatory work on the programme, and, as a special present for Charles I, painted a highly political allegory of *War and Peace*, which in the words of Charles I's surveyor, Abraham van der Doort, was *'an Emblim wherein the differencs and ensuencees betweene peace and warrs is Shewed',* a subject very relevant to the European peace the artist had been negotiating. (Mars, the god of war, is driven off by Minerva, the goddess of wisdom, who protects a woman suckling a child, probably Pax and the infant Plutus, the god of wealth.)

In 1632 Van Dyck was lured back by Charles I to England, where he was to spend most of the remaining nine years of his life. Traditionally it is said that the King's pleasure with the *Rinaldo and Armida* (Museum of Art, Baltimore; see *The Low Countries* 1993-94: 311), which he had commissioned two years earlier, is supposed to have been responsible for the invitation. If so it is ironic that Van Dyck was required to spend the rest of his career painting portraits of the royal family and the court. The *Cupid and Psyche* (H.M. The Queen), painted towards the end of his life, remains the only known surviving mythological picture from the years in England. Its purpose is unknown, but it represents the culmination of Van Dyck's love affair with Venetian sixteenth-century painting, above all with that by Titian. The wonderfully varied range of colours in a high key – above all the pinks and the blues – combined with the elegance and delicacy of the figures and their actions show the artist at the furthest point from the wholeheartedly Rubensian works with which he had begun his career. It is not difficult to imagine that this picture would have been warmly received by an English Court infatuated with Venetian painting. The only mystery is why he was never invited to repeat the exercise.

There was another side to the taste of the King and his fellow collectors, a penchant for ingenious and meticulously executed works on a small scale. The Haarlem painter Hendrick Pot was called on to paint the King and

Peter Paul Rubens,
War and Peace. 1629.
Canvas, 203.5 x 298 cm.
National Gallery, London.

Queen in a style and size recalling an enlarged miniature. Charles had a particular liking for the ingenious perspectives and architectural scenes, with their romantic atmospheric effects of nocturnal interiors, by the Antwerp artist Herman van Steenwyk the Younger, who was active in England from 1617 until 1637; the more prosaic perspectives of the Dutch artist Gerrit Houckgeest were no less popular with the King. In landscape this taste was met by, amongst others, the works of Cornelis van Poelenburgh, who appears to have made several journeys from Utrecht to London in the late 1630s, and who collaborated with the Antwerp painter Alexander Keirincx, who on a second visit in 1639 shared a house in Westminster with him. Apart from painting views of castles and towns for the King, Keirincx provided the landscape for figures probably added by Poelenburgh in the *Wooded Landscape,* painted for Charles, which was later sent to The Hague with other Dutch pictures by William III and never returned.

England during the Civil War was no place for a foreign artist, although Peter Lely, who arrived in London from Haarlem just as it began, was able to survive remarkably well during the war and the subsequent Commonwealth. At the Restoration he was promptly appointed Principal Painter by Charles II. Regarded as the natural successor to Van Dyck, like his predecessor he realised that portrait painting was the principal requirement and quickly abandoned the pastoral and mythological subjects with which he had begun his career, such as *The Concert.* This lyrical picture is probably to be understood as an allegory of Music, here personified by the singer, the flautist and the bass violinist (probably a self-portrait), in the service of Love and Beauty, exemplified by a half-naked woman seen from the back and

Alexander Keirincx and Cornelis van Poelenburgh, *A Wooded Landscape.* c.1639 (?). Panel, 64 x 92 cm. Mauritshuis, The Hague (inv. no. 79).

Peter Lely, *The Concert.*
Late 1640s. Canvas,
122.9 x 234.5 cm.
The Courtauld Institute
Galleries (Lee Collection),
London.

the woman on the right who silences her dog.

With the accession of Charles II in 1660, the crown no longer played the dominant role in patronage that it had done under his father. Although he was assiduous in trying to reassemble his father's dispersed collection, Charles II proved himself a far less discerning and active patron of living artists. Moreover, although the art of the Netherlands remained the principal overall cultural influence, royal taste veered towards French and Italian art, with erotic mythologies appealing to the King and religious subjects meeting the devotional requirements of his Catholic wife, Catherine of Braganza. But artists from the Low Countries were to serve a purpose. Charles II had a passion for the events of his own life, particularly his escape from the Roundheads during the Civil War and his journey to France in a Brighthelmstone (Brighton) coal-brig; after his restoration, the ship was converted into a yacht and renamed the *Royal Escape,* in which state it was painted by the younger Willem van de Velde presumably on commission from the King (H.M. The Queen). Charles' departure from Scheveningen at the time of the Restoration represented a more triumphant moment in the King's career and the subject of his embarkation on the beach became a popular subject with Dutch artists. Allied to this penchant for his own life-story went his interest in landscape to provide records of his possessions. The Dutch artist Hendrick Danckerts, was, for example, commissioned by the King to paint royal residences, such as Greenwich, Windsor Castle and Hampton Court, and naval ports, such as Plymouth, Portsmouth and Tangier. The latter subjects would particularly have appealed to the nautically minded King, as well as to his brother, the Duke of York, later to be James II, and this aspect to their taste undoubtedly led to their patronage of the elder and the younger Willem van de Veldes, who probably arrived in England in or shortly after 1672, when Charles II issued a declaration inviting people from the Low Countries to come and settle in England.

With patronage no longer very largely centred on the Court, many foreign artists found employment with patrons who in these happier times were building and embellishing their homes in and around London. In fact some artists from the Low Countries had no contact with the King and were entirely dependent on commissions from outside the Court. While Ralph Montagu was building the first Montagu House in London 'in the French taste', the Duke and Duchess of Lauderdale were active in enlarging and redecorating their house at Ham in the early 1670s. They employed, in addition to some Dutch joiners, a team of Dutch artists and under the controlling hand of the Duchess they produced a very distinctive ensemble which still happily exists today. Much of the painted decoration consisted of overdoors and overmantles, which included landscapes by Dirck van der Bergen and Abraham Begeyn, a battle-piece by Jan Wyck, three seascapes by the younger Van de Velde, his first recorded commission in this country, and an alchemist's den by Thomas Wyck. This was only one part of a sumptuous ensemble of wall-hangings and furniture all designed in the most fashionable taste of the period, which led John Evelyn to describe the interior as *'furnished like a Great Prince's'* and to claim that it was *'inferiour to few of the best Villas in Italy itself'*.

Sir Thomas Willoughby, another active patron of artists from the Low Countries, commissioned topographical landscapes of his houses at Wollaton and Middleton Park from the Antwerp painter Jan Siberechts, who came to England in the 1670s. By abandoning his natural bent for landscapes with peasants and animals, Siberechts built up a thriving and distinguished practice producing views of country seats. Both Danckerts and Jan Griffier the Elder, followed later by Leonard Knyff, were also busily producing country house 'portraits' for a wide variety of owners around the country. Willoughby also employed Egbert van Heemskerk, another emigrant artist with a very different specialisation, to paint a series of six drolleries. The Haarlem artist went on to illustrate events of local history, such as the *Oxford Election* (Corporation of Oxford) and the *Quaker Meeting*, which offered a satirical comment on the Society founded in 1647; the latter proved a popular subject which was repeated in numerous painted versions as well as being engraved.

Samuel van Hoogstraeten, *A View down a Corridor.* 1662. Canvas, 264 x 136.5 cm. The National Trust / John Hammond (Blathwayt Collection), Dyrham Park.

One of the most admired qualities in painting during the reign of Charles II was that of verisimilitude. Its representation, which was principally provided by artists from the Low Countries, found an eloquent admirer in Samuel Pepys, who on being taken to Simon Verelst's lodging in London was shown *'a little flower-pott of his doing, the finest thing that ever I think I saw in my life – the drops of Dew hanging on the leaves, so as I was forced again and again to put my finger to it to feel whether my eyes were deceived or no'*. On another occasion he enthused about a picture in the manner of the 'miscellanies' produced by the Leiden artist Evaert Collier, who spent a short time in London. It is, he said, *'so well painted that in my whole life I never was so pleased or surprised with any picture … even after that I knew it was not board, but only the picture of a board, I could not remove my fancy'*. And his enjoyment of the ingenious is reflected in his repeated pleasure in the power of spatial *trompe l'oeil;* visiting the house of Thomas Povey in Lincoln's Inn Fields in 1663, he wrote: *'above all things I do the most admire his piece of perspective especially, he opening the closet door and there I saw that there is nothing but a plain picture hung upon the wall.'* The work described is very probably to be identified with the *View down a*

Corridor painted the year before by Samuel van Hoogstraeten, who was in London from 1662 to 1667, and which passed from Povey's possession to that of his nephew, William Blathwayt of Dyrham Park, where it has hung as a *trompe l'œil* ever since.

If not a great work of art, the picture known as *The Tichborne Dole* (Mrs John Loudun, Tichborne Park), painted by the little-known Flemish artist Gillis van Tilborch in 1670, provides one of the richest documents of English social history. Standing before their Tudor house, Sir Henry Tichborne and his family, accompanied by their various retainers and watched by tenants and villagers, are about to distribute bread to the poor, following a family tradition supposedly going back to the thirteenth century. In this wide composition, recalling Dutch and Flemish paintings of the subject of the distribution of bread, the entire spectrum of a village society dependent on the grand house, including an engaging variety of dogs, is painstakingly recorded.

James II, whose taste matched that of his brother and who had particularly patronised the Van de Veldes, had little time as monarch to attract new artists to England. William and Mary, as might be expected, turned to artists from the Low Countries, but perhaps deliberately reacting against the taste of their two predecessors chose to employ different artists. Jan Wyck, who had been in England since 1674 but who had never carried out any work for the Crown, was now given commissions. Godfried Schalcken, the master of candle-light scenes, which sometimes included portraiture, was encouraged by William to make several visits to England in the 1690s. According to Arnold Houbraken, the flower painter Maria van Oosterwijk also worked for William and Mary. The Van de Veldes however, so popular with Charles II and James II, were ignored by the new monarchs; yet so much did they appeal to English taste that they readily continued to find patronage. Willem van de Velde the Younger lived on until 1707, into the reign of Queen Anne; regarding his search for light and atmosphere there is a nice account of his *'going a skoying'* given to the English artist William Gilpin by an old Thames waterman who *'had often carried him (i.e., Van de Velde) out in his boat, both up and down the river, to study the appearances of the sky. The old man used to say, they went out in all kinds of weather, fair, and foul'*. It was a practice which was followed by so many English artists in subsequent centuries.

CHRISTOPHER WHITE

FURTHER READING

BROWN, C., *Van Dyck*. Oxford, 1982.

MILLAR, O., *Sir Peter Lely 1618-80*. London, 1978.

WATERHOUSE, E., *Painting in Britain 1530 to 1790*. New Haven / London, 1994.

WHINNEY, M. and O. MILLAR, *English Art 1625-1714*. Oxford, 1957.

WHITE, C., *The Dutch Pictures in the Gallery of H.M. The Queen*. Cambridge, 1982.

urner's

Holland

Reflections after a Pioneering Exhibition in London

From July till October 1994 a special exhibition was on show at the Tate Gallery, London, entitled *Turner's Holland*. As such, it filled a gap in Turner studies. For J.M.W. Turner (1775-1851) was not only Britain's greatest landscape and marine artist but also a most compulsive traveller in Europe. Accordingly, dozens of books and numerous exhibitions have been produced on *Turner and Italy, France, Switzerland, Germany,* or even *Luxembourg.* But never before one on *Turner and Holland.*

It is true that of Turner's more than 500 authenticated pictures only some 24 can be described as 'Dutch', and of his roughly 15,000 sketches only about 600. There are three facts, however, whose proper evaluation make this neglect difficult to countenance. The first is the artist's *'Ah! That made me a painter!'*, an emotional confession recorded when, long after he had already acquired fame and fortune, he found himself suddenly confronted again with a particular Van de Velde engraving.[1] The next is that, at the age of fourteen, he became a pupil at the Schools of the Royal Academy whose President, Sir Joshua Reynolds, had written in 1781: *'Painters should go to the Dutch School to learn the art of painting, as they would go to a Grammar School to learn languages.'*[2] And the third is that his major commission as a budding artist was for a pendant to another Van de Velde – a pendant which, as *Dutch Boats in a Gale*, became Picture of the Year in 1801.[3]

The story of Turner's 'Dutch connection' begins with the Van de Velde engraving that caused him to reveal the origin of his career. It could be traced because Walter Thornbury, the biographer to whom we owe the anecdote, had specified: *'... it was a green mezzotinto, a Vandervelde – an upright; a single large vessel running before the wind, and bearing up bravely against the waves. That determined his genius to marine painting.'*[4]

When considered in the light of Turner's dismal early life, Thornbury's conclusion seems convincing. Turner grew up as the only surviving child of a barber in Covent Garden, a short walk from the Thames and the Pool of London. His mother's increasingly frequent attacks of schizophrenia made the nearby river – and at times a brief stay with an uncle at Margate – his most effective escape from domestic upheaval. This helps to explain his lifelong attachment to water, ships, the sea, and simple fishing-folk. And it may also have been the source of his obsession with skies and half-light. Out there, angry winds, near-blinding mists and rain-darkened clouds would alternate as rarely with heartwarming sunshine as, according to the state of his mother's affliction, the atmosphere at home would in an already by itself dark and depressing area of London. He would have learned soon enough to *'bear up bravely against waves'* whipped along by forces way beyond his ken. Subconscious identification with the image of a storm-tossed ship in a printseller's window close to his father's shop must, for a boy gifted with what was clearly an intense urge for pictorial expression, seem only natural. It was drawings resulting from this urge that proved arresting enough for his enlightened father to procure him an apprenticeship as an architect's draughtsman and in 1789 enrol him at the Academy Schools.

Turner's successes began with topographical watercolours. But his debut in oil at the Academy's annual exhibition was a partly Dutch-inspired marine, *Fishermen at Sea* (1796). And when five years later the above-mentioned *Dutch Boats in a Gale* – significantly titled in full *Fishermen Endeavouring to Put their Fish on Board* – reaped that rapturous reception, Benjamin West, Sir Joshua's successor as President R.A., even pronounced the picture *'What Rembrandt thought of but could not do'*.[5]

If we ask what it was that in Britain, in 1801, the so greatly admired Dutch Master could be considered unable to do, the answer may be found in contemporary art theory. For, viewed in this context, the answer would lie in the boldness of a young artist introducing an eighteenth-century trend into a composition mirroring a seventeenth-century model, i.e. in the seamless integration, in this mirror-image, of Burkean 'Sublimity'.

Ever since the appearance in 1757 of Edmund Burke's immensely influential treatise on *The Origin of our Ideas of the Sublime and Beautiful*, the 'Sublime' – unlike our definition of it – was associated with all that was *'vast, rough, awe-inspiring, and deadly dangerous';* the 'Beautiful', on the

J.M.W. Turner, *Dutch Boats in a Gale; Fishermen Endeavouring to Put their Fish on Board.* 1801. Canvas, 162.5 x 222 cm. National Gallery, London.

other hand, with everything that was *'small, smooth, peaceful and life-enhancing'*. The novelty in Turner's *Dutch Boats in a Gale* was that, to an audience still constitutionally familiar with the basics of sailing, the fishermen in the foreground would at once be recognised as being on a terrifyingly obvious collision course with the two central vessels; depicted as risking a catastrophe in the execution of their job, they thus embodied 'Sublimity'.

The situation resembled that of a Swiss mailcoach about to crash into an abyss, or a mountain-hut about to be overwhelmed by an avalanche. In the Romantic era, viewing near-catastrophes in man's struggle with the invincible forces of Nature evoked a feeling of intense exaltation, of 'sacred horror'. What Turner had achieved was the successful translation of land-Sublimity into marine-Sublimity. Or rather, while faithfully adhering to his Dutch model's composition and *chiaroscuro,* he had added, as a rider, this element of Sublimity – one of the most typical artistic criteria of his time and country.

It had not been easy. His preliminary studies show how painstakingly he had experimented with possibilities for this dramatisation.[6] But the end-result was so gratifying that he repeated the pattern time and again. His *Calais Pier, with French Poissards Preparing for Sea; an English Packet Arriving* (1803) shows the same 'Sublime' situation in the near-collision between an outward-bound French fishing-boat and an incoming English ferry. Only, now he also added the diametrically opposed motif of the 'Ridiculous' – which was expressed in a clumsy *'poissard'* attempting with one oar to save his little lugger from being smashed against the pier, while his woman is handing down a bottle of presumably 'Dutch courage'.

Turner had evidently been seduced by the principle that *'One step above the Sublime makes the Ridiculous; and one step above the Ridiculous makes the Sublime again'*[7]*;* it was the equivalent of the well-known *'du sublime au ridicule il n'y a qu'un pas'* which he may well have picked up in 1802 when studying the Louvre exhibits on his first continental visit during a short peace with revolutionary France. The Sublime-cum-Ridiculous motif became a favourite formula of a side of Turner that, at bottom, was deeply pessimistic about human endeavour – a trait which was also responsible for the frequency of caricatured staffage in his pictures and for his long, unfinished poem on the *Fallacies of Hope.*[8]

By now another aspect, too, had made its appearance, viz. that of a political message derived from past or present Dutch history. Like *Calais Pier* (which was painted when a resumption of the war was already on the cards), *Fishing-Boats Entering Calais Harbour,* his second picture of the port most frequented by travellers wanting the shortest possible time at sea, graphically asked his audience by implication *'How close to the wind can the British afford to sail?'* – in their dealings with Napoleon.

In this vein Turner painted *Boats Carrying out Anchors and Cables to Dutch Men-of-War, in 1665* (1804). With its explicit historical reference to former disastrous English complacency (the 1667 Dutch raid on the Medway), this spelt out the warning that, like the seventeenth-century Dutch, the nineteenth-century French might also refit their invasion-fleet a good deal sooner than expected: complacency after some initial successes in the resumed war might be fatal.

As a picture, and perhaps understandably, it did not on the whole meet

J.M.W. Turner, 'Antwerp'. *Waterloo and Rhine* sketchbook, 1817. (TB. CLX, p. 17). Tate Gallery, London.

with a favourable reception. The one that did was *Dutch Boats and Fish-market* (1807) with its remarkably integrated echoes of Cuyp, Van de Capelle, Van de Velde and Teniers. The original title was *Sun Rising Through Vapour, Fishermen Cleaning and Selling Fish* and its special interest lay in Turner's rendering of peaceful morning-mist seen from a beach on which a Dutch low-life scene, complete with – at dawn! – unlikely wine-swilling, created a contrast which forcefully demonstrated how the Burkean 'Beautiful', and not only the 'Sublime', could also be '*one step above the Ridiculous*'.

It was to be another decade before Turner actually set foot on Dutch soil. This happened at Ostend (present-day Belgium and Luxembourg having been joined to the old Dutch Republic in 1814 to form the new 'Kingdom of the United Netherlands'). The occasion was his wish to produce a counterblast to the chauvinistic compositions submitted in the then competition for a 'Grand Historical Painting' commemorating the Battle of Waterloo.

Swamped by publishers' orders for engravings, it was not until August 1817 that he was free to cross over and, sketching all the way, reach the battlefield via Ghent, Bruges and Brussels.[9] In one day he made sixteen sketches on the spot, some quite moving in their inscriptions of e.g. '*4,000 killed here*' or '*Hollow where the great carnage took place of the Cuirassiers by the Guards*'. In the meantime, a trip to Waterloo had become a kind of pilgrimage for gloating battlefield tourists.

What Turner painted after his return, therefore, was not a Paean of Glory but an Elegy of Grief. Based on a sketch of the fortified manor-house with the inscription '*Gate of Hougomont forced 4 times*'[10], *The Field of Waterloo* (1818) depicted the site on the evening after the battle with women searching by torch-light for their nearest and dearest in a heap of corpses.[11] The background is formed by the burning ruins of a place whose holding had been the hinge, as Wellington put it, on which the outcome had turned. Behind this the sloping field is lit up by a flare, fired to frighten off rapacious marauders.

In the press, the picture was descried as '*unpatriotic*', '*an abortive attempt*', '*a failure*' etc., and worse. Turner withdrew it and it has only recently been on show again. But the *Waterloo* was not the only fruit of his tour. The other 'Dutch' composition to come out of his 1817 visit was the glorious

The Kingdom of the United Netherlands, 1814-1839, with Turner's routes in 1817 and 1825. When travelling to Switzerland and Italy he also passed through a number of times in transit (British Library, London).

201

J.M.W. Turner, *The Field of Waterloo*. 1818. Canvas, 147.5 x 238.8 cm. Tate Gallery, London.

J.M.W. Turner, 'Scheveningen Beach'. *Holland* sketchbook, 1825 (TB. CLXII, p. 35). Tate Gallery, London.

Dordrecht. The Dort Packet-Boat from Rotterdam, Becalmed (1818). This picture could be seen as the painter's psychological counterpart to the former, each embodying one of the two Burkean notions.

What had happened was that, after his harrowing day on the battlefield, Turner had travelled on to Cologne and up the – pictorially newly discovered – Rhine to Mainz. Having gone down-stream again he had then traversed Belgium back to Antwerp for the coach-service to Rotterdam in order to 'do' Holland next. He went as far as Amsterdam, returned via Utrecht and Dordrecht, and finally embarked at Rotterdam for his sail home.

Conceiving and producing *The Field of Waterloo* in his studio during the euphoria that had taken possession of British minds must have been a veritable *tour de force*. Only a few poets such as Coleridge, Southey, and Byron had expressed in verse what had driven Turner to do the same on canvas and present a fiercely anti-war picture. To the death-obsessed painter of the *Waterloo* the memory of the sun-drenched peacefulness of Holland's rivers could not have been more different. The material for these pictures was contained in the *Waterloo and Rhine* and the *Dort* sketchbooks[12]; but their spirit could only have been rediscovered in what each time his sketches must have recalled for him both of the *genius loci* and of the essence of his most beloved Dutch Master: Aelbert Cuyp.

J.M.W. Turner, *Dordrecht. The Dort Packet-Boat from Rotterdam, Becalmed.* 1818. Canvas, 157.5 x 233 cm. Yale Centre for British Art, New Haven (CT).

Turner's fabulous memory, and the associative function he used it for, again come out strongly in the third picture painted after this tour, his *Entrance of the Meuse, Orange Merchant Going to Pieces on the Bar* (1819) with the singular addition of *Brill Church Bearing S.E. by S., Maesensluys E. by S.*. The composition shows once more a combination of the 'Sublime' (people desperately trying to leave the shipwreck) and the 'Ridiculous' (scavengers eagerly trying to salvage oranges from the merchant vessel's cargo). But the message was undeniably political.

In 1819 King William I of Orange, formerly a refugee in London and soon dubbed the 'Merchant-King' for his eagerness to fund industrialisation in his new state, had sustained heavy losses when the Bank of England went off the gold standard. This pained friends of Holland and resulted in financial rescue attempts. It was all recorded in the media – as was also the actual wrecking on the South coast of a trader carrying oranges. On his way home, Turner's ferry would have passed one or more wrecks on the dangerous Meuse shoals off the Hook. Someone would have enlightened him about their position. This information Turner was now happy to use in order, on the strength of his own sketches, to make unassailable the credibility of his unusual composition.

Fully eight years later, in 1825, he toured the Dutch Kingdom again. The resulting *Holland* and *Holland, Meuse and Cologne* sketchbooks are filled with an astonishing wealth of impressions of towns, people, and above all of inland shipping.[13] In the intermediate years his output had gone from strength to strength. His annual summer-trips took him to France, Germany, Switzerland and especially Italy, and his pictures covered a wide range of themes, either narrative or purely descriptive, inspired by what he registered

J.M.W. Turner,
The Rotterdam Ferry-Boat.
1833. Canvas, 92.7 x 123.2
cm. National Gallery of Art,
Washington D.C.

– or found clamoured for by his patrons. But the memory of Dutch light and Dutch art remained with him always, as his lectures as the Academy's Professor of Perspective since 1811 abundantly – and poetically – prove.[14]

A new series of Dutch-inspired canvases appeared between 1827 and the early 1830s. The Low Countries were increasingly in the news, developments in Belgium clearly leading to a conflict which in fact broke out in the summer of 1830. In Turner's oeuvre this brought another wave of interest in Dutch Old Masters, producing a skilful Rembrandt-fantasy, *Rembrandt's Daughter* (1827) and a striking marine, provocatively titled *Port Ruysdael* (1827) and based on his old *Studies in the Louvre* sketchbook. Then came the curious, very Rembrandtesque *Pilate Washing his Hands* (1830).

From the same period date the first two of the painter's four beautiful *Admiral Van Tromp* pictures, a series of historical seapieces culminating in 1832 in *The Prince of Orange, Embarked from Holland and Landed at Torbay, November 4 1688, after a Stormy Passage* (1832) and *Helvoetsluys, the City of Utrecht, 64, Going to Sea* (1832) portraying one of the Prince's flagships leaving their naval base. The series was rounded off by two intriguing river-views, *The Rotterdam Ferry-Boat* (1833) and *Antwerp. Van Goyen Looking out for a Subject* (1833).

The background to this spate of Dutch compositions was the painter's feeling, shared with more than one of his Whig friends, that the new Dutch Kingdom was being left in the lurch by Whitehall which, for purely political reasons, had been largely responsible for its creation in the first place. The pictures' messages were loud and clear: '*Fellow-Britons, think what we owe to Dutch initiative in the past; those Dutch Masters are as essential to*

J.M.W. Turner, *Antwerp. Van Goyen Looking out for a Subject.* 1833. Canvas, 91.8 x 122.9 cm. Frick Collection, New York.

the evolution of our art as the Glorious Revolution was to our democracy, right up to the present!'

In the meantime, the outcome of the Belgian conflict, secession, was becoming inevitable. Turner must have felt this, too, as may be witnessed by his pair of river-pieces. In both *The Rotterdam Ferry-Boat* and *Antwerp. Van Goyen Looking out for a Subject,* the central vessels, although expertly painted, provide food for thought. The former shows a small sail-boat carrying only women and children across the Meuse while a huge merchantman is bearing down on them and a seventeenth-century warship lies at anchor behind them; the latter shows the Scheldt with a boeier-yacht, identified by the (historically impossible) initials 'V G' on her stern and prominently carrying a figure in a plumed hat: evidently the Dutch Master who is known to have indeed sketched at Antwerp.

Since it had proved senseless to try and preserve the new Kingdom of the United Netherlands, what should be secured, Turner seems to suggest in the *Ferry-Boat,* is a future with the instruments of war immobilised, commerce forging ahead, and the people safe in the Dutch market. At the same time, in Rotterdam's Belgian counterpart, *Antwerp,* political independence could and should once more reunite artists from North and South, in a shared Low Countries culture.

After an interval of another eleven years, Turner for the last time painted Dutch pictures. In 1844 he exhibited *Van Tromp Going about to Please his Masters, Ships a Sea, Getting a Good Wetting,* then *Fishing Boats Bringing a Disabled Ship into Port Ruysdael* and finally *Ostend.*

The message of the *Van Tromp* (with anachronistic initials in his burgee)

J.M.W. Turner, *Ostend.*
1844. Canvas, 92.9 x 123.2
cm. Neue Pinakothek,
Munich.

was clear: no war hero should sulk and refuse to serve his country – a reference to Cornelis Tromp's quarrel with De Ruyter, patched up in 1672, the
Dutch 'Year of Disaster' – and presumably aimed at the aged Wellington.
In the second *Port Ruysdael* picture, a wrecking has apparently been
avoided and the situation promises salvage money to whoever will lead the
big 'disabled ship' to a safe haven. As for the *Ostend,* the little sailboat at
the centre will evidently succeed in clearing the dangerous pier on her lee
and, after a timely gibe, be able to follow the other boats – likewise to safety.

   In each of these, the mood seems one of dogged determination to survive;
but each could also be called a 'return picture'. Did the 69-year-old painter
imagine himself as a man in need of reconciliation with his critics and a
return to his artistic roots? Did he feel himself physically, if not spiritually,
'disabled'? In his prime the sight of a Dutch image had 'made him a painter'.
In mid-life Ostend had literally been for him the gateway to the land that had
enabled him to 'flesh out' a Dutch connection that his oldest *guru* at the
Royal Academy had wanted to be a 'school' for artistic expression in the
way a Grammar School was for linguistic expression. Turner's language
had soon acquired many modes. But what it all adds up to is that, precisely
because of his seeming abuse of great models and mistakes in historical
detail, the limited number of pictures that make up his 'Dutch connection',
spread out as they are over his entire oeuvre, demonstrates all the better the

importance for him of 'Holland'. But then, when towards the end of his life he would still receive the odd visitor on his home-made roof-terrace in Chelsea, he would point inland saying *'My English prospect'* and down-river whispering *'My Dutch prospect'*. Could anything be more suggestive – in retrospect?

FRED G.H. BACHRACH

NOTES

1. THORNBURY, W., *The Life and Correspondence of J.M.W. Turner.* London, 1877, ed. 1970, p. 8.

2. REYNOLDS, J., *Works … Containing the Discourses …[and] A Journey in Flanders and Holland.* London, 1809, vol. 2, pp. 359-64.

3. Willem van de Velde the Younger's picture was *A Rising Gale,* acquired by the Duke of Bridgewater in 1798 (M. Butlin and E. Joll, *The Paintings of J.M.W. Turner.* London, 1977, pp. 11-12).

4. See note 1; the mezzotint was engraved by Kirkall and printed in green ink in 1724.

5. FINBERG, A.J., *The Life of J.M.W. Turner.* London, 1961, p. 71.

6. See his *Calais Pier* sketchbook (TB. LXXXI, pp. 106/7, 108/9, 122/3, and 126/7)

7. See his *Cockermouth* sketchbook (TB. CX, p. 1) in which he copied the phrase from Tom Paine, *The Age of Reason.* London, 1795, Pt. II, p. 20.

8. WILTON, A., 'Sublime or Ridiculous? Turner and the Problem of the Historical Figure', *New Literary History,* vol. 16, pp. 343-376. Also CHUMBLEY, A. and T. WARRELL, *Turner and the Human Figure.* London, 1989, pp. 7-11.

9. See his *Itinerary Rhine Tour* sketchbook (TB. CLIX)

10. See the *Waterloo and Rhine* sketchbook (TB. CLX, pp. 17-26).

11. In the catalogue Turner quoted the line *'Rider and horse, friend and foe, in one red burial blent'* from Byron's *Childe Harold's Pilgrimage.* London, 1816 (Canto III, stanza 28).

12. The *Dort* sketchbook (TB. CLXII) also contains numerous views of Rotterdam and other places in the area.

13. TB. CCXIV and CCXV.

14. DAVIES, M., *Turner as Professor* (Tate Gallery exh. cat.). London, 1992.

FURTHER READING

BACHRACH, FRED, *Turner's Holland* (Tate Gallery exh. cat.). London, 1994.

BUTLIN, M. and E. JOLL, *The Paintings of J.M.W. Turner.* London / New Haven, 1977, 2 vols.

FINBERG, A.J., *A Complete Inventory of the Drawings of the Turner Bequest.* London, 1909, 2 vols.

WILTON, ANDREW, *Turner Abroad.* London, 1982.

ooking

for the Other Self

The Work of Kristien Hemmerechts

In a relatively short time Kristien Hemmerechts (1955-) has become one of the most prominent of her generation of authors, a large group who are innovative in different fields. In the second half of the eighties, that group brought a long period of impasse and hesitancy in Flemish literature to an end. In 1990 Kristien Hemmerechts received the three-yearly State Prize for prose, the official literary recognition bestowed by the Flemish Community, for her novel *Broad Hips* (Brede heupen, 1989). She was one of the youngest authors ever to have been awarded that prize. Every new novel or collection of short stories she publishes, without exception, remains on the list of best-selling books for weeks, and she often appears in the media, as author, literary critic, or spokeswoman for the emancipation of women on both the social and the personal level. When she was studying English she found that her teachers did not pay much attention to the great contribution made by women authors to literature written in that language all over the world. She is trying to remedy this in the course on the short story she teaches at the Catholic University in Brussels. In a short biographical note for a brochure put together by her publisher she writes: *'I know it was important for me to be intensively engaged with texts written by women. I don't know if there is such a thing as a specifically feminine style. I do know, though, that the writings of women often inspire me more than those of men, and that reading their work helped me find my own voice.'*

Hemmerechts was born in Grimbergen, a small town on the edge of Brussels, and studied in Brussels, Leuven, Amsterdam and Cambridge where Malcolm Bradbury, the novelist and academic, encouraged her to write. Her first three stories, written in English, appeared in the series *First Fiction*, published by Faber and Faber. They were later translated into Dutch. In 1986 she was awarded her Ph. D. with a dissertation on the work of the British writer Jean Rhys, author of *Wide Sargasso Sea* (1966) and other novels.

The influence of her intensive study of literature written in English, and especially of the short story in which she excels, is obvious in her first novel, *A Pillar of Salt* (Een zuil van zout, 1987). In that novel a young woman, Anna, returns to her parents' house from Amsterdam after her father's death.

Her father has left newspaper clippings lying around all over the house. Anna tries to sort them because she wants to write a paper about them to try to reconstruct the image of a period. Anna is pregnant with the child of an American globetrotter, but she rejects a well-organised family life of the kind her sister has made for herself. Although such a life offers more certainties, it fails to offer greater satisfaction and it ends up in the type of life led by her grandmother, who spends her days in an old people's home, blind and listless. During one of her visits to her grandmother Anna, who occasionally takes a bath in the home, unexpectedly gives birth. The baby is stillborn. Afterwards the grandmother appears to have turned into stone.

Even though gripping events take place in this story, there are no emotional peaks. This makes the subtle game with symbols all the more obvious. There is the cycle of being born and dying that is rounded off in the home, but also immediately broken off – there is no vision of any future. There are also the different shapes in which water appears in this story: drinking water, rain water, bath water, amniotic fluid … water that gives solace, purification, life. There is finally, most obviously, the quest, without success, for the method that made her father put the newspaper clippings in what were obviously carefully selected places. This quest might bring an order of its own into Anna's life, provide it with the sense she is now forced to find. She suspects the solution is in her father's study, but she does not dare enter it, for fear she might discover that, to quote Shakespeare, there really was no 'method' in his 'madness' after all, and that he died at his wits' end, unable to fathom the meaning of life, unable to view it as a coherent whole.

The central theme in Kristien Hemmerechts' work is that of the relationship between people, between parents and children, brothers and sisters, spouses and lovers. Not infrequently these people remain at a distance from each other, and that distance is not easily bridged, in spite of various forms of intimacy. Parents are often expected to be able to answer the crucial questions of life which plague their grown-up children. In the very moving story 'Back' ('Terug') from the collection *Long Ago* (Lang geleden, 1994), a daughter spends a week with her parents – and without her partner – at their holiday home in the South of France. The daughter measures the relationship between her parents against that of James Joyce and Nora Barnacle – she happens to be reading a biography of the latter. She also compares her mother to Nora and to herself: two older women who have found certain answers, she thinks, as opposed to a third who still finds herself in the stage of complete confusion. The father has also ordered his life around fixed principles and rituals (*'On the way to the beach he picks up litter and carries it with him till he finds a litter bin, even if it is really filthy litter'*). For the parents the roads have been mapped, the river-beds eroded, and what they managed to get out of life turns out to be rather modest. When the daughter looks across the chasm between herself and her parents she becomes melancholic.

Structurally Kristien Hemmerechts often confronts extremes with each other in this way: life and death, hope and failure, with a turning-point that is just as often situated off-screen, outside the boundaries of the actual story. It is impossible to fathom the mechanism, the process that brings about that turning-point. What goes wrong between hope and failure, between a sense of enterprise and final resignation, remains opaque. The writer investigates reality by registering it, but she keeps a certain modest distance from the unknowable, the unfathomable of what drives people and defines their lives.

The father figure is among the most obviously recurrent characters. Sometimes he is dead or absent, which causes a sense of something missing, a lack of direction, and vague nostalgia in the children as they are growing up. In *Broad Hips* Laura, the secretary, never knew her father because he died in an accident. As a result she allows surrogate fathers to define her life for her. She had worked in London for a month and met a man there who treated her as his daughter. She allows her boss to shape her into what he thinks is a modern woman as if he were another Pygmalion, selecting hair-does, make-up, lingerie, expensive dresses, high heels for her. He regularly takes her to a blindingly white hotel room after a dietetically responsible meal and has distant sex with her. He later complains that she remains so indifferent to him.

In most cases, however, fathers refuse to play their parts: the father of Laura's little daughter, for instance, leaves her just before the birth. Women suffer more from life in Hemmerechts' stories, everyday life weighs more heavily on them than on men, hence the use of 'broad hips' as a symbol. But even though they are vulnerable and uncertain, they also appear to be able to fight back. In their striking resignation they are able to cope with a life that is not very inspiring.

Another very incisively drawn character is that of the protagonist's sister who is in an institution. When Laura's sister Elza, who is two years older than the protagonist, is admitted to a psychiatric institution, family life with her mother and two brothers is put under severe strain. Elza has always been prettier and more successful than Laura, but in her youth she always came to Laura for protection against her fears. In another story, 'Little Child and Orange, Orange and Little Child', ('Kindje en Appelsientje, Appelsientje en Kindje'), from *Long Ago,* Kristien Hemmerechts evokes youth and the symbiotic relationship between two sisters, one of whom is very fickle and domineering. They have such a symbiotic relationship that one of them, now a young woman, identifies with her sister when she visits her in the institution to which she has been admitted after pathological behaviour. As if inspired by telepathy, she feels there is something wrong in the institution and she does, indeed, stumble on a dehumanising scene. Then she thinks, about herself: *'This room is her whole life. This is her life and if she ever doubted it she knows it now: this is it and she has to accept it, she has to embrace it. All the rest is smoke and mirrors.'* This character most strongly embodies the protagonist's fear of loss of control and degeneration in the face of life, the unfathomable, and personal emotional instability.

Hemmerechts' most recent novel, *Many Women, a Man Now and Then* (Veel vrouwen, af en toe een man, 1995), also features two sisters. In this case the author adopts the point of view of the more unstable of both sisters. The life of this character is compared to the lives of women of two generations ago. Once again this is a novel which examines the concepts of identity and personality; it deals with the impotence of women – in different times and under changing circumstances – to free themselves of emotional inhibitions and obstacles, and to be happy in an unrestricted way.

In the novel *White Sand* (Wit zand, 1993) the characters move around in

a general atmosphere of growing loss of control, dismay and despair. Paul and Elisabeth, mature lovers, spend a weekend in a hotel on the coast in Northern France. When it's over, Elisabeth goes back home. She idealises her father and she is always preoccupied with herself. As a result, her children feel emotionally abandoned. Paul, who has no children, gets involved with murky social situations in and around the hotel: the owner's handicapped child, who dies in an accident after falling down the basement stairs, or a single mother in the neighbourhood. The characters are weighed down by the emotional burden of their past: they always appear to be looking for something to hold on to, for a kind of constancy in their lives. The underlying tone of the characters' hopeless expectations in a disjointed world gives the novel a sombre timbre indeed.

The greatest thematic constant in Kristien Hemmerechts' prose is the unquenchable longing her characters have for security and for the fulfilment of their emotional desires. The fact that this longing for fulfilment is never actually 'fulfilled', causes a constant gnawing sense of lack in their lives, a lack of satisfaction that makes them wander around disquieted and disoriented and sometimes causes illogical and inexplicable behavior. This sense of lack is most obviously symbolised in Victor's two missing fingers in the novel *Without Boundaries* (Zonder grenzen, 1991). Victor wanted to become a doctor, but he had to break off his training as the result of a stupid accident. The metaphor is further clarified in a key passage in which Victor goes out to buy gloves. Because the novel's chronology is scattered, the passage only occurs toward the end of the book and in that passage the author gives a cynical twist to the whole story of attempts to compensate for what is lacking, of missed opportunities and emotional misunderstandings.

Yet Victor is not the main character in this novel; the three women who surround him are. Two of these women are his wife Petra and his daughter Emilia who are looking for a new meaning for their lives in travel and work abroad after the divorce and subsequent disintegration of the family. The third woman is Hannah Prat, a seedy revolutionary who exerts a peculiar attraction on the bourgeois Victor. She moves around in a secret world full of signs, rituals, and dreams, in caves, holes, corridors, and slums in the city, a kind of underworld that is a symbol for the uncontrolled, the unfathomable, and the unreasonable in man, the dark side of the personality, at once fascinating and a little frightening. Through his relationship with her, Victor makes contact, in a strange way, with a part of his personality he has never been able to define before. She opens a door for him to a world whose existence he had only suspected, to a non-defined longing that was never satisfied in successive previous relationships with women, in short: to his other self. Using this character, Kristien Hemmerechts clarifies the motivations driving many protagonists in her work.

Kristien Hemmerechts' prose has a strongly Anglo-Saxon character. That is no accident: through deep study she has taken over the sober, realistic, and at the same time psychologically revealing style of, say, Jean Rhys and Katherine Mansfield. Her emotionless style, full of suggestions and understatements, does indeed strike the reader, as does the special attention she devotes to plot, character, and the structuring of narrative elements. This creates the impression that her characters have no emotional ups and downs, that they submit to their lives with a certain sense of resignation, and that they do not have a grip on the world around them.

But one can also recognise methodological features of Virginia Woolf's work in that of Kristien Hemmerechts, although those features are much less obvious. They surface in the treatment of chronology and consciousness. Thematically Kristien Hemmerechts' work is reminiscent of the female awareness in the work of Margaret Drabble, and of the undirected investigation of the psychology of mainly solipsistic characters in the novels of Iris Murdoch. There is also a degree of affinity with authors like Jenny Diski and Alan Hollinghurst. But Kristien Hemmerechts reworks all these real or imagined influences into a literature that is outspokenly of our time, a time without moral bearings, a time of uncertainty, superficiality, splintering and seediness, which causes great emotional lack of fulfilment. Against this background she puts people into poignant psychological situations, surrounded by questions about their identity, about the content of their life and its meaning, seized by a vague fear of advancing time and death, and longing for the fulfilment of their lives that are full of contingencies and short-lived, indifferently conducted relationships. They look at life with a great lack of understanding and a great sense of wonder; they find it hard to emerge from the confusion in which it appears to them, and they only do so with limited success. In their lack of control and their failure to view life as a coherent whole, they testify to a very 'postmodern' powerless sense of life. The representation of their wry sense of uneasiness in a world full of disjointed dimensions leads to a reading experience that is at the same time fascinating and profoundly disquieting.

JOS BORRÉ
Translated by André Lefevere.

Kristien Hemmerechts
(1955-) (Photo by Filip
Claus).

Extract from 'Back'
by Kristien Hemmerechts

A woman is spending a week in the South of France with her parents. She is reading a biography of Nora Barnacle, James Joyce's wife, and occasionally thinking of her husband back home.

Something I love: showing my mother the blouse I have just bought and both of us feeling the material. We let it glide between our fingers with a gesture which in some countries is used to indicate that something is expensive. If you ask me it's got acrylic in it, says my mother. No, no, I say, it's viscose. Yes, says my mother, but they mess around with viscose a lot. She looks for the label. One hundred per cent viscose, it says. My mother looks doubtful. She is not at all convinced. I prefer wearing viscose, I say firmly. It's a natural product, made of wood fibre. The pronouncement makes little impact. Cotton is still the best thing to wear, she says. Are those buttons sewn on properly? Probably not, I say, deflated. My mother tugs gently at a button. Not as bad as you might think, she says, those machines have improved a lot in the last few years. Just give me all your things with buttons on, and I'll put in an extra stitch to secure them. Officially my mother is supposed to have arthritis in her fingers. Sometimes she cannot hold a needle.Sometimes she herself suggests sewing on buttons.

It is odd how I gradually forget him and see only her. She is the core. If he were not there she would behave in exactly the same way. What he would do, I have no idea. What clothes would he wear? What would he eat? He does odd things, like standing on his head for minutes on end at the side of the swimming pool. Daddy, you're an exhibitionist. Darling, I've been doing this all my life. It's very good for you. You're still an exhibitionist, I say. On the way to the beach he picks up litter and carries it with him till he finds a litter bin, even if it is really filthy litter. That's the boy scout in him, the man who keeps himself and his surroundings clean. On the beach he sometimes reminds me of a Roman senator. He stands looking out to sea with a towel around him. Daddy, why are you standing there with that towel wrapped around you in that silly way? Darling, it's very hot today, you have to be careful you don't burn. His skin is dark brown. No, no, he doesn't want any suntan oil, the towel will protect him. After his swim he washes himself on the terrace with a bucket of water. When he has lathered himself all over, he empties the bucket over himself. Then he goes and stands on his head for a bit longer. (Wouldn't this kind of psychology be neat: she flirted a lot and liked giving men the come-on because her father regularly stood on his head, and in public too, which he possibly liked most of all?) The best tactic, says my mother, is to ignore his little eccentricities, even when he says things like: There's no respect for trees these days. In the dead of night their Swiss neighbour cut back the trees that were blocking his view, without first asking the permission of the owners of the trees. To make matters worse, he did not prune them but had the temerity to chop them down to half-size. In the old days that would have been inconceivable, says my father, people had respect for trees then. That is how he talks: one man does something, and he concludes that everyone does it. There's a malaise, he says. And he calls it typical of the spirit of the age. An ill omen. The writing on the wall.

But the trees are not what it's about. It's about my fear of the severity of his judgement. One of the things he confides to me is: I would never have wanted to try anything on with any woman except your mother. You have to put not just your penis into a woman like that, but all your intellectual energy too, says my father. My father is fond of quips. When I suggest that there are a few fascinating women around besides Mummy, he looks sceptical. I suspect he does not think much of me either, compared to her.

The Joyces were not strict at all with their children. When there were problems, they blamed the outside world. Low marks at school: school no good. That kind of parent. They spoiled each other too, 'Indulged' says the biography. 'They indulged one another.' He let her buy the hats and clothes she dreamed of, she never carried out her threat of walking out if he went on drinking so heavily. They were a couple, and pretty possessive about each other. No one else was allowed to call him 'Jim'. (I wonder if Lucia thought: You and your Jim, *your* Jim, he's my Jim too, my father.)

She talks a lot. She talks non-stop. Moves noisily about the house. When she takes a siesta, she'd like everyone to take one. This week teaches me how

I've grown used to silence, even though I don't live alone. It is the only thing I find a problem here: the fact that the conversations start off at breakfast time, heated conversations on subjects on which we all have different views. As a starting signal, my father announces the main points of the news, and everyone has their say. As always I am caught up in this, even though I find the exchange of views exhausting. The Mule Family, I think, because none of us will give an inch. We're convinced that we're right. Can't keep quiet.

Later I sit at the bottom of the garden against the umbrella pine and think: It'll be quiet when she dies. I imagine sitting at her deathbed and saying: Sleep now, relax, everything's all right, no one will hurt you any more, no, you don't have to tell me what once happened or what you were frightened of in that stuffy little house, my God, I've slept there too, had nightmares there too, your mother, her mother … My eyes fill with tears, so vivid is the picture of this mournful deathbed scene. Be my child now, I whisper, relax, let yourself go, be my baby so you can die, but you put up a fight, you struggle, you wrestle with it, what am I thinking of, and sure enough, two seconds later there you are in front of me with your shopping bag, alive and kicking. Do I need anything from the shop?

No. Do you mind if I don't come?

Of course not.

I close my eyes and see Nora Barnacle sweeping past like a sailing ship. Her bosom is imposing and she has an enormous hat on. At her side are a skinny, indecisive man and a surly-faced girl. The biggest problem whenever they moved house were Nora's hats. There were boxes for them but they got lost, so new boxes had to be bought each time.

Perhaps, I suddenly think, my mother once wanted to be a woman like that, perhaps she thought she should at least give it a try. Her own mother was a bit like that. When she visited us she wore an astrakhan coat and hat, and lots of gold and rings. These are women who have invested their whole lives in these status symbols of successful spousehood. My mother has little interest in fur or astrakhan. She explains to me how the first coins originated in Lydia and the techniques used to try to determine the date of the *Odyssey*. Then she gets carried away.

Nora Barnacle was not a slave to her Jim. For example, she did not type his manuscripts, or keep his correspondence up to date. But she identified completely with the masculine point of view. It was she who had joined her fate to that of James Joyce, and not the other way round. In her vision of the world men were more important than women, whatever the size of their hats. But Lucia was more intelligent than her dull brother. How could she believe that he was more important than her?

I was at a party with my mother once and heard a woman say to her: Female solidarity has meant a lot to me. Whereupon my mother – without a trace of irony – asked: What's female solidarity?

After Lucia Joyce was committed to a mental institution, Nora never saw her again. In the period leading up to the committal, she had become a danger to her mother. Nora had struck Lucia occasionally, but Lucia openly assaulted her mother. Who was jealous of whom? Did Lucia also want a writer to note down her childhood memories, and incorporate her love letters in his novels, down to leaving out the punctuation? If she could not have her Daddy, did she want someone who could compete with him? Is that why she fell hopelessly in love with Samuel Beckett? Do-it-yourself psychology.

Whatever happens to the children, says my mother, it's always the mother's fault. She says: the mother always gets the blame.

Three pearls, I think, one for each nipple, one for my clitoris, like that, with nothing else on, I'll lie in bed and wait for you. The nicest thing of all would be a letter from you asking me to adorn myself for your visit with three choice pearls.

Going away from you does not help. Quite the reverse. (On the few occasions when Nora and Jim were separated from each other by force of circumstance, they wrote each other randy letters. How long would I have to stay away before I got a letter like that from you?)

In the months preceding her eventual committal, Lucia Joyce displayed great sexual boldness. She sat on the lap of a total stranger and unzipped his fly. Then she burst out laughing.

Tell me, Mummy, when you're on your deathbed, what it is that made you afraid. Why are you closed as tight as an oyster, so that I look and listen to you without ever discovering who you are, what you really think? What is it that you are anxiously keeping secret? You say: Why do you want to know that? Why do you refuse to believe that there's nothing to know? And if there were anything to know, she says after a brief silence in my imaginary deathbed scene, would you really want to know it?

My daughter says: Listen, Mummy, it's very simple: on one side there are words, on the other side things. For instance, there's the word 'dog', and then there's the thing 'living creature with four legs, fur and a wet nose', and the two go together. I envy her that no-nonsense view of things, but maybe she's right.

Take the word 'foot'. My father admires his feet, thinks they are the best part of his body, they are not only well-shaped feet, but feet that can carry him for miles. They don't make feet like that any more, he says. I've got very difficult feet, says my mother. Look, not an ounce of fat on them and so narrow, I can seldom find a shoe to fit me. Her mother has 'unfortunate' feet: feet with bumps which push her shoes out of shape and make walking difficult. Though my mother does not have 'unfortunate' feet, like her mother, she cannot wear shoes without socks. In the summer they wear 'hosettes'. I have never known anyone else who wore hosettes, somewhere there must be a factory producing hosettes just for my mother and grandmother. Hosettes are flesh-coloured and cover your toes and ankles. They are edged with elastic. You pull them over your toes at the front and stretch them over your ankle at the back. Somehow foldable, translucent rain hoods belong with hosettes. Never leave home without them. Unbelievably convenient: weighs nothing, takes up no room in your handbag and your hair never gets wet. For years my mother went on slipping me hosettes and rain hoods in vain. You've got good feet, she says now when she sees me wearing shoes without stockings or hosettes. But what can you expect with feet like mine: not an ounce of fat. There's no fat on my feet either, I say indignantly.

Be smart in life, says my mother, popping a rain hood into her bag. A thousand-and-one tricks for outwitting life. For not getting caught out.

Man: no wet nose, no fur, two legs, sometimes three. Never let him leave home on three legs. Be smart.

The day before I leave the inevitable question comes: Do you miss him?

Yes, but I didn't want to talk about it. I wanted to be with the two of you. But now she asks questions and I answer. One of the things I say is: I hope he's bought me flowers. Later, when I get back from the beach, there is a bouquet lying on the table for me. If he's forgotten about flowers, she says, then you'll have had some anyway. She has got my father to write a few lines on a card. Yes, it's been a very good week. We dare not look at each other, otherwise we'll start snivelling.

They see me to the bus. My mother is wearing her straw hat, not the one she can fold up and put in her bag, but a larger one with a ribbon. She is wearing a full green dress and blue shoes. She looks young, radiant, happy that the week has been such a success. We agree not to say goodbye, we say cheerio as if I'm going shopping. So I get a shock when after buying my ticket I take a window seat and see him standing there, as though wanting to give me an image to remember. Tanned, a little red sun hat, a pink T-shirt, blue checked shorts, hand raised, bye. We are practising farewells. I think: If he hadn't been standing there, I wouldn't have cried.

Later, when I walk into town for a bit because I am far too early for my train – you'd better get that bus, then you'll be sure of catching your train – she walks ahead of me, behind me, to the left and right of me with her straw hat and her green dress and her shopping bag. The images come closer, merging with each other and with me till she walks right into me. She says: Why are you always trying to understand me? What secret are you trying to get to the bottom of? You and I are the same. I am as much of a closed book as you.

In a baker's I buy two croissants with my last few pence and eat them slowly on the station steps. Shortly I'll be taking the train to the house where he may or may not have put out flowers for me, but for now I sit on the steps and think of the bouquet which I hung to dry on a branch of the umbrella pine. There's no point sticking those flowers in a vase, said my mother, they'll wither just like that. Where did Mummy pick them? No, no, not from people's gardens, she said, I'd never do that, there are lots of flowers by the side of the road. I smile and think: There's no respect for flowers these days. I expect she could see that I didn't believe her. The way she shrugs her shoulders or feigns indignation when we laugh at her because her lies are so transparent. I take the card that she got my father to write out of my bag and read it for the umpteenth time. Then I get up.

From *Long Ago* (Lang geleden. Amsterdam / Antwerp: Atlas, 1994, pp. 10-18)
Translated by Paul Vincent.

Margriet

de Moor's Defeat of Loneliness

Margriet de Moor (1941-) suddenly emerged as a writer at the age of forty-six. Her first book, a collection of seven short stories published in 1988, was acclaimed as a real achievement. Literary critics as well as the reading public hailed a mature author. *Seen from the Back* (Op de rug gezien) was nominated for a well-known literary prize and shortly afterwards it was awarded the *Gouden Ezelsoor* (The Golden Dog-Ear), a prize for the most successful debut of the year. Eighteen months later her second publication, *Double Portrait* (Dubbelportret, 1989), containing three long stories, proved an even greater hit, and won her another prize. And her first novel, *First Grey, Then White, Then Blue* (Eerst grijs dan wit dan blauw, 1991) not only gained her her third successive award, the lucrative, much publicised AKO Prize, but proved to be a public success as well: in less than three years it went through twenty-one printings (135,000 copies). Her most recent novel, *The Virtuoso* (De virtuoos), appeared in 1993. Again the book was nominated for a national prize and again it proved to be a bestseller. Thus, in the course of a few years Margriet de Moor has become one of the best-loved of Dutch novelists. And not only in the Netherlands: her four books have appeared in Germany, where one critic called her *'the darling of the reading public'*, and her first novel has been translated into several languages. The English translation of this novel was on the shortlist for the 1995 *Independent* Foreign Fiction Award.

De Moor's career is all the more remarkable because she makes hardly any concessions to her readership. On the contrary: her work demands a discerning reader because of its complicated structure, but her craftsmanship is such that she creates an impression of natural ease.

A few strongly-held convictions about human existence constitute the basis of her work. The first of these is that it is impossible to go beyond the boundaries of one's own personality, and that consequently everything one assumes or concludes about the views, nature and emotions of other people, or about the situations in which one is involved, is basically no more than purely subjective speculation. Every individual is living in a world of appearances mainly of his own making, groping in vain for some kind of certainty. As a logical consequence of this view of the *condition humaine,* nearly all her stories are presented from one single point of view: that of the protagonist. Only in dialogues, either recollected (and therefore subjectively transformed or even warped), or taking place at the actual moment of telling, is the reader given any insight at all into the views and emotions of other people. And in keeping with this conception, the author refrains from making explicit philosophical or moralising comments on her characters' ways of life or on the course of events. *'The story itself is of my own invention and that is quite enough'*, she once said. It might seem that this solipsistic view of human life should result in a simple, maybe monotonous or even dreary, kind of story-telling. But this is not the case. Her evocation of people, the things they do and the surroundings in which they live, is lively and graphic, and she generally succeeds in avoiding overemphasis or purple patches, so that most of the time the result is natural and convincing. The curious thing is that her characters' ways of life, however out of the ordinary they may be, are invariably credible under the circumstances. For instance, one rarely encounters a story in which the sexual aspects of life are integrated so naturally, even when they occupy a central position, as in *The Virtuoso*.

To enliven the single viewpoint in her work the author uses a blend of explicit and interior monologue, real or imagined dialogue and free indirect style. However, this method could lead to considerable problems in a novel. To avoid these in *First Grey, Then White, Then Blue,* Margriet de Moor applies a method used by Joyce Cary in his two trilogies and by the Flemish author Louis Paul Boon in his novella *Minuet* (Menuet, 1955). The same complex of events is related in four successive parts of the novel by a friend who discovers the dead body of a woman with her husband, who has stabbed her to death, sitting beside her, by the husband himself, by the murdered woman herself, and by the friend's wife. The tragic enigma is not solved – each individual's view has its subjective validity, but, in the end nothing is really cleared up, and even the immediate motive remains a matter of speculation: it is not given to man to fathom his own acts, let alone those of his fellow-creatures. One thing, however, is evident: the husband, and *a fortiori* his wife, are the victims of his uncontrollable and foredoomed urge to master, to absorb, to incorporate, outside reality into his own existence, whether it be the landscape through his paintings, or the life of his wife. In her most recent book, *The Virtuoso,* the author has tried – not entirely successfully – to find a solution for the difficulty of the single viewpoint by inserting an 'Intermezzo' of fifteen pages two thirds of the way through the novel. This serves to tie up a number of loose ends by presenting the life of an old woman, a servant of the family, from the viewpoint of an omniscient author. The fragment provides the reader with the outline of the story and even with events that will take place in later years.

A second principle which underlies Margriet de Moor's stories is her conviction that it is fundamentally impossible for man to live purely in the present. Everything he thinks or does is irretrievably mixed up with, and to a large extent determined by, his past experiences. And again her way of story-telling is a true reflection of her beliefs: continually, and often hardly perceptibly, present and past experiences are intermingled and the reader is expected to make the necessary distinctions. She manages to fuse what is, what has been, and sometimes even what will be, into one inextricable complex; and she does it in a way which is generally convincing.

Margriet de Moor (1941-)
(Photo by Patrick de Spiegelaere).

Despite the fact that the author's conception of human life and its vicissitudes is not all that reassuring, given the inescapable loneliness of man, the impossibility of coming to grips with reality and its ever-elusive appearances among which we are doomed to wander, her stories have an inherent vitality. Her characters are nearly always active, creative even. *'I am certainly not a pessimist'*, the author once said in an interview. And however sad and frustrating the experiences of many of her characters may be, she is undoubtedly right; not only in the case of *The Virtuoso*, which she has dubbed *'a divertimento about lust and beauty'*, but hardly less so in her other work.

Enigmatic as the advent of every good author or artist may be, De Moor's case is special because her books give no indication that she went through a period of apprenticeship. A literary talent was suddenly there, in full bloom.

As a girl, the fourth child in a Roman Catholic family of ten, she had been a voracious reader of bulky novels, but at secondary school she wanted to become a psychologist. Suddenly, however, she decided to become a pianist instead. But she finished her musical education at the Royal Conservatory in The Hague, an institution with a remarkably lively and stimulating artistic and intellectual atmosphere, as a talented singer with a predilection for the Viennese avant-garde repertoire. Her love of music is apparent in the stories 'Variations Pathétiques' and 'Chosen Landscape' ('Verkozen landschap'), in each of which a woman, a piano teacher in the first and a concert singer in the second, is the protagonist, and particularly so in *The Virtuoso*. In this novel about an eighteenth-century Neapolitan opera singer, a castrato, she displays a solid knowledge of all aspects of the art and technique, and also of the *mores* of the period. Of far greater importance, however, is the fact that her musical schooling, together with her intuitive feeling for interrelations, for harmonious parallels, inversions, allusions and oppositions, for changes of mood and tonality, is apparent in her way of writing: she succeeds in transposing these musical structures into her literary work. Maybe De Moor's detailed picture of an illustrious opera star could be interpreted as a kind of compensation, not to say a revenge in a different field, for a personal deficit: although apparently a very good singer, she was excessively nervous when she had to face an audience and consequently never made a successful professional career.

The next formative influence on the future author was her marriage to the sculptor Heppe de Moor: *'He made objects, concrete palpable things'*. She was fascinated by his craftmanship. And that is how she came to look at her own work, later on: as a craft first of all, a professional skill, and not a kind of divinely inspired art. Together with her husband she also organised a *salon* at their home, for which she composed video-portraits of the participating artists.

After some years of studying art history and classical archaeology she wrote a paper on a Greek vase-motif: the god Hermes weighing the souls of Achilles and Hector. Afterwards she said of her own writing: *'I suppose I am like Hermes, searching for a kind of balance between conflicting forces and passions.'*

It is hardly possible to explain creativity or specific artistic talents. The course of any life is determined as much by chance as by inclination, intelligence and intuition, but it may be helpful to know what Margriet de Moor's background was, when at the age of about forty-five she, again, suddenly decided to become an author. A first attempt at writing a novel was a failure, but after that she had apparently found her bearings: *'I like things that are well-constructed. (...) In my view form is the most important aspect of art.'* Her husband's constant struggle with his resistant raw material had also helped to impress her with this essential truth.

One of Margriet de Moor's most characteristic stories is 'Chosen Landscape'. The title is a quotation from Paul Verlaine's poem 'Clair de Lune' – or rather, as the protagonist Mira, a professional singer, says, from a song by Fauré ('Votre âme est un paysage choisi'). When Mira parks her car on the opposite side of the street, coming home after a rehearsal, she sees an unknown woman sitting in her place at the family table. She is struck by the thought that she is standing there, *'observing a scene of everyday happiness, in the sad way of a character from a fairy-tale. As if she wanted to copy its secret. As if she wanted to hide this secret under her coat, never to forget it again, not even when sleeping'*. Confused and disorientated she walks aimlessly through the little town where she lives, clutching her music books to her breast, until at last she gets back to her home and is introduced to the woman who has taken her place at the table.

It appears that the woman, Karin, has taken Mira's little girl home because her husband could not be there on time, and has stayed on to cook a meal for the family. From the very start Mira feels her own personality endangered, invaded, by the other woman, however sincerely interested, kind and helpful she appears to be. At the end of the first chapter Karin leaves Mira's house in her silvergrey sports car: *'Fast as a fish of prey the car shot off into the rain.'* Mira feels that her life is being relentlessly encroached upon. There is no immediate reason for jealousy with regard to her husband, but in spite of an apparently harmonious marriage the situation makes her realise how he has essentially remained a stranger to her: *'She had no idea who he was. Not at the time and not later on. She only knew that her existence apart from him had become inconceivable.'* Even her sense of affinity with her father appears to be based on an illusion. At a certain moment she picks up and sings Schubert's 'Winterreise': *'Fremd bin ich eingezogen, fremd zieh' ich wieder aus'* ('as a stranger I came in, as a stranger I leave again'). It is in her calling and her profession that she finally finds the one and only foothold for the defeat of loneliness: *'With the pianist as a shadow behind her she unhurriedly stepped forward. She bowed and took up her position. She smiled. Small sparks flickered round her ears.'* This is Margriet de Moor all over.

A.L. SÖTEMANN

TRANSLATIONS

First Grey, Then White, Then Blue (Tr. Paul Vincent). London, 1994.
A translation of *The Virtuoso* is in preparation.

Extract from 'Chosen Landscape'

by Margriet de Moor

Having been adopted as a baby by a childless couple, Mira has always felt a close bond with her adoptive father; in her musings his wife, now dead, is called 'Auntie'. In an earlier section of the story she remembers a scene from her childhood:

'Look hard. Try to remember this always.'
Her father had stopped at the bend in the road.
We are at the bend in what we call the Lovely Road. It is the only asphalt road in the village. From here the fields stretch all the way to Haarlem. I look where he is looking. Our eyes see nothing unusual: waves of images and colours in which one can make out a shed, a rectangular haystack or a gate, as the case may be, and suddenly, startlingly close, a cow foaming at the mouth. As usual, I take my time, knowing his hands are gripping the handlebars on either side of me, catching the faint whiff of cigars, the sky is blue and flies are walking across the cow's warm eyeball. Look hard … The moment slips into me, dazzling me, overwhelming my memory so that I will supposedly forget it, will never breathe a word of it, not to my husband, not to my daughter, not to anyone. My three-year-old eyes see that the true nature of the landscape is not the landscape itself.
   Kennst du das Land, wo die Zitronen blühn …

Mira is spending a few days with her father.

Later that evening she took off her shoes and stretched out full-length on the sofa. Under one of the cushions her fingers discovered a volume of poetry without a cover. Languidly, half dreaming, she occasionally read a few lines. It was quiet. She never played records when she was back home. Music was one of the few things that she did not have in common with her father. She heard the soft scratching of his pen. He was sitting at the table writing up his notes on the history of the village during the German occupation. Suddenly the memory surfaced of the time when Auntie had given her a snood with imitation pearls in it: an ill-chosen present more suitable for a schoolmarm, but why should it provoke such a ridiculous, embarrassing flood of tears in her, Mira?

He looked up with a rather dazed expression and said, 'She kept herself going with the thought of a nice sunny chicken coop and a bunch of Barneveld hens which would lay every day.'

At night it blew a gale. She listened. It was the same gale as always. With whistling, slamming, a tin can rolling across the road, the sudden silences filled with snoring on the other side of the wall, warmth, wonderful sleep and then, in the morning when she woke, the intense peace of her parents' house.

They breakfasted in silence. Elbows resting on the table, they read the paper, drank coffee with hot milk and looked out at the fields which lay there like old hessian sacks. At about ten Mira went shopping.

'There was a phone call for you,' said her father when she returned.

With her back to him she went on putting her purchases away.

'A woman,' she said afterwards.

'Yes. Rather harsh voice. She'll ring back later.'

However, when the phone rang a second time she was not even called to it. She heard the voice, quacking like a duck, and her father's reticent answers. His eyes roamed about, occasionally lighting on her for a moment with a vacant look in them. She knew there was something he could not fathom. He could not fathom why he was being told, not once but twice, not to disturb his daughter after all, absolutely no need, a message would suffice. The friend informed him that the new carpet that Mira and Paul had ordered had arrived that morning, it had been no trouble for her to stay in the house for a bit to take receipt of it, it was beautiful, blue-grey with a border of ivory animal figures. Apart from that everything was fine, Jeanne had had a nasty fall in the playground but Mira needn't worry about a thing, there had been plasters and iodine to hand. Finally she inquired about him. His back trouble. How nice it must be to have his daughter back with him.

He put down the receiver in astonishment.

She was standing at the window. He looked at her pale morning face without make-up, her shoulders in the ribbed sweater. She had grown sturdy. There was little left to remind him of the girl of seven he had once found shuffling along the hall, the frightening dream still nestling in her eyes, in her open mouth, heavy and warm. He had stroked her hair, her fat bare feet. She had not been able to put the nightmare into words.

She turned her head towards him.

'That was Karin,' she whispered.

She had been standing at the checkout.

Because she was going to stay with her father for a few days, she wanted to get in all the shopping she needed. She was going to prepare the meals in advance, feed the plants and leave funny notes on her husband's and daughter's pillows. Everything had been planned to perfection. She would leave the car behind; no help from friends would be required. Jeanne's school had restarted, and Mira had found a nice sixteen-year-old girl who was prepared to come and play with the child from three-thirty till dinner time. She could leave with her mind at rest. She needed to go. Paul had said so too. He thought she was seeing ghosts. She thought the world was growing absurder every day.

The young man ahead of her paid for his cigarettes. Now it was her turn. Looking up, she saw the grey car approaching through the spotless plate-glass windows of the supermarket. Instantly her heart started playing up, before she herself had even realised it was happening again and that nothing could be done about it. For some time now a quirk of coincidence had contrived to arrange these meetings almost daily, and God alone knew the reason for the mounting, sickening apathy which rendered her incapable of defending herself against the faint smiles, casual questions, against what might be intense mockery. She no longer slept at night.

As she pushed the trolley forward, she saw the car make a difficult turn, come back and pull up right behind hers. 'This time I won't bat an eyelid!' she thought.

The woman strolled in in her boots. Taking a packet of sugar off the first shelf she passed, she walked round the central display and joined the only customer at the checkout. 'Hey, hello!'

And though Mira kept her lips absolutely still and stared straight ahead, nothing could prevent the other woman from openly checking on how she was intending to provide for her family in the next few days: the white coconut slices, the pear jam and the crackers to brighten up breakfast, the cinnamon rusks to have with tea, the tea itself, lemon-flavoured this time … Under her vigilant gaze Mira's hand placed the items on the moving belt one by one, the chopped chicken for the rice curry, of course they would want to have prawn crackers and cocktail onions with it, then there was the usual supply of milk and, just to be on the safe side, fresh toothpaste and soap … Her movements became slower … The net full of oranges turned out to be torn, and scarlet-faced, almost in tears, she emerged from behind the sweet stand to put the two culprits back with the rest, wasn't it moving, she thought, to see every-thing a man and a little girl needed for their existence displayed like this … She noticed that it was a pleasant distraction for her to see each item stand-ing there for a moment in all its lonely innocence before being assessed for usefulness, price and affection quotient, she noticed that it was if she were seeing these kinds of objects for the last time, she noticed that she had to fight back her tears.

At first they both felt awkward. How fast should she push the wheelchair? She decided to walk at a brisk pace. He had always been a lot taller than any man she knew. Taller and, as the years went by, baggier, more ponderous. They had always been used to walking next to each other. She had never had the grey back of his head in front of her for so long, it was really strange that it reached only to chest height. They had not wasted too many words dis-cussing the blanket, the temperature was near freezing and she had tucked it in up to his waist. Now she was reminded of a stiff old dog in a cart, and the eighteen inches between them was unpleasant: sitting on a child's seat on your father's handlebars, you can feel his breath, the strength of his muscles, your soft hair blows against his chin.

It was about a twenty-minute walk. The last stretch, along the asphalt road, was very easy. There was scarcely any traffic. At this time of year there were no tractors or lorries and the bulb farmers were at home having lunch or abroad on business.

There was the bend. She pushed the wheelchair onto the verge.

Everything was different, of course. There were winter colours now. The muddy pools. The bare bushes between the road and the fields. Bolt upright, with his back to her, her father sat looking straight ahead. She knew he was seeing the same landscape that she was. The fields drawn in pale ink, which no longer extended into infinity, but stopped at the edge of a new estate. The old farm had been done up. A seagull soared around the television mast. She was sure that at this moment he was remembering what she was remem-bering. It had always been like that, they were alike, everyone said so. The way she walked, talked, most of her preferences: she had inherited it all from him. Up to then there had been only one thing which sometimes made her curious: her voice, her addiction to music, which surely could not derive from him … The wind brushed her face, fresh, easy to inhale. Close to them, on the spot where the cow had been, a piece of black agricultural plastic was flapping about … Suddenly it struck her that her love of music might, in some incomprehensible way, be simply a continuation of that one moment back then, when she had looked out over the summer fields with her father. She had grasped it with both hands, that moment, and taken it with her into her later, self-constructed life. A lasting talisman. It came from home.

She squatted beside him.

'Do you remember?'

He gave her a very absent look.

'Do you remember bringing me with you, on the bike?'

His hair was blowing across his forehead. She could see he was cold. He seemed to have little interest in where he was and still less in her question.

'She always liked going to the seaside best,' he said.

She put her arms round him and pressed her face against his gaunt cheek.

'Come on,' she said, pulling the wheelchair onto the road. 'We've got the wind behind us.'

That evening she insisted on him coming to hear her in mid-March.

He was not used to going to concerts. Buying a ticket, sitting in rows, the jostling and public transport afterwards: he disliked all of it. At first he and Auntie had occasionally travelled to concert halls. It had embarrassed all three of them having to meet in a dressing room late in the evening, having to talk about the dress and the lovely voice; she had left home ages ago and saying goodbye at a tram stop in the rain had always left each of them with a vague feeling, something like pathos, like impoverishment, as though their home had been burgled in their absence and as yet they knew nothing about it.

But now she wanted him to come again. When she broached the plan, she was a little drunk. Her glass had kept her father's glass good company. It was late. The scent of havanas hung in the room. She lay drowsily watching him, his look of delight at having found a document he thought he had lost among his papers, and mentioned the evening of Romantic songs. Paul would come and collect him in the car, they would have aisle seats, he would stay over with them afterwards.

He agreed at once and even seemed to be looking forward to it.

'Fine,' he said. 'I'll come.' Then, immediately afterwards: 'And I'd like to go back to Echternach again too, some time.'

She did not understand what he meant, but before she could ask anything, he said in a commanding tone, 'It's bedtime, daughter.'

She left late the following afternoon. She took the bus and then the train; halfway home, when it was already getting dark, it began snowing. Staring at the beautiful tiny flakes, she nodded off for a while. Paul and Jeanne picked her up from the station and all three of them felt like going to a restaurant. It was Friday evening. The few places to eat in the small town were crowded, but they still managed to find one with a couple of tables free. Was it really such a tremendous coincidence that another family – husband, large wife, boy with hunched shoulders – should have hit on the idea of dining out too?

Mira saw them come in, the pleasantly surprised Karin leading the way.

'How was it at your father's? I spoke to him on the phone. He seems like a sweetie.'

Paul looked embarrassed, Mira said nothing, further on a waiter beckoned. The newcomers had no alternative but to go on. However, no one could stop the woman putting out her hand as she went past and stroking the soft curly hair of Jeanne, who had a corner seat.

It was a very tender gesture.

From *Seen from the Back* (Op de rug gezien. Amsterdam: Contact, 1988, pp. 176-182).

Translated by Paul Vincent.

Between

Christendom and Christianity

The Church in Flanders

(Photo by Jean Mil).

A Catholic region of old

Flanders remained a strong and homogeneous Roman Catholic area until
shortly after the Second World War. From the time of the Reformation up
to the French Revolution, Emperor Charles v, Philip ii and the later
Hapsburgs managed to ensure that the Flemish region remained within the
Catholic faith; though not without a struggle. Limburg was part of the
prince-bishopric of Liège until 1795. There had, however, been a tremendous drain on the population in the sixteenth century: a whole elite was put
to death because of its Calvinist inclinations, and between 1585 and 1588
the richer half of the metropolis of Antwerp moved to Amsterdam where it
contributed to the blossoming of the northern Netherlands.

Flanders meanwhile became a powerful bastion of the Counter-Refor-
mation. The episcopate, and in particular the recently formed Jesuit order,
acted forcefully to implement the decrees of the Council of Trent, with pos-

itive results for the intellectual and moral standard of the clergy. Many imposing baroque churches were built in the course of the seventeenth century. There was a strong emphasis on proper religious instruction, particularly for children. The Church was supported in this by great painters like Peter Paul Rubens, and Flanders produced famous missionaries such as Ferdinand Verbiest, who worked as an astronomer at the court in Peking.

Though the Enlightenment influenced a limited group of intellectuals and helped lay the foundations for the sometimes strongly anti-ecclesiastical freemasons' lodges that still exist today, practically the whole population remained Catholic. This was demonstrated partly by the intensity of the school funding controversy (1878-1884), when the Catholics defended their own school network from nationalisation, but also by the fact that Marxist socialism did not take such a firm hold on the workers as it did in Wallonia (the French-speaking part of Belgium). Yet the shilly-shallying of part of the episcopate towards the just demands of the workers prior to the First World War and, even more serious, the at times exasperatingly negative attitude of (in particular) Cardinals Mercier (1906-1921) and Van Roey (1926-1961) towards the aspirations of the Flemish Movement, inflicted deep wounds on the minds of the people and its leaders. Mercier stubbornly opposed a Flemish university: science was only possible in the French language!

The school funding controversy reopened (1954-1958) after the Second World War, a sign that the vast majority of the population was prepared to defend free Catholic education. The controversy resulted in the recognition and financing of this free school network through the 'school pact', whereby the three national parties (Christian Democrats, Socialists and Liberals) reached a compromise settlement which was gradually modified.

When in 1966 the episcopate, led by Cardinal Suenens (1961-1979), rejected the complete 'dutchifying' of the Catholic University in Leuven, the whole of Flanders rebelled. Even schoolchildren sullied the walls of the episcopal palaces with graffiti. The bishops had to give way and the Université Catholique de Louvain (UCL) was founded in Louvain-la-Neuve. Like the Katholieke Universiteit Leuven (KUL), it now has some 25,000 students and cooperation between the two universities has very gradually been restored. In 1968 Pope Paul VI published the encyclical *Humanae Vitae* banning the use of contraceptives. Its cautious interpretation by the episcopate did not prevent the majority of the population distancing itself even further from the Church as an institution.

Yet, despite all this tension, to this day no single ecclesiastical area in the world has established such strong 'Christian' structures; and, though small, it has done much to influence the world far beyond its borders, as the following facts serve to illustrate. Between c.1880 and 1960, Flanders sent thousands of missionaries to every continent; hence the saying: *'Flanders sends out its sons'* (no mention was made of 'daughters', notwithstanding the large number of nuns). The international Catholic employees' organisation, the World Labour Union, and the employers' organisation, UNIAPAC, both have their headquarters in Flanders.

It would be hard to overestimate the influence of the theology faculty of Leuven on Vatican II: Professor Philips was the key figure in the writing of the most important conciliar texts and Bishop De Smedt (Bruges) pushed through the declaration on the freedom of religion. Nowhere is there such a

The Cathedral of Our Lady in Antwerp (1352-1521; dome restored in 1536).

dense network of Catholic educational institutions and Catholic hospitals. Free subsidised education (almost exclusively Catholic) accounts for 65% of all school-goers (1991-1992), while 45% of the welfare institutions come under Caritas Catholica (and as many as 90% of the psychiatric hospitals).

The Christian employees' groups have far-reaching influence: the employees' umbrella organisation (ACW), the tradespeople's organisation (NCMV) and the Farmers' Union (Boerenbond), which defends the interests of farmers, easily surpass their parallel organisations both in number and strength – and thereby influence politics, especially through the Christian People's Party (CVP), which has been the main source of Prime Ministers in recent decades. One example will suffice. Flanders has two large employees' trade unions, the Christian ACV and the Socialist ABVV. In 1991, 68% of all union members belonged to the ACV.

When it comes to women's and youth movements, the relative scale of the Christian organisations is even greater. The three women's movements: KAV (female workers), KVLV (rural women) and CMBV (middle-class women) have a total of some 550,000 members. They joined forces in criticising the apostolic letter *Ordinatio Sacerdotalis* in which Pope John-Paul II endeavoured to put an end once and for all to the discussion about the ordination of women to the priesthood. As regards culture, the long-standing Davidsfonds (formed in 1875) with its some 80,000 members is still very active in almost all municipalities and did much to stimulate the federalisation of Belgium.

In 1995 we can rightly state with the religious sociologist Karel Dobbelaere that 'sociocultural Christianity' has never been stronger. Even if it appears to be declining gradually on a party political level, 'pillarisation' is a fact of life, as it was in the Netherlands, but with a much more powerful hold and greater permanence. And unlike the Netherlands where all the great Roman Catholic newspapers have disappeared, the daily press in Flanders is still overwhelmingly Christian in attitude.

'Christendom' versus 'Christianity'

Like Sweden, Great Britain and Germany, Flanders is still very much part of 'Christendom' (with, for example, high figures for christenings and church funerals, 83% and 89% respectively in 1990; for church weddings only 65%). But what of 'Christianity' and the 'professed Christians', as Dietrich Bonhoeffer called them?

After Vatican II every effort was made to spread the conciliar spirit. In 1970 an Interdiocesan Pastoral Consultative Body was set up as the highest public democratic organ for all the Flemish dioceses. This interdiocesan body is unique in Europe and exercises much influence as a sort of ecclesiastical parliament, even though only with consultative powers. It represents the dioceses and the main movements and groups and has made a stand in practically every field, from the attitude to immigrants through to the ordination of women to the priesthood. Following every Roman synod of bishops, the bishops were asked to give an account of the proceedings in what were sometimes very turbulent general meetings. Meanwhile, pastoral councils were set up in all the dioceses and most of the parishes, which resulted in a climate of democratisation at the grass roots. Great efforts were made to bring about liturgical reform (about a thousand people take part in the annual Flemish Liturgical Days), as well as to adapt religious instruction for the benefit of young people and adults alike (the Christian Forum in Ghent and in Hasselt is very well attended). Sometimes inspired by the Latin American model – the influence of the murdered Archbishop Romero of El Salvador still runs strong – hundreds of 'basic communities' were created, from extreme left to rather right-wing. At the same time tensions arose among believers everywhere: some want to go further than Vatican II, others have kept to the letter of the Council or want to return to a protective, authoritarian Church. A noisy rearguard continues to interpret Vatican II in minimalist fashion.

The Abbey Church in Grimbergen (1660-1698).

In contrast to the Netherlands, the episcopate largely succeeded in suppressing tension within the church, not least by infrequent or rather vague declarations. It proceeded with extreme caution and did not engage in radical innovative initiatives, partly because of its concern to avoid polarisation and running into trouble with Rome. This caution was justified in the case of the Catholic University of Leuven, for example, which has a very important medical faculty, in order to protect it in the bioethical dispute. Consequently, the reaction to the publication of *Ordinatio Sacerdotalis* was a sobering eye-opener for the bishops: the papal refusal to further discuss the ordination of women was the famous drop which caused the already full bucket of concealed dissatisfaction to overflow, and that in the most church-going part of the population: women.

Neither the dynamic approach summarised above nor the episcopal cautiousness could prevent an ever deepening crisis. The increasing individualisation throughout Europe, the complex secularisation, the ideology of pluralism (in the church as elsewhere) brought about a change the like of which had never been seen before. The democratisation of education and the media as well as the emancipation of women diminished the impact of every uncritical repetition of 'tradition for tradition's sake'. In the eyes of many – even within the church – the gap between the people's culture, language and symbolics and the general policy of the Church was almost unbridgeable. Many have come to realise – as in Scandinavia – that faithful Christians are in the minority.

Yet the vast majority still have a link with the Church because they hold on to the so-called 'rites of passage' (baptism, marriage, funeral). But here too alienation from the church is gathering speed. In Table 1, Flanders is compared to the other two parts of Belgium.

Table 1. Church practices (in %)

region	year	weekly Sunday mass	baptisms / births (total)	church weddings (total)	church funerals (total)
Flemish dioceses	1967	52.9	95.9	91.5	91.4
	1990	21.3	83.1	64.5	88.8
Walloon dioceses	1967	34.0	92.7	83.3	78.9
	1990	14.6	74.3	58.1	76.8
Brussels	1990	8.8	34.4	28.1	60.4
Belgium (total)	1967	42.9	93.6	86.1	84.2
	1990	17.9	75.0	59.1	81.4

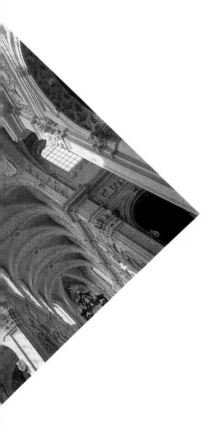

It goes without saying that this evolution has led to a blurring of the traditional religious content, as the Belgian part of the European Values Study (1990) illustrates. To the question of whether people find support in religion only 42% in Flanders (and in Wallonia) answer in the affirmative; yet 68% claim to be 'a religious person' and only 5% say they are 'a confirmed atheist', a figure which tallies with the average for Western and Eastern Europe. Only 72% claim they belong to a religious denomination (66% in Wallonia, 56% in Brussels) and of these 97% say they are Catholics. In the 18 – 24 age group, 45% (for the whole of Belgium) say they do not belong to a church. If we take a look at the usual doctrinal points, that erosion becomes even more apparent: believe in God 64%, believe in a life after death 36%, in heaven 28%, in the devil 16% and in hell barely 14%. Sin, however, continues to score high, with 41%. Despite all the Sunday sermons only 25% say they believe in the Resurrection. With the 10% who believe in reincarnation, Flanders clearly falls below the European average (21%) and way below Switzerland (c.30%). Among young people, belief increasingly takes on New Age interpretations. Thus, in 1988 M. Elchardus stated that among women aged under 30, 46% believe in astrology and 22% in reincarnation (28% and 17% respectively of young men). Increasingly, each individual puts together his own assortment, rather like at a cold buffet, with the feelings of the moment determining the choice.

Meanwhile the attitude towards the Church as an institution has also changed. Flemings are more critical of the Church than Walloons. To the question of whether a person has a lot or a reasonable degree of trust in the Church (1990), 44% in Flanders answered positively; in Wallonia the figure was 59% (in Brussels 49%). Only 25% think that the Church responds adequately to individual moral questions and family issues and when it comes to the country's social problems, the figure is not even 18% – notwithstanding all the Christian social organisations. Only spiritual needs achieve a higher score, but still only a minority of 37% (below the Walloon and Brussels average). The days when Flanders was 'high church' are apparently over. Asked whether it is good that the Church speaks out on certain issues, the majority answered in the affirmative only with regard to third-world problems, racial discrimination and disarmament – again the Walloons score higher, except on the subject of disarmament. And only 14% – and then mainly among the elderly – believe that the Church should say something about government policy. Clearly the negative experiences of the past are imprinted on the collective memory.

Should we say that we are evolving towards a *'Church without believers'* (Bert Claerhout in *De Standaard,* June 1994) or towards *'Christians without a Church'* (Jan Kerkhofs in *Streven,* May 1991)? In any event, from a historical viewpoint we have come to an all-time turning point.

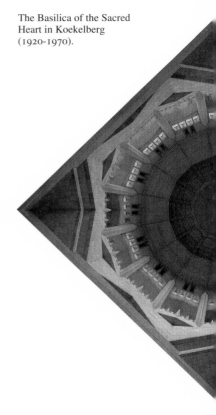

The Basilica of the Sacred Heart in Koekelberg (1920-1970).

Priestless parishes and empty cloisters

Naturally, this whole development has had repercussions for priests and those in religious orders, as it has in the rest of Europe. The cold language of figures is again the most telling. The number of priests has declined continuously both in Flanders and in Wallonia. No separate comparative data for Flanders are available but developments in Belgium as a whole regarding diocesan priests and the religious are symptomatic: the former fell from 10,450 (1961) to 6,832 (1990), the latter from 12,725 (1947) to 3,722 (1993). Their average age in most dioceses and religious institutions is over 65 years.

In Flanders we see the same process for the nuns: in the apostolic institutions the membership fell from 23,371 (1970) to 15,377 (1990) and among the contemplative orders from 1,642 to 1,103. Meanwhile hundreds of convents have been closed or regrouped. In the space of a few decades, nuns have practically disappeared from schools and hospitals where, up until about 1950, they were a typical presence with their colourful habits and wimples. Everywhere their place has been taken by lay people. The figures in Table 2 (men in religious orders) conceal the aging process: the average age is not far off 70 (1993).

Table 2. Men in religious orders in Belgium and Flanders (1974-1993)

Categories	Belgium		Flanders	
	1974	1993	1974	1993
1. Monastic Orders	1,276	822	908	581
2. Apostolic Orders	4,328	2,821	2,644	1,883
3. Missionary Institutes	870	824*	734	631
4. Institutes of Brothers	2,254**	1,170	1,635**	888
Total	8,728	5,637	5,921	3,983

* The majority in this group are retired missionaries who have returned from abroad

** Including Brothers in institutes for priests

The search for answers to this crisis within the framework of the Church has led to new forms of participation, as volunteers or through part-time or full-time involvement. The number of permanent (male) deacons has gradually risen (212 in 1990). Not unlike the Dutch model, and especially in the dio-

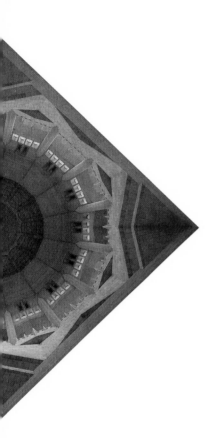

cese of Antwerp and in the Flemish part of the archdiocese of Mechelen-Brussels, 'pastoral workers' have been trained and deployed in parishes, action groups and hospitals. Between 1958-1959 and 1993-1994 more than 1,200 lay-persons have graduated from the theological faculty of the Catholic University of Leuven; half were women. In the last fifteen years, three times as many lay students as diocesan student-priests have completed their higher theological studies. Clearly the classic image of leadership in the Church is changing.

The contribution made by lay-persons is impressive. On a popular religious level they organise national and international mass pilgrimages (Banneux, Beauraing, Lourdes, Medjugorje), but it is mainly practising Catholics – and so older people – who take part. The Pax Christi Vlaanderen peace movement, easily the most important in the country, is very influential. Caritas Catholica, the Broederlijk Delen (a Lenten appeal which raises money for developing countries), the Welzijnszorg Advent appeal and the Kerk in Nood foundation (which works mainly on behalf of the Church in Eastern Europe) channel impressive sums of money – a multiple of all the other appeals – to needy countries and groups. The Justice and Peace Committee has gained recognition even beyond Catholic circles for its views and publications (from the ethics of banking to the 1994 world population conference in Cairo). At the same time, hundreds of action groups work on behalf of the handicapped, immigrants, drug addicts, AIDS patients, asylum seekers, the sick, etc. Life is clearly stronger than the decaying church structures; and however estranged young people may be from the Church, the Catholic youth movements still form the vast majority of the organised groups of young people.

A complex balance

So the general picture of the Flemish Church is multifaceted: collapse and creative construction go hand in hand. Yet the whole evolution points in the direction of an ever more depleted flock on a narrow path. This prospect has great consequences for 'pastoral strategy'. The relationship between Church and State has changed. The episcopate avoids all meddling in party politics. People are moving away from compulsion and towards an emphasis on conviction and testimony. Yet the minority church lacks homogeneity. Alongside the – few – fundamentalist groups, the observer sees a majority of open and even strongly progressive communities, sometimes with an ecumenical or even interreligious structure. Yet ' the peripheral Christians' are growing in number: people want to go on believing but feel largely alienated from a Church institution which is all too often felt to be static, with too little room for individual consciences. The traditional loyalty to Rome – still very apparent during the festive welcome of Pope John-Paul II in 1985 – is dwindling fast, as the general rejection of the papal dictate against the ordination of women revealed. The writing on the wall can be seen in that silent exodus, not only of young people but of all the age groups under fifty.

We cannot deny that, as in neighbouring countries, a sort of 'Scandinavianisation' is taking place: Christian values (like solidarity, tolerance, freedom) are endorsed, but acceptance of the specific content of the

Christian faith is becoming blurred. There is a yawning gulf between the official language of faith, the language that is used in preaching, and the language of today. That much became clear, for example, from the Vatican *Catechism of the Catholic Church* (Catechismus van de Katholieke Kerk, 1992), which, like the *Book of Faith* (Geloofsboek, 1987) of the Belgian bishops, is little read, and from the encyclical *Veritatis Splendor* (1993), fiercely criticised by the professors of moral theology at the Catholic University of Leuven. People are faced with symbols, thought systems, rules of law and policy practices which are still often reminiscent of feudalism. Earlier generations produced great Catholic men of letters. There is no sign of them whatsoever today.

Increased tolerance with regard to those of other faiths is a positive sign. The old anticlericalism and clericalism are dying out. The ecumenical movement is generally accepted, notwithstanding the small number of Protestants. Jewish-Christian discussion groups are building bridges. The Church's critical attitude towards racism is appreciated. Its open stance towards dialogue with Islam, however, meets with resistance mainly in radical Flemish milieus and among the lowest income groups, even though integration of the important Islamic minority – the second religion in the country, way ahead of Protestantism – is inevitable. The whole process also means a gradual decline of the so-called 'pillarisation' in mentalities, though less so in structures. Whereas the majority of Catholics used to be supported from birth to death by Catholic institutions and were informed by Catholic media, the sense of belonging is gradually on the wane. Not only are the Catholic institutions increasingly pluralistic internally, families, too, are losing their homogeneity. Anyone who wants to be a Christian will do so today far more out of conviction than out of habit or under social pressure, and will look for his knowledge of the faith to progressive writers like H. Küng, L. Boff or Bishop J. Gaillot (not least because of the Altoria publications of the Abbey of Averbode). People seek support in communities of like-minded people, such as bible study groups, the charismatic movement, the 'focolare' (a small group of convinced young laics), and in circles connected with abbeys and centres of contemplation. They have brought the Church in Flanders into a whole new phase. The change is gathering momentum. It is impossible to predict what the Christian scene will look like a decade hence. In the meantime the scene is still profoundly characterised by thousands of churches and monuments, the result of 1,500 years of Christendom, and no alternative has yet succeeded in replacing this Christianity as a meaningful ideology.

JAN KERKHOFS
Translated by Alison Mouthaan-Gwillim.

FURTHER READING

DOBBELAERE, KAREL, 'Secularisation, Pillarisation, Religious Involvement and Religious Change in the Low Countries', in: Th. M. Gannon (ed.), *World Catholicism in Transition.* New York / London, 1988, pp. 80-115.
The Church in Belgium, in: *Pro Mundi Vita Dossiers,* no. 18. Brussels, 1982.

Reynard the Fox

The Triumph of the Individual in a Beast Epic

Reynard the Fox (Van den vos reynaerde) was written around 1260 by a certain Willem, part of it being an extremely free version of a French tale. Around 1400 this text was reworked and provided with a sequel, under the title *Reynard's History* (Reynaerts historie). Scholars refer to these as *Reynard I* and *Reynard II* respectively.

Reynard is charged before King Noble's court with the most villainous crimes. First Bruin the bear and then Tybert the tomcat are sent to bring him before the court, but he is able to fool both of them with the prospect of an irresistible feast. They fall into the trap and barely escape with their lives. Reynard does finally accompany his nephew Grimbert to court. He is sentenced to death, but with the noose already round his neck he succeeds in deceiving the King and Queen with a tale of conspiracy and buried treasure. As a result he goes free, while his opponents are severely punished. *Reynard II* goes through the whole case again, expanded with a number of new anecdotes and a sequel in which a duel between the fox and

Even if Reynard the Fox is portrayed as a ruthless villain, it is actually inconceivable that he should ever be regarded as anything but the waggish rogue who above all exposes a thoroughly rotten society rooted in authority and power. Does he not demonstrate the age-old truth that evil can only be countered with evil? One after another he makes a mockery of court procedures and conventions in high society. These are seen to be only a veneer on the meanest egotism. And all this is presented in the manner of a mordant parody of the courtly literature of the time, which, while entertaining the courtiers, also provides them with a firm historical basis for their lofty status.

Right at the start, in the prologue, all the typical conventions of chivalric literature are so thrown off balance that the listener realises straight away that he has entered the upside-down world of the animal kingdom. An author's name is submitted – Willem – presumably known to the public since it is said that he wrote *Madoc*. That text has not survived, but there are somewhat mysterious references to it in a number of other medieval texts. Apparently it is a Celtic tale about a seafaring prince, ruler of an equally topsy-turvy world of heresy and superstition. In the earliest surviving manuscript with this passage the copyist (or his master) has decided to remove this dubious commendation by scratching the ink off the parchment. In the space this left, he then wrote the anodyne *'vele bouke'* ('many books'), thus turning Willem into a garrulous hack instead of the consummate satirist who turns the established order upside down.

A little later in the prologue, a second author makes his appearance, a certain Aernout, who has apparently only described some of the fox's escapades. This provides Willem's main motive. He intends to complete the job, by searching out anew the *'vijte'* (the 'hagiography'!) of Reynard in French sources and presenting this in its entirety in (Middle) Dutch. Two authors in the given combination, French models, scholarly accuracy and the credibility of the life of a saint provide the accepted opening of chivalric literature. In addition the author must give his professional assurance that he has sacrificed endless nights' sleep for the sake of his irrepressible poetic drive.

the wolf Isengrim determines which of them is in the right. Reynard is victorious and his whole family is rehabilitated. These Middle Dutch versions of the animal stories involving the crafty fox stimulated the dissemination and popularity of Reynard texts throughout the world. William Caxton's 1481 English translation and the Low German translation of 1498 played a key role in this. Willem's text provides a judgment of traditional court-centred power as entertaining as it is sharp, exposing its basis of self-seeking greed. Such an approach strikes a chord with the new spirited attitude of the urban nobility and patricians, with its emphasis on the intelligence of the individual rather than the brute force of hereditary power. This infectious vision enabled the text to conquer the world.

(Tr. Tanis Guest)

As part of this parodied setting, we also have an attack, typical of this kind of epic, against dolts and other rustic trash, who will understand nothing of the tale and who had better stay away. Just so long as they never dream of messing up the text with their wrongheadedness. As a parting shot comes the lady of rank who has persuaded the authors to write this verse-tale full of obscene derision of life at the court. This lady *'accustomed to invest / All that she does with courtesy'* inevitably becomes a voluptuous creature now that she stands four square in the ranks of a palace society that Willem exposes so ruthlessly.

Anyone familiar with medieval chivalric literature can guess what to expect after this prologue. Is that not reinforced straight away, by the little dog Cortois that can only yap in French? In his name and behaviour he is the embodiment of the brainless courtier full of arrogant airs. No sooner has the wolf Isengrim made his serious accusation – Reynard has raped his wife and blinded his children by urinating on them – than the lapdog comes up with the ridiculous complaint that the fox has stolen a sausage from him, his only possession. This sausage, it later transpires, actually belongs to Tybert the tomcat, who in his turn had stolen it from a miller. At the court everyone lies and cheats. And in this nasty world homosexuality too is in its element. This was considered in the Middle Ages to be a lascivious bent inspired by the devil, that could only be referred to in covert terms, as it is here. At the end of the tale another such pansy little dog appears, a certain Rine. Reynard is undoubtedly taking him off when he, lamenting, recalls him as *'Sweet Rine, Dear companion, nobly-bred harrier'*.

However you look at it, the Flemish court could feel itself very exposed and attacked. In the thirteenth century it was entirely Gallicised and included in its patronage the poet of Arthurian tales, Chrétien de Troyes, who can be seen in both Cortois and Rine. But these are only incidental jabs that cannot conceal the fact that *Reynard the Fox* (Van den vos reynaerde) in reality attacks the whole ethos of the court, using the weapon of their own favourite literature. The only difference is that the knights and ladies are now animals which never abandon their profiteering natures although they have human names. Reynard is even introduced as if he were the hero of a chivalric tale: *'The fierce one with the ruddy beard'* which reminds us of other epic characters such as Ferguut, *'the knight with the white shield'* or Walewein, *'the father of ventures'*.

Yet this scenario of a roguish fox exposing the nobility throws up a number of problems in view of its date of origin. The text must have been written about 1260 in the north east of Flanders, partly as a creative adaptation of a French text and thereafter continued in an equally individualistic way. At that time literature in the vernacular was normally patronised by the higher aristocracy, and just occasionally by the Church. Both these estates and their institutions, however, come in for such a drubbing that it is almost inconceivable that they sponsored such a fierce chastisement.

Another problem is that the fox at that time was by no means the crafty and also amusing animal that we like to see in him. For people in the Middle Ages he is a ruthless thief and murderer, very much feared in the countryside because of his limitless decimation of their poultry. The terms *'fierce'* and *'roguish'* denote these dreadful characteristics, and in the Middle Ages carry none of the crafty and enterprising connotations that we nowadays associate with these attributes. It would have been quite impossible to identify oneself with such a blackguard, since even his revelations of the evil in others were as nothing compared with his own savagery. In the thirteenth century that would not have been its primary purpose. Does the text then only show that everyone starts acting bestially as soon as he loses control of his Christian thinking or whatever makes him human, distinguishing him from the animals? Inevitably then, the tale must address the theoretical structure of the three traditional estates on earth, whose representatives so often fail in practice: nobility, clergy, commoners. But the question remains: at whose expense and for which audience or readers was this text written in the first place? And above all, by what kind of a poet? And now it's high time to return to the work itself …

At a court hearing the absent Reynard is accused of all kinds of crimes. Only his uncle, Grimbert the badger, speaks in his defence. During this very defence a cock and chickens appear with the funeral procession of the hen Coppe, whose head has just been bitten off by the accused. Bruin, the bear, is ordered to go and summon Reynard. Reynard lures him to a tree containing honey in which Bruin gets trapped, only to be thrashed by the furious villagers. Tybert the tomcat is then sent out on the same mission. He too is easily duped, this time with the promise of tasty mice in the pastor's house. But he likewise ends up in a trap and is roughly treated by the reverend's whole family. Like Bruin he only escapes by the skin of his teeth. The third one to fetch Reynard is Grimbert, and the fox does go along with this member of his family. On the way he confesses his misdeeds. At the court, further accusations ensue, after which he is sentenced to the gallows. With the noose round his neck he is allowed to make a public confession. He concocts a conspiracy against King Noble involving Bruin and Isengrim as well as his uncle Grimbert and his father. The huge treasure that financed the plot was stolen by him and buried in a secret place. As soon as Reynard reveals this, Noble and his wife become very interested. In exchange for the treasure, Reynard may go free. The others will set off to collect it, but without the fox since he must first do penance with a long pilgrimage. Bruin and Isengrim are severely punished. Reynard escapes to his family, where he murders his travelling companion Coward the hare to provide supper, saddling the ram, Beline, with the blame for that.

About one and a half centuries later, around 1400, this text was revised and extended with a sequel under the title of *Reynard's History* (Reynaerts historie). This longer version is really little more than a repetition, amplified with new anecdotes. Bruin and Isengrim are rehabilitated, further charges are brought against Reynard. He is again summoned, but this time a duel with Isengrim must settle the issue. Reynard wins, and this means that his and his family's name is cleared. This sequel also is partly derived from one of the many branches of the French *Roman de Renard*.

Towards the end of the Middle Ages, in about 1475, this second Reynard text was rewritten by a certain Heinric van Alcmaer in four books and seventy-four chapters, accompanied by headings and moralising explanations. Only fragments of one single copy have survived, in an edition of 1487 printed by Gerard Leeu in Antwerp. But we have a complete version of it in the Low German translation, *Reynke de Vos,* printed at Lübeck in 1498. In

Anton Damen's Reynard monument (1938) in Hulst (Zeeland Flanders).

1479, in Gouda, Leeu published Van Alcmaer's version reduced to forty-four chapters and without headings and glosses, as *The History of Reynard the Fox* (Die hystorie van Reynaert die vos). This printed text has been the source of numerous reprints, adaptations and translations, including those in Latin, German, English, Danish, Swedish and Icelandic, down to the present day.

An important member of this group is the English translation, made by William Caxton, the first English printer, who published his text at Westminster in 1481. This was frequently reprinted by himself and others. Because of his years of activity in Bruges and Cologne as printer and diplomat in the King of England's service, he had an excellent command of Dutch. That he included so many Dutch words in his translation should not therefore be attributed to his ignorance, but rather to the fairly extensive spread of Dutch in England due to the intensive mutual trade. Nor do the mistakes indicate a lack of knowledge, but merely (excessive) haste and carelessness. When, in his *The History of Reynard the Fox,* he translates '*Segt ons Bellijn'* as '*Says on Bellyn'* he is simply not looking properly, because of course Caxton knows perfectly well what '*ons*' ('our') means in Dutch.

We may reasonably assume that even in the Middle Ages various Reynard versions were written to appeal to the shifting questions and expectations of different social strata. Where Willem's text predominantly parodies chivalric literature and court life in general, this gradually dissipates in later versions, until it is scarcely visible in the prose editions. Meanwhile the moralising tendency takes over, thus emphasising the human characteristics of the animals.

Nevertheless in all these versions the instructive and amusing basis of these beast epics remains paramount. This was the function, too, of the fables from the animal world in the earliest cultures. They presented an inverted world in which an amusing display was made of what happens in the real world when people abandon basic human values and virtues. Classical traditions surrounding Aesop meet up with early German traditions in the Middle Ages. The tales about a fox appear to have their origins in his clashes with the wolf, whose power and strength can only be mastered by the fox's guile. This all starts with the anecdote about the sick lion. The wolf accuses the fox of wilfully neglecting the king on his sickbed. The fox admits this, but gives the reason that he was searching for a remedy for the lion. This he has now found. They have to wrap the king in a wolf's hide, and the warmth will cure the king. That is what happens, and the king recovers entirely while the wolf stands wretchedly in the cold. Since then wolf and fox have been implacable enemies. In both Latin and French this encounter is further embroidered with various anecdotes in which they are both the protagonists among an increasing number of other animals.

Undoubtedly the substantial Middle Dutch beast epic which Willem created stands supreme among these animal tales. That is clearly evident from all the many derived versions, and no less so from the numerous laudatory references to it in other medieval texts. The fox has acquired a remarkable leading role and appears unaided to defy every authority and even the organised animal kingdom in its entirety. His main weapon is his tongue that conveys his utter lack of scruples, recognising only his own advantage and that of his wife and children.

But who on earth could have enjoyed this ruthless humiliation of the tra-

Title page of the chapbook *About Reynard the Fox* (Van Reynaert die Vos), published in Delft in 1589.

An illustration from the edition of *Reynard's History* (Reynaerts historie) printed by Gerard Leeu (Antwerp, c.1487).

ditional power of the noble courts, brought about moreover by a universally hated animal? The assumption that it expresses a kind of introspection in those circles overlooks the harshness of the satire, leaving as it does no stone standing in the foundations of feudal society and its aristocratic keystones. And is that fox really such a despicable animal? His cunning in the face of the stupid authorities and their brazen egotism was surely irresistible, certainly for the urban classes rising in society, who with their wealth and marital arrangements were striving to establish a new kind of power. It is also scarcely conceivable that a medieval text would become popular if it depended from start to finish on a negative hero with which no one would ever wish to identify himself.

This new zest in society appeared unmistakably at this time in the new aristocracy of a Flemish city like Ghent. This then consisted of a *nouveau riche* nobility amongst ambitious merchants. In this fluid situation there was no place for the old values increasingly cultivated in a vacuum by the mouldering courtly society, bolstered by a nostalgic chivalric literature that only offered emulation of a life that died with Charlemagne and King Arthur.

In contrast to this, a more pragmatic approach to life was emerging, with eyes rather on the street and everyday reality. This was nurtured on the one hand by new ways of life in the towns, based on categories of labour, capital assets and investments, and on the other hand, since the twelfth century, by a growing individualism where the emphasis lay on personal responsibility instead of unquestioned loyalty and obedience to the overlord. This zest, stimulated by the towns, could spread within and outside their walls through all the strata of society, whether it be the nobility or the clerical hierarchy, the international merchants or the guild master-craftsmen. Together they formed a new power, based on personal skill and business acumen, and there was soon open competition with the traditional authority of the sovereign powers.

In a number of places Willem refers in his text to Ghent and the bordering Waas region. This topography is so important because Ghent was the one city conspicuous among the others for its more than adequate capital, intelligentsia and mentality to appreciate *Reynard the Fox* as the interpreter and resonance of this new zest.

It is striking that it was in the thirteenth century that popularity shifted to texts that showed how an individual with practical ingenuity could take on the whole world and take good care of himself under all circumstances. These often comic exercises in the most inconceivable cunning have in common that the hero and protagonist cocks a snook at all the traditional values, whistles at court mores and every other kind of accepted behaviour, yet accepts them with alacrity if that is to his advantage. Reynard constantly gives stimulating examples of this. He knows the ceremonial of legal proceedings off pat, and so he can faultlessly exploit the weaknesses in the system. He remains courteous where that yields results, for instance towards King Noble and his wife Gente. It is in this way that he softens them up for his unmitigated con-tricks.

It is as if the tale of Reynard's triumphs blazed a pioneer's trail for the later picaresque tales, which, attuned to the burgeoning power of the urban elites, enjoyed an increasing popularity. Then came the ruses of hyper-individualists like Marcolphus, Aesop, the quasi-Villon, Aernout, Everaert,

Title page of the 1485 edition of *Aesop* (Esopus).

Uilenspiegel, the pastor of Kalenberg, Virgil, Heynken de Luyere and many more. The *Aesop* printed in 1485 even carries a prologue commending it as a manual of survival based on personal guile. This underlines the assumption that the animal fable had precisely that function.

If the fox in the Middle Ages, despite its infectious exposure of the stupid brutality of the leaders, should still appear offensive in the tale, there was always the justification of the animal fable. It was, after all, only literature; animals cannot speak, and identification with the protagonist could be withheld at any time. And doesn't Reynard simply act according to his nature, stealing chickens and killing a young hare to satisfy his wife and children's hunger? And all the other cruelties are brought upon the powerful creatures like the wolf, bear and tomcat by themselves, as the deserving victims of their own greed and exploitation.

Not least among the tale's qualities is the nice balance between human and animal characteristics in each animal. Reynard has a name, goes on a pilgrimage and owns a castle. But Bruin has to wait outside because he is too large to go in, so that the castle then turns back into a fox's earth.

First page of *Reynard's History* (Reynaerts historie, c. 1400).

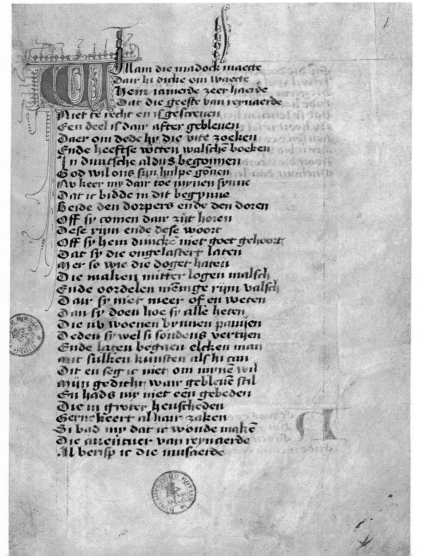

Willem, who laboured to indite
Madoc in many a wakeful night,
Willem took it much to heart
That one adventure of Reynard
In Dutch remained as yet untold,
Which had not been writ of by Arnold.
For that legend he made a search
And began to tell it in Dutch
After the French in which it was made.
May God grant me his aid!
Now I would with all my heart
Make a request at the start,
To every fool and country clown,
If they happen to come to town
And hear these rhymes read in Dutch,
Which will not benefit them much,
That from carping they refrain –
They're like the raven ever fain
To croak some impertinence.
They'll say – those verses make no sense –
Though they know of poetry nothing at all,
As little as I know what to call
The folk now living in Babylon.
'Twere well they left such things alone.
I say this not for my own sake.
I would not presume to make
A poem but for the request
Of one accustomed to invest
All that she does with courtesy.
She it was who persuaded me
To tell this adventure of Reynard.
Against carpers I'm on my guard,
Fools and bumpkins, the whole crew.
Rather would I be listened to
By such as observe etiquette
And have their minds ever set –
Rich or poor, whichever they be –
On behaving courteously.
Mark my words without fail.
Now listen how I begin my tale.

Translated by A.J. Barnouw.

Reynard makes his confession to Uncle Grimbert. But just after that he is mightily distracted by a yard full of hens, so great is the temptation that Grimbert more or less has to hold onto him. Even so he almost manages to grab a fat cock. A subtle strand running right through the text is the variation between the normal posture on four legs and the times when he stands on his hind legs like a human. Reynard operates within a similar duality, sometimes as an animal hunting for food, at other times as a mastermind capable, in the human world too, of establishing a new hegemony.

Reynard may expose a rotten status quo, but his popularity is primarily due to his display of a practical and apposite guile that in reality has a democratic bearing: anyone can acquire this if he wants, whatever his birth, wealth or status. Though the exposure of the traditional power of the overlords by means of parody is undoubtedly the main theme of Willem's original text, the infectious craftiness of a loner under attack from all sides appears to be its passport to success in later centuries – right up to the present day. And why not for ever and ever?

HERMAN PLEIJ
Translated by Peter King.

NOTE

The translations of the text are from: A.J. Barnouw and E. Colledge, *Reynard the Fox and Other Mediaeval Netherlands Secular Literature.* Leiden / London / New York, 1967.

FURTHER READING

Texts: *Van den vos reynaerde. 1. Teksten.* (ed. W. G. Hellinga, Zwolle, 1952) is a diplomatic edition containing all pre-1550 texts. The fragments discovered in 1971, now in the Koninklijke Bibliotheek in Brussels, have been published by W.E. Hegman in *Zestig jaar Oudheidkundige Kring 'De Vier Ambachten'. Jubileumboek 1988-89,* pp. 14-37. Modern critical editions are: *Van den vos Reynaerde* (ed. F. Lulofs, Groningen, 1983); and, with a facsimile, *Van den vos Reynaerde, Het Comburgse handschrift* (ed. J. Janssens *et al.,* Leuven, 1991). An English translation can be found in: A.J. Barnouw and E. Colledge, *Reynard the Fox and Other Mediaeval Netherlands Secular Literature.* Leiden / London / New York, 1967. The first English translation appeared as early as 1481: William Caxton, *The History of Reynard the Fox* (ed. N.F. Blake, Oxford, 1970).

Other literature in English: JACOBY, F.R., *Van den Vos Reinaerde. Legal Elements in a Netherlandic Epic of the Thirteenth Century.* Munich, 1970.
PEETERS, L., 'Hinrek van Alckmer and medieval tradition. The Reynardian interpretation of a man and his world', *Marche Romans,* 29 (1978), pp. 89-110.
SANDS, D.B., 'The Flemish Reynard: epic and non-epic affiliations', in: H. Scholler (ed.), *The Epic in Medieval Society.* Tübingen, 1977, pp. 307-325.
WACKERS, P., 'The use of fables in Reynaerts Historie', *Niederdeutsche Studien,* 30 (1991), pp. 461-484.
WACKERS, P., 'Words and deeds in the Middle Dutch Reynaert stories', in: E. Kooper (ed.), *Medieval Dutch Literature in its European Context.* Cambridge, 1994, pp. 131-147.

Flemish

Miniatures for England

In 1479 the King of England, Edward IV, paid a merchant called Philip Maisertuell *'for certaine boks by the said Philip to be provided to the kyngs use in the partees beyond the see'*. The King's commission had been for the purchase of manuscripts in Flanders. His interest stemmed from a long tradition, for one of the striking aspects of Flemish miniature painting in the late Middle Ages was the connection with England – to the extent that a thorough survey could be written just using those codices which were sent there or which were produced as a result of commissions from England.

This interest can be explained by the many dynastic, political and economic links between the two. Since the twelfth century English wool had played a central role in the economy of Flanders, and this led Flemish weavers to press for good relations with England. Later, the Flemish representatives in London of the Hanseatic League organised trade with both England and Scotland; and in 1344 the Merchant Adventurers set up their headquarters in Bruges. Edward III married Philippa of Hainault in 1328 and in 1339 was supported by Flanders in the Hundred Years' War. He was often at his headquarters at Antwerp and Ghent, where Philippa had her court. And it was during this period too that people from Flanders built up the cloth industry in England. In 1335, for example, a colony of Flemish weavers was established in Norwich with the King's support.

Despite the interruption in the export of English wool during the second half of the fourteenth century, economic links remained; although it needed a fair amount of negotiation to keep these going. Well known in this connection was the pro-English position of James van Artevelde. In 1382 his son Philip went to England to conduct negotiations accompanied by two artists.

Religious links also existed. The Abbey of Eeckhout at Bruges, for example, was in contact with religious houses overseas. And there were cultural links too: the city accounts of Bruges contain a number of entries for musicians and singers from England who had appeared at ceremonies in the city.

The oldest reference to the presence of Flemish artists overseas is to the painter Giles le Fleming from Bruges, who was working in Norwich between 1286 and 1298. But it was above all from the second half of the fourteenth century that East Anglia and London began to attract many different kinds of art and artists. Monumental brasses, pottery and paintings were all imported from Bruges. Where the art of the miniature is concerned the first traces of Flemish influence can be found shortly before 1350; in, for example, a Psalter of around 1350-1360, now in Paris (Bibliothèque Nationale, Ms. lat. 765), which was made for a member of the Fitzwarin family from Somerset, and a number of manuscripts made between 1361 and 1399 for the Bohun family, one of the most prominent in England. From 1337 William de Bohun spent a good deal of time in Flanders as a counsellor to Edward III. Even more specifically Flemish are the codices made for Humphrey de Bohun, seventh Earl of Hereford and Essex, who died in 1372, and for his two daughters. It is clear that a Flemish illuminator, whose work bears strong similarities to books made on the continent, played an increasing part in the Bohun workshop at Pleshey Castle, which worked exclusively for the family. The broad architectural designs which frame the pictures are a particular characteristic of these manuscripts.

It was during this period that pre-Eyckian miniature painting blossomed. It is characterised by a concern for the accurate portrayal of the individual, materiality and the incidental in man and his surroundings. Paintings were of plastically modelled figures with naturalistic faces, solid bodies, and expressions suitable to the subject matter. Landscapes and interiors gave a good impression of space. Realistic details received particular attention. Considerable imagination was used to enrich and bring up to date traditional biblical themes with anecdotal, 'apocryphal' details. This art was different from the High Gothic as it was found in France and elsewhere, which was characterised by courtly and idealised forms, by mannered poses and flowing draperies. That Flemish art developed differently was without doubt because it arose from, and was destined for, a world that was of an essentially urban nature; a world of rich merchants, bankers, high officials and bourgeois patricians. They were all men who had experienced reality in a quite different way from kings, princes and courtiers who had never had to provide for their own needs. In order to be able to survive at the political, economic and social level, citizens and merchants had to take into account the smallest details of everyday reality. This trend in art was a forerunner of the work of the Flemish Primitives and of Jan van Eyck in particular. He was to bring this realistic composition to its highest form, which is why this particular period in Flemish art is described as pre-Eyckian realism.

The English art of miniature painting underwent a revival at the end of the fourteenth century as a result of the presence in England of manuscripts and illuminators from Flanders. A key manuscript is without doubt the Carmelite Missal, made in 1391-1398, probably for the Whitefriars Church in Fleet Street in London (London, British Library, Add. Ms. 29704-5, 44892), of which only a few cut out illustrated initials now survive. A number of miniature-painters collaborated on this missal; the work of some of them displays all the characteristics of pre-Eyckian realism, such as naturalism, narrative

Presentation in the Temple, illustrated initial from the Carmelite Missal, Bruges Master in London, end fourteenth century. London, British Library, Add. Ms. 29704-5, 44892, f. 93.

St George Slaying the Dragon, illuminated page from a Book of Hours and Psalter, Bruges, 1401-1415. London, British Library, Ms. Royal 2.A.xviii, f. 5v.

structure and emotional expressionism. They worked together under the leadership of an artist from Bruges, and indeed these miniatures show a clear connection with other manuscripts produced at Bruges. Another example is the Lapworth Missal, a large and richly decorated work of 1398 (Oxford, Corpus Christi College, Ms. 394), in which the Calvary is ascribed to the Brugian Master of the Carmelite Missal. This group of Flemish artists later obtained commissions from the House of Lancaster, as is apparent from the *Great Cowchers,* a book of 1402-1407, with copies of the official possessions of Henry IV (London, Public Record Office, DL 42 1/2). The same artist can be met again in Henry's *Big Bible,* of about 1412, which got its name from its huge format (62 x 42,5 cm) (London, British Library, Ms. Royal 1.E.ix)

In this milieu there appeared Herman Scheerre at the beginning of the fifteenth century. He worked both with the miniaturists at the Court school at Westminster and with those on the continent. Scheerre lived in London in Paternoster Row close to St Paul's, where a number of booksellers lived. His work displays certain Flemish characteristics, though the origin of these is a matter of dispute among scholars. According to some he can be identified with a certain Herman of Cologne, who in 1402 was involved in the decoration of the Moses well in the Carthusian monastery at Champmol. He is thought at this point to have come in contact with the work of the painter Melchior Broederlam from Ypres; or he might have got to know Broederlam's work in Ypres before he himself emigrated to England. Others assert that there are good grounds for considering him of Flemish origin. The name Scheerre (= *'lakenscheerder'* or cloth shearer*)* seems to indicate that he came from a region where cloth was manufactured. The work of this illuminator is not so distinctly naturalistic as that of his Flemish contemporaries. It is marked by a delicate use of colour and by doll-like faces. He often embellishes the background of a painting or clothing with inscriptions to which he sometimes adds his name. In other places he puts his motto: *'Omnia levia sunt amanti. Si quis amat non laborat'* ('All is easy for one who loves; he who loves toils not').

Both the Flemish masters of the Carmelite Missal and Herman Scheerre were responsible for the changes in style in England at the beginning of the fifteenth century and their influence was to remain noticeable for a long time.

The same can be said of the anonymous Master of the Beaufort Saints. He was called this because of the very detailed representations of saints in a Book of Hours commissioned by an unknown English patron. Later on it was apparently owned by a member of the Beaufort family and about 1460 it came into the hands of the English royal family. This Psalter, now at Rennes (Bibliothèque Municipale, Ms. 22) was made in London and illustrated by Scheerre or someone in his circle, although the full page miniatures of the *memoriae*, or prayers to the saints, are attributed to the Beaufort Master. Even before the end of the fifteenth century most of these had been removed from this manuscript and added to a Psalter and Book of Hours, produced in London in 1440 (London, British Library, Ms. Royal 2.A.xviii). We do not know why this was done or on whose instructions. The miniatures in the *memoriae* were created between 1401 and 1415 and represent saints. They are large bold figures in interiors or landscapes, placed under canopies which strengthen the feeling of space. The male figures have expressive faces with accentuated eyebrows and cheekbones. The faces of the female figures are more refined. In concept, colour and iconography these paintings have a distinct Bruges character about them. Until recently it was thought that the Beaufort master had worked with Scheerre in London. The discovery that all the illustrations in this Book of Hours had been stuck into places reserved for them and only later given English margins makes plausible the theory that they were actually made in Bruges and from there sent to London – particularly as other manuscripts prove that this master and his collaborators were indeed active in Flanders itself.

Around 1400 the growing tendency to private devotions led to the increased use of illuminated Books of Hours. Recent research has shown that the export of Books of Hours from Flanders and more specifically from Bruges, which had by this time developed into a major centre of book manufacture, had reached far greater proportions than had previously been thought. This large scale export trade was the result of the direct trading links between Flanders and England. The manuscripts followed the same routes along which other luxury goods were exported. In these Books of Hours the content is more or less fixed, adapted to the English liturgy which first developed in the diocese of Salisbury (Sarum) and then spread widely throughout England. The calendar contained typical saints such as Edmund, Dunstan, Oswald, Magnus, Hugo of Lincoln and Etheldreda. After the calendar follow the *memoriae,* in which Thomas Becket is usually included as well as prayers to the Trinity and the true face of Christ. A typical feature is that the shortened version of the Hours of the Cross is inserted into the Hours of the Virgin. Equally characteristic is the presence of certain special prayers, such as a paraphrase of the *Salve Regina,* a meditation on the Wounds of Christ, on the Instruments of the Passion and on the Seven Words of the Cross. The iconography was adapted to take into account the fact that they were intended for England. Thus the Hours of the Virgin are usually illustrated with a Passion cycle, whereas on the continent the preference was for scenes from the life of Mary. The representation of angels

The Murder of St Thomas Becket, illuminated page from a Book of Hours, Bruges, c.1390-1400. London, Sotheby's, 2-9 March 1937, f. 23v.

raising the souls of the departed to God the Father in a sheet in the prayer for the *Commendatio animarum,* as well as the presence of the portrait of Thomas Becket in the *memoriae,* point specifically in this context to the English destination. However, the name and depiction of this saint were often deleted or mutilated after 1538 when Henry VIII struck him off the calendar. These full-page miniatures were painted on individual sheets so that they could be prepared in advance, perhaps even in quantity, and were only added at the binding stage.

These export manuscripts show many signs of use. Prayers and personal marks of ownership in English were often added shortly after their arrival in England. And later, even centuries on, owners would insert texts or personal notes. Some of the Hours were intended for English soldiers, who occupied large areas of Northern France after the Battle of Agincourt in 1415.

Colophons confirm that these books originated in Bruges. A Book of Hours now at Ushaw College in Durham (Ms. 10) contains the information that the transcription was completed at Bruges on 21 January 1408 by Johannes Heineman. The oldest of these codices date back to the end of the fourteenth century and are outstanding testimony to pre-Eyckian realism. The export of this kind of book continued to the end of the fifteenth century. So far, more than two hundred examples have been catalogued, and it is more than likely that many more were lost with the rise of Anglicanism.

The exploration of reality: the rule of the dukes of Burgundy (c.1430 – c.1475)

Philip the Good personally commissioned hundreds of fine manuscripts, which even today compel our admiration. They were made in a number of well organised workshops in Flanders. The illuminators were among the very best artists in Europe and were, therefore, on a par with the Flemish Primitives. The books they created were not just ornamental treasures; they provided moral models which the prince could use to support his political aspirations and to justify his activities. Many members of Philip's retinue followed his example in their love of books, among them Antoon and Karel van Croy, Lodewijk van Gruuthuse, Nicolas Rolin and Jean Chevrot. The illuminators refined further the trends which had developed during the period of pre-Eyckian realism. Although the personages are often portrayed in a mannerist fashion, they are nonetheless individualised and events are rendered in a naturalistic way. The landscapes are deep and often poetic in character. The scrupulously detailed representation of clothing, objects and decor makes these pictures an accurate reflection of the daily milieu and lifestyle of the period. The high standard was maintained under Philip's successor Charles the Bold and his third wife Margaret of York.

Margaret of York was the daughter of Richard, Duke of York, and Cicely Neville. In 1461 her brother had deposed Henry VI and assumed the crown as Edward IV. Her marriage to Charles the Bold in 1468 brought Margaret into the glittering world of Burgundy. Between 1468 and 1477, the year in which her husband died, Margaret built up a personal library. She was indeed the most important female patron of the arts among the Burgundians of this period. She acquired for herself mainly books of devotion and religious treatises suitable for the devotions of a woman of her status. What is

particularly noticeable is the attention she paid to her own portrait. She is portrayed at prayer or performing good works. Pictures like this have a political purpose in that they show her moral responsibility as Duchess and so display her authority.

At least eight manuscripts were produced as a result of her commissions. A number of the illuminators who worked on them had already previously worked for Philip the Good. Nicolas Finet, a canon at Cambray, was commisioned by her to translate the treatise *Benois seront les miséricordieux* (Brussels, Koninklijke Bibliotheek, Ms. 9296). This was illustrated by the Master of Girart de Roussillon, who was active in Brussels from about 1450 and has sometimes been identified with Dreux Jehan whose name is mentioned in documents of Philip the Good. This artist was primarily a sensitive colourist. He paints charming landscapes in pastel shades with a strongly atmospheric perspective. In the manuscript in question he illustrated two pages. In the first, Margaret kneels in a landscape with the church of St Gudule and the Town Hall of Brussels. She is supported by her patroness, St Margaret, and surrounded by four Fathers of the Church. This is one of the first pictures to portray recognisable buildings. In the second miniature Margaret, supported by Christ, is herself performing the Seven Acts of Mercy. In several places a coat of arms draws attention to the direct connection between the princess and this book. The same artist provided the illustration for another text by Finet, *Le dialogue de la duchesse de Bourgogne à Jésus-Christ* (London, British Library, Add. Ms. 7970). In this the risen Christ appears to Margaret, a composition inspired by Christ's appearance to His mother after the Resurrection.

Margaret of York and the Seven Acts of Mercy, illuminated page from *Benois seront les miséricordieux,* Master of Girart de Roussillon, c.1468-1477. Brussels, Koninklijke Bibliotheek, Ms. 9296, f. 1.

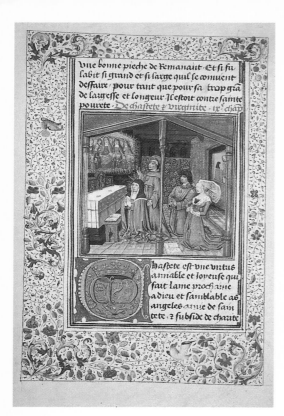

St Anne Appears to St Colette, illuminated page from the *Vie de Sainte Colette,* Bruges circle of the Master of Margaret of York, c.1468-1477. Ghent, Arme Klaren, Ms. 8, f. 40v.

Acheron Swallowing the Avaricious, miniature from *Les visions du chevalier Tondal,* Simon Marmion, c.1475. Malibu, J.P. Getty Museum, Ms. 31, f. 17.

A series of manuscripts can be grouped round a codex of Margaret containing works by the chancellor of the University of Paris, Jean Gerson (Brussels, Koninklijke Bibliotheek, Ms. 9305-06). The illuminator was given the name of the Master of Margaret of York in view of the fact that she commissioned this codex. He was active in Bruges between 1470 and 1480. The quick drawing is striking. The layers of paint are transparent. The perspective is inaccurate, his figures are rather stiff and marionette-like and his clothing modelled with vigorous hatching. This artist is easily recognisable by his treatment of buildings. He leaves the fronts open, while the interiors are supported by glass-looking pillars. The grey walls are embellished with blue and red gold-brocaded tapestries.

A richly decorated life of St Colette, written shortly after her death in 1447 by her confessor Pierre de Vaux, was commissioned by the Duchess at Bruges and presented by her to the Poor Clares at Ghent (Ghent, Arme Klaren, Ms. 8). The book contains thirty-one pictures. Since there was no earlier illustrated example, the artists had to create their own originals; the style is very similar to that of the Master of Margaret of York. In the picture of the appearance of St Anne to Colette, Charles the Bold and his wife appear as witnesses.

Margaret was also interested in visionary literature. As well as an Apocalypse and a Purgatory of St Patrick she owned copies of *La Vision de l'âme de Guy de Thurno* and of *Les visions du chevalier Tondal* (Malibu, J.P. Getty Museum, Mss. 31 and 30 respectively). The first is the story of a rich burgher of Verona, whose spirit comes to visit his wife after his death. The second text, written c.1149 at Regensburg by an Irish monk, tells the story of a knight called Tondalus who falls sick and dies. His soul journeys through Hell to Purgatory and then to Heaven. There are more than 200 known copies of this text, in fifteen different languages, but Margaret's copy is the only one which is illustrated. According to a colophon the text was copied at Ghent in 1475 by David Aubert, formerly court scribe to Philip the Good, who was given a number of other commissions by Margaret. This masterpiece is ascribed to Simon Marmion, one of the best known illuminators of the second half of the fifteenth century. He too had received a number of commissions from Philip the Good. From 1458 until his death in 1489 he worked at Valenciennes. His work shows what a good narrator he was with his brush, able to portray with power the psychology of a situation. He achieved brilliant atmospheric effects with his use of particularly delicate colouring. At the same time he succeeded in reproducing the innate texture of materials. The *Visions* offered him a marvellous opportunity to use the play of light and shade to evoke the atmosphere of Hell. The way in which he does this anticipates the work of Hieronymus Bosch and he led the way into the final phase of Flemish miniature painting.

Reality surpassed: the Ghent-Bruges School (c.1475 – c.1520)

Around 1470-1480, Flemish illuminators underwent a final period of radical innovation. Illusionistic effects were used to break through the flat plane of each decorated page of vellum. The illuminators were able to create in their landscapes much more sense of depth than previously, and to give complex structures to their interiors. The studied handling of light and shadow enabled them to portray depth. Each scene was viewed as if through a window. Through the new strong narrative interpretation of traditional themes and through various artistic tricks they succeeded in strengthening the impact of the representation on the viewer. But the most striking innovation is the use of *trompe l'œil* in the marginal decoration. Highly realistic motifs, such as flowers, insects and objects, throw shadows on the coloured surface of the vellum. This innovation was first introduced in workshops in Bruges and Ghent, hence the term 'Ghent-Bruges School'. It was the anonymous Master of Mary of Burgundy who played the pioneering role here. The new style contained such qualities that it was copied almost immediately throughout Western Europe and foreign kings, nobles and prelates turned to the Flemish workshops for their most precious manuscripts. Among them were, for example, Isabella of Castille, Joanna the Mad, James IV of Scotland, Maximilian of Austria, Cardinal Albrecht of Brandenburg, and the Infante Dom Fernando of Portugal.

Among these manuscripts in the new style, one of the first is a breviary of Margaret of York produced around 1476 (Cambridge, St John's College, Ms. 215). Margaret's brother Edward IV also acquired many Flemish manuscripts. These were to form the basis of the English Old Royal Library. In 1470-1471 Edward lived as an exile in Bruges at the house of Lodewijk van Gruuthuse and he was to have contacts again later on with this prominent bibliophile. Edward was so taken with Burgundian court ceremonial that he asked Olivier de la Marche, the Duke's master of ceremonies, to prepare a description for him of the Duke's household. His purchase of illuminated manuscripts in Bruges dates from about 1479-1480. He bought among others from Philip Maisertuell, who is mentioned in the opening sentence of this article. He was particularly interested in French historical texts with a narrative and moralising content, which he probably intended for the education of his sons. The text and the illustrations are similar to those made for Lodewijk van Gruuthuse himself. It seems probable, therefore, that he acted as intermediary in their acquisition.

The Master of Edward IV, who was working in Bruges around 1470-1490, takes his name from a 1479 *Bible historiale* made for the King (London, British Library, Ms. Royal 14 D.i., 18 D ix-x). The miniaturist is distinguished by his broad compositions full of variety, his wide range of representations of clothing and head-gear and pleasing use of colour. An artist in the circle of this Master produced a copy of the second part of the anonymous translation of Flavius Josephus' *Antiquités et Guerre des Juifs.* This was begun for Gruuthuse. On folio 140, however, Gruuthuse's coat of arms is overpainted with that of Edward IV (London, Sir John Soane's Museum, Ms. 1.). Each chapter is introduced by a large picture. Particularly striking is the exaggerated rising perspective as a background for the figures which adopt a wide variety of poses and make pronounced gestures. Under the influence of the School of Ghent and Bruges, the white background on which flowers and leaves were depicted, was overpainted with gold. It seems probable that Gruuthuse either sold or presented this book to the King.

Another person who was well acquainted with Burgundian culture and art was William, Lord Hastings (c.1430-1483). He had a significant part to play in some of the moments of drama in the English royal house, which is why Shakespeare gave him a role in his play *Richard III.* Hastings was friend and counsellor to Edward IV and headed the Burgundian party at the English court, and had also played a part in the negotiations concerning the marriage of Margaret of York. His sister Elizabeth and her husband, Sir John Donne, commissioned a retable from Hans Memling in Bruges (see *The Low Countries* 1994-95: 85). Donne also owned some Flemish manuscripts, among them a copy of *Les Faits d'Alexandre le Grand* by Quintus Curtius (London, British Library, Ms. Royal 15 D.iv), which he had probably obtained from Margaret of York. About 1480 Donne had two Books of Hours made in Flanders (London, British Library Add. Ms. 54782 and Madrid, Museo Lázaro-Galdiano, Ms. 15503). These are masterpieces of the early Ghent-Bruges school, ascribed to the Master of the Older Prayerbook of the Emperor Maximilian, who probably worked in Ghent. He refined still further the innovations of his predecessor, the Master of Mary of Burgundy. This is why the patronage of Hastings was so important for the evolution of the Ghent-Bruges style. The perspective is wonderfully done and the landscapes extremely realistic.

Flemish Books of Hours and breviaries were still being sent to England around 1500. Their export even reached a new highpoint. One fine example is a Book of Hours according to the Use of Sarum in the Ghent-Bruges style (Stonyhurst College, Ms. 60). Above the miniature of the raising of Lazarus is written: '*Pray for the soules of Dame Cattrayn Bray and of Ion Colett den*

Herod's Soldiers Drowning Aristobulus, illuminated page from Flavius Josephus, *Antiquités et Guerre des Juifs,* Bruges, c.1470-80. London, Sir John Soane's Museum, Ms. 1, f. 1.

St Elizabeth of Hungary, illuminated page from the Book of Hours of William, Lord Hastings, Ghent, the Master of the Older Prayerbook of Maximilian, c.1480. London, British Library, Add. Ms. 54782, f. 64v.

of Paules'. The reference is to Katherine Bray (died 1507), the wife of Sir Reynold Bray, Knight of the Order of the Garter and Treasurer to Henry VII. The second name is that of John Colet, the friend of Thomas More and of Erasmus: in 1509 he was Dean of St Paul's London. It seems probable that Katherine presented the book to Colet and he wanted to keep the memory of both of them alive by the request for a prayer.

A noteworthy offshoot of this export of paraliturgical manuscripts is the fact that the first printed Sarum breviary appeared at Leuven in 1499 and the first Sarum missal at Antwerp in 1527. Throughout the whole of the sixteenth century many printers, binders and booksellers in Flanders worked for the English market or actually went to settle there. In this context we should note William Caxton, who went to live in Bruges around 1444 as a cloth merchant. In 1462 he was head of the English community and a diplomatic representative of the King of England. His interest in literature brought him into contact with workshops producing manuscripts. In 1471, encouraged by Margaret of York, he translated into English Raoul Lefèvre's *Recueil des histoires de Troye,* which had originally been made for Philip the Good. During a stay in Cologne in 1471-1472 Caxton learned the art of printing. In 1473 he returned to England and set up his own publishing and printing business at Westminster. His *Recuyell of the Historyes of Troye* was the first book to be printed in English. He dedicated it to Margaret; the frontispiece of the book depicts the scene.

One of the last important artists of the Ghent-Bruges school was Gerard Horenbout, a master at Ghent from 1487. In 1515 he became court painter to Margaret of Austria, Regent of the Netherlands. Both his son Lucas and his daughter Suzanna were also illuminators. In 1522, when he was about 60, he and his family moved to England, where he worked for Henry VIII; later he returned to Ghent, where he died in about 1540. The charm of his work lies in his rich palette, in his masterful handling of detail and in his narrative structure. At a time when the printing of books was expanding rapidly and therefore becoming a formidable competitor for the manuscript, his contribution was to ensure that the art of the miniature enjoyed a brilliant swansong.

In view of these facts, Horenbout's sojourn in England is hardly surprising. He probably understood that the English public showed a lively interest in Flemish manuscripts and that Flemish miniaturists were appreciated in that country. In fact he was perpetuating a tradition which had existed for more than 150 years.

MAURITS SMEYERS
Translated by Michael Shaw.

FURTHER READING

About Flemish Miniature Painting:
DOGAER, G., *Flemish Miniature Painting in the 15th and 16th Centuries.* Amsterdam, 1987.
Vlaamse miniaturen voor Van Eyck. Ca.1380-ca.1420 (exhibition catalogue), *(Corpus of Illuminated Manuscripts Low Countries Series,* 6, ed. M. Smeyers). Leuven, 1993.

About the relationship with England:
BACKHOUSE, J., 'Founders of the Royal Library: Edward IV and Henry VII as Collectors of Illuminated Manuscripts in England in the Fifteenth Century', in: D. Williams (ed.), *Proceedings of the 1986 Harlaxton Symposium.* Woodbridge, 1987, p. 30 ff.
MCKENDRICK, S., 'Lodewijk van Gruuthuse en de librye van Edward IV, in: *Lodewijk van Gruuthuse, mecenas en diplomaat ca. 1427-1493* (exhibition catalogue). Bruges, 1992, pp. 153-154.
PLOMER, H.R., 'The Importation of Books of Hours into England in the Fifteenth and Sixteenth Centuries', in: *The Library.* 1923, pp. 146-150.
SIMPSON, A., 'English Art during the Second Half of the Fourteenth Century', *Die Parler und der Schöne Stil,* 5. Cologne, 1980, p. 137 ff.
VERTONGEN, S., 'Herman Scheerre, the Beaufort Master and the Flemish Miniature Painting. A Reopened Debate', in: *Flanders in a European Perspective. Manuscript Illumination around 1400 in Flanders and Abroad. Proceedings of the Colloquium, Leuven, 8-10 September 1993.* Leuven, 1995, pp. 251-266.
WRIGHT, S., 'Bruges Artists in London: the Patronage of the House of Lancaster', in: *Flanders in a European Perspective. Manuscript Illumination around 1400 in Flanders and Abroad. Proceedings of the Colloquium, Leuven, 8-10 September 1993.* Leuven, 1995, pp. 93-110.

The

Poet in the Mixer

The Work of Breyten Breytenbach

Breyten Breytenbach (1939-) (Photo by Jerry Bauer).

The South African poet and artist Breyten Breytenbach (1939-) once said that he wrote in a 'bastard language', Afrikaans.[1] Nowadays he publishes mostly in English, having turned his back on the Afrikaans literary establishment which once showered him with prizes and accolades. In his uneasiness with his own cultural heritage Breytenbach is by no means unique, coming as he does from a country with eleven official languages, and where ethnic conflicts have been the thread running through the patchwork that is South African history.

Novelist Chris Barnard once remarked that Breyten Breytenbach's alliterating name sounded as if it had been 'thought up'. The poet started life in two other 'B's', Bonnievale, a small town in the Cape region of the Boland. No other area in South Africa is so quintessentially Afrikaans; even the accents sound as if they were made for TV programmes about wine and regional cooking.

Living in self-imposed exile in Paris – he married a French-speaking Vietnamese in the early sixties, to the chagrin of the apartheid authorities back home who initially refused her a visa to visit the country – Breytenbach poured out his love for his native Boland in poems, even whole anthologies, such as the following poem about his father in the town of Wellington, also in the Boland:

I will die and go to my father
to Wellington with long legs
gleaming in the light
where the rooms are heavy and dark
where stars sit like gulls on the roof
and angels dig for worms in the garden
I will die and be on my way with little luggage
over the mountains of Wellington
between trees and twilight
and go to my father
the sun will throb in the earth
the surf of the wind makes the joints creak

we hear the tenants'
shuffle above our heads
we'll play checkers on the backporch
— cheat daddy —
and listen to the news of the night
on the radio

friends, companions in dying
don't fear — now life hangs like flesh around our bodies
but death doesn't let you down —
our coming and our going
is like water from the tap
like sounds from the mouth
like our coming and going:
our legs will know freedom —
come along
in my dying and going to my father
to Wellington, where the angels
fish fat stars from the sky with worms —
let's die and perish and be merry:
my father has a big boarding-house

(Translated by Ria Loohuizen)

The paradox of Breytenbach's poetic sensibility is to be found in the tension between his attachment to a small-town upbringing, as enunciated in this poem, and his exposure to the cosmopolitan world of Paris with its political and cultural fashions. Zen Buddhism, which had its heyday in the Paris of the sixties, became a major influence in Breytenbach's work, especially in his two properly 'Zen' works, *Lotus* (1970) and *In Other Words* (Met ander woorde, 1973). Echoes of the Dutch poet Bert Schierbeek, himself a follower of Zen, can be found in various parts of Breytenbach's work, as well as other Dutch Experimentalist poets from the Fifties Movement such as Lucebert and Gerrit Kouwenaar. In his work as a visual artist, too, Breytenbach embraced a form of later surrealism not too far removed from that of the CoBrA group of Karel Appel, Corneille, Alechinsky, Constant, Asger Jorn and others, to which authors of the Fifties Movement such as Lucebert and Hugo Claus also belonged.

Apart from Zen, the left-wing atmosphere of 1960s Paris also left its mark on Breytenbach, so that he became more and more attracted to the role of revolutionary, struggling against apartheid and capitalism — two notions that, until recently, used to be easily equated. The rest of Breytenbach's trajectory, his ill-fated involvement with an obscure underground movement known as Okhela, clandestine visit to South Africa in 1975, and subsequent arrest and tragic incarceration, is fairly well-known. His release from prison after eight years of confinement was followed by a spate of publications, including a considerable body of poetry in Afrikaans, as well as a kind of prison notebook, *The True Confessions of an Albino Terrorist* (1984).

In his diaries, politically inspired polemics, novels and other prose works, Breytenbach loves to mix fantasy and reality, narrative and moralising, often choosing various aliases for himself, such as B.B. Lazarus, Panus or Jan Blom, with whom the narrator engages in fanciful dialogues that are sometimes peppered with scatological puns.

In one of the many ironies of the post-apartheid era, Breytenbach has now become something of a political anomaly and finds himself rejected by a younger generation of sycophantic intellectuals who are pandering to the jargon and African self-righteousness of the new regime. Increasingly therefore, the figure of Breytenbach the activist and aspiring politician is fading on the new-South African stage, in favour of a more classical image of the poet / artist doubly exiled from his country and from himself, celebrating that age-old loss of identity that is synonymous with creative being. As a reader one is drawn irresistibly towards his earlier work, where the *mot juste* often crops up amid a simple, guileless celebration of love or domesticity, as in the famous poem, 'The Hole in the Sky' ('Die gat in die lug').

THE HOLE IN THE SKY

(for our house)

my house stands on high legs,
I live in the attic,
ho ho
I'm happy here
stoke the fire,
blow my flute;
when a visitor arrives
he knocks at the door,
I just open the window,
the sun comes to drink
with a clear tongue
the wine in my glass

Breyten Breytenbach, *Untitled*. 1967. Water colour on paper, 55 x 55 cm. Private Collection.

and I can't complain;
sometimes the thousand-eyed rain
watches at panes
but can't find a foothold,
little tadpoles slip to the ground

I've chairs and a table,
books and oranges,
a wife,
a bed that folds like muscles around me

in the evening my house is an observatory;
this coach pulls up at the eyepiece
and a martian climbs out:
come come
I scratch my crotch,
let wind into my shoes;
no thanks, I'm happy here

stoke the fire,
blow the flute;
I shake my hands out,
doves gallop through the air:
go tell the politicians
and the other idiots
my life is without purpose,
a grave, a hole in the sky,
but I'm happy here

in the morning my house is a boat;
I stand at the prow,
my fingers set
to plumb the uncharted coast,
limbs of trees in the yard
flashing past the porthole

the tree:
the tree grows red leaves,
the leaves eggs, eggs become fists
and moult and die
like old bloodroses;
but my house is sound,
that's where I walk around
like a tongue in its mouth;
tongues decompose?
the lean man wastes away?
mould covers bones?

ah the earth shudders,
the walls show through,
the floor splits open: fruit;
my doors are hoarse,
the windows gape,
my wine turns sour,
it snows in the summer,
the rain wears glasses, small rose hands,
but I am happy here

(Translated by Denis Hirson)

This translation comes from the Canadian selection *Sinking Ship Blues* (1977), but the original was published much earlier in the collection *The House of the Deaf One* (Die huis van die dowe, 1967), the title being a reference to Goya's residence in Madrid, *'la quinta del sordo.'* It is a good example of the earlier poetry in that it combines Zen-type allusions to a void or nothingness – in this case the portrayal of the house as a hole in the sky – with the intensely personal nature of Breytenbach's poetic activity. (His predilection for the first person singular was initially denigrated as *'ekkerigheid'*, an untranslatable neologism that could approximately be ren-

Breyten Breytenbach,
Untitled. 1972.
Canvas, 150 x 200 cm.
Collection Dado.

dered as 'me-obsessed'.) The enumeration of personal possessions here can be seen as an exposure of the self, a common theme in his work, which is also very compatible with the kind of Oriental *Weltanschauung* normally associated with Zen.

Roland Barthes once referred to a form of textual voyeurism as *'scopophilia'* ('love of seeing'). The depictions of the rain as having vision and also 'wearing glasses' are also very typical Breytenbach devices – be they insects or secret policeman, a lot of his creations are provided with spectacles of one sort or another. Not only does the rain look in, but he looks out from his *'observatory'* so that one is very much persuaded of a universe of beings peering at one another.

Breytenbach has probably never read Kant, but his notion of the artist's life as being futile *('go tell the politicians / and the other idiots / my life is without purpose, / a grave, a hole in the sky')* is open to a Kantian reading of the 'disinterestedness' of aesthetic contemplation, and indeed, judgment; but this would take one too far away from the current summary of the salient elements of his poetry. However, if one lumps together his multifarious remarks on poetry and art, in and outside his poems, Breytenbach did develop a kind of aesthetic. In various respects Breytenbach is a very *self-conscious* author, also in the Anglo-American sense of the term which denotes a certain self-referentiality in a text. Compare in this regard the penultimate stanza above *('I walk around / like a tongue in its mouth'),* which focuses attention on the fabricated nature of this poem.

The apocalyptic element in the final part of the poem where the carefully

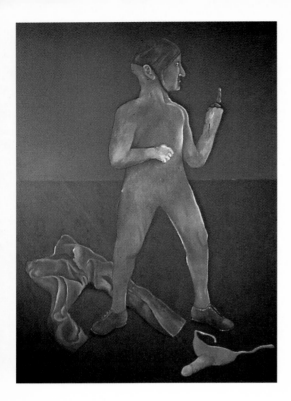

Breyten Breytenbach,
The Bat. 1983. Canvas,
185 x 150 cm. Collection
Nationale de France /
Musée de Dôle.

constructed house of words is made to break down in some tremor, is also very characteristic of Breytenbach. In another well-known poem, *'Populated Death'* ('Bevolkte dood'), he describes a painting by Hieronymus Bosch, the apocalyptic painter *par excellence.* The title of the anthology that contains this poem is *Kouevuur* (1969), which means 'cold fire', but also 'gangrene'. The view of a gangrenous world where everyone is accompanied by his own death, is very much Breytenbach's. In *Kouevuur* and elsewhere he created a kind of topsy-turvy symbolism in which the colour black stood for all good things like Africa, the home country, the chaos of life, and white for everything associated with death, disease, Europe and the white man / albino.

There is an intimate link between Breytenbach the poet / author and Breytenbach the artist / painter. In his paintings and drawings the apocalyptic and grotesque elements of his work seem to attain an even greater prominence. Human figures are usually depicted with malformed faces and limbs, often with impaired sight, their genitals pathetically exposed, stumbling half-blind through a hostile universe. As a motto to his first prose publication in 1964, the collection of short, surreal pieces *Catastrophes* (Katastrofes), he quoted Jean-Paul Sartre: *'No, the universe remains dark. We are animals overcome by catastrophes ... But I have suddenly discovered that alienation, exploitation of man by man, malnutrition, push the metaphysical evil which is a luxury into the background. Hunger is an evil: that is all ... I am on the side of those who think that things will go better if the world has changed.'*

The phrase *'animals overcome by catastrophes'* retains its appositeness regarding the portrayal of *angst*-ridden humanity both in the written oeuvre and in the visual one. However, especially in the bright blues and reds of his paintings and illustrations, there is a rough, child-like quality that is lacking in the relatively smoother, more contrived nature of the poetry. It is as if in this field Breytenbach has allowed himself a greater freedom to overthrow convention and the exigencies of academic stylistics than in his poetic production.

In the cultural turmoil of the new South Africa, Breytenbach's former role as poet laureate to dissident Afrikanerdom has certainly changed. But his quest for freedom and his scintillating phrases will haunt and inspire many generations to come amid the never-ending difficulties of the South African situation.

DAN ROODT

NOTE

1. In 1652 three ships belonging to the Dutch East India Company cast anchor in a bay at the foot of Table Mountain, near the Cape of Good Hope. The Europeans aboard the ships were under the command of the Dutchman Jan van Riebeeck. Their task was the establishment and manning of a supply station for ships on their way to the Indies and back. Van Riebeeck's companions were for the most part sailors and farmers from the provinces of Holland and Zeeland. Their seventeenth-century dialects formed the basis of the present Afrikaans language, which to many Dutch-speakers resembles a kind of simplified Dutch. The reasons for this grammatical simplification have been explained in different ways, some linguists emphasising the influence of other languages (native African tongues, Malay, English, …), others stressing the internal dynamic of Afrikaans itself.

LIST OF ENGLISH TRANSLATIONS AND PUBLICATIONS

Sinking Ship Blues (Tr. André Brink, Ria Loohuizen, Denis Hirson). Toronto, 1977.
And Death White as Words: An Anthology of Poetry (Selected and edited by A.J. Coetzee). Cape Town, 1978.
In Africa Even the Flies Are Happy (Tr. Denis Hirson). London, 1978.
Mouroir (Mirror Notes of a Novel). London, 1984.
Notes of Bird. Amsterdam, 1984.
The True Confessions of an Albino Terrorist. Johannesburg, 1984.
A Season in Paradise. London, 1985.
End Papers: Essays, Letters, Articles of Faith, Workbook Notes. New York, 1986.
Judas Eye; and, Self-Portrait / Deathwatch. London, 1988.
Memory of Snow and Dust. Johannesburg, 1989.
All One Horse: Fictions and Images. Johannesburg, 1990.
Painting the Eye. Cape Town, 1993.
Return to Paradise. London, 1993.

Piecing

the Scraps Together

Roel D'Haese and his Sculptures

The Flemish sculptor Roel D'Haese casts bronze sculptures using the 'lost wax' process. This technique was developed more than four thousand years ago in order to make durable bronze casts from fragile, complex three-dimensional models. The model is covered with a thin layer of wax and then a heat-resistant substance. The layer of wax corresponds exactly to the thin skin of the bronze casting and of course disappears on heating; hence the term 'lost wax' as, in French, *'cire perdue'*. The mould, too, is chopped away afterwards. The execution of the process itself is usually left to the craftsmen, the bronze-founders, while the artist or designer concentrates on modelling the object in clay and supervising the finishing of the bronze after it has been cast. Roel D'Haese, however, has succeeded in transforming this laborious traditional procedure into a creative process in its own right. *'The lost wax technique is as simple as using a pencil',* says D'Haese.

Roel D'Haese was born in Geraardsbergen (East Flanders) in 1921. The family later moved to Aalst. Albert D'Haese, father of ten children, was a lawyer, journalist, Aalst's alderman for education and an MP. When faced with his son's artistic ambitions, he said, *'become a pharmacist, then you'll have lots of spare time, and after work you can play the artist'.* But Roel wanted to follow in the footsteps of his uncle, Frans Tinel, and become a sculptor. His younger brother Reinhoud and his sister Begga, in their turn, followed the example of their elder brother, and another brother became a musician.

At the Academy in Aalst the young Roel realised that he really did have artistic talent. He was then apprenticed to an ornamental metalworker and a wood carver, and they taught him the tricks of the trade. D'Haese has always remained grateful to these simple craftsmen. In fact he regrets the fact that in modern art education training in craftsmanship is being displaced by the attention devoted to artistic training. He values rather less his studies with Oscar Jespers, at that time one of the most important sculptors in Belgium. D'Haese studied under Jespers at the La Cambre Institute in Brussels from 1938 to 1942. In the years immediately after this he would continue to work with the chisel, taking Jespers and Brancusi as his example. In the works he produced during that period he was aiming for simple and flawless design.

He achieved his first successes but was later to dismiss this work as a mistake. When open-air exhibitions were organised in the Middelheim Park in Antwerp, from the fifties onwards, D'Haese was one of the artists shown (see *The Low Countries* 1994-95: 119-124).

In the meantime, artists and enthusiasts in Brussels were making passionate efforts to integrate the local art world into the international avant garde and put an end, once and for all, to traditionalism and provincialism. The most important initiative was undoubtedly the establishment of CoBrA in Paris in 1948. The Belgian Christian Dotremont, the Dutchmen Karel Appel, Eugène Brands, Corneille and Constant and the Dane Asger Jorn wanted to join forces against the domination of artistic life by the Parisian avant garde, and against the dogmatism and formalism of surrealism and the avant garde. Belgian artists did not actually contribute a great deal to the development of the characteristic CoBrA idiom; Dotremont was a poet. Even so, Asger Jorn and his associates, with their world of childlike dream creatures and their spontaneous way of working, later exercised a great attraction on various Belgian artists. And the slogan *'poetry, revolution and love'* (read *'self-expression, subversion and lust'*) was taken up by many at that time.

Roel D'Haese lived very near Brussels, in St-Genesius-Rode, and followed movements in the art world closely. In 1955, together with his brother Reinhoud, the poet Hugo Claus (see *The Low Countries* 1993-94: 17-24), the painters Pierre Alechinsky, Wallasse Ting and Serge Vandercam, he appeared alongside Asger Jorn in the exhibitions at the Taptoe arts centre in Brussels.

Every one of the works Roel D'Haese made during this period was evidence of his quest for a medium that would allow him to create figures unpremeditatedly, as if on impulse, just as the painters did: a three-dimensional form of automatic writing. He hoped that an intuitive feel for the material and the firm hand of the craftsman would be enough to conjure up sculptures free of preconceived objectives and artistic conventions: the creative process should simply happen to the artist. It was at about that time that he discovered himself as a sculptor, as he himself states.

In 1954 D'Haese welded and screwed iron motifs together into images which are reminiscent of reptiles or standing figures, such as *Lizard*

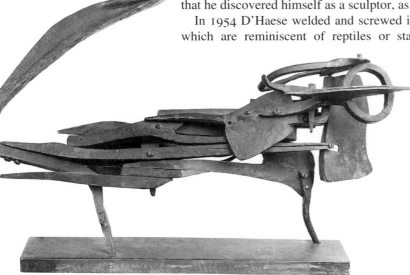

Roel D'Haese, *Lizard Movements*. 1954. Wrought iron, 44.5 x 69.8 x 26.3 cm. Koninklijke Musea voor Schone Kunsten van België (B. & A. Goldschmidt bequest), Brussels.

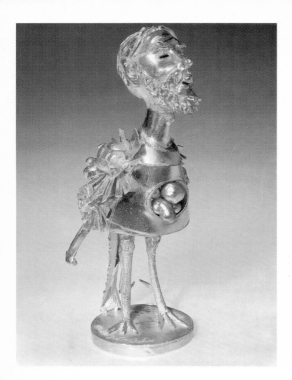

Roel D'Haese, *The Midnight Cuckoo (Ensor)*. 1969. Gold, H 20 cm. Private Collection.

Roel D'Haese, *Bronze Tower*. 1955. Bronze (sand mould), 77 x 30 x 28 cm. Koninklijk Museum voor Schone Kunsten, Antwerp.

Movements and *The Warrior*. These assemblages immediately won him the new Prize for Young Belgian Sculpture. A sculpture like *Lizard Movements* probably arose out of the fortuitous but striking resemblance of a piece of old iron to a natural motif. The artist's actions are limited to sawing, bending, welding and bolting together the available material. So the way the image is brought into being is determined to a large extent by the evocative power of the objects available.

D'Haese had hardly launched into iron work when he started working copper and steel sheets too. The metal sheeting was cut and bent into elongated, shell-like elements that were then welded together. This is how the *Mythical Animals* originated. D'Haese occasionally used this technique later on too, and his brother Reinhoud used it to produce a virtuoso oeuvre.

In 1955 D'Haese also started casting in bronze, working entirely alone in his own foundry until 1964. In the beginning he used the sand mould process. Various objects are pressed into a bed of sand, producing the cast in high relief. The various casts are then welded together. The *Bronze Tower* shows clearly the much greater element of chance in this method. The accumulation of disparate motifs produces a figure whose expressiveness is to a great extent dependent on the arbitrary surfaces of the various parts. The figures are grown over, so to speak, by a carapace of ribs and projections. This way of working was undoubtedly a forerunner of the assemblage art that was to become popular in the sixties.

It was not very long before Roel D'Haese gave up his welding and joinery work, his copper sheeting and the sand mould process. In 1957 he discovered the lost wax method as incomparably the most creative way of working. This technique incorporates and surpasses the possibilities of welding and joinery, the working of copper sheeting or the assemblage of sand-mould bronzes. D'Haese modelled the parts of a sculpture – shapes, motifs and details – directly into soft, warm wax. The bronze cast makes an extremely detailed and faithful reproduction of the original model; here and there the traces of dripping liquid wax were also reproduced in bronze. The layer of wax is sometimes supported by gauze and you can clearly see how D'Haese has tried to exploit this surface effect, particularly in the later bronzes. This concern for a refined texture has also occasionally led him to leave some of the white traces of the mould on the cast, producing unplanned tonal effects.

Some of the wax forms can afterwards be cut up like fabric. Since D'Haese discovered that he could easily hang these forms from the ceiling with string, he has had greater freedom in the assembly of the fragile wax shapes. He can commence the assemblage of wax forms with the top, the body, a minor part or the base. Working with wax also freed the artist from the inherent content of found materials, since he makes the parts himself. In addition, working with warm wax compels him to work at speed.

Afterwards, the assemblage has to be dismantled, its individual parts cast in bronze and finally welded back together again. The artist can also make alterations in this final stage. The traces of welding are usually clearly visible.

At first D'Haese consistently tried to construct the sculptures discontinuously, to let creation simply 'happen'. So the first lost wax bronzes display abrupt articulations between one part and another, as well as unexpected combinations. In later sculptures too, such as *Jason,* from 1974, the long, solid upper legs support the hero's bust, with nothing in between. His behind looks like the upper half of an enormous pumpkin. The commanding arm of the ruler appears behind his back. On his shoulder he is wearing the skin and head of a ram (the Golden Fleece), while Jason's enormous head almost entirely blocks our view of the body of a dying young Negro on his other shoulder. In order to grasp D'Haese's sculptures fully you have to walk

Roel D'Haese, *Mythical Animal.* 1955. Copper, 39.1 x 35.5 x 18.5 cm. Koninklijke Musea voor Schone Kunsten van België (B. & A. Goldschmidt bequest), Brussels.

round the figure, crouch down and stick your head between your legs.

These sculptures are startling, absurd, frightening and ludicrous. D'Haese has always resisted the 'Expressionist' label, though he does create distinctly grotesque images. The artist is an admirer of James Ensor (see *The Low Countries* 1994-95: 156-167) and he may well at times have come under the direct influence of Ensor's discomfiting deceptions and masked scenes – until now not the slightest attention has been paid to the iconographic, technical and stylistic sources of D'Haese's work; in other words it is not easy to discover where he sought inspiration. But in any case, in D'Haese's work the popular, and typically Western, preference for the primitive occasionally shines through. The artist himself maintains that his taste is determined primarily by Leo Frobenius' *Cultural History of Africa* (Kulturgeschichte Afrikas, 1933): *'This seemed to be something I would one day be able to achieve. I didn't dare say so, but I found it much more beautiful than Michelangelo, who always has something of the boredom of sitting in church about him. (…) We are still the same people as our forefathers in the Stone Age, except that we are less handy and less inventive.'*

Roel D'Haese, *Jan de Lichte.* 1987. Bronze (lost wax), H 333 cm. Middelheim Museum, Antwerp.

Round about 1961 D'Haese's work underwent a change. The sculptures became more realistic and less chaotic. Perhaps he realised that the pseudo-spontaneous and pseudo-organic method brought him dangerously close to breaking the decorative taboo. But because he rejected the methods of Pop Art and Minimalism, all that remained to him was to return to a more traditional artistic outlook, and so he offended against the modernist ban on true-to-life, narrative images. *'Artists make things they would like to see or of which they dream. Narration, that's as old as the world itself. I don't see why that should change',* says D'Haese. Of course, he remained true to his love for the primitive and the grotesque, and the design of the sculptures is still determined to a large extent by the separately conceived parts or *'scraps'*, as D'Haese calls these limbs and other motifs.

Since D'Haese opted for a narrative conception of sculpture he has also taken on the interpretation of traditional sculptural themes. The equestrian statue *Song of Evil* dates from 1964 and is the last sculpture D'Haese cast entirely on his own. He called the work *'almost a manifesto'*.

As far as humanity is concerned, D'Haese's views are pessimistic: *'the white man is fundamentally evil'*. And during the production of *Song of Evil,* the artist was totally under the spell of Billy the Kid and other trigger-happy outlaws. This equestrian statue is clearly not intended as a consecration of the mounted ruler, the sovereign figure. But who, without a label, would recognise, in the comical figure on the back of the baying horse, an unmasking of the stupid, cruel white man?

Since 1958 D'Haese has handed his works over to the Paris dealer Claude Bernard. In 1965 his work was exhibited next to that of Cesar and Tinguely in the Musée d'Arts Décoratifs in Paris. He is also known in Germany. Nevertheless, critical interest in his work comes almost entirely from Belgium. Given the indisputable monumentality of sculptures like *Song of Evil* or *Jason,* it is remarkable that D'Haese has never been granted an official commission.

The Flemish writer Louis Paul Boon died in 1979. He came from the same area as D'Haese and they both held the same anarchist views. Boon had written a book about the life of Jan de Lichte, who was executed in Aalst

Roel D'Haese, *Song of Evil.*
1964. Bronze (lost wax),
227 x 87 x 273 cm.
Koninklijk Museum voor
Schone Kunsten, Antwerp.

in 1748. In Boon's book the thief and sex-murderer was presented as a resistance hero. D'Haese decided to make a portrayal of Jan de Lichte in memory of Louis Paul Boon, and hoped that the sculpture would be set up on the Market Square in Aalst. The execution of this project was of course endangered by the controversial subject, the size of the work and the dynamic approach of the artist and his supporters. The sculpture was cast in 1987 and ultimately placed in the Middelheim Open Air Sculpture Museum in Antwerp.

Roel D'Haese did not try to portray Jan de Lichte as a romantic rebel, let alone as the brutal ruffian who lives on in oral tradition. He calls the ragged lad *'a poor soul':* the umpteenth alter ego of the existentialist artist who in the West, according to D'Haese, *'enjoys only one freedom: a miserable death'.*

HERWIG TODTS
Translated by Gregory Ball.

FURTHER READING

Bert Popelier's *Roel D'Haese (Beeld / Spraak)* (Ghent, 1987) contains the best biographical and bibliographical survey and three interviews with the artist.

Chronicle

Contents

A Brightly Coloured Ocean Liner
The New Groninger Museum

In the autumn of 1994 the skyline of the Dutch provincial capital of Groningen was dramatically transformed by the building of the Groninger Museum. It isn't architecture, it isn't design and it isn't art. This striking construction, which houses a highly diverse collection of art both ancient and modern, can best be described as a work of total art. Sited opposite the station, this complex aptly illustrates the motto of its director, Frans Haks: *'Look and Wonder'*. The building is a showcase for contemporary architecture and, just like art, it is intended to delight. The visitor is gradually seduced into abandoning himself to the show, in which no distinction is made between art and design or between art and architecture. Once inside, all contact with the outside world is broken. There are no windows in the museum's rooms, there is in fact no daylight at all. Haks considers that daylight would distract the visitor too much; moreover, it cannot be stage-managed.

He can create any atmosphere he likes using artificial light. This is because Haks wants not only to entertain the visitor, but to stimulate him too. Just like Goethe, he believes that the human being needs constant change. This was why he chose to take the diversity of the collection, a mixture of old and new, from East and West, (inter)national and regional, as the point of departure for the new museum. He gave the commission for its design to the versatile Italian Allessandro Mendini who, apart from being an architect, is also a poet, a designer, a visual artist and a writer, and in whom Haks saw a kindred spirit.

In accordance with the wishes of the director, Mendini in turn employed several guest architects including the French designer Philippe Starck and the Viennese architects of the Coop Himmelb(l)au. The result of this collaboration is entirely original and looks like no other existing building. A colourful procession of architectural shapes has come to a halt on a dream of a site, in the middle of an expanse of water. The whole thing looks rather like a colourful ocean liner, one built from a model kit and not intended ever to sail the seven seas.

From the outside the most conspicuous feature is the thirty-metre high, gold-coloured storage tower, the museum's 'treasure-house', 'Groningen's sun', doing battle with the church towers behind it. In most museums, the stock of works of art is stored in the cellar and the visitor ascends to view an exhibition. Not so in Groningen. Here the museum itself is underground, and the visitor stands up to his waist in water.

On both sides of the tower are the heaped pavilions of the museum, each showing by means of its style and form which part of the collection it houses. So the fortress in dark brick is home to archaeology and regional history. In the profusely decorated box on the other side is the modern art. The higgledy-piggledy roof in steel plate covers the section on ancient visual art. This specimen of modern architecture, designed by Coop Himmelb(l)au, reflects the chaos of our times and puts the strict equilibrium of Mendini into perspective. It is the only one of the pavilions whose exterior was not designed by the Italian master, and also the only building with windows.

Inside, the museum does not immediately reveal what a hallowed atmosphere awaits the visitor in the underground vaults. The entrance hall is a public area and provides a wide view over the outskirts of the city. From its centre a spectacular mosaic stairway leads down to where the museum itself begins. There are no windows in the exhibition rooms.

The route to the pavilions is short and clear, but then the wandering begins. The Italian guest architect Michele de Lucchi has created a breath-taking environment for the regional art. A narrow passageway enveloped above, below and at the sides in a brilliant terracotta colour, opening into small rooms on each side. Here the art is no longer restricted to the walls. The visitor is surrounded by the works and is sucked in among them. The open ceilings with terracotta-coloured service ducts form a pleasant game of stray-

Mendini's pavilion for temporary exhibitions and contemporary art, and Coop Himmelb(l)au's pavilion for ancient art (Photo by John Stoel).

Studio Mendini's model of the Groninger Museum (Photo by Jan Stock).

ing paths and the indirect lighting with its high-tech mirrors is a delight to the eyes.

One floor higher, inside an aluminium cylinder, the Frenchman Philippe Starck has given the section on the applied arts a serene, fragile look. The path to be followed is determined by a fanciful route of double white curtains lit by fluorescent tubes. Porcelain from a ship sunk in the South China Sea floats in an aquarium inhabited by goldfish. For the other side of the central hall Mendini designed a symmetrical, classical museum layout in the decorated box. Every detail is perfect. No shadow on the wall is allowed to disturb the hallowed atmosphere. Not a hint of white is to be found anywhere. The pastel violet rooms with their angled skirtings and doorposts tapering to a point are intended for temporary exhibitions.

On the first floor are the rooms where the Dutch light-artist Peter Struycken has provided the contemporary art with a theatrical lighting programme. The vivid pink, purple and deep blue gives a hallucinatory splendour to the kitsch of, for example, Rhonda Zwillinger or Thomas Lanigan-Schmidt.

The oblique display walls in the Himmelb(l)au pavilion, which can be moved within the space with great flexibility and on which the ancient art is displayed, received the American Association of Museums Award before the museum was even opened.

It is not often that so much beauty can be admired in the Netherlands. Architecture and art are entirely absorbed into each other. And that is also the only negative point to be detected in this ultimate museum. The presence of the public can only disrupt the existing harmony and has in fact become superfluous. There is only one thing left to the visitor and that is to submerge himself completely in the aesthetic bath that Haks, Mendini and partners have prepared for him.

MARINA DE VRIES
Translated by Gregory Ball.

ADDRESS
Groninger Museum
Museumeiland 1 / 9711 ME Groningen / The Netherlands
tel. +31 50 366 65 55
Opening hours: 10 a.m. - 5 p.m. (closed on Mondays)

Kattenbroek, a Provocative Housing Development

Amersfoort is a town of some 115,000 inhabitants, right in the centre of the Netherlands. Between 1982 and 1994 it needed to expand its housing stock in an accelerated tempo: 17,000 new dwellings – 5,000 in the existing town and 12,000 in the north as a 'new town' area. In the same period the employment situation had to be given extra impetus by the creation of 16,000 new jobs, and the development of new facilities in the old city centre and the surrounding residential areas. In short: the task was the creation of an environment in which it was good to live and good to work.

The physical aspect of the town of Amersfoort derives its pronounced identity from the old inner city with its medieval structure. This centre is like the heart of a flower, around which the petals of ten different residential areas have been successively built between 1880 and 1980. Amersfoort's situation at the meeting point of various landscapes – moorland with sand hills and woods, a valley with streams and a river delta with pasture-land – forms a natural basis for a great diversity of residential environments.

After a period of enquiry and taking stock, of brainstorming and reflection, in March 1988 Ashok Bhalotra, associated with the firm of Kuiper Compagnons of Rotterdam, was commissioned to produce a development plan for the last 5,000 dwellings to be built in the northern 'new town' area. This new district is known as Kattenbroek, after a very old fortified farmstead whose name is all that has survived the passage of time. Kattenbroek is the keystone and the apotheosis of this remarkable achievement of expanding Amersfoort's housing stock as rapidly and soundly as possible.

The terms of reference were: to make a master plan based on a vision derived from the old city of Amersfoort. To offer a project, whose coherency should be such that during the 5-year realisation period all those engaged in its execution would derive ever-increasing pleasure from sustaining the project. No standard procedure with a standard product, no monotonous streets of terraced houses, no depressing, people-unfriendly public spaces. Away with the cynical plan, lacking heart and soul, which appears far too often in the peripheral areas of Dutch towns. Give imagination full play. The town must stimulate the senses agreeably: large structures, which guarantee spatial unity, can be made exciting through attractive detail and diversity. The design of the neighbourhood must be structured around cohesive public spaces, which should offer a perspective to both residents and passers-by.

One of the main desiderata for housing in the years ahead is that everyone shall be able to achieve his own lifestyle and the corresponding domestic culture, as future housing development will offer a sufficient range of choice. That rich and poor, young and old, large and small households shall live alongside one another without irritating each other. The basic principle here is that the different social strata of the population should be housed in among one another in comfortable coexistence, instead of the various groups each being housed in their own separate location.

The old city centres, which took shape organically in the course of the centuries, teach us that this sort of mixed population greatly enhances the quality of life and the liveliness of the town.

In short: no 'apartheid' to satisfy the wishes of the property developers in the short term, but a society, which creates the conditions in the long term for a state of tolerant humanity. Indeed, this housing policy was based on an ongoing survey of housing wishes, which was annually translated into a development plan.

Ashok Bhalotra's design is based on a conceptual

Views of Kattenbroek.

view of the way people live. Obvious as this principle may sound, many town planners consider this view too romantic, too emotional, and contrary to the prevailing idea that town planning must first and foremost be rational. Bhalotra believes that people want to feel 'at home' in their residential environment, because it appeals to them and stimulates their senses. On the other hand, people want to go out, undergo new experiences and explore the unknown. Travelling and being at home, those are the themes which have been elaborated in Kattenbroek.

The principal housing groups have been given metaphorical names, such as the Ring, the Mask, the Avenue of the Interior Courts, the Creek, the Hidden Zone. By using these metaphors it was possible to alert the participating architects to the underlying emotional values of the master plan and to transmit the imaginative power behind it.

In implementing the plan a great deal of attention was paid to the characteristics of the existing landscape. For example, tree-lined canals, a series of old farmhouses, the contiguity to the country estate to the south and Park Schothorst and the huge play area on the old cover sand ridge. The different social housing categories are represented in each of the five themes by very varied atmospheres, which are also accentuated by the names of the housing clusters, such as The Quiet Alley, The Wood of Villas, The Fort, The Marsh Houses and so on. In the meantime the phased construction of Kattenbroek has been completed. The lay-out is divided into 'conceptual areas', where the residents

can derive their own values from their particular housing experience.

The project was supervised from the first drawing to the last paving stone by Ashok Bhalotra; he advised the client on the choice of architects and stimulated everyone involved in the project not only to sustain his master plan, but also to reinforce it in the course of its implementation.

Kattenbroek has broken the mould of planological thinking, so that since 1990 the urban landscape in the Netherlands has been acquiring a slightly different aspect.

FONS ASSELBERGS
Translated by Rachel van der Wilden.

The Gothic Revival in Britain and Belgium

The English influence on Art Nouveau and Belgian Symbolism has often been emphasised. Thus we know that in 1893, Victor Horta chose English wallpaper for his pioneering house Tassel, and that Ferdinand Khnopff was greatly inspired by the Pre-Raphaelites. Henry van de Velde and Gustave Serrurier-Bovy, with their social approach to interior design, also followed in the footsteps of William Morris and the Arts and Crafts movement.

This fertile assimilation of ideas and forms was, however, merely the creative culmination of a long process which began as early as the end of the eighteenth century. In the field of Gothic artistic expression in particular, a remarkable interplay appears to have existed between England and Belgium (primarily between England and Flanders). This interplay was a leitmotif for the special exhibition *The Gothic Revival in Belgium* held in the Bijloke Museum in Ghent during the autumn of 1994.

Before 1850 Belgium was principally influenced by France, while other influences were only indirect. But here, too, the fashion for English gardens, with Gothic pavilions, was introduced in all manner of publications. One of the earliest preserved examples is the gatehouse of Moregem Castle (c.1792-1798). In the same spirit, the Lille architect Benjamin Dewarlez built the half-oriental, half-Gothic pavilion for the St Joris shooting club in Kortrijk.

After Belgian independence in 1830 the contacts became more direct, probably helped by the excellent relations between Leopold I and Queen Victoria. The Gothic Revival spread from the gardens to the country houses themselves, and the buildings acquired more English features.

One of the most typical buildings of the period is Castle *Les Masures* near Pepinster, which P. Colman rightly called *'the Strawberry Hill of Wallonia'*, after Walpole's famous house. Built between 1835 and 1837 to the design of Auguste-Marie Vivroux, it was later completed with the addition of an imposing bridge and gatehouse in the Tudor style. The patron, Edouard de Biolley, was a businessman whose connections presumably brought him into direct contact with British culture. The English style remained especially fashionable for country houses: a striking late example is Castle *Tudor* at St Andries Bruges, built in 1904.

In towns and cities too, representative buildings were built in the 'national' Gothic style. Often the stylistic features came from English design books, either for the sake of convenience or through a highly conscious effort to be picturesque. The episcopal Palace in Ghent (1841-1845) has interiors in an early 'Gothick' which, across the Channel, had been out of fashion for decades. The architect Joseph Jonas Dumont studied the pioneering prison architecture of England *in situ*. His prisons in Leuven (1846), Brussels (1847), Liège (1850), Verviers (1850), Dinant (1851) and Charleroi (1851) were largely inspired by the English style.

At that time the Antwerp Academy was one of the international keystones of the romantic plastic arts, inspired largely by the Middle Ages. The Dutchman Alma-Tadema was a pupil of G. Wappers, N. De Keyser and H. Leys, before, as Sir Lawrence, he

E.W. Pugin, *Drawing of the basilica of Dadizele* (1860).

The Blue Room in Caloen Castle (Loppem), designed by J.B. Bethune.

created a furore in England with his Roman tableaux. His early work consists of medieval scenes such as *The Destruction of the Abbey at Doest in Flanders* (1857) and *Clothilde at the Grave of her Young Children* (1859).

The one-way artistic influence did not remain so for very long. English antiquarians and antique collectors scoured the country, among them the leading light of the Gothic Revival, Augustus Welby Northmore Pugin, who, for example, used Flemish antiques for the chapel of his beloved Oscott College. The craftsmanship of the wood carvers and the precious-metal workers, which had suffered less than that of other countries from the consequences of revolution and industrialisation, was much appreciated abroad. The Gothic Revival choir stalls in the cathedral at Antwerp, begun in 1839 by the Leuven sculptor K.H. Geerts, for example, were acclaimed well outside Belgium.

Around 1850, the city of Bruges became the focal point in a new phase of artistic influence, this time directly from England. Bruges, for a long time a stop on the tourist route to Waterloo, Cologne and Aachen, was home to a large colony of Englishmen, mostly of independent means. Thanks in part to the enlightened patronage of Mgr J.B. Malou, Bruges became one of the focal points of Puginesque Gothic Revival on the continent. In 1844 the English architect R.D. Chantrell designed a remarkable new spire in advanced neo-Roman style. An edited translation of Pugin was published in Bruges by Thomas Harper King under the title *Les vrais principes de l'architecture originale ou chrétienne,* and became the artistic bible of the Belgian Gothic Revival. King was also involved in the design for the Magdalena Church in Bruges which, by analogy with Hamburg's Nikolaikirche, was set to become the prototype of artistic innovation. The style books which he published contributed much to the spread of the Gothic Revival on the Continent, and at once ensured that continental medieval art became more widely known in Britain, where it became an important source of inspiration. A great number of workshops in Bruges concentrated on production according to Pugin's theories; one example is the gold embroiderer Louis Gossé, whose shop had a London branch in Baker Street for quite some time. The basilica of Dadizele (1859 ff.), which was designed by Edward Pugin (Augustus' son) at the request of Mgr Malou, is one of the most monumental reminders of the High Victorian Gothic Revival outside England.

Puginesque Gothic Revival only truly caught on in Belgium under the influence of Baron J.B. Bethune, with his personal variation on this style which was adapted to Belgian taste. Early on, Bethune's childhood friend, George Mann, introduced him to British culture and Bethune remained in regular contact with Pugin from 1843 onwards. He began his artistic career as a glazier, influenced by the technical knowledge made available to him by Pugin's associate John Hardman. Bethune concentrated increasingly on architecture after 1858, when he took over the wharf of Caloen Castle at Loppem from Edward Pugin.

Sir John Sutton of Norwood Park, who published *A Short Account of Organs* with Pugin and founded the English Seminary at Bruges, worked with Bethune on the restoration of the church and famous medieval organ of Kiedrich in the Rhineland.

Bethune's associate, the antiquarian James Weale, christened him *'the Pugin of Belgium'*, because he approached more closely than any living architect the style of his great English mentor. Bethune's excellent knowledge of Belgian medieval art enabled him, in his personal works, to adapt Puginesque Gothic Revival to continental taste and tradition, as in the village complex of Vive-Kapelle (1860-1867) near Bruges, and the abbey at Maredsous (1872-1888).

Meanwhile the characteristic High Victorian style, with its powerful language of forms and pronounced colours, had also become popular in Belgium. It was introduced there by, among others, Edward Pugin and William Curtis Brangwyn. The latter drew plans for the interior of the Chapel of the Holy Blood in Bruges. The High Victorian style was also copied in the work of – among others – Eugène Carpentier and August van Assche.

There was also a close spiritual bond between the Pre-Raphaelites and the Belgian historical-realist school. Dante Gabriel Rossetti visited Bruges in 1849 and was greatly impressed by the Chapel of the Holy Blood, *'a wonderful little place'*. Like their contemporaries across the English Channel, Hendrik Leys, Pieter van der Ouderaa and Théophile Lybaert also looked back to late-medieval art, and maintained an almost photographic realism in order to convey 'genuine ideas' of a largely moralistic nature. The Bruges artist Edmond van Hout was hailed by English critics as 'the Belgian Pre-Raphaelite'.

Export across the Channel was an important source of income for the Gothic Revival firms, which were now sprouting like mushrooms. In 1886, for example, the De Clerq brothers of Merelbeke proudly reported in their firm's prospectus that they were making a pulpit for St Mary's, a communion rail for Halifax, a triptych for Skipton and a colossal statue of Our Lady, with pedestal, for Glasgow. The 'liturgical workshops' of the Bruges artist Louis Beyaert, a pupil of the English sculptor Alfred Gilbert, concentrated on the Anglo-Saxon market (e.g. work on the Catholic Westminster Cathedral).

It must be said that the constant English influence was balanced by equally intense contact with France and Germany. It is precisely through this melting-pot effect that Belgium became, as it were, a microcosm of contemporary Europe, which explains why this small but relatively prosperous and centrally situated country became one of the most important laboratories of a new artistic synthesis, the pinnacle of which was Art Nouveau.

JEAN VAN CLEVEN
Translated by Yvette Mead

FURTHER READING

VAN CLEVEN, JEAN, et al., *Neogotiek in België*. Tielt, 1994 (ill., with extensive critical bibliography).

Cultural Policy

Brussels Calling Live from Flanders

The voice of Flanders is heard all over the world. It is the voice of a small community with its own cultural identity within the Kingdom of Belgium. The 'voices' are those of the staff of the Flemish world service, RVI (Radio Flanders International – *Radio Vlaanderen Internationaal),* a department of the public broadcasting corporation BRTN (Belgian Radio and Television, Dutch-language broadcasts – *Belgische Radio en Televisie, Nederlandstalige Uitzendingen),* which serves the Flemish Community within the Belgian state.

The Flemish world service, RVI, works within the structure of the public broadcasting corporation and is quite independent of other public or private bodies. The RVI editors, like those of the BRTN, are legally bound to be objective in all their broadcasts, and the broadcasting legislation expressly forbids any form of political or other censorship. The service is financed from the funds of the public broadcasting corporation, without support from any other organisation.

Radio Vlaanderen Internationaal has been the official name of the Flemish world service since the autumn of 1992. It had begun life in what was at the time Leopoldstad (now Kinshasa), the capital of the Belgian colony of the Congo (now Zaire), and went on air for the first time on 16 May 1943. The name includes all the transmissions in the six languages in which the corporation broadcasts. In addition to its own Dutch, these are: English, French, German, Spanish and Arabic. The various language broadcasts go out as, respectively, *Brussels Calling, Ici Bruxelles, Hier ist Brüssel, Aqui Bruselas* and *Hoena Bruxelles.*

The job of the Flemish world service is twofold: to maintain contact with Flemings and to act as a mirror of life in the Flemish community and in Belgium as a whole. The service seeks to maintain links with fellow countrymen who, for whatever reason, are in some other part of the world, on land, at sea or in the air; with Flemings who have settled abroad permanently, but also with those who are away from home for a brief period or who are travelling. These might be missionaries or seamen, aid workers, lorry drivers, business people or holiday makers taking a short break or perhaps wintering abroad.

This provides a permanent and clearly rewarding job for the ten members of the editorial team, who encounter their most exciting challenges in so-called times of crisis. This was the case in 1951 during the war in Korea, where the Belgian detachment included many Flemings. There were peaks of drama in 1960 when the former colony of the Congo declared its independence from Belgian rule – and later in the Gulf, in Somalia and recently in the former Yugoslavia, Ruanda and Burundi. Many Flemings abroad find their most tangible contact with the mother country in their world service's broadcasts of normal daily Dutch-language programmes, either in their entirety or in part, just as they are heard at home.

But besides making contact with fellow countrymen abroad, the RVI also attracts listeners within Belgium whose mother tongue is not Dutch. Representatives of the main world languages – one thinks of the EU, NATO and the business world – can, for instance, obtain information in their own language on medium wave about the country where they are permanently or temporarily resident. This is an extremely important part of the RVI's job; it is particularly significant in a community with a minor European language, for foreign guests in Belgium are traditionally and almost exclusively informed by French-language media. This has given (and still gives) rise to inaccurate reporting, misunderstandings and disinformation.

The mirror function consists in making the world more familiar with Flanders. Most countries regard this as the principal task of a world service; serving as an ambassador for the sociocultural and political-economic individuality of a country, a nation, a people. With the RVI that responsibility has taken on a broader and more fundamental significance since the spring of 1992, when the French-language Belgian broadcasting corporation (RTBf) was forced for financial reasons to dispense with its world service.

It is a well-known fact that in many countries world broadcasts are subject to governmental influence or control. In Flanders, too, the question has been raised as to whether a world service should not come under a government department such as the Ministry of the Interior or of Foreign Affairs rather than the public broadcasting company. Belgium has resisted that ministerial temptation, realising that political and economic propaganda and promotion should form no part of a broadcasting company's brief.

The RVI now has at its disposal three short-wave transmitting stations, a medium-wave station and a satellite channel. The satellite channel enables people to listen to programmes of FM quality as far afield as Dublin and Warsaw, Oslo or Stockholm, Rome or Tangiers. The satellite channel is received via Astra 1 C, horizontal polarisation, on 10,920.75 GHZ frequency, audio channel 7.38 MHZ. The signal can be picked up with a 20 to 60cm dish. In Belgium, cable networks ensure that reception of RVI programmes is first-rate. It is now possible to listen to RVI pretty well all over the world, though it still does not have enough powerful broadcasting or relay stations at a few vital points around the globe.

Since March 1994, *Brussels Calling* has been relayed by World Radio Network in London. WRN is a private enterprise which produces a summarised edition twenty-four hours a day of English-language news and current affairs programmes from Europe (RVI, BBC, the Netherlands, Finland, Ireland), the USA (National Public Radio) and Australia. The WRN programme is transmitted in Europe via the Astra satellite and in North America via the Galaxy satellite as a sub-carrier of Turner Broadcast Systems. The programme is relayed by cable networks in Europe and Canada as well as in the USA, where it is also transmitted in part by the C-Span audio network.

The thirty-minute English-language programme, *Brussels Calling,* is put out six times a day by the RVI: in UTC time, at 7.30 a.m. (Australia, Europe), 10 a.m. (Africa, Southern Europe), 2 p.m. (North America), 7 p.m. (Africa, Europe), 10 p.m. (Europe) and 12.30 a.m. (North and South America). The English-language broadcasting section has a number of its own features: daily News and Review of the Press, of course, and also Belgium Today, Living in Belgium, Focus on Europe, Tourism in Flanders, The Arts, Around the Arts, Green Society, Economics, North-South, Radio World and Music from Flanders.

In 1994 *Brussels Calling* received 2,730 letters. Of those 40% came from Europe, 25% from North America, 15% from Africa, 15% from south-east Asia and 5% from Australia and New Zealand. Clearly the voice of Flanders does not go unheard in the wilderness of the world.

HUIB DEJONGHE
Translated by Alison Mouthaan-Gwillim.

Information about broadcasting schedules and RVI frequencies (they vary each season) are available free of charge from: RVI / P.O. Box 26 / 1000 Brussels / Belgium tel. +32 2 741 38 02 / fax +32 2 732 62 95

Seventy-Five Years of Dutch Studies in London

1994 marked a milestone in Dutch Studies in the United Kingdom: it was precisely seventy-five years since the foundation of the chairs in Dutch Language and Literature and in Dutch History at the University of London. In the early 1980s these two departments were reunited at University College London, where they were both originally housed in 1919 (see *The Low Countries* 1993-94: 209).

The Department of Dutch at UCL offers both undergraduate and postgraduate courses. Undergraduate students can opt for a 'Single Honours BA degree in Dutch', a range of combined study degrees such as Dutch with German, Dutch with History of Art, etc., or a degree in Modern European Studies with Dutch. No prior knowledge of Dutch is required for these courses.

1986 saw the founding of the Centre for Low Countries Studies, which had the dual aim of promoting the interdisciplinary study of the society, history and culture of the Low Countries and of promoting 'Low Countries Studies' in the English-speaking world. The Centre also supervises the interdisciplinary MA course in the History and Culture of the Dutch Golden Age.

A number of academic publications are produced and distributed via the Centre for Low Countries Studies. First and foremost there is *Dutch Crossing,* which was launched in 1977 as *A journal for students of Dutch* and has now grown into a *Journal of Low Countries Studies.* The journal also functions as the Dutch-language periodical for the Association for Language Learning in the United Kingdom. It currently appears twice a year and the editorial flavour reflects the interdisciplinary approach taken to Dutch Studies at UCL, with disciplines such as geography, politics and environmental studies finding a place alongside topics from the field of language and literature. As might be expected, a good deal of attention is also given to history and the visual arts. Several issues of *Dutch Crossing* also contain translations of Dutch literature which had not previously been published elsewhere. A cumulative index (1977-1993) appeared in 1994 and is available free of charge from the Centre on request.

The Centre also publishes the book series *Crossways.* Unlike *Dutch Crossing,* which is aimed at the interested layman and the well-versed academic alike, the *Crossways* collections are aimed primarily at an academic readership. Two volumes in this series have appeared since 1991. The second volume, which appeared in 1993, is a book numbering 344 pages and bearing the title *From Revolt to Riches: Culture and History of the Low Countries 1500-1700. International and Interdisciplinary Perspectives.* The essays in this publication are the written record of papers presented at the conference *The Low Countries and the World* in April 1989, which was the first international conference to be organised by the Centre.

The second 'International and Interdisciplinary Conference of Low Countries Studies' was held in December 1994 as the crowning point of this jubilee year. The central theme this time was *Presenting the Past.* More than seventy academics from the United Kingdom, the USA, Canada, the Netherlands and Belgium presented papers on the portrayal and treatment of the (national) past in literature, the visual arts, historiography, etc. Special mention should be made of the fact that this successful conference concluded with a plenary lecture by Jonathan Israel, Professor of Dutch History and Institutions at UCL. Professor Israel is also the author of the recently published *The Dutch Republic: Its Rise, Greatness, and Fall 1477-1806* (1995), a tome of more than 1,000 pages and a standard work in the series *Oxford History of Early Modern Europe* (see p. 282). Anyone wishing to acquaint themselves with the erudition of the other speakers at the conference will have to be patient for a little while longer, until the publication of the third volume in the *Crossways* series.

FILIP MATTHIJS
Translated by Julian Ross.

ADDRESS
Centre for Low Countries Studies

Foster Court 316 / UCL / Gower Street / London WC1E 6BT / United Kingdom
tel. +44 171 419 3113 / fax +44 171 916 6985

From Civil Servant to Entrepreneur
The Privatisation of National Museums in the Netherlands

On 1 July 1995 the last of the twenty-one Dutch national museums were freed from their state ties and began a new, more independent existence. Since that day the billions of guilders' worth of antiquities and other treasures from the worlds of the arts, natural history, books and anthropology which were previously in the possession of the State, or which had been entrusted to it, is managed by (private sector) foundations. The linking of the word 'foundation' *('stichting'* in Dutch) to familiar names such as the Rijksmuseum or the Kröller-Müller Museum symbolises the way in which the Dutch State has distanced itself from the national treasure houses of cultural heritage: driven not by indifference, but by the desire to give the museums more scope to manage and display their collections more efficiently and effectively.

The museums concerned are the Rijksmuseum, the Vincent Van Gogh Rijksmuseum, the Netherlands Maritime Museum (all three in Amsterdam), the National Museum of Natural History, the Boerhaave Museum (History of the Natural Sciences and Medicine), the National Museum of Antiquities, the National Museum of Ethnology and the National Cabinet of Coins and Medals (all five in Leiden), the Catharijneconvent (Christian Culture in the Netherlands) in Utrecht, the Zuiderzee Museum in Enkhuizen, the Het Loo Palace National Museum in Apeldoorn, the Kröller-Müller Museum in Otterlo, the Royal Mauritshuis Picture Gallery, the Meermanno-Westreenianum Museum (Museum of Books) and the Mesdag Museum (all three in The Hague), and finally, two castle museums, the Muiderslot near Muiden and Slot Loevestein near Brakel.

A number of support services will also be freed from state control, namely the Restorer's Training Centre and the Central Laboratory for the Study of Objects of Artistic and Scientific Value (both in Amsterdam), the National Department of Visual Arts and the National Art History Archive, both in The Hague.

Until privatisation all these institutions operated under the umbrella of the Ministry of Education, Culture and Science (formerly the Ministry of Welfare, Health and Cultural Affairs). Part of the reason for the move to give them autonomy was the publication of a critical report on national museums by the General Chamber of Audit in 1988. In its report this august body, which monitors the effectiveness and justifiability of government spending, observed that the preservation of the museum collections was under threat due to inadequate registration, serious backlogs in restoration work and inadequate storage conditions. Accessi-

The library of the
Meermanno-Westreenianum
Museum in The Hague.

bility to the public was also found to be below standard, and major improvement was needed in order to create a rational funding system for the museums. Moreover, the Chamber considered that the way the museums were run was not sufficiently in line with their purpose.

In order to protect the valuable collections from further deterioration, the then Minister Mrs Hedy d'Ancona made a sum of 40 million guilders (approx. $ 26.5 million / £ 16 million) available for a period of five years. She also set in motion a process of privatisation, designed to turn the national museums into effective and efficient organisations. The structure chosen was such that the Minister would not relinquish the state ownership and trusteeship of the collections.

The management of a national museum ('rijksmuseum') was fraught with problems: as part of the state apparatus, a national museum was subject to the great mass of government bureaucracy. For example, personnel policy was decided by the Minister of ˌthe Interior, while the accommodation was a matter for the Ministry of Housing (Government Buildings Department). The financial accounting had to be carried out in accordance with the rules set by the Minister of Finance, as laid down among other things in the Accountancy Act. The budgeting system meant that there could be no question of a commercial accounting system with opportunities for investment. Income generated by the museums went by definition to the Minister of Finance and not to the institutions themselves. All in all, then, a director of a national museum was tied hand and foot to government rules, and was more of a civil servant than an entrepreneur.

In order to create the necessary room for manoeuvre, the Minister opted for a system whereby the museums were placed outside the state machinery. In consultation with the museum directors she opted for (private sector) foundations, on account of the fiscal advantages (exemption from corporation tax and from gift and inheritance tax) and because this offered greater scope for attracting friends, sponsors and volunteers than would be the case if they were public limited companies. Another consideration was the fact that the foundation is the usual legal form for cultural institutions in the Netherlands.

Although the national museums have been turned into private foundations, it is certainly not the case that the Minister of Culture no longer bears any responsibility for them. The State will continue to own the collections and the greatest part of the museums' income (80-90 %) still comes from state subsidies. The national museums also hold a prominent position in the Dutch museum system as a whole. The Minister's influence is apparent, for example, from the right to appoint the Supervisory Boards of the independent museums, which in turn appoint the directors. The Minister is also empowered to inspect the collections, which in all cases have been loaned to the museums for use or management. Since most of the museums are housed in high-maintenance listed buildings, the buildings have remained the property of the State and not been transferred to the museums themselves, as is the case in Great Britain, for example. Maintenance will therefore continue to be a task for the experts at the Government Buildings Department.

An important factor in the success of the privatisation operation was the guarantee given to staff (a total of 1,500 excluding volunteers) that their net pay and pension rights would remain intact when they lost their status as civil servants.

The total government budget for the national museums is 152 million guilders, which covers the cost of staff, equipment and buildings. Funding takes place in the same way as with other cultural institutions, through subsidies. The Minister grants subsidies on the basis of approved long-term policy plans and budgets. Within these long-term frameworks, each institution is free to spend the subsidy as it sees fit.

The path towards privatisation has led to considerable changes in the museums involved. A more professional and active orientation to the public is reflected in public surveys carried out by new marketing and public relations staff, in the introduction of new facilities and the expansion of activities such as courses, lectures and concerts. The management of the collections has also greatly improved. Major investments in the renovation of accommodation will remove once and for all the traditional 'dusty' image of the national museums.

ROB BERENDS
Translated by Julian Ross.

FURTHER INFORMATION

Autonomy for the National Museums in the Netherlands / La privatisation des Musées Nationaux aux Pays–Bas / Verselbständigung der staatlichen Museen in den Niederlanden (Rijswijk, December 1994, ISBN 90-7436497-7).
Available from: Hageman Verpakkers bv / P.O. Box 281 / 2700 AG Zoetermeer / The Netherlands

Wim Vandekeybus and the Answer of Body Language

In 1987, during one of the famous 'Mondays' on which short artistic projects were presented, the Fleming Wim Vandekeybus (1963-) danced a short duet with Eduardo Torroja to the accompaniment of what has since become the famed 'Table Percussion' of Thierry de Mey. With a tremendous display of energy, power and agility, the two dancers flung themselves into a furious, intensely dynamic torrent of movement. They performed huge tiger springs, launched themselves backwards into the air, catching each other with a dazzling fleetness of foot ... or not, so that the leaping dancer fell roughly to the floor, rolling hither and thither in a whirl around the stage, then suddenly throwing his body in a different direction, bounding horizontally from the floor, sometimes over the body of the other dancer, as if driven, like a bouncing ball, by some powerful unseen force from below. There was a steely tension between the dancers and the breathless audience.

Vandekeybus immediately received offers from a series of foreign producers to develop a full performance built on this initial showing. A few months later the production *What the Body Does Not Remember* had its premiere in the Toneelschuur in Haarlem. The title suggests intuitive bodily thought and action, automatism and impulsive reactions. But the production also features all manner of 'stunts', in which the element of danger has the audience on the edge of their seats. Dancers throw heavy stones at each other's heads, send razor-sharp darts thudding into the floor at each other's feet, or launch themselves into the air to be swiftly caught by a 'chance' passer-by. The realisation that every movement has to be carried out with absolute precision of timing, however nonchalant it may appear, and above all the total confidence which the dancers have to have in their own ability and that of their colleagues, generates a sense of awe.

The dance is driven by an unrelenting dynamism, which in turn derives its energy from the pulsating music. Movement, energy and sound are juxtaposed in equal doses, in structured segments of time and space, lending an unexpected sense of harmony to the overall image of apparent chaos. In 1988 Vandekeybus received a Bessie Award for this work, the highest dancing award in the United States.

Two years later Vandekeybus received the Bessie Award again, this time for *The Bearers of Bad Tidings* (Les Porteuses de Mauvaises Nouvelles), which was described as *'best foreign production in the New York season 89-90'*. The same work also earned him the First International London Dance and Performance Award. Between the razor-sharp, dynamic movements, this new choreography also contains more intense, even intimate gestures interspersed in a sensi-

tive, almost sensual way within a still sharper juxtaposition of energy, space and time, thus creating a deeper theatrical fascination. The ingenious scenery and remarkably subtle lighting complete the beautiful visual image.

Vandekeybus, who in a former life was a photographer, gradually began turning his attention to video and film productions which, while based on his dance work, are situated in an autonomous space-time framework. The images create a kaleidoscopic portrayal of the physical structure of the dance, amplifying its energy and, with a fresh rhythm and an excitingly different visual design, lending a totally new dynamism and – literally – a new dimension to the whole. It was therefore no surprise when *Roseland* (1990), made together with video-film specialist Walter Verdin and based on the choreography of *The Weight of the Hand* (Le Poids de la Main), walked off with several prizes at video dance festivals, such as the 1991 Dance Screen Award.

Vandekeybus once acted in Jan Fabre's production *The Power of Theatrical Madness* (De macht der theaterlijke dwaasheden). Now he is invited to stage his own productions at the greatest temples of culture in the world – with a series of successful performances in London in 1994, for example. He is introducing more and more theatrical and anecdotal elements into his work, resulting in extreme but always fascinating, sometimes even poetic, moments, as in *Always the Same Old Lies* (Immer das Selbe Gelogen, 1991), in which he portrays his meetings with an eccentric old man. Gradually, the furious, hyper-dynamic, almost rough scenes, in which partners passionately push each other away and violently draw together, are interspersed with greater intimacy and even tenderness, expressed for example in delicate touches and embraces. The driving flow of energy which by turns pushes Vandekeybus' dance forwards and continually throws it off course with its unpredictable cross-currents, gradually becomes more and more restful, like a blown-out storm, giving way to calm, intimate moments. These herald the introduction of unusual actors / dancers, who are present on the stage or in the projected film images, nearby or far away, in another country, another decor. They are figures who have been chosen much more for their personality than for their dancing skill, like the old man in *Always the Same Old Lies* (1993) or the blind people in *Her Body Doesn't Fit her Soul,* each of which brings its own small world, with its own emotions, thoughts and actions, still virgin and unadulterated, to the performance.

In his most recent work, *Mountains Made of Barking* (1994), the blind Said Gharbi is actually the leitmotif running through the whole performance. Past and present, here and there, are kaleidoscopically juxtaposed by interspersing film images of the protagonists in Gharbi's birthplace in Morocco with the action on the stage. Extreme images are reinforced on the stage by the presence of sheepskins, strange hairy masks, characters in white dinner jackets and fragments of text. Gharbi with his inner despair, his strength and his optimism; intimate scenes split asun-

Wim Vandekeybus, *Her
Body Doesn't Fit her Soul*
(Photo by Danny Willems).

der by energetic dance passages. With the aid of the powerful, time-shaping music of George Alexander van Dam and Peter Vermeersch, Vandekeybus appears to be attempting once again to manipulate time, to delay or accelerate it – an attempt which, in the interference of the film images with the stage scenes on the retina of the observer, in his intuitive observation, is successful. The boundaries between sense and nonsense, between beautiful and ugly, between the imaginary and the tangible, between theatre and reality, are no longer an issue. Perhaps the body language alone is capable of providing a reasonable answer. Because then people understand each other at a different level.

KATIE VERSTOCKT
Translated by Julian Ross.

Fifty Years of Shakespeare in Diever

The fifty-year-old tradition of the open-air theatre in Diever, a village of around two thousand souls in the province of Drenthe in the northeast part of the Netherlands, may confidently be said to be unique. Not only because the Netherlands is not particularly blessed with theatrical traditions, but also because the Diever amateurs consistently play the work of a single author – Shakespeare, whose most popular plays seem to lend themselves exceptionally well to open-air production.

Every year some ten thousand theatre-lovers visit Diever's beautiful theatre in its woodland setting, where every summer there are twelve performances of a Shakespeare play in Dutch. Like many other open-air theatres, Diever has known hard times in its by and large glorious history. Its heyday in the early sixties was followed a decade later by a disturbing decline in the number of visitors. But Diever survived, won the public back, and appears to be alive and kicking even in 1995.

Moreover, when one counts the total number of open-air performances in recent summers, it is evident that there is a surprising revival. The thirty-odd open-air theatres in the Netherlands seem to be developing once more into competitive summer attractions. In the Summer of 1994 three of these theatres put on a version of *A Midsummer Night's Dream* (with varying degrees of adaptation) – one in the northern province of Friesland (in Frisian) and two in the southern province of North Brabant.

Naturally this thriving recovery pales into insignificance beside what is to be enjoyed, year in, year out, by way of open-air performances in the native land of the world's greatest dramatist. Thus for many years *A Midsummer Night's Dream* has been among the best attended productions on the grass of Regent's Park in London, the beloved Shakespeare plays are always to be found at various outdoor locations in and around Oxford and Cambridge, and in Lincolnshire the Stamford Shakespeare Company gave at least three performances in 1995 at the Rutland Open-Air Theatre.

It is notable that although it is situated in a pre-eminently tourist area, Diever does not owe its present success primarily to summer recreation. Because players and assistants value their own summer holidays highly, the Shakespeare performances are given immediately before or immediately after the so-called high season, and therefore in a period when tourism in Drenthe is not at its peak. However, by establishing the Friends of the Shakespeare Plays Foundation, among other things, Diever has built up a network of benefactors

Toneelvereniging Diever,   Toneelvereniging Diever,
1950, *Hamlet*   1993, *King Lear*
(Photo by Wim K. Steffen).   (Photo by Bert Wieringa).

and regular visitors throughout the whole country.

The man behind the Shakespeare tradition in Diever is the popular village doctor, L.D. Broekema. It was on his initiative that the Toneelvereniging Diever *(Diever Theatre Association)* was set up in May 1946; it made its debut in the summer of the same year with *A Midsummer Night's Dream.* Broekema's greatest virtue is undoubtedly that he managed to bring together, in a convincing way, a relatively uneducated post-war rural population and the grandeur of Shakespeare, which many hold to be beyond the powers of amateurs. The quotation which adorns the company's dressing-rooms as a sort of apologia and motto is revealing: *'For never can anything be amiss, when simpleness and duty tender it.'* These are the words of Theseus to Philostrate in the last act of *A Midsummer Night's Dream,* and that was Broekema's message to his players.

When Broekema died unexpectedly in the Spring of 1979, immediately after the start of rehearsals for *The Merry Wives of Windsor,* it became clear just how much Shakespeare fever had seized some of the local population. Broekema's assistant shouldered the burden without hesitation, and in the ensuing summer there was still fine acting. To this very day Mrs Wil ter Horst is director of the Diever Theatre Association, which has therefore known only two directors in its half century of existence. The director is the only paid worker; all the other jobs – from dressing-room maintenance to playing King Lear – are undertaken by actors, assistants and supporters on a voluntary basis.

Photographic material from the Toneelvereniging's archives shows how strongly, over the years, Diever has maintained a fairly conventional notion of theatre and a somewhat orthodox style of directing. Without doubt, this approach stems from the tone set originally by Broekema, which the older actors were reluctant to depart from in any great measure after his death. Although on the professional theatre circuit of the eighties topicality and commitment were the rule rather than the exception, and contemporary elements were not entirely lacking at Diever, Broekema's successor understood what are the prime requisites for attracting the public to open-air theatre in large numbers – a public that comes above all for entertainment. To this day the exuberant atmosphere of the Diever productions is characterised by a strongly physical style of acting, solid stage-properties, and historical costumes. The translations (always very true to Shakespeare) are undertaken by the company itself, thus avoiding high copyright fees.

The choice of repertoire over the years (with, for instance, seven *Midsummer Night's Dream*s, five *Twelfth Night*s, and four *Taming of the Shrew*s) also demonstrates that the entertainment aspect has a high priority in Diever. This is borne out by the fact that a play such as *The Merchant of Venice,* which is felt to be controversial and politically sensitive, was only brought back into production again in 1995, after an absence of more than twenty years.

Among the memorable moments in the history of Diever is without question the visit, in 1987, of the Mayor of Stratford-upon-Avon to the Diever production of *The Tempest.* This visit led to an invitation to the Diever group to play *A Midsummer Night's Dream* at the Stratford-upon-Avon Festival during the following summer, and everyone involved considers this a real milestone. It demanded an enormous physical and organisational effort on the part of actors and assistants, but the effort was matched by the result. The local press was enthusiastic: *'It was a play that kept the audience engrossed in the actions and expressions of the actors, negating the language barrier, each actor putting on a convincing and immaculate performance.' (Stratford-upon-Avon Herald,* 5 August 1988.)

The success of the excursion to England convincingly underlines the topical significance of the Diever Shakespeare tradition. It is a small miracle that the theatre-lovers of Diever have managed to keep alive to this day the lamp lit by Dr Broekema in 1946. Not how to initiate, but how to maintain a tradition – *'that is the question'.*

JOS NIJHOF
Translated by Sheila M. Dale.

ADDRESSES
Toneelvereniging Diever
Attn. Mrs T. Kerstholt-Doddema (secretary)
Gerritstraat 20a / 7981 BS Diever / The Netherlands
tel. +31 521 59 17 48

VVV Diever (tourist information)
Brink 7 / 7981 BZ Diever / The Netherlands
tel. +31 521 59 13 50

Dominique Deruddere, a Flemish Anglophile

The Flemish film industry has never really amounted to much on the international scene, and that is still the case. Many reasons for this can be cited, but two stand out: the unavoidably small scale of the national industry itself and the lack of a universal thematics. For decades the Flemish film climate was dominated by three genres: peasant or 'hearth and home' movies, proletarian pamphlets, and comedies, often burlesque. A handful of French-speaking directors, from Paul Delvaux to Gérard Corbiau, have, therefore, been mainly responsible for the international resonance of the Belgian film industry.

But things are changing for the better: some young Flemish directors are looking beyond their own borders and tackling themes capable of addressing an international audience. Flemish director Stijn Coninx (who made the much-acclaimed *Daens;* see *The Low Countries* 1993-94: 275-276), for instance, is at present hard at work on the Belgian-American co-production *Damian of Molokai,* a film on the life of the Belgian priest Father Damiaan in the leper colony of Molokai, Hawaii. But the most international director in Flanders is probably Dominique Deruddere (1957-).

Dominique Deruddere,
Wait until Spring, Bandini
(1989) (Photo UIP).

Dominique Deruddere,
Suite 16 (1994)
(Photo Independent Films).

Sympathy for the weak or the less fortunate of this world is a film-theme that is as classical as it is praiseworthy. Deruddere has given that theme a nostalgic and ironic treatment in his first full-length feature *Crazy Love* (1987). The film is based on the story 'The Copulating Mermaid of Venice' by the American writer Charles Bukowski. Deruddere and Bukowski met on a number of occasions, and the famous writer was very pleased with the way in which the Fleming filmed his story, a compliment that was to prove of crucial importance for Deruddere's later career. *Crazy Love* tells the life story of Harry Voss in three instalments. The child Harry Voss sees his first sexual dreams repressed by many taboos. The adolescent Harry Voss is ostracised by his environment (including girls) because of his severe and persistent acne. The adult Harry Voss becomes a bum. The only way he can find the White Fairy Of His Dreams is to steal the corpse of a young woman and to commit necrophilia on it. This kind of plot is almost guaranteed to lead a film astray, but *Crazy Love* proved to be very successful indeed: Deruddere managed to find the right tone, a mixture of bitterness and nostalgia, cruelty and sympathy, sarcasm and despair.

The film's success, but above all Bukowski's favourable comments, resulted in a second project for Deruddere. He filmed the book *Wait Until Spring, Bandini* (1989) by the Italian-American novelist John Fante. Fante, who wrote mainly autobiographical novels about the hard life of poor Catholic Italian immigrants to the US, never became a writer of best sellers, but his books became 'hot' again in Hollywood a few years ago, to the extent that he was called *'the hottest dead man in town'* by the magazine *American Film*. Deruddere was given the chance to make the film for Francis Ford Coppola's Zoetrope Studios. He produced excellent work. *Wait Until Spring, Bandini,* with Faye Dunaway, Joe Mantegna and Ornella Mutti, turned into a sensitive portrait of the Bandini family, which tries to survive in an unfriendly and inhospitable little town in Colorado. The story of the adulterous and unemployed father is told through the eyes of the eldest son, Arturo, who tries to preserve at least some optimism among al the misery and manages to keep the family together with something approaching cunning. The verdict of critics and connoisseurs was unanimously positive, but the film may well have proved somewhat too subtle, too full of nuances, and too introspective for the American film market. It was not a box office success.

This film revealed the stark choices facing a Flemish (or European) director who wants to work in the States while keeping a 'European style'. Many Europeans tried the Big Crossing after becoming successful on their own continent, and 'didn't make it' by American standards. Among them Wim Wenders, Neil Jordan, and now also Dominique Deruddere. It would seem that the laws of Hollywood do not leave much room for compromise, and that only those who adapt, like the Dutch director Paul Verhoeven, the maker of such blockbusters as *Robocop* and *Basic Instinct,* manage to hold their own.

He has made three full-length feature films up to now, and all three have been closely tied to English-language culture. Deruddere is a child of his generation, which means that he grew up with British pop music, American TV serials and American movies. Most Flemish (and European) young people have grown up like that since the sixties, but Deruddere has built a very personal cinematic oeuvre for himself on the basis of those cultural acquisitions.

Few people have ever seen Deruddere's short film *Vodka Orange,* yet much of his talent is encapsulated in those few minutes' worth of celluloid. The film is both a nostalgic and a cynical portrayal of the final days of a father, demented as the result of alcohol abuse, who is visited by his son in the hospital. The father is desperate for the alcohol that is now strictly forbidden, and his son helps him in an ingenious manner by bringing oranges he has previously injected with vodka into the hospital. That way the father absorbs his alcohol quota unnoticed and can drift off into his nth delirium.

Deruddere made the inverse mistake with his third and, for the moment, final film: he wanted to make a Hollywood movie in Europe. *Suite 16* (1994) is an 'erotic thriller' of the *Fatal Attraction* and *Basic Instinct* type. This story of a young gigolo and a rich, physically impaired, lascivious man who heavily manipulate and abuse each other was intended to become a subtle mixture of sex and violence, with an existential-Freudian sauce added, but it turned out to be Deruddere's weakest effort yet. In spite of the wonderful *huis-clos* set (a fantastic Art Déco apartment on the French Riviera), everything else in the film tends to fall flat: plot, acting, directing. *Suite 16* is neither erotic nor gripping, because it falls between two stools. Not a hard-boiled commercial sex movie, but not an artistic film either, no flashy plot structure, but also no *conte moral*.

Seven years elapsed between *Wait Until Spring, Bandini* and *Suite 16*. During that time Deruddere put a great deal of work into the *Dipenda* project, that was supposed to turn into a grandiose film about the colonial past of Belgians in the Congo. But problems with the plot and, especially, with finance have put the project (temporarily?) on ice. This is the real weak spot of the Flemish (and, by extension, European) film industry: there is a lack of professional purveyors of capital and of institutional structures capable of creating a European film industry in which big commercial projects would help defray the costs of smaller productions. The present half-hearted 'Euro-pudding' policy has not been able to rescue productions like *Suite 16*.

MARC RUYTERS
Translated by André Lefevere.

A Fresh Look at Old Material
The Netherlands Film Museum

Like every other self-respecting country, the Netherlands has its own national film museum. This institution combines the tasks of maintaining an archive with conservation and educational activities, and its film library plays an important role in showing specimens from international film history.

For many years, the Netherlands Film Museum led a wretched existence. Housed in a wing of the Stedelijk Museum of Amsterdam, it suffered increasingly from an absence of public interest and inadequate governmental support. Under the direction of founder Jan de Vaal, whose passion for collecting films had resulted in the birth of the museum in 1946, the museum evolved into a closed bastion where only the highly motivated dared to venture. De Vaal's priority was especially aimed at maintaining the archive and conserving old nitrate films. In 1994 he was given the Netherlands Cultural Prize for his excellent work in this area.

But after De Vaal retired, the policy was drastically altered. What the foundation's board of directors and the governmental subsidisers had in mind was a more

The Netherlands Film
Museum in the Vondelpark.

publicly-oriented museum. In July 1987, Hoos Blotkamp-De Roos, formerly head of the plastic arts section of the Ministry of Culture, was appointed director. This was followed six months later by the naming of jack-of-all-trades Eric de Kuyper as assistant director. Until that time, De Kuyper had been a university teacher of film science, a writer, theatrical director and filmmaker.

Thanks to Blotkamp's organisational talent and De Kuyper's passion for films, the programme of activities grew at an explosive rate. The museum moved to Amsterdam's Vondel Park to a beautiful nineteenth-century pavilion, purchased by the government, whose gates opened wide to give the public a hearty welcome. And come they did, stumbling over scaffolding and paint pots, for at the same time that a number of presentations were being shown the renovation was proceeding on this exceptionally fine building.

With backing from sponsors, the building now has two cinemas at its disposal. In the existing theatre was installed the impressive art deco interior of Amsterdam's oldest cinema, the *Cinema Parisien* (now closed). The new theatre, formerly the library, had its nineteenth-century interior restored. At the same time the theatre was adapted to modern requirements, making it possible to show 70-mm films, and was equipped with Dolby Stereo sound equipment.

These two cinemas provided a place not only for representatives of films from the distant past but also for those from a living present as well as from the future-anticipating avant-garde. These possibilities were based on the belief held by the museum directorate that the past can only be understood from the present, and the present can be better appreciated with knowledge of the past. NFM / International Art Film, the museum's own government-subsidised distribution department, makes it possible for the Film Museum to let the public peruse the newest artistic expressions of domestic and foreign cinematography.

Another important task of the Netherlands Film Museum is the maintenance of its archives. The poster archive contains 35,000 film posters that have been classified and made ready for use; the same is true for the collection of around 300,000 photographs. The library, located in a nearby building, has some 10,000 books, 250,000 articles and 150 film magazines available to those who are interested. In addition to temporary exhibitions (such as the show of collages and paintings by the Georgian filmmaker Sergei Paradzianov in 1994), the pavilion contains a permanent exhibition of antique film equipment from the museum's own collection.

The conservation of archival material always has priority. Although government cutbacks have hit the museum hard, the work goes on as best it can. It is concentrated in an annex to the museum located on the Dutch coast, where about five million metres of nitrate film lie in vaults and await restoration. Surprising discoveries are still frequently being made, from missing film fragments from the oldest Disney animated films to the 'missing links' of Dutch feature films from the teens, twenties and thirties that had been given up for lost. Thus after careful restoration and reconstruction, the first Dutch sound film, Gerard Rutten's 1931 production *Terra Nova,* was given a festive second premiere in the Film Museum. During the International Documentary Film Festival 1994, newly-preserved early films from the 1920s such as *Rain* (Regen) and *The Bridge* (De Brug) by the Dutch documentary maker Joris Ivens were shown as well as a newly-found version of the working copy of *Borinage,* Ivens' view on the living conditions of Belgian miners in the 1930s.

This direct presentation of newly-preserved material and the museum's thematic programming is evidence of the importance that the museum directorate attaches to serving the public. Over the years, people have been able to expand their knowledge of international cinema, film genres and influences with programmes such as 'The Western', 'The British Gainsborough Productions of the Thirties', 'The Indian Film as Melodrama', 'The Japanese Avant-Garde in the Twenties' and 'The Silent Film's Foreign Language'. There have been retrospectives of early and more recent filmmakers such as George Melies, Jevgeni Bauer, Frank Borzage, George Stevens and Howard Hawks.

With the departure of assistant director De Kuyper and the arrival of his successor, programming director Peter Delpeut, more and more attention was paid to the similarities and differences between classical and modern films in a unique kind of programming that compares the old with the new. Working close to the source – the museum's archives – and with the approval of director Blotkamp, Delpeut has developed into a successful found-footage filmmaker. For example, he provided archive material of North Pole expeditions with a newly-recorded frame narrative in the prize-winning film *The Forbidden Quest* (1993). It's convincing proof of the museum directorate's firmly-held belief that a fresh look at old material can open up new worlds.

GERDIN LINTHORST
Translated by Nancy Forest-Flier.

ADDRESS
Netherlands Film Museum
Vondelpark 3 / 1071 AA Amsterdam / The Netherlands
tel. +31 20 589 14 00 / fax +31 20 683 34 01
Opening hours: 10 a.m-5 p.m. (Monday-Friday)

History

Women of the Golden Age

The articles in this collection derive from a master class entitled *Women of the Golden Age,* held at the University of Utrecht (1-2 July 1993). Coinciding with the master class was an exhibition in Haarlem of Judith Leyster, *A Dutch Master and her World.* Another master, Simon Schama, considers women in his 'House-wives and Hussies' chapter of *The Embarrassment of Riches,* but only in relation to men. The master class format is an interesting choice. In the first place, there is an actual dialogue with various 'masters', specialists in a variety of disciplines, including English and Dutch history, Dutch, Italian literary history and art history, who were invited to be present to respond to the papers presented. Moreover, the collection engages polemically with an absent master, Simon Schama, the highly influential interpreter of the Dutch Golden Age. In fact, Schama's perspective has proved so controversial that Els Kloek wittily refers to him as *'a modern Saint Sebastian', 'pierced by so many arrows of Dutch criticism'.* To which this collection now adds the arrows of feminist historians, although occasionally the link with Schama in the papers themselves seems tenuous.

Part 1 of the collection discusses images of seventeenth-century women as presented in the work of three male writers. A. Agnes Sneller's opening article offers a deconstructive reading of Jacob Cats' *Touch-stone of the Wedding Ring* (Proefsteen van de Trouringh, 1637), a collection of historical and biblical stories in verse by the popular Dutch moralist Jacob Cats. Often presented as a champion of women who expresses the new attitude towards a companiate marriage, Cats' lexicon and his treatment of biblical sources indicate that these texts consistently present the woman's 'free' choice of a husband-master. This husband and his willing servant are to form the nucleus for a patriarchal Dutch republic. In his response, A. Th. van Deursen points to the basic 'unoriginality' of Cats in his un-selective dependence on the holy source of the Bible. He also presents a more positive interpretation of seventeenth-century marriage texts, promoting the protection of the weaker party.

Lia van Gemert's essay discusses Schama's ambivalent perspective on women with reference to the Dordrecht moralist and city physician Johan van Beverwijck. His *On the Excellence of the Female Sex* (Van de utnementheyt des vrouwelicken geslachts, 1639) presented an idealised picture of women, while the trilogy *Treasury of Health, Treasury of Sickness and Surgery* (Schat der gesontheyt, Schat der ongesontheyt, Heel-konste, 1636-1645) offers health advice and perhaps a more realistic picture of women's daily lives. Reading Van Beverwijck's work as an example of the Dutch ideal of a balance of extremes, Schama underestimated the classical medical principles underlying his work. Moreover, Schama's polarisation of women into the clean housewife and the filthy whore is a basic stylistic device. Van Gemert concludes that the *'need to reconcile is Schama's'*. In response, Marijke Spies agrees with her interpretation of the plurality of Dutch society, pointing out, however, that for seventeenth-century Holland, difference and plurality were not yet regarded as integral to an ideal society.

Giesela van Oostveen asks the question whether Bredero's *Farce of the Miller* (Klucht vanden molenaer, 1613) offers information on implied sexual values and gender. Bredero's farce discusses the position of eroticism as detestable outside marriage but acceptable within. It further suggests male fears of female potency and sexual hunger, warning a middle-class audience against an unorderly world which exists amongst the lower classes. Maria-Theresia Leuker's reaction stresses the need to consider these texts' function in their historical context. They should not be read as the product of artistic originality but as part of a philosophical or moralist discourse on gender, marriage and sexuality.

Part II focuses on historical 'traces' of the social and cultural aspects of women's lives. Thus, Lotte C. van de Pol, departing from the popular pennyprints describing the lives of female servants, investigates female migration to Amsterdam. Using the registers of intended marriage in Amsterdam as primary sources, she concludes that female migration has been both overlooked and underestimated by researchers. Mainly haling from inland areas, these female immigrants remained unmarried to a much greater extent than had been thought. Van de Pol points to the deficiencies of marriage registers in tracing women, indicating the many, unmarried female servants who remain invisible to the modern historian. In response, Jan Lucassen asks additional questions: whether labour opportunities for women during the Golden Age doubled as they did for men, what sectors they were employed in, etc.

Marybeth Carlson delineates an alternative to the picture of the seventeenth-century maid servant as the *'Trojan horse of worldliness'*. A lack of sources again makes it difficult to contradict the picture of the quarrelsome, lazy wench lusting after the household's men. Carlson looks for traces of these women in notarial archives, in their depositions for lawsuits, their contracts and wills. These can go some way to dispelling the negative image, pointing to occasional alliances between mistress and servant against bad husbands. While foreign servants abound in literature, only a minority of maidservants were in fact immigrants. On average as literate as the rest of the population, a significant proportion of them remained unmarried, choosing service for reasons of security. Their behaviour as consumers suggests that they identified

Pieter de Hooch, *Interior with Women beside a Linen Chest.* 1663. Canvas, 72 x 77.5 cm. Rijksmuseum, Amsterdam.

'A monstrous shape or a shapeless monster. A description of a female creature borne in Holland ...' (Anonymous woodcut, 1640).

with the middle-class values of their employers. Rudolf Dekker suggests counterbalancing the limitations of the notarial sources by reading memoirs and diaries by servants such as Elisabeth Strouven or Maria van Antwerpen, or by their masters and mistresses.

Heidi de Mare discusses the *'spatial interpretation of gender'* in *Huysbou,* an architectural treatise by the Flemish engineer Simon Stevin which describes a town and housing blocks for burghers. De Mare warns against Schama's anachronistic reading of this text in terms of polarities between private and public, between the home and the prostitute's anti-home. Interpreting Stevin from the perspective of seventeenth-century epistemology, on the other hand, De Mare contends that Stevin's classification of space along gender lines is part of a larger classification system in which both people and things are organised according to age, kinship, usage. His architectural design includes practical inventions but also posits the house as part of the larger cosmological order. Brita Rang questions this latter statement, and provides further counterpoints to this essay by stressing the areas of transition and overlap rather than the gender boundaries in Stevin's designs. She also sees Stevin as part of an 'enlightened' interpretation of space, responding to the new, companiate model of marriage.

Finally, departing from the representation of Dutch women in the travel accounts of male foreign visitors, Anne Laurence asks whether English women in the seventeenth century were less free than their Dutch counterparts. Investigating women's public presence and economic activity, she concludes that the greater perceived 'freedom' of Dutch women stems from a more urbanised society than that of England, from the fact that in a mercantile republic men were more likely to be absent for prolonged periods, and from the Dutchwoman's greater legal right to engage in trade. Mary Prior's response focuses on a comparison between the English painter Mary Beale, whose supportive husband allowed her to continue working and managed her affairs, and the Dutch Judith Leyster, who was able to manage her studio and apprentices independently and held a power of attorney for her husband's affairs.

Part III contains papers on a number of women who transgressed gender codes; women like Anna Maria van Schurman and Antoinette Bourignon, who subscribed to non-orthodox, non-Calvinist religious movements. Mirjam de Baar describes their strategies for making this acceptable. While the theologian, philosopher and author Van Schurman derived authority from her learning and scholarship in explaining her religious choice, the uneducated visionary Bourignon employs traditional gender roles: she presents herself as mother to her followers, and as a vessel used by God. Helen Wilcox's response refers to 'A Monstrous Shape', a 1640 English ballad and woodcut about a demurely dressed woman with a pig's head. Her rhetorical question suggests that the *'monstrous shape'* can be both the woman rebel, and the woman who submits to her traditional gender role.

The formula of a 'master' responding to the paper of a (pupil?) lecturer may seem overly hierarchical at first. It does, however, offer the reader a variety of perspectives on an academic argument, rather than limiting the audience to the impenetrable, well-defended paper of the traditional academic collection. Its interdisciplinary offers a prismatic view of gender in the Golden Age, as well as demonstrating the very urgent need for further detailed research. Occasional translation and editing problems notwithstanding, this successful collection offers a challenging start to further research into femininity and gender in the Dutch Golden Age.

SABINE VANACKER

Women of the Golden Age. An International Debate on Women in Seventeenth-Century Holland, England and Italy (ed. Els Kloek et al.). Hilversum: Verloren, 1994; 190 pp. ISBN 90-6550-383-8.

The Anglo-Dutch Connection in Prints and Drawings

The Atlas Van Stolk collection, housed in the Schielandshuis in Rotterdam, is a unique assemblage of drawings, prints, photos and posters. This 'atlas' of Dutch history, started in the nineteenth century by Abraham van Stolk, a Rotterdam timber merchant, and carried on by his descendants, has since 1967 been maintained and managed by the Rotterdam Historical Museum.

From 4 February to 28 May 1995, fifty of the prints from this collection were exhibited under the title of *Friend or Foe. Prints and Drawings about the Relationship between the Netherlands and England.* This exhibition also marked the official opening of the jubilee year of the Anglo-Netherlands Society. This association, whose aim is to strengthen the bonds of friendship and culture between the two countries, celebrated its seventy-fifth anniversary in 1995.

At the entrance to the exhibition hung two allegorical prints (c.1760), one referring to the Dutch and the other to the English. The symbolic print *Batavus* refers to a *'cold and watery country with simple people'* and the picture entitled *Anglus* describes England as *'a damp country with amiable inhabitants'.* Even so, the rest of the exhibition demonstrated that they could not really be called kindred peoples. The history of Anglo-Dutch relations has a distinct smell of gunpowder about it.

First of all there were three maritime wars in the second half of the seventeenth century. Just how tense the relationship between the two countries was, can be seen from a Dutch print (in three languages) about the Great Fire of London in 1666. One month before the catastrophe, an English squadron led by Admiral Robert Holmes had set Terschelling ablaze. The English immediately suspected Dutch retaliation, and so the English caption to the print mentioned above also says that *'divers strangers, Dutch and French, were during the fire, apprehended, upon suspition that they contributed mischievously to it'.* Another symbolic print about the same disastrous episode shows that the Dutch interpreted the Great Fire rather as a form of divine justice.

More than a century later, from 1780 to 1784, the fourth war between the English and the Dutch was fought. One of the reasons for this conflict was the salute to American ships fired by the Dutch on St Eustatius (in the Dutch Antilles) on 16 November 1776. This shot counted as the first official recognition of the flag of the 'rebels'. The gesture was not greatly appreciated by the English. On top of this, St Eustatius was an important arms store for the American troops. For this reason an English invasion fleet occupied the island on 2 February 1781. In a hand-coloured print from the same year, with the caption *The Dutchman in the Dumps,* an Englishman is consoling a distraught Dutchman who has just heard of the loss of St Eustatius by holding a bottle of Hollands gin under his nose.

When it came to fighting, though, the English and

the Dutch were not always facing each other with weapons drawn. Sometimes they were even the best of mates, as in 1588, when they together gave the Spanish Armada the push. And in an etching called *Glorieuse Expedition des Anglois et des Hollandois a Vigos,* the English and the Dutch are fraternally stowing away the cargo of a captured French silver fleet.

The exhibition did not consist entirely of pictures of military history. Another important subject was the link between the houses of Orange, Stuart and Hanover. There was quite some intermarriage between the Dutch stadholders and members of the English royal family. *Friend or Foe* had pictures of the marriages between William II and Mary Stuart (1641), William III and Mary Stuart (1677) and William IV and Anna of Hanover (1734).

The rulers of England and the Netherlands were actually linked in yet another way. On 4 February 1613, Prince Maurice of Orange, as depicted in an etching by S. Frisius, received the Order of the Garter in the name of King James I. Since then, all Maurice's descendants, stadholders and kings, have been members of this order. A hand-coloured etching by J.C. Philips, for example, shows the investiture of the four-year-old William V by his grandfather, King George II, in 1752.

Only one descendant of the House of Orange, King William II, missed out on the Order of the Garter. This may have had something to do with his broken engagement to Charlotte, daughter of the Prince of Wales (the later King George IV), in 1814. The way the then crown prince and future hero of the Battle of Waterloo was rejected is depicted in the cartoon *The Dutch Apollo!*. From the text in the balloons it appears that even William's impressive trousers were not able to charm the princess.

What is exceptional about the Atlas Van Stolk is that the collection has been kept up to date to the present day. This explains the numerous pictures from the present century in the exhibition. One remarkable work, for example, is L. Jordaans' drawing of Winston Churchill as the sprightly little man on the whisky bottles of John Walker & Sons Ltd. His 1961 drawing of Prime Minister MacMillan for the newspaper *Het Parool* is equally amusing. It shows MacMillan's timid attempt to approach a united Europe: the British Prime Minister – in his bathing apparel – dips his big toe tentatively into the apparently chilly waters of the Channel, while Adenauer and De Gaulle, cheerfully splashing around, encourage him to take the plunge.

This exhibition included only a selection from the material on the 'Anglo-Dutch connection' in the possession of the Atlas Van Stolk. It is to be hoped that, one day, someone will find the time and the means to make a marvellous book out of it.

FILIP MATTHIJS
Translated by Gregory Ball.

'The Dutch Apollo!'. Caricature on the broken engagement between Prince William and Princess Charlotte, 1814. Coloured etching published by W. Holland, London, 29 June 1814 (Stichting Atlas van Stolk, Rotterdam).

Winston Churchill as Johnnie Walker. Drawing by L. Jordaan, c.1951 (Stichting Atlas van Stolk, Rotterdam).

The Dutch Republic

Ever since Sir William Temple published his *Observations upon the United Provinces of the Netherlands* in 1672, the English-speaking world has remained intrigued by the sensational success (and the no less dramatic demise) of the Dutch Republic. Several excellent surveys of its history exist in English (e.g. by K.D. Haley and Ch. Wilson), but no full-scale history has appeared in either English or Dutch since Pieter Geyl's well-known work of the 1930s. We should therefore be grateful to Jonathan Israel for dedicating his considerable skills to the daunting task of composing a new synthesis.

The Dutch Republic: Its Rise, Greatness, and Fall 1477-1806 is an astonishing work. The reader is dazzled by its sheer magnitude and its exceptionally wide scope. In no fewer than 1,231 pages the history of the Republic is traced from Holland's earliest land-reclamation projects in the thirteenth century to the collapse of the Batavian Republic (the United Provinces' French-dominated successor-state) in 1806. Yet the focus of this work is firmly on the Golden Age: 65% of the text deals with that period, against 20% for the

Hapsburg period and the Revolt, and 15% for the eighteenth-century denouement. It deals with all aspects of the history of the Republic, political, military and diplomatic as well as social, economic, religious, intellectual and cultural. It deals even-handedly with all seven provinces and avoids the excessively Holland-centred approach that has impaired earlier works, while still doing full justice to the overwhelming preponderance of Holland over the other provinces, tracing its ascendancy back to the thirteenth century.

Israel's history of the Republic is admirably set in its wider international context. Not only is there a wealth of solid information on international relations, a field in which the author is an expert, but he also takes pains to elucidate the wider European significance of purely Dutch phenomena. He stresses, for example, that the Republic's elaborate system of public welfare, as a strategy for controlling the workforce, had no counterpart elsewhere. Similarly, in one of the most exciting chapters, dealing with late seventeenth-century intellectual life, he underlines the striking originality of radical Cartesian philosophy and liberal Coccean theology. The author also pays more than usual attention to the impact of the Republic on the adjoining German border-areas and on the Spanish (later Austrian) Netherlands.

The Dutch Republic is a book of immense learning. The bibliography fills almost sixty densely printed pages, an estimated 1,400 titles, more than three hundred of which relate to primary sources; and a number of references reveal that Professor Israel has more than occasionally backed up his reading with solid archival research. He never sits on a fence; there is always an argument. He is never afraid of overturning accepted truths and cherished historiographical beliefs. It is delightful to see how skilfully he arranges the evidence so as to lure the reader into sharing his view of a particular case. He argues, he debates, and then he stuns the reader with a sweeping statement: the *'Calvinist revolution'* of 1618 marked *'one of the most fundamental shifts of the Golden Age',* and the demise of William III heralded *'a profound change'* in the character of the United Provinces. But since he writes for a general public, his revisionism never turns into polemicism.

The most far-reaching instance of revisionism concerns the separation between north and south. Since Pieter Geyl, historians have been accustomed to regard the seventeen provinces of Charles V, despite their considerable mutual differences, as an increasingly coherent entity. Before the Revolt, it is argued, no meaningful distinction between north and south existed. The outcome of the Revolt, two separate and culturally distinct communities, was largely accidental, due to geographical and military factors, and had no roots in the past. Against this widely accepted view Jonathan Israel argues that the seven provinces north of the rivers Rhine and Maas did in fact have a distinct identity of their own. They constituted a separate political arena, had a well-defined common economic orientation and shared a number of cultural characteristics (though not,

of course, a north-Netherlandish 'national' awareness). Seen from this perspective, the revolt of 1572 and the ensuing separation between north and south were merely the logical outcome of a duality that had existed for centuries.

There is no doubt that this thesis, directed against one of the most central tenets of Dutch and Belgian historiography, will provoke intense debate. Although Israel is right in stressing the long-term continuity in the relations between Holland and the north-eastern provinces, I would personally be inclined to discern at least four different areas: a highly urbanised, commercially and culturally advanced nucleus in the west (including Flanders and Brabant as well as Holland and Zeeland); the recently conquered, but highly independent north-east; the Walloon provinces with their aristocratic and clerical preponderance; and the backward, semi-feudal south-east, which played no significant role at all. This arrangement makes for a much more complex interplay of forces, which does not point to any 'logical' outcome of the Revolt. In fact, the Revolt enjoyed its most substantial support in the western core-provinces that were split in two in the course of the struggle.

However that may be, Jonathan Israel's *Dutch Republic* is an immensely stimulating book, a thoughtful synthesis that is scholarly, intelligently argued and elegantly written. It is indispensable for anyone interested in the history of the Netherlands or of early-modern Europe in general, a master-work bound to set the standard for future generations of historians.

HENK VAN NIEROP

Jonathan Israel, *The Dutch Republic: Its Rise, Greatness, and Fall.* 1477-1806. Oxford: Oxford University Press, 1995; 1,231 pp. ISBN 0-19-873072-1.

Language

Multilingual Speech Technology from West Flanders

Conversations with computers are occurring on a regular basis.

Caller: I would like some information on *restaurants* in the Ghent area.
Computer: What type of restaurant would you prefer?
Caller: I prefer *Chinese* food.
Computer: On what day would you like to eat?
Caller: I want to have dinner on *Thursday.*
Computer: How much money do you want to spend?
Caller: About *800 francs* per person.
Computer: In the Ghent area there are two Chinese *restaurants, open on* Thursday, *where you can eat for approximately* 800 francs *per person. Do you want to make a* reservation?

283

Caller: Yes, make a reservation for four please.

All around the world people are talking to computers, *and* the computers are talking back. Sounds like science fiction, but in reality it is becoming commonplace. Since it was founded in 1987, Ypres-based Lernout & Hauspie Speech Products has become a world leader in the development and marketing of multilingual speech technology. Lernout & Hauspie Speech Products, commonly known as 'L & H', develops and markets a family of speech technologies for integration in a range of desktop multimedia and portable computing devices, consumer electronics, telecommunication and automotive products. Its speech technology enables electronic equipment to recognise human speech as a form of input *(speech recognition)*, transform computer readable text into speech *(text-to-speech)*, and efficiently store and replay speech and music *(speech & music coding)*.

In 1987, L & H acquired the exclusive licence of groundbreaking speech technologies from the universities of Ghent, Mons and Leuven. It later fine-tuned and expanded these technologies for commercial applications. After extensive world-wide market research, founders Jo Lernout and Pol Hauspie, (both from the Ypres area), found that Belgian institutions had the unique multilingual approach that guaranteed a truly global market offering. Institutions both in the USA and in Japan proved to have extensive developments in the field of speech, but were limited by a uni-lingual approach. L & H technology is currently available in American and British English, Dutch, French, German, Spanish, Italian, and Korean; Japanese, Mandarin, Hindu, Tamil and Arabic languages are on the way.

Why will speech technology, in the coming years, be an ever more important element of the man-machine interface of all kinds of electronic devices? The human brain processes spoken information very efficiently. The fastest way to go from thoughts to expressed information is *to speak* the results of such a thought process aloud. Most people think at an average rate of about 1,000 words / minute. Most people speak (in a continuous mode) at an average rate of 150 words per minute. Skilled typists type at an average rate of 60 words per minute. Two finger typists type at an average rate of 30 words per minute. Handwriting is usually at an average rate of 20 words per minute. So, what faster way is there in the foreseeable future then to simply have a 'chat' (in continuous spoken speech) with your PC, car phone, VCR, or by telephone with a computer to give it commands, enter data, enter pass-words, or even dictate texts?

One can therefore expect, with a high degree of certainty, that such speech technology will be incorporated as 'standard' in all types of electronic devices which are routinely used by humans. It will be just an integral part of the man-machine interface, in combination with all other means of interfacing.

The obvious next question: Why hasn't this 'dream interface' been realised yet? It is so obvious, isn't it? First, the speech technology that enables people to exe-

An example of a speech-enhanced application running under WINDOWS ᵗᵐ (Photo Point Studios).

cute such a 'chat' efficiently and effectively has only now become mature. Moreover, only very recently has speech technology left the labs of universities, small specialised companies and internal labs of large corporations. This has to do with the fact that only over the last couple of years has enough inexpensive computing power been available in those labs to conduct all the research necessary to produce technology that both did the job and was able to work on low-cost, mass-volume hardware. Secondly, only now is mass-market electronic equipment – such as personal computers, electronic organisers, telephone servers and in-car electronic equipment such as navigation systems – equipped with low cost but high performance semiconductor technology to execute such 'gourmand' speech technology code.

The sociological impact of the massive spread of this new man-machine interface (versus more traditional 'speech-loss' man-machine interfaces) will be much greater than just increasing the comfort of users. In a seamless way, many millions more people will now use technology which they would not have used before. Even illiterate people will ultimately use advanced technology, thereby skipping some intermediate stage in the use of technology in general.

Voice technology, when properly applied, has the potential to propel people of all nations, at all stages of development, into a much broader use of the latest available technology, boosting their productivity level to unknown heights.

JO LERNOUT

ADDRESS
Lernout & Hauspie Speech Products
Sint-Krispijnstraat 7 / 8900 Ypres / Belgium
tel. +32 57 22 88 88 / fax +32 57 20 84 89

Frisian Language and Culture Today

The ongoing debate in the Low Countries about the future of the Dutch language took an interesting turn at the end of 1994, when Professor De Bot of Nijmegen

University presented a scenario in which English could well become the dominant *lingua franca* in the Netherlands in the domains of trade, industry, education and administration. He further envisaged a situation of diglossia, in which the Dutch language would increasingly be relegated to the more informal domains of language use. Early in 1995, Mr Jan Timmer, president of Philips, took this one step further when he advocated a linguistic unification of the European Union, urging Brussels to adopt English as the only language of administration. Meanwhile, others were advocating an intensification of German language teaching in the Netherlands, since Germany is now the dominant power in the European Union and good working relations with this closest neighbour are obviously important.

Looking at this debate, it is useful to keep in mind that Dutch is the official language of the Netherlands and Belgium and the natural medium of communication for 20 million native speakers. The language is learned on a large scale by children as their first language, it has a well-established written standard, it is widely used in the media, and there is an extensive and lively literature in Dutch. Moreover, in January 1995 the Dutch and Flemish governments issued a joint declaration emphasising the importance of a full recognition of Dutch as an official language of the European Union. All of this lends support to Uhlenbeck's view that whatever challenges the Dutch language may be facing, the threat of rapid language death is not one of them (see *The Low Countries* 1993-94: 30). For the time being, the Dutch language is reasonably safe.

By contrast, the Frisian language, which is used in the northern province of Friesland, is in a quite different and far more endangered position. Frisian enjoys official status in the province, which is officially bilingual, and use of the language is allowed in a number of domains – the courts, the administration, the education system. But Dutch is clearly the dominant and more prestigious language: the higher someone's socio-economic position, the more likely he or she is to make use of Dutch rather than Frisian.

In Friesland today, about half of the 600,000 inhabitants have Frisian as their first language at home. When we include Frisian speakers living elsewhere in the Netherlands, the total number of native speakers comes to 400,000. At the same time, there is a continuing influx of non-Frisian speaking immigrants, resulting in Dutch speaking pockets in the towns and the new suburbs. In the countryside, mass tourism and second homes facilitate the further penetration of Dutch. As a result of these developments, there are no monolingual speakers of Frisian any more.

Looking at the ecology of Frisian, we note a number of worrying trends. In the schools, children are taught both in Frisian and in Dutch, but 70 of the 580 primary schools have been exempted from the obligation to teach Frisian; while at secondary level, in 1990 there were no candidates for the final school examinations in Frisian (in 1995: 16). There is also a decline in the intergenerational transmission of Frisian: especially in mixed marriages, parents increasingly cease to educate their children in Frisian. Frisian is used in the media, but Frisian television is facing enormous financial difficulties and the two largest newspapers in the province have only one page per week in Frisian; they will not increase this for fear of losing subscriptions. In business, Frisian is used with clients but not in documents; only 10% of the Frisians can write Frisian, even though there is an established written standard. When local authorities in Friesland attempted in the eighties to have their documents published in Frisian only, the Dutch Supreme Court forced them to provide free Dutch translations for those who did not know Frisian.

In this unequal diglossic situation, Frisian survives mostly as a spoken language with considerable dialect variation. The standard for Frisian therefore remains fluid, and the language is an easy target for mixing with Dutch. Dutch words and constructions are often unconsciously adopted by Frisian speakers, and Frisian is giving way, especially in the towns, to an urban Dutch dialect with Frisian features. In recent years, moreover, there appears to be a trend away from Frisian: according to a recent survey, between 1980 and 1994 some 40,000 Frisian speakers seem to have abandoned their mother tongue.

The various developments sketched above, together with the impact of urbanisation and modernisation, market forces and immigration, may well lead to a situation, in the near future, when Frisian speakers become a minority even in their own province.

While all this is cause for serious concern about the future of the Frisian language, we may also note the following positive factors and developments.

First of all, the Frisian language enjoys a positive image and the active commitment of those who speak it. There is an active language policy, supported by a sound institutional framework. New immigrants are expected to learn Frisian, and courses are available from the Centre for Frisian Language Education (AFUK). The Fryske Akademy in Ljouwert (= Leeuwarden) is an active centre for research in Frisian Studies with an international reputation. The Dutch government has drafted a new law for the use of Frisian in administration, and the Frisians have been officially recognised as a linguistic minority in the European Union. The Frisians are actively involved in the European Bureau

Sticker with the Frisian flag and a piece of advice:
'You can say it in Frisian!'

for Lesser Used Languages, where they work together with the Welsh, the Basques and the Catalans, among others, to improve the situation of Europe's linguistic and cultural minorities. Diversity of culture and language is, after all, the indispensable spice of European life. In this context, and given the seriousness of the threat faced by the Frisian language, it is of the greatest importance that the Frisian authorities intensify their efforts for the promotion of Frisian language learning, especially among the younger generation.

Secondly, there is in the Frisian community, small though it may be, an active and attractive literary and cultural climate. New initiatives are being taken to strengthen the Frisian cultural profile, as when Ljouwert presented itself as the cultural capital of the Frisians with the production, early in 1995, of the first Frisian opera, *Rixt*. Each year, about a hundred Frisian books are published, ranging from new works of fiction to a succesful series of Frisian Classics, from a translation of *Alice yn Wûnderlân* to the humorous children's books of Diet Huber, from the poetry of Tsjebbe Hettinga (the Frisian Dylan Thomas) to the work of the poet, critic and novelist Anne Wadman. Recent years have seen the success of two full-length Frisian films, *The Dream* and *The Lighthouse,* both made by Pieter Verhoeff, the Frisian Bertolucci. And everywhere in the province there are active local amateur theatre groups keeping alive the tradition of Frisian popular theatre. At the same time, we find a modern and innovative group such as Suver Nuver and its recent taboo-breaking production *Negro Fear* (Negerangst, 1994) in which the emotional complexities of ethnic and race relations were explored by Frisian and black actors, whose performance caused quite a stir when they took it to the Zagreb Theatre Festival in May 1994.

Such efforts and initiatives in the field of Frisian cultural and linguistic policy and the production of new and succesful works of art and imagination in Frisian do enhance the quality and diversity of Frisian cultural life. In this respect, they offer a much needed focus of inspiration for the Frisian future.

REINIER SALVERDA

FURTHER READING

BREUKER, PH. and REINIER SALVERDA (ed.), *The Frisians. Language, Literature, Cultural History.* Special theme issue of *Dutch Crossing,* vol. 18, 2, Winter 1994.
JELLEMA, R., *Country Fair. Poems from Friesland since 1945.* Grand Rapids / Kampen, 1985.
JELLEMA, R., *The Sound that Remains. A Historical Collection of Frisian Poetry.* Grand Rapids, 1990.
OLDENHOF, B., *Frisian Literature Today / Friesische Literatur heute.* Ljouwert, 1993.

ADDRESSES

Fryske Akademy
P.O. Box 54 / 8900 AB Ljouwert / The Netherlands
tel. +31 58 213 14 14 / fax +31 58 213 14 09

AFUK
P.O. Box 53 / 8900 AB Ljouwert / The Netherlands
tel. +31 58 213 80 45

Frisian Literary Museum and Documentation Centre
P.O. Box 884 / 8901 BR Ljouwert / The Netherlands
tel. +31 58 212 08 34 / fax +31 58 213 26 72

Stichting It Fryske Boek
Dimpte Haven 11 / 9001 AX Grou / The Netherlands
tel. +31 566 62 35 00

Literature

Total Writing An Anthology of New Flemish Fiction

Many magazines have devoted special issues to Dutch-language poetry; a few, even, have attempted to give an idea of what is going on in the Dutch-speaking area in both poetry and prose, notably *Dimension*'s bilingual issue (University of Texas, Summer 1978) and the final issue of *Contemporary Literature in Translation* (Vancouver, 1980). The *Review of Contemporary Fiction*'s present anthology is more ambitiously courageous in limiting itself to innovative currents in Flemish fiction. The editors have made a good job of it but, naturally, have had to confine themselves for the most part to extracts from recent novels by the authors concerned. It is therefore still worthwhile getting hold of those other special issues which contain earlier and different work by several authors featured in this latest anthology.

Also included here is an eleven-page checklist of Dutch fiction in translation published since 1980, which at first suggests a healthy climate of interest. In fact, the majority of authors appeared in five anthologies, two of science fiction and fantasy, a further two published by Guernica, a small but enthusiastic Canadian firm. Again, the majority of these authors are from the Netherlands. Only Hugo Claus and Mark Insingel, of those included in this anthology, have had complete novels published in the last fifteen years (and Ivo Michiels during the seventies). This anthology is therefore the more relevant in indicating the richness of a writing so far overlooked.

New Flemish Fiction sets out to present only those authors who demonstrate soundness of style and technique and depth of approach. In his introductory essay Hugo Bousset places them in the context of postmodernism, largely because of their questioning of our perceptions of reality. Though this sounds daunting, the texts are accessible enough and range through fantasy and near-pornography to the playfully ironic.

The work of two short story writers is included, but the episodic nature of some new writing in Flanders allows complete sections from the novels concerned to be presented, in themselves differing little from short stories. The standard of translation is high; that is to say, the English flows naturally but one gains a clear idea of the register and rhythm of the original. In the Flemish context not everything can be suggested, in that many people speak dialect (or use dialect expressions) and use standard Dutch only in writing. Some of the richness of Leo Pleysier's *White Always Looks Good* (Wit is altijd schoon, 1989) is lost, therefore (since it is written entirely in 'dialect'), but otherwise its repetitive colloquiality is well rendered.

A fair idea of how Pleysier's marvellous work would strike a Flemish audience can be gained by reading Faulkner's *As I Lay Dying*. But whereas the American novel consists of the monologues of all those concerned with the woman's funeral, Pleysier restricts himself to the monologue of the deceased (his mother to himself). The two works complement each other and Pleysier's is by no means diminished in the comparison.

The work of other authors suggests further interesting comparisons. Paul de Wispelaere's *The Charred Alphabet* (Het verkoolde alfabet, 1992) is autobiographical, but moves swiftly between different layers of time, viewpoint and subject matter. One is irresistably reminded of the equally fragmented diary genre *(nikkō)* of the Japanese, as represented by such masterpieces as Sei Shōnagon's *Pillow Book* or Kenkō's *Essays in Idleness*. In all these one finds the same skilful transitions between fragments of memory and current reportage, between subjective and objective record. De Wispelaere's approach is typical of that of other contemporaries. It probably owes nothing to the Japanese. All the more strange that writers from so dissimilar a culture should virtually reinvent the charm of that genre for themselves.

The most innovative and challenging of those included is Mark Insingel who, in *That Is To Say* (Dat wil zeggen, 1974), presents language as process and, in analysing its elements, demonstrates that reality is merely a fiction composed in much the same way. We make a choice between coherent elements in presenting either a text or a view of reality. Manipulation of language and interpretation go hand in hand. Insingel is making no merely aesthetic gesture here. His writing encompasses the minatory political dimension to this and so joins hands with more narrative-based authors who also include similar considerations, either overtly

or as implicit in the fiction-making process. But Insingel is of further interest in that his text includes frequent repetition and these elements take on added meaning from their new contexts. The touchstone here is Alain Robbe-Grillet's script for the film *L'Année Dernière à Marienbad* (1961). One has, in brief, the framework of the *nouveau roman* without the tedium of having to read one!

The anthology, then, is challenging and stimulating, but it has its weak points. Walter van den Broek's *The Siege of Laken* (Het beleg van Laken, 1985) is a tedious reworking of Kafka's *The Castle*. For all its technical tricks, hardly suggested in the extract translated, the work seems banal and derivative. Another point arises from the despairing vision which is something of a Flemish trademark. In the absence of an alternative vision, or treated in the rather understated manner of some authors, too much of this strikes one as gutless and inhumane. So bleak a vision only becomes credible when combined with energy, whether it be the driving rhythms of Daniël Robberechts' prose, the satirical vision of Hugo Claus or the anger of Monika van Paemel, the best of the three women included here.

Such hiccups apart, the final impression one gains of Flemish writing is of strength, not simply of the writing but of the personality of the authors. This is no light-weight commodity but a total writing; everything they are and have is put into it.

YANN LOVELOCK

'New Flemish Fiction' (guest editors: Hugo Bousset and Theo Hermans), *The Review of Contemporary Fiction,* Vol. XIV, no. 2 (Summer 1994), pp. 7-185. Normal (IL). ISSN 0276-0045.

Against the Natural Order of Things
The Novels of Renate Dorrestein

'Who wants to write like a woman?' was the title of a hugely succesful lecture by Renate Dorrestein (1954-) when she was 'writer-in-residence' at the University of Michigan in 1986-1987. Why wouldn't a man try to write like Virginia Woolf? This pattern of thought and method is characteristic of feminist writer Dorrestein. Every page of her work – which earned her the biennial Annie Romein prize in 1993 – attests to this. *'I'm not the kind of person who always fearfully hastens to declare: "No, no, I'm not really a feminist"'*, the self-assured Bonnie says in *Unnatural Mothers* (Ontaarde moeders, 1992).

Dorrestein was already well-known as a journalist when her first book *Outsiders* (Buitenstaanders) came out in 1984. This was followed by a number of novels which in their focus on the fantastic, the violent, the grotesque and the gruesome are reminiscent of the gothic novel. According to Dorrestein this genre,

• NEW FLEMISH FICTION •

THE REVIEW OF CONTEMPORARY FICTION

SUMMER 1994 • EIGHT DOLLARS

Renate Dorrestein (1954-)
(Photo by Corinne Noordenbos).

mostly executed by women, has produced quite a few *'feminist novels of protest avant la lettre'* and that is why she likes to see herself placed within the tradition of the 'female gothic novel'. However, this genre-typing must not be taken too strictly in Dorrestein's case: many of her books contain elements of the whodunit, satire and the psychological thriller.

My interest in Dorrestein's writing dates from her autobiographical book *The Perpetuum Mobile of Love* (Het perpetuum mobile van de liefde, 1988). In it she deals with her feelings of guilt about the suicide of her younger sister, who suffered from bulimia nervosa. Dorrestein attributes her own compulsion to write to her sister's fatal 'fall' and thus discloses the principal source of her authorship. Her ideas about the position of women also become evident in this book; cynically she speaks of the almost uncontrollable inclination women have to let themselves be messed around *'in the name of love'*, and about *'the crying shame that in the twentieth century the body you're born with still determines what sort of life you're allowed to lead'.*

The fact that men and women cannot lead the same kind of life is a great injustice, according to Dorrestein. Throughout her oeuvre she is fighting against the ingrained, social idea of *'the natural order of things'*, in which the roles of men and women are strictly separate; what men can do, women can do – and vice versa. Dorrestein consistently demonstrates in her work the lack of necessity to comply with traditional, sex-determined expectations. Because the division between that which is considered specifically masculine and explicitly feminine is made at an early age, it is the upbringing which often gets the blame in her books. The idea that, if fathers would share in bringing up a child, that child won't make any distinction between women and men anymore, can be found in Dorrestein's finest novel *Unnatural Mothers*. From a 'compensatory' point of view, men play only a minor role in her books, but in *Unnatural Mothers* she actually breaks through that pattern: the main character is a man. Of course this is not an ordinary man: he manages to rear his daughter on his own.

Dorrestein's feminist principles may be radical, but in her prose at any rate she is not dogmatic; her entertaining, thrilling, often funny and provocative books fortunately aren't exclusively worth reading by her partisans. Dorrestein's writing technique, which she herself has called *'The Laws of Dorrestein'*, is to thank for this: *'1. a number of witticisms, 2. a number of blows below the belt, 3. at least one sentence in which I say something intelligent, 4. an ending in which I turn the whole thing completely upside down.'* She also often uses clichés from trivial literature, which contributes to the entertaining, old-fashioned narrative style. The reader is comforted by the familiarity, and perhaps accepts the modern, unconventional ideas more easily because of it.

The psychological thriller *Unnatural Mothers* is about the disentangling of a horrible family secret, about mothers and daughters, about a father who has to play the role of a mother, psychological and physical violence, rape, responsibility and love, and several other subjects. A variety of unnatural mothers files past: the independent career woman Bonnie who left her husband years ago, thus saddling him with the care of their daughter Maryemma, Bonnie's sister Meijken, eighteen years older than herself, who in the past had been forced to deny her motherhood, their 'Mother' who found her own longing for a child more important than Meijken's happiness. Three unnatural mothers spread over different generations, all of whom are unable to escape the fatal inheritance of evolution. In the way she sketches the inadequacy of her characters and the misunderstandings between them, Dorrestein has mercilessly chronicled human deficiency. She doesn't supply any moral judgement: everybody is irrevocably a victim of something or other. But the one who is most victimised in this timeless interpersonal drama is the touchingly described, defenceless, fearful, eleven-year-old child Maryemma, who is at the mercy of the whims of unpredictable parents and who time and again has to wait and see whether anyone wants to take care of her. That child thus becomes a good measure of the effects of unnatural motherhood. Bonnie, however, provides a different theory: *'Later, when she's old enough, she'll thank me. None of that stifling symbiosis for her – and believe you me, I know what I'm talking about. I was myself left to the mercies of a mother. Weren't we all? So we should all know better.'*

JEROEN VULLINGS
Translated by Ria Loohuizen.

Renate Dorrestein, *Unnatural Mothers* (Tr. Wanda Boeke). Seattle (WA): Women in Translation, 1994; 232 pp. ISBN 1-879679-06-X.

'The Rustling of Clothes'
The Poetry of Eddy van Vliet

The contemporary poet fights his own art, its blandness, its flatness, the laconic understatement so difficult to avoid because it has become the very essence of what poetry is nowadays. *Farewell and Fall* (1994), a bilingual collection of the Flemish poet Eddy van Vliet's poems, does not avoid this built-in difficulty, naturally, but frequently manages to overcome it by the use of an image here, the suggestion of a story there, a rapid brushstroke in an unexpected place sometimes making an unexpected point, as in 'Morning' ('Ochtend'):

My favourite sound is the rustling of clothes
as they take on their shape again
from which love has driven them for hours.

Many of these poems yield some surprise of vision, offer some turn of perception, or even provide some extraordinary sense of an all too ordinary occurrence, as when one of them, 'In Love' ('Verliefd'), characterises that emotion by its common mishaps:

Between thumb and index finger, like burning ashes,
the wrongly gathered phone number.
Parks too wet, hotel too full, Paris too far.

This ability to capture a feeling or situation is not all that marks Van Vliet (1942-) as a poet. As critics have noted, his best poems appear almost to create the situations he depicts. He has famously said that poetry allows you to say what you can't in other ways, but evidently it also allows you to invent and to create what you otherwise can't have. In a poem called 'Birds' ('Vogels'), he recounts a childhood experience of creating for a photograph *a forest of birds* by first covering up the wire of their cages with twigs and leaves. The poem speaks of conjuring and eternalising, and this appears very much to be at the heart of Van Vliet's talent. And one guesses that it was some such drive to arrange, organise and shape that drove Van Vliet into the discipline of poetry – the attorney, now in his fifties, practicing law in Antwerp, speaking one language, the poet moulding another.

This sounds more joyful than it is. The most powerful poems in *Farewell and Fall* are deeply melancholy. 'In Light-Blue Pants' ('In een lichtblauwe broek'), a surreal account of a party, *'cast in silver'*, is as luridly mournful as Oscar Wilde's 'The Harlot's House'. And indeed the gloom as well as an almost appealing decadence are there:

(...) In filtered light and with the conceit
of living persons, the dance was lit. Sad
as a brothel after the doors were closed.

Another poem ('Party') features another party, where the party-goers have not seen each other for a while, *'the sons the image / of the father'*. Time has done its work, and of course implicitly death is everywhere. It is a measure of the poem's success that we feel this before we come to its aphoristic conclusion:

The names of the dead are exchanged like addresses
on the last holiday. Apparently the one someone
wanted to ask something, was already buried.

Within this poem indirectness has turned to directness. No such turn in a small masterpiece called 'Death' ('Dood') which asks, no, tells, death not to dither but to

'Wipe your feet and make yourself at home', to keep the poet – all of us? – from its usual settings and diversions, from *'pointless hours in classy clinics'*.

Most of these poems were translated by John van Tiel, who performed a truly difficult job. The translator of modern poetry too fights the art. One longs to see a number of different translations and compare which best render into English the simple but elusive diction of Eddy van Vliet's poetic language.

MANFRED WOLF

Eddy van Vliet, *Farewell and Fall* (Tr. Matthew Blake, Theo Hermans, James S Holmes, Peter Nijmeijer and John van Tiel). Dublin: The Dedalus Press, 1994; 77 pp. ISBN 1-873790-55-4.

Translator or Actor?

I find myself asking myself more and more: *'Why do you sit translating?'* What are the deeper-lying, the ultimate reasons for it? After all, for years I have objected to being referred to as *'James Brockway, the translator'*, for translating is only one of the things I have done in the Netherlands since the war. Writing about British authors in Dutch and about Dutch authors in English often amused me more. I never needed to translate and in recent years I have confined the activity mainly to poetry, and to poets of my own choice too. An exception is translating for the *Poems on Walls* project, whereby poems in various languages, with translations, are painted up on outdoor walls in the university town of Leiden, the work of an enterprising group of people.

The other day I found myself translating a story by Jan Siebelink as I might have been doing years ago – that is to say: to commission, because I had been asked to – and as I sat writing, I became aware of an old contentment. I was sitting there, quietly enjoying myself. Why? I asked myself, and then the answer came, shot up out of my unconscious of its own accord.

As a youth, for six years, I played a highly active part in school dramatics as an actor, a producer, even writing a play, and producing it and acting in it myself. These were some of the happiest, most fulfilling hours of my life. I suppose I should have become an actor – for the answer to my question was: for me translating was the next best thing to acting.

As a translator, one is always acting a part, pretending to be someone else – as I was, as a flyer in the war. That wasn't me. When I am translating the poems of Dutch poet Rutger Kopland, I am trying to become Kopland. When Achterberg, I am trying to become Achterberg (difficult!). I have also tried to become female writers like Maria Dermoût, Vasalis, even Andreas Burnier. Perhaps I was fairly good at it because at school I was often called upon to take on women's roles. Yes, translating, I am play-acting.

There were some translations, however, I was required to do which I found harder – because the author was so different from myself. Flemish author Herman Teirlinck, for example, with his great, grim, cold novel *The Man in the Mirror* (Zelfportret of het Galgemaal, 1955), stern and severe in matter and style. But what a challenge! I found I got another sort of satisfaction from assuming similarly difficult roles and deliberately took on translating Jan Wolkers and Heere Heeresma by my own choice. I proved good at it – a thing I could always tell from the responses I received from British editors, who often took the work eagerly. As for the critics, the reception in the London press of Heeresma's brilliant novella *A Day at the Beach* (Een dagje naar het strand, 1962) was so positive it surprised me. It resulted in Roman Polanski buying the film rights in my English version, though the film was never released. More's the pity – but it justified my taking on the translation myself when the official 'Powers That Be' had said it had no chance and refused their support. Moreover, once my English version had appeared, it was followed by at least a dozen in other languages – English being the key to the world.

This brings me to the question: translate to commission or independently? The former guarantees some income, but not much, and had, for me, several drawbacks. Would work done to commission even be published? That matter was, after all, then in different hands. It is a fact that much of the work I did to commission did not get published, whereas work I did independently usually did – because I had certain editors in mind and knew what they would and would not like. When third parties were involved, difficulties would arise which never occurred when I worked on my own. True enough, I had to submit four stories by one Dutch woman author before I could convince a certain editor that she could write. And in another case the translation of a novel by Jaap Harten misfired because the first publisher who took it was bought up by another and the second one went bankrupt. But usually, when the contact was direct, so was the acceptance.

Another drawback of translating literary work to commission is that the wonderful incentive of risk – shall I or shan't I succeed? – is missing. I think the element of risk was one of my main incentives and added to the excitement. No one on my very insular island was waiting for Dutch writing, no one was crying out for it. I wanted to do something about this and wrote wherever I could about authors like W.F. Hermans, Gerard Reve, Harry Mulisch (the Holy Trinity). I knew it was important to place information about their work next to work by British authors like Evelyn Waugh, Cyril Connolly, Ted Hughes, and I did.

The publishing situation fluctuates. Only recently I heard from a publishing acquaintance in London that the outlook for translated fiction in Britain was hopeless, impossible. They were taking nothing on. The American 'blockbuster' mentality is partly to blame for this. I have always preferred to go for what are misleadingly called the 'little magazines'. From the literary angle, there is nothing little about such a magazine as *London Magazine,* first under the editorship of John Lehmann and for thirty years now under Alan Rose,

himself a writer and poet. The work I placed with them was spade-work, pioneering work, but I think it helped to open up the field. Recently Ross has published work by poets Rutger Kopland and Anton Korteweg, also a story by the Jewish author, Frans Pointl. We shall continue.

I can, however, recall a commissioned project which was wholly satisfactory and enjoyable and which threw up no difficulties. It concerned a series of radio talks on Dutch and Flemish writing for Radio Netherlands World Service, and I took it on only on condition that I had a free hand to re-write the talks, where necessary. It was and I did, for authors like J.C. Bloem, Achterberg, Adriaan Roland Holst, among the poets, were missing and no postwar writers were mentioned. It meant translating poems and prose extracts by about seventy different authors, ranging from the anonymous author of the medieval *Egidius* to Jos Vandeloo and Remco Campert, for I added a talk of my own about then younger figures. The talks were broadcast and later appeared in book form as *A Sampling of Dutch Literature.* This was an exercise in discipline which I enjoyed – especially the re-writing bit.

Nevertheless, I prefer my 'game of literary roulette', as I call the independently done translation. I could have done ten times more, it is true, but, after all, when I came to the Netherlands in 1946 it was to pursue my own writing and I became *'the translator, James Brockway'* only by accident. By mistake.

A word before leaving about the difference between translating prose and poetry. There is a world of difference. Poetry that really is poetry – much of it isn't – is a very special, highly concentrated, subtle and roundabout, oblique way of saying something so that it will stick and live on in the mind. It is far more difficult to translate, especially if your aim is to remain true to the original and yet produce a translation that is, itself, a poem. According to Dutch poet J. C. Bloem, that is the most difficult task of all in writing and I love trying to prove American poet Robert Frost wrong when he defined poetry as *'what gets lost in translation'.* It need not get lost.

But now I must go away and pretend I am Pessoa, Cavafy, Ingeborg Bachmann, H. Marsman and Frederik van Eeden, for those charming *Poems on Walls* people. It gives a special satisfaction in a money-based society to be doing something that has nothing to do with money. An act of defiance, if you like. As long as he can still put up poems (with translations!) on walls, there is still hope for man.

JAMES BROCKWAY

James Brockway's latest collection of translations is *Singers behind Glass. Eight Modern Dutch Poets* (Lincoln, 1995).

One of the AMVC
repositories
(Photo by Joris Luyten).

Hendrik Conscience could be called the Flemish
Walter Scott: his historical novel *The Lion of Flanders*
(De Leeuw van Vlaenderen, 1838) gave Flemings a
mythical and heroic past. On his death the City of
Antwerp acquired a substantial part of his literary
estate and in 1912 a magnificent Conscience exhibition
was assembled from these manuscripts, books and trib-
utes. The overwhelming success of the exhibition
helped convince the municipal authorities that a space
was required for the permanent preservation and display of these and other archive materials. However, it
was not until 1933 that these plans were realised, with
the foundation of what was then called the Museum of
Flemish Literature. From the outset a number of those
behind the project argued that the field of collection
should be extended to the broad spectrum of cultural
life in Flanders.

This aim was certainly soon achieved in practice,
with drama, music and the visual arts featured alongside literature. In addition, a mass of archival and
documentary material was soon acquired from the
flourishing cultural societies and from figures and
groups associated with the Flemish Movement. The
Flemish struggle for liberation aimed not only at the
political and social equality of Flemings and Franco-
phones, but was also intended to create a Flemish cultural identity. Thanks to the breadth of vision of a succession of curators, among them Ger Schmook, a
wealth of important cultural-historical source material
has been preserved.

In 1945, which in many respects marked a 'fresh
start', the museum was renamed and became the
Archive and Museum of Flemish Culture (AMVC),
which certainly accorded better with the institution's
complex nature and wide field of collecting.

Today the AMVC is the central archive and documentation centre for Flemish literature, the Flemish
Movement, music, and the dramatic and visual arts in
Flanders since c.1750. At present it holds some
1,000,000 letters and manuscripts, 100,000 photographs, 25,000 posters, as well as countless sculptures,
paintings, prints and audiovisual items.

Of course not all the dossiers are equally substantial,

but a number of archive collections which have grown
organically should be mentioned here. For example,
the AMVC houses the archives of men of letters like
André Demedts and Maurice Gilliams, composers and
music-lovers like Lodewijk de Vocht and Denise de
Vries-Tolkowsky, plastic artists like Alfred Ost and
Jozef Peeters, theatrical companies like the Royal
Flemish Opera and the New Flemish Theatre, the
Antwerp mayors and politicians Camille Huysmans
and Lode Craeybeckx and all kinds of organisations,
down to the complete administrative archive of the
Antwerp 1993, Cultural Capital of Europe project. It
goes without saying that the majority of acquisitions
result from donations: the available budget unfortunately leaves no scope for a systematic purchasing
policy.

In addition the AMVC is building up a contemporary
documentation centre. All Flemish newspapers and the
most important periodicals and magazines are combed
daily: the relevant articles are cut out, backed with low-
acidity paper, and added to the appropriate dossier with
an indication of the source. The extensive collections
can be accessed through a computerised index (available on-line), and catalogues of the Antwerp university
libraries and the Municipal Library. The index contains
over 25,000 headwords: names of persons, institutions,
societies, magazines and movements are listed alpha-
betically, with their dossier number, a short identifying
note and a list of the archive material and documents
held by the AMVC. The inventory of letters can also be
retrieved using this computerised database. The letters
themselves, however, together with other (autograph)
personal documents, may be consulted only with the
express written permission of the author (and, in the
case of letters, of the addressee) or his / her heirs for
fifty years after the author's death.

Letters are an important source for any literary-his-
torical research. Since only letters received are generally found among posthumous papers, a great many
foreign celebrities figure in the AMVC's letter collection; they include Lenin, Friedrich Engels, Charles de
Gaulle, Winston Churchill, Victor Hugo, Alphonse
Daudet, Anaïs Nin, Rudyard Kipling, Tristan Tzara,
Pablo Casals, Auguste Rodin, Charles Ricketts, Peter
Ustinov, John Galsworthy and many others.

The reading room of the AMVC is open to all readers
over the age of 17. It is visited by academics, students
and journalists, as well as interested members of the
general public in search of material or information on
cultural life in Flanders in the last 250 years.

Cultural history is also evoked in the permanent
exhibition, which takes up most of the display areas.
All aspects feature in the wealth of varied material
from the AMVC's own collection; surrounded by statues, paintings, photographs, manuscripts and other
exhibits, the visitor wanders through two centuries of
Flanders, from Hendrik Conscience to Hugo Claus.

Oases of calm are provided by several 'cabinets': a
reconstruction of the cluttered study of the remarkable
Miss Marie-Elisabeth Belpaire, founder of a magazine
and a college for women, both of which still exist, and

at the other extreme an avant-garde suite of furniture made in Paul-Gustave van Hecke's Brussels studio *Sélection* for the journalist Gabriël Opdebeek, who under the pseudonym Geo de la Violette wrote a series of erotic stories about his *Miss Mary.*

The AMVC also mounts a number of temporary exhibitions each year on a particular figure, movement or aspect of its collection. The 1994 diary, for instance, contained the following varied programme: a spring exhibition on the Naturalist writer Lode Zielens, a summer collection of post-mortem photographs and death masks and in the autumn a selection from the AMVC's extensive collection of menus and cookery books. There is usually an accompanying exhibiton catalogue, which appears in the SB / AMVC series of publications.

The AMVC's brief, then, is a wide one. It is a unique institution, which helps ensure that authentic source material, on which all scholarly research must be based, is preserved and made accessible.

LEEN VAN DIJCK
Translated by Paul Vincent.

ADDRESS
Archive and Museum of Flemish Culture
Minderbroederstraat 22 / 2000 Antwerp / Belgium
tel. +32 3 232 55 80 / fax +32 3 231 93 10
Opening hours: Reading Room, 8.30 a.m.-4.30 p.m. (Monday to Friday)
Museum, 10 a.m.-5 p.m. (Tuesday to Saturday)

Music

'Bitten by the bug' Peter Greenaway Goes Opera

British film-maker Peter Greenaway regards himself as *'almost, in some senses, an honorary Dutchman'. 'I've felt very much at home here',* he continues, *'I feel very much supported by notions of Dutch society, what it stands for, its history, certainly its incredibly rich pictorial history which I've always admired and respected.'*

Greenaway's first screen triumph, *The Draughtsman's Contract* (1982), was made in the Low Countries, and saw the beginning of his long-standing association with producer Kees Kasander. *A Zed and Two Noughts* (1985) was shot in Rotterdam's Blijdorp Zoo. Greenaway has now made fourteen films in the Netherlands, including five feature-length films. Apart from locations, the sincerity of Greenaway's respect for Low Countries artistic creativity is evidenced by his collaborations with Dutch set designers and his documentary about the work of Flemish choreographer Anne Teresa de Keersmaeker. Dutch seventeenth-century still-life painting (including Rembrandt's arresting meat carcasses) is an obvious reference point for visual images which recur in his films, and now in his first venture into opera.

Louis Andriessen and Peter Greenaway, *Rosa* (Photo By Rosa Boosey & Hawkes).

No wonder, then, that he chose Amsterdam for his debut in a new performance art form, opera. *Rosa: A Horse Drama* premiered on 2 November 1994 at the Amsterdam Muziektheater, with the Australian baritone Lyndon Terracini in the title role, Australian soprano Marie Angel as his lover Esmeralda, and Dutch soprano Miranda van Kralingen as Madame De Vries.

Amsterdam was also the obvious choice of venue for the first performance of an opera whose music was written by the contemporary Dutch composer Louis Andriessen. Talking to Andriessen for the BBC radio 3 arts magazine programme *Night Waves,* on the day of the final dress rehearsal, I asked the composer if he was worried that opera-goers might find *Rosa* too avant-garde – both musically and in its staging. He shrugged off any such anxiety. Amsterdam audiences, he said, were well used to the avant-garde, and his post-minimalist music had a steady and committed following in the city quite large enough to fill the Muziektheater for the half-dozen performances for which *Rosa* was scheduled. The very characteristics which had drawn Greenaway to Andriessen's music – the spare, allusive forms, and *'a certain sort of detachment from conditions of high melodrama which I think both intrigues and excites both of us'* (as Greenaway put it to me) – draw capacity houses whenever his work is performed (in Amsterdam his stature is comparable with Greenaway's other composer-collaborator, Michael Nyman).

Rosa is the story of a Brazilian composer – Juan Manuel de Rosa – who died in Uruguay in 1957 under mysterious circumstances. The programme notes tell us that *Rosa* is the sixth (but the first to be executed) in an ambitious programme of ten operas which Greenaway intends to write, charting the bizarre similarities linking the circumstances surrounding the violent deaths of ten composers, from Anton Webern's in 1945 to John Lennon's in 1980. *'I've always been intrigued by those works of art which I suppose are maybe self-indulgently self-reflexive'*, Greenaway told me just before the opening performance. *'If you're going to make a work about a composer you ought to make it in musical terms. So already maybe ten or twelve years ago (maybe more) the notion of making an opera around Webern's death was circulating in my mind. Then in 1980 came the death of John Lennon – another mysterious death under strange circumstances where it's very difficult to believe in the accepted verdict, the notion of a man who kills John Lennon for reasons of notoriety.'* The ten-year-old Mark Chapman appears in *Rosa,* learning how to kill off composers. As with all of Greenaway's work we are lured into looking for structure and connections between surreally meaningless (and gruesome) incidents, but the unfolding drama constantly withholds from us the key facts which could turn wild speculation into substantiated conspiracy.

I asked Greenaway if opera lent itself particularly well to his self-referential and self-ironising form of dramatisation – one which constantly draws attention to its own techniques and formalisms. He was quick to agree that the suspension of disbelief required of an opera audience was so extreme as to cry out for deconstruction: *'The opera tradition is full of the most ridiculous and preposterous conventions which have to be leapt over in order to engage in what's going on on that stage.'* He was equally clear that one of the things which had drawn him towards Louis Andriessen as a composer was his artistic self-consciousness. *'Anyone who is going to collaborate with me needs a great delight in the medium per se. If my cinema is about anything it's about cinema, it's about the actual vocabulary of making, manufacturing, using, processing images. And I think Andriessen's music and his ideas are very much part and parcel of that.'*

One of the challenges to the conventional expectations of opera which Greenaway was anxious to stress was his treatment of the soprano heroine – Rosa's lover Esmeralda. *'There are I suppose what could be called disturbing sequences in "Rosa", but that's intended to be doubly ironic. When you think of the role of the female in traditional opera, she is often an extremely passive emotional object who suffers all sorts of humiliations, but the opera tradition somehow deodorises them, sanitises them, is very censorious about them, turns her grief into pretty music. In "Rosa" there's a serious attempt to make the audience rethink the sexually humiliated traditional operatic female. There is, right in the centre of the drama.'* Anyone familiar with Greenaway's films might immediately anticipate the kind of raw physicality and explicit representation of studiedly perverse sexual behaviour we saw in *The Cook, the Thief, his Wife, and her Lover* (1989). The real Rosa was rumoured to go in for 'unnatural practices' with his favourite horse; his lover Esmeralda was the daughter of the local abbatoir-owner (abbatoirs as

an unmoralised, shocking spectacle crop up again and again as a visual counterpart for gratuitous violence in Greenaway's cinematographic repertoire).

Rosa in the auditorium, however, defies any kind of reassuringly intellectualised critical assessment – from beginning to end it is raw, violent, visually disturbing and musically challenging. Blood runs down the walls in sheets, and animal carcasses are gutted by teams of naked men and women. Film-footage of cowboys is projected on the semen- and blood-stained sheet where Rosa has humiliated his adoring Esmeralda. Stage directions and glosses on the plot, blown up into over-sized texts, compete for the audience's attention with the more-or-less traditional formalisms of opera. Musical idioms collide; musical quotation is used ironically to counterpoint the stage action. The diva sings her most important arias naked and daubed with black paint. Taken together, the result is an unforgettable opera experience, and one which, as far as I was concerned, really worked, both at the level of intellectual challenge, and (perhaps more importantly) as an aesthetic triumph, combining the strengths of both film and opera traditions.

Some older members of the Muziektheater audience at the first night seemed stunned (some left before the end); the predominantly youthful majority, however, gave *Rosa* a rapturous ovation. As for Greenaway himself … this is certainly not the last the opera world has seen of him: *'Just watching people at work on the proscenium stage night after night after night has given me a hundred new ideas for all sorts of other exciting possibilities. I've been bitten by the bug now.'*

LISA JARDINE

The Splendour of Flemish Polyphony

Four hundred years ago, on 14 June 1594, the death occurred of Orlandus Lassus, one of the principal figures in Flemish polyphony. It was the celebration of this centenary that prompted the Davidsfonds cultural foundation and publishing house, and its record label Eufoda, to embark on an ambitious project – the production of ten CDs and a book under the joint title of *Flemish Polyphony* (De Vlaamse polyfonie). The project was directed by Professor Ignace Bossuyt of the Musicology Department of the Catholic University of Leuven. The musical realisation was undertaken by Erik van Nevel, conductor of the Concurrende Consort and of the Capella Sancti Michaelis. The music we are concerned with here dates from the fifteenth and sixteenth centuries, the period in which not only trade but also the arts and scholarship blossomed in the Southern Netherlands under the Dukes of Burgundy and, later, the Hapsburgs (see *The Low Countries* 1993-94: 39-50).

Between around 1420 and 1600 the musical life of cathedrals and royal houses throughout more or less the whole of Europe was dominated by five generations of composers from the Southern Netherlands, French-Flanders, Artois, Hainault and Liège. They laid the foundation for genres, styles and techniques of composition which became typical of Renaissance music in Europe. Those five generations comprised several dozens of composers, and literally thousands of compositions which are to be found in libraries all over Europe. The Davidsfonds production includes recordings of some two hundred works by forty-two composers, among them Dufay, Ockeghem, Josquin des Prez, Philippus de Monte, Lassus …

In handbooks of the history of music they are referred to nowadays as the Dutch School, the Franco-Flemish School, or even the Burgundian School. Ignace Bossuyt chose the term 'Flemish Polyphony' because in their own period the composers in question were all known and renowned as *'I Fiamminghi'* or the *'Capella Flamenca'*. The term 'polyphony' refers to the fact that this is part-singing: the simultaneous execution of several melodies (horizontality) according to established standards for harmony (verticality), in an ordered rhythm and measure. The interplay of horizontality and verticality gives the counterpoint, of which these composers were such great masters. Moreover, their contrapuntal constructions had a hitherto unknown euphony and were rich in emotional expression. This was true of both religious and secular music, whether it was in Latin or in Dutch, French, Italian … in an array ranging from the mystical Latin motet to erotic French *chansons.*

Professor Bossuyt's beautifully illustrated book *Flemish Polyphony* is a brilliant synthesis of the evolution of that polyphonic music over two centuries, and of the most interesting composers. The first part of the book places polyphony in context – political situation, geographical location, previous musical history, various genres, manuscripts and publishers. The second part covers composers and their work. Bossuyt divides the book into chapters, each of which concentrates on one principal figure, the environment in which he worked and appropriate contemporaries. For instance: Ockeghem and France, Dufay and Burgundy, Willaert and Italy, Gombert and the court of Emperor Charles v. The ten chapters correspond to the ten CDs, so that reading and listening can be juxtaposed in a fascinating manner.

The CDs and the book are 'interactive'. Each CD illustrates a chapter from the book by means of an extensive selection of works. In addition, attention has been paid to the mix of genres (masses, motets, psalms, madrigals, chansons, villanellas), and considerable care has also been taken to include composers less well-known but of equally high quality. Conductor Erik van Nevel has ensured variety in the performers as well: choir or group of soloists, purely vocal or with suitable instrumental accompaniment. The renderings are excellent: extremely well-balanced, with clear differentiation (in the expression of words, among other things) according to the stylistic evolution from the early, barely medieval polyfony to the late Renaissance, in which certain Baroque characteristics are beginning to be apparent.

An interesting extra is that the handbook which

The Munich choir, directed by Orlandus Lassus, in the St George's Chapel of the Neuveste, which was the residence of the dukes of Bavaria. This plate is from the Mielich Codex, p. 186 (Bayerische Staatsbibliothek, Munich).

accompanies each CD not only includes the texts of all compositions performed, but also gives translations in French, German, English and Dutch. Whoever reads *Flemish Polyphony* and goes on to listen to the music with the texts of the songs to hand, receptive in body and soul, surely cannot fail to be impressed by this beautiful music from one of the most magnificent periods in Flemish cultural history.

HENDRIK WILLAERT
Translated by Sheila M. Dale.

Ignace Bossuyt, *De Vlaamse polyfonie.* Leuven: Davidsfonds, 1994; 176 pp. ISBN 90-6152-843-7.
De Vlaamse polyfonie. 10 CDs under the direction of Erik van Nevel. Eufoda, CDs 1160-1169.
The CDs are also available separately. Those subscribing to the complete series of CDs will receive a free copy of the book (available in Dutch only).

The More Breuker, the Better

Is Willem Breuker (1944-) the biggest comic turn in Dutch jazz, or just the worst-dressed jazz musician in the Netherlands? The answer is: he is both. Such at least was the conclusion of the jury which awarded Breuker the 1993 Boy Edgar Prize. This verdict did not, of course, rest merely on the above considerations but, rather, on the jury's recognition of Breuker's *'dedication to "Good People's Good Music"'* and their appreciation of him as *'a musician who infuses all aspects of both composition and interpretation with this dedication.'*

Willem Breuker is the only musician who has carried off the premier Dutch jazz trophy twice. The previous occasion was in 1970, when he won the Wessel Ilcken Prize, an award to encourage up and coming talent. At the time, Breuker did not have any substantial oeuvre to his name. In 1980, that award was renamed the Boy Edgar Prize, which officially became the VPRO / Boy Edgar Prize when the VPRO broadcasting corporation pledged 25,000 guilders (c. $ 16,000 / £ 10,000) in sponsorship and a radio broadcast. In mid-1994, at the Concertgebouw in Amsterdam, Breuker received the prize with due formality from the then Minister of Welfare, Health and Cultural Affairs, Mrs Hedy d'Ancona.

The extent of Willem Breuker's contribution to Dutch jazz and improvised music is virtually beyond measure. Its value is, perhaps, summed up as succinctly by the slightly tongue-in-cheek tag *'The More Breuker, the Better',* coined years ago by co-rebel and fellow saxophonist Hans Dulfer, as by his own battle-cry of *'Good People's Good Music'.*

Over the past quarter century, the composer / player has evolved a personal, irreverent brand of politically committed music theatre, composed film scores, and engaged in all manner of other creative activities. One of these is the Willem Breuker Kollektief, the most polished jazz orchestra in the Netherlands. About to celebrate its twentieth anniversary, the Kollektief can play any audience off its feet. Abroad too – and that includes the United States, the home of jazz – the orchestra has an established reputation and has for many years been something of an ambassador for Dutch jazz and improvised music.

Another venture, but on a more limited scale, is *The Crowning Touch* (De Klap op de Vuurpijl), the annual festivity which Breuker organises during the Christmas season to see in the New Year with fitting cheer. The fact that he invariably manages to rise to this occasion in his persona of performing animal is a testimony to his indestructible workaholic drive. Breuker lives, breathes and eats music. During the *Crowning Touch* event, he always features new contemporary work alongside jazz and improvised music. This takes some guts. Guts in the sense that Breuker has no qualms about matching his playing, his group and his compositions with the very best in an environment geared to *'outstanding quality'* and *'significant musical developments'.* He runs the risk, in other words, of showing up badly, or of being overshadowed by others. But he takes this gamble voluntarily – and that he should do so speaks volumes for the man's integrity.

Breuker's own record label, BV Haast, similarly provides a platform for his own and other music and musicians. Here again, his sole criterion for the music he backs is that it lives up to his yardstick of *'Good People's Good Music'.* For the rest, anything goes, be it *musique concrète,* film music, or fairly conventional types of jazz. For all the panache, the idealism and the funny clothes, though, the Breuker enterprise is no shoestring art for art's sake operation. He conducts his affairs with a steady, professional hand; from those who work with him, he expects as much as he puts in himself.

The music which Breuker composes for his core group, *The Willem Breuker Kollektief,* and for the many other ensembles which play his work, is exceptionally multi-facetted. A typical characteristic is how he unites musical depth with a sense of the theatrical, approachability and a sense of humour (he is, actually, one of the most humorous people in Dutch musical circles). As an instrumentalist, his mastery of the tenor and bass saxophones and of the bass clarinet is such that he can in the blink of an eye switch seamlessly from a flowing classical line to a breezy jazz rhythm that could bring a Christmas turkey back to life.

The report of the Boy Edgar Prize jury put it thus: *'Whether he picks up a police whistle, a mouth organ or the accordion, he knows how to extract an utterly individual sound. As a vocalist (…) he has succeeded in elevating the art of singing out of tune into a wholly sublime genre of its own, which he deploys in inimitably inventive ways in concert and on the music theatre stage. His audacity imbues his musical activities with a freshness and vigour which is typically Amsterdam and cosmopolitan, and couldn't be further from the conventional idea of the stolid Dutchman!'*

All of this however, has not necessarily rendered him equally popular in all quarters. Critics regard him as a groucher, forever indignantly up in arms for his achievements which, he feels, are undeservedly under-appreciated. Be that as it may, it is a fact that the first serious study of Breuker was not written by any compatriot, but by the French husband and wife team of musicologists, Françoise and Jean Buzelin.

KEES POLLING
Translated by Sonja Prescod.

SELECTIVE DISCOGRAPHY
Baal Brecht Breuker Handke. BV Haast, CD 9006.
Bob's Gallery. BV Haast, CD 8801.
Metropolis. BV Haast, CD 8903.
Parade. BV Haast, CD 9101.
This Way, Ladies. BV Haast, CD 9301.
Overtime / Uberstunden. NM Classics, CD 92042.

Willem Breuker (1944-)
(Photo by Frans Schellekens).

From Looms to CDs The Museum for Industrial Archaeology and Textiles in Ghent

The city of Ghent (capital of the Province of East Flanders) is often mentioned in the same breath as Bruges. Scores of buildings serve as reminders of a magnificent, mainly medieval, past. However, tourists who venture beyond Ghent's historic centre are likely to find themselves in the 'nineteenth-century belt', a jumble of narrow streets lined with small workers' houses. Though many of these houses have been atractively restored, the area still conjures up memories of the dire living conditions of a sizable urban proletariat. Many of those who lived there were employed in the mechanised flax and cotton industry which determined the visual aspect of the city in the nineteenth and even well into the twentieth century.

In 1976 the City Council decided to set up a museum which would tell the story of this industrialised society from around 1750 to the present day; and so the MIAT (Museum for Industrial Archaeology and Textiles) was founded. The collection expanded very rapidly, causing a chronic shortage of space. Before long the museum acquired the use of a former cotton spinning mill, though at first this served only as a storage area. Gradually the old mill was turned into a museum, and a modern reception area, which includes a museum shop and a multi-functional room, was built onto the main building. The new complex opened at the end of 1994.

The MIAT collection now extends over five floors – each measuring almost 1,000 square metres – within the main building of the former mill, whose layout closely resembles that of mills of the same date in Manchester. Scores of machines, including the museum's showpiece, the Mule Jenny, are on display. The plans for this mechanical cotton spinning machine were smuggled out of England by the Flemish industrialist Lieven Bauwens in the 1790s, and with that the Continent was able to embark on the industrial revolution.

However, the museum is not devoted exclusively to technology. It also looks at the political, socioeconomic, social and cultural developments which went hand in hand with successive industrial revolutions, covering themes such as the living conditions of the factory worker, employment in smaller trades (laundries, cooperages, printing works, etc.), heavy industry (steel works), child labour, social conflicts and strikes, distribution and transport, banking, education, the increase in leisure, sport and tourism. Recent phenomena such as nuclear energy, space travel, the modern media, information science and biochemistry are also illustrated. All these themes are presented by means of a great diversity of machines, paintings, photographs, reproductions and information 'blocks' with short introductory texts. An annex houses a richly stocked library.

The MIAT is primarily concerned with industrial developments in and around Ghent, yet there is no geographical limitation. Attention is also paid to parallel changes in other countries such as the Netherlands and the German-speaking areas. England, as the birthplace of industrialisation, is also given wide coverage. For example, as well as a copy of the first social legislation, we find the harrowing account of a young English orphan who worked in a factory in the most inhumane conditions.

The MIAT can certainly be described as an impressive achievement, not only because of its extensive and varied collection but also because of its convincing combination of economics, politics, society and culture. Moreover, it is located just outside the centre of Ghent and so is easily accessible.

HANS VANACKER
Translated by Alison Mouthaan-Gwillim.

ADDRESS
Museum for Industrial Archaeology and Textiles
Minnemeers 9 / 9000 Ghent / Belgium
tel. +32 9 223 59 69
Opening hours: 9.30 a.m.-5 p.m. (closed on Mondays)

The Solar System in the Living-Room
The Eise Eisinga Planetarium

The stars were unfavourable in the Spring of 1774; at least, that was the opinion of Eelco Alta, the pastor of Bozum, a small village in Friesland. Early in the morning of 8 May there was to be a rare conjunction of the moon with the planets Mercury, Venus, Mars en Jupiter. Five heavenly bodies so close to each other in the sky could only be a bad omen. Maybe the conjunction was a portent of the end of the world. Alta decided to write a book to put the fear of death into the Frisian farm folk. Prayer and attendance at church might yet stave off the crack of doom.

The pastor was wise enough not to publish the book under his own name. He called himself *'a lover of truth'*. There is no historical evidence as to whether church attendance in Bozum increased in 1774, but it is a fact that Alta's book of doom led indirectly to the building of one of the most unusual places of interest in the Netherlands – the Eise Eisinga Planetarium.

Eise Eisinga was a Frisian amateur astronomer who had been aware for a long time of the exceptional conjunction. Eisinga, the son of a wool carder, had studied mathematics and astronomy and when he was only eighteen years old had written books on sundials and eclipses of the moon, among other things. In 1774 – Eisinga was then thirty – he became so incensed at the foolish superstition of his fellow countrymen that he decided to build a planetarium, a moving scale model of the solar system which would show everyone how the planets really moved and why there was nothing to fear from apparent conjunctions.

Eisinga's wife, Pietje Jacobs, heavily pregnant with

The Eise Eisinga Planetarium.

her first child, agreed to the planetarium being fixed to the living-room ceiling of their house by the canal in Franeker. The intricate clockwork was constructed in the attic. However, Pietje was not prepared to have the pendulum of the master clock in the matrimonial cupboard-bed. Eisinga had to shorten the pendulum, which meant re-calculating all the cog-wheels.

Eisinga worked on the planetarium for seven years, working in his spare time only: by day he earned his living carding wool, just as his father did. He made a false ceiling in the living-room, with circular openings in it corresponding to the paths of the planets. There were rods through these openings to which the balls of the planets were attached. Thus the planets travel close to the ceiling to exactly their real orbit times: the golden ball representing Jupiter makes one orbit every 11.87 years. Saturn takes almost thirty years for a single orbit. Consequently anyone visiting the museum is unable to see anything moving: the movements of the planets cannot be speeded up.

All the movements in the planetarium are driven by a single master clock by means of intricate cog-wheels. Eisinga made all the cog-wheels himself. Often they are large wooden discs into which iron pins (which he also made himself) are stuck – about ten thousand in all. The smallest wheel in the enormous mechanism makes one revolution every forty-five seconds; the largest (that of the planet Saturn) makes one revolution every twenty-nine and a half years. In order to replicate exactly the irregular planetary movements and the complicated movement of the moon around the earth, Eisinga designed special eccentric cog-wheels.

In the planetarium one millimetre represents one million kilometres. Thus the earth is fifteen centimetres from the sun; the planet Saturn 1.43 metres. In 1781, the year in which Eisinga completed the planetarium, the English astronomer William Herschel dis-

covered the planet Uranus; the orbit of this distant planet would never have fitted into Eise's and Pietje's living-room.

Apart from the actual scale model of the solar system Eisinga also made numerous clocks and dials which show all kinds of interesting things: the times when the sun and moon rise and set, the phase of the moon, the appearance of the sky, the day of the week, and so forth. In 1995, more than two hundred years after the planetarium was built, everything is still in working order. There is hardly any sign of wear: the enormous Saturn wheel has only made a little over seven revolutions.

In 1825, three years before Eisinga died at the age of 84, his life's work was purchased for ten thousand guilders by King William I, but since 1859 it has belonged to the town of Franeker. The Eise Eisinga Planetarium, where many other instruments of historical interest are to be seen, attracts some thirty thousand visitors a year. They can see with their own eyes, just as Eisinga's contemporaries did, how harmless conjunctions are.

That this sort of education is still necessary is apparent from the fuss that is already being made over a similar conjunction in the Spring of the year 2000. A few years ago a book was published in the United States in which this conjunction was described as a portent of the end of the world. It would seem there will always be a need for the likes of Eise Eisinga.

GOVERT SCHILLING
Translated by Sheila M. Dale.

ADDRESS
Eise Eisinga Planetarium
Eise Eisingastraat 3 / 8801 KE Franeker / The Netherlands
tel. +31 517 39 30 70
Opening hours: 10-12.30 a.m. / 1.30-5 p.m. (closed on Mondays between mid-September and mid-April)

Jean Bourgain and the Fields Medal

For the second time in only a few years a Belgian mathematician has received the Fields Medal. This prize is awarded every four years by the International Association of Mathematicians to mathematicians aged under forty; it is the highest distinction in this field and is comparable with the Nobel Prize. This time the prizewinner is a Flemish mathematician: Jean Bourgain (1954-). He won this distinction – along with two French mathematicians and a Russian – for his work on the geometry of Banach spaces, harmonic analysis and non-linear partial differential equations.

Jean Bourgain's work lies in the field of functional analysis. It was Bernard Riemann in the middle of the nineteenth century who introduced this modern branch of mathematics, which expresses the traditional problems of mathematical analysis in terms of function spaces.

Originally, Hilbert spaces had been used for that

purpose. Though of infinite dimension, they closely resemble the space of the geometry we are familiar with. The latter is three-dimensional, with one-dimensional subspaces – lines – and two-dimensional ones – planes. All planes are alike, as are all lines. Each plane has a perpendicular line; together they generate all space. The same applies to Hilbert spaces. Two subspaces of equal dimension are alike. Each subspace has a perpendicular subspace; together they span Hilbert space.

This elegant construction quickly proved too simplistic to accommodate the more complex problems of functional analysis. Banach spaces went some way towards filling this gap. Jean Bourgain began his career by resolving numerous questions relating to Banach spaces: their subspaces, the interaction between their geometry and their properties of continuity. In particular he studied the classical function spaces, resolving many conjectures on that subject. He also constructed counterexamples to other conjectures, which had been regarded as highly plausible.

Since then Jean Bourgain's centres of interest have expanded considerably. Let us take a brief look at three of these.

Harmonic analysis is a branch of mathematics which has its origins in the study of periodic phenomena. These occur in many branches of science and consequently have very varied aspects. For instance, Jean Bourgain has studied the minimum of a sum of cosines or sines, and applied his results to number theory.

He has also contributed to ergodic theory, which deals with evolutive properties of complex systems – such as many particle systems in physics. From there he moved on to dynamic systems, which are particular types of ergodic problems.

Thirdly, let us move on to the theory of partial differential equations. Most physical problems which relate to a phenomenon described by a function (field of gravitation, electromagnetic wave, temperature inside a body) lead to one partial differential equation, or a system of these, which the function must satisfy. For example, in non-relativistic quantum mechanics a particle is described by a wave function whose square measures the probability of the particle finding itself in the vicinity of the point. This wave function is a solution of the Schrödinger equation. The large majority of equations studied to date conform to the principle of superposition: if two functions satisfy the equation, so does their sum. This principle, which is for example at the basis of interference phenomena, derives from the linearity of the equations used. Since many natural phenomena are fundamentally non-linear, this type of equation has its limitations. Chaos theory, to which Ilya Prigogine – another Belgian scholar – made important contributions, is an example of this. However, non-linear partial differential equations are much harder to tackle. Jean Bourgain has recently obtained very interesting results on this type of equation, particularly on non-linear generalisations of the Schrödinger equation, thereby contributing to the creation of a more suitable mathematical tool for the sciences of the twenty-first century.

After the rapid development of mathematics in the second half of the nineteenth century and the crisis which rocked its very foundations at the beginning of this century, many mathematicians have taken an interest in mathematical structures. Jean Bourgain returns to more traditional preoccupations, tackling basic problems and resolving them positively or negatively, as the case may be. His success in this is due partly to his vast knowledge, but above all to his use of tools deriving from different fields of mathematics.

Jean Bourgain began his academic career at the National Research Fund and at the Free University in Brussels. He is currently a professor at the Institute for Advanced Scientific Study at Bures-sur-Yvette near Paris and is on secondment to the Institute for Advanced Study in Princeton, two of the most prestigious mathematical research institutes in the world. Let us congratulate him on his fine career to date, a career which is full of promise for the future.

FRANZ BINGEN
Translated by Alison Mouthaan-Gwillim.

Society

Floods The Netherlands Attacked from Behind

The threat of danger by water had always come from the sea. Few people realised that that same water could also creep up on the Dutch from behind. Yet at the beginning of February 1995 the government ordered some quarter of a million Dutch people to leave their comfortable homes. They spent almost a week in large sports halls located on higher ground or took refuge with relatives in a different part of the country.

For a while, the old battle against the water evoked good old-fashioned patriotic feelings to which the customary wrangling among parties and interest groups, as well as the question of guilt for the drama, had to yield. But immediately after the end of what were mostly smooth-running evacuations based on well-rehearsed scenarios, the question arose as to whether all those evacuations had really been necessary. Only in one place had a dike come close to bursting, but nowhere had the water risen much beyond the previous year.

Experts had pointed out years earlier that the dikes were in need of strengthening and raising in the river region in the Central Netherlands where the Maas and Rhine branch into many streams enclosing very low-lying areas. But the decisions were postponed time and time again. Dike reinforcement had come up against objections, mainly from newcomers from the Randstad (the urban agglomeration of Western Holland) who had discovered that this picturesque area made an ideal weekend retreat. They were afraid that the fine scenery

The Netherlands, February 1995: sandbags, boots and high water

(Photo by Marcel Antonisse / ANP).

would be irrevocably spoiled if the plans of the Department of Public Works – the body responsible for drainage and the condition of the dikes – were to be given the green light. The Department wanted to streamline the dikes to increase safety: cutting off corners and even heightening and widening the dikes. It would mean the end of many houses and characteristic little roads. The objectors won the sympathy of the environmental movement and found a willing ear in Parliament. Thus the original plans were swept aside and replaced by ingenious designs which would largely spare the landscape. But this approach required more money and so its implementation was spread over a period of many years.

Experts had also pointed out that the character of the great rivers has changed considerably over the centuries. The rivers were only diked at the beginning of this century. Before that they would freeze over, and it was this that often led to flooding. The discharge of cooling water from nuclear power stations now means that the chance of the rivers icing over is minimal. A second factor which has brought about a radical change is urbanisation on higher ground along the basins of the large rivers. Furthermore, sewer systems convey water quickly whereas it used to drain away into the soil or at least reach the river much more gradually. And finally, the Rhine and Maas are canalised in many places: their beds have become narrower and the water, being confined, rises faster.

Yet all those changes seemed to have produced few consequences. The water meadows alongside rivers like the Maas were last flooded in 1926 and there was a growing tendency to go and build on them. After all, there were fewer and fewer people who could remember the disaster of 1926.

The hydraulic engineer from Delft, Cees van den Akker, believes that the Low Countries will have to reckon with calamities of this kind more and more frequently in years to come, for the enormous volumes of water which converge in the Dutch delta area are simply not always manageable. Aware of this fact, in past centuries people would site important buildings on artificial mounds or dikes inside the polders. Nowadays all these basin-shaped areas, seemingly protected by high dikes, are fairly built up.

At the height of the difficulties Prime Minister Kok announced that a delta plan for the river region would be drawn up as quickly as possible. The name 'delta plan' refers to the famous plan devised after the Netherlands was struck by a real flood disaster in 1953: some 1,800 lives were lost when the sea dikes in the Province of Zeeland broke. In accordance with that plan the sea dikes were raised and strengthened substantially, and a flood barrier was built at the mouth of the Eastern Scheldt.

The new delta plan is more modest in scope. The dikes will be heightened. The weakest areas, some sixty kilometres, have to be reinforced within the first two years and the Cabinet is introducing an emergency law designed to make it possible to shorten the procedures which have been dragging on for years. Safety first is now the motto. The environmental movement has already made it clear that it will not take all this lying down. Naturally it has never been against safer dikes, it claims, only against the way in which the work is carried out.

The Dutch government is also keen to confer with its neighbours. For if the developments which caused the flooding in the Netherlands continue, then the Netherlands will be the hardest hit. And by itself it will never really be able to cushion the blows.

PAUL VAN VELTHOVEN
Translated by Alison Mouthaan-Gwillim.

Blacks in the Dutch World

Blacks in the Dutch World (1994) is part of a series: *'Blacks in the Diaspora';* it is the second volume in this series to be written by Allison Blakely (Professor of European History and Comparative History at Howard University), his first being *Russia and the Negro: Blacks in Russian History and Thought. Blacks in the Dutch World* does not, therefore, emerge from a Dutch Studies context. That, in itself, is probably no bad thing. Race is not necessarily best studied as a feature of individual European nationalities or cultures, it can be understood to emerge from a general, shared, white sense of the world. Coming from the outside, a general historian can ask questions of the particular circumstances drawn from a broader overview.

Chapter 1 describes the 'Dutch World', the history of conquest and trade, one shaped by European rivalries. Chapter 2 explores the transforming mythologies of blackness within the Netherlands, the folklores and belief systems which gave meaning to and were in turn responses to contact with blacks. Chapter 3 surveys the representation of blacks in the visual arts, high and popular, and Chapter 4 covers the same topics in literature and other (arbitrarily selected, one feels) writings. Chapter 5 deals with a complex web of accommodations in religious thought and practice; the Dutch exported every aspect of their religious culture but its tolerance (revealing, perhaps, tolerance in the Netherlands as the pragmatic and contingent accomodation it really was). Chapter 6 gives a compendious account of black lives and careers in the 'Dutch World'. Chapter 7 provides a summary of the themes and arguments in the book and seeks to address the topic as stated in the title of the book.

This is a very ambitious book. Race and gender studies are anyway confronted with the problem of re-sorting and retelling histories of the world simply to get to their starting points. Even if we cannot believe that it is written out of a profound understanding of a vast number of specialist fields of study, the notes show that the author has familiarised himself with an impressive range of secondary documentation. Professor Blakely seeks to tell a story that touches upon all aspects of Dutch society at home and abroad, over a period stretching from the Middle Ages to the present, in fewer than 300 pages. One must expect to find such an account suffering from (for general readers) over-compression and confusion, and (for specialist readers) omissions and a general feel of slightness.

But then, it is a pioneering work. It seeks to under-stand a series of discrete historical topics (periods, mentalities, art history, literary history, religious his-tory, etc.) within an all-embracing topic: *'The Evo-lution of Racial Imagery in a Modern Society'*. This begs a lot of questions. Certainly, few blacks in the historical record have been responsible for their own representation; these images (in art, literature, jurispru-dence, religious doctrine) are evidences of the white societies that made and consumed the representations. Therefore this must be a history of white society's changing view of the world.

To a large degree Professor Blakely does a good job of combining narration and interpretation to produce a coherent account. But the organisation of the book, described above, was perhaps not the best way to do it. There are quite useful categories into which a history of transformations of this kind could have been fitted (Enlightenment, Romanticism and Modernism; 'Dis-covery', Colonialism and Imperialism; Superstition, Ethnology and Racial Science) any of which would have been the product of a slightly different set of assumptions about the historical task. But as we can see, the book is organised by source material, or sub-ject-based topics. This organisation obscures the con-cept of 'Evolution' as a broader feature of Dutch soci-ety and problematises an overall conception of 'Imagery'. And how does the conception 'Imagery' relate to such, perhaps more useful, terms as 'mental-ity' or 'ideology'?

If there is a story, then, it has to be read out of a num-ber of topical accounts. Those factors which made John Maurice occupy the north-east corner of Brazil in the seventeenth century are part of one account (the history of the West India Company and the trade war with Spain and Portugal); John Maurice's employment of, among others, Albert Eckhout to portray the flora and fauna (including human inhabitants) of this ephemeral Brazilian empire belongs to another. And perhaps the absence of any topical category of 'the his-tory of ethnology' (into which Eckhout's work could also fit) means that other important documentation

such as the Gordon Atlas (now in the Rijksmuseum printroom) does not get any mention at all.

But then some aspects of the history of ethnology are well covered in various parts of the literary survey. It emerges in brief but telling accounts, such as that of Petrus Camper who sought to categorise blacks not by skin colour but by physiognomy. This was a 'typically' Enlightenment rationalisation of racial difference to fit into a set of classifications by formal criteria; a norma-tive 'aesthetic' of the various races as degradations from the ideal from of Greek sculpture. Camper's clas-sification was used by other scientists to place the black races at some indeterminate point between humankind and the beasts. And the complexity of the task of setting this kind of enterprise against the con-temporary enthusiasm for the 'noble savage' (also not far from the primitive Greek ideal) does not make for easy, linear accounts of evolutions of racial imagery. The chapter on the Black and religious traditions re-presents the complexities of the conflicts of inherited prejudice and experience very well indeed.

This is a stimulating and frustrating book. Too short to do anything more than indicate a set of issues, but indicating a set of issues that offers us the prospect of a library of books. The organisation suggests a confi-dence in the tellability of the story, but the contradic-tions and problems of the content indicate that the story cannot be told without endless, cleverly inflected repe-titions. Most of the issues are still alive and threatening us all with an appalling racial disaster – if, that is, we do not believe that our world is already in a state of racial disaster.

CHARLES FORD

Nicolaes Berchem, *A Black Moor Presenting a Lady with a Parrot*. c. 1665.

Canvas, 93.7 x 88.9 cm. Wadsworth Atheneum, Hartford (CT).

Allison Blakely, *Blacks in the Dutch World: The Evolution of Racial Imagery in a Modern Society.* Bloomington / Indianapolis: Indiana University Press, 1994; 336 pp. ISBN 0-253-31191-8.

In the Belgian Château
THE SPIRIT AND CULTURE OF A
EUROPEAN SOCIETY IN AN AGE OF CHANGE
Renée C. Fox

Belgium and the Outsider's Perspective

In the Belgian Château (1994) doesn't have a real castle on the jacket, but rather Magritte's *Empire of Lights* (1954), a mysterious mansion in fascinating chiaroscuro. The subtitle, *The Spirit and Culture of a European Society in an Age of Change,* makes clear that this book is not a tourist guide like Frommer's *A Masterpiece Called Belgium.* Actually it is an exceptionally astute analysis of the relationship between character and society. On the basis of thirty-five years of fieldwork the eminent American sociologist Renée Fox shows that Belgium *'makes a difference',* no matter how obstinately separatists have been maligning their country as a non-state, an unfortunate union of Dutch- and French-speaking areas.

Dr Fox first descended on Belgium in 1959 to investigate medical research. She shrewdly managed to penetrate into the symbolic temples (or castles) of the Establishment, and her portraits in Part One ('Public Houses') include Jacques Errera (the then Commissioner of Atomic Energy), Corneel Heymans (a Nobel Prize-winning medical scientist), and Jean Willems, the director, vice-president, treasurer *and* dinosaur of the National Research Fund (who disliked her for spilling the beans about flaws in Belgian science policy, particularly inbreeding).

From the second part, ('Private Houses'), we gather how the scope of her investigations widened so as to include average Belgians as well as artists. She takes her cue from her friend Michel de Ghelderode in explaining her attraction to Belgium as a felicitous coincidence of *'obsessions and cosmic phantoms'.* This social scientist is not afraid to expose herself as a self-avowed romantic, thus affirming a truly humanising scepticism about neutral perception. Her way of rendering a young woman's death and the family's mourning implicates her at every point, showing how narrative cannot be bypassed when defining what life is all about.

A third part deals with her experiences in Zaire, the land that *'provided Belgians with a horizon, and with*

an existential as well as geographical frontier'. Regrettably, the loss of this horizon in 1960 contributed to Belgium's becoming too self-absorbed. While often preferring the company of Africans to that of Belgians, not only for purposes of participant observation but also out of genuine sympathy, she wisely refrains from idealising the liberated Africans. One of the most amusing passages relates how she was warned against 'the Flemish': *'There was a certain irony in the fact that Papa Cyrille and other Congolese employed the term "Flamands" in the derisive way they had heard many of their French-speaking Belgian colonisers apply it to Flemish compatriots.'*

Dr Fox's gift of wonder exudes perhaps most intensely from the final chapter, 'Belgium Revisited', based on her latest visit in November 1993. While the media coverage of King Baudouin's death reaching her in Philadelphia had led her to believe that this event was evidence of Belgium's resurgence, she was at first *'perplexed'* to get the inside line from Belgians about the crucial difference between the realm of *'symbolic reality'* and the *'instrumental reality'* of the country's everyday life. It transpired that the latter was very much fraught with negative competition between vying groups, each of which defined itself as an oppressed minority. However, on closer inspection this insight fitted into the complex culture pattern she had encountered throughout her decades of questing: *'the tendency of Belgians to be highly sensitive to the sphere of their individual and collective existence where emotions and beliefs, values, and symbols reside, while verbally denying their importance in daily life and systematically excluding them from their intellectual and scientific work.'*

As a part-time Freudian I'd like to venture the educated guess that this denial of uncomfortable knowledge is typical of a country that kept on excluding Freud even half a century after he had been productively assimilated in the Netherlands, thus perpetuating cultural deprivation and a terrible inferiority of Belgian mental health care to boot. While the American literary scholar Frederick Crews may deplore his culture's indulgence in Freudian platitudes, surely a culture steeped in pre-Freudian platitudes is much worse … As Luc Huyse has argued, Belgians do not really *want* to know certain societal data which are readily available in neighbouring countries, especially the Netherlands. Hence eye-openers from foreigners are very useful for recognising flaws, for even if these were pointed out by native writers (e.g. Louis Paul Boon in *Chapel Road* – *De Kapellekensbaan,* 1953), such intuitive political analyses were not taken seriously until they were independently conceptualised by American political scientists. Subsequently these inspired the pioneering work of Huyse and his associates about the lack of transparency in Belgium's *'tutelage democracy'.*

Hopefully, Dr Fox's masterpiece of intercultural perception will equally inspire Belgian researchers to pursue her lines of investigation in a rapidly changing scene, where early in 1995 the latest government crisis was not settled in a château, where the King prefers an easygoing style, and where the rise of European regionalism encourages both Flemish and Walloon leaders to steal the show, leaving the federal authority with a stigma of outdated Belgian patriotism …

Meanwhile, this exciting and enlightening book should be translated with alacrity into French and Dutch. Not into 'Flemish' of course, as Dr Fox misleadingly calls the language used in Flanders: it differs no more from the Dutch used in the Netherlands than the French of Walloons does from the language of France. While refraining from indulging in pipe-dreams about a reunification of the Low Countries, it is sensible to affirm the necessity of a standard language for the approximately 21 million users of Dutch. Cherishing cultural diversity does not mean encouraging variants to such an extent that it interferes with communication. Ironically enough sociolinguists advocating a return to 'Flemish' are antisocial, unconcerned about repercussions for, say, a Flemish waiter who needs to work in the Netherlands

However, this peccadillo and some printing errors apart this innovative work of creative nonfiction offers food for thought to all those who realise that self-imaging is always inadequate and needs to be complemented by the outsider's perspective. The publisher Ivan Dee deserves praise for having taken the risk of printing a book considered irrelevant by the big publishers, dealing as it does with a country that looks smaller than a postage stamp on the globe. For those who subscribe to the 'Small is beautiful' ideal, however, this book is a rare treat.

JORIS DUYTSCHAEVER

Renée C. Fox, *In the Belgian Château: The Spirit and Culture of a European Society in an Age of Change.* Chicago: Ivan R. Dee, 1994; 339 pp. ISBN 1-56663-057-6.

The 'Pasar Malam Besar' The Largest Indo-European Festival in the World

Just fifty Dutch cents was enough to gain admission to the first *Pasar Malam* held in the Netherlands in 1959; children were admitted for only twenty-five cents. A small hall in the Zoo in The Hague was turned into a great *koempoelan* (gathering) of Indo-European people; they came from all corners of the land, all of them having some connection with the Indonesian archipelago. They came to meet one another, to eat Indo-European food, to fire catapults and to listen to their own music. For the visitors in those early years it was all about being together, about exchanging experiences in their own environment and atmosphere. It is not for nothing that Indonesian culture is sometimes referred to as a 'home culture'. Since the start of the twentieth century, inhabitants of the former Dutch East Indies – today's Indonesia – had had to behave in as 'Dutch' a way as possible in order to be accepted. True mixed culture was confined to the home. When they moved to the Netherlands, things were no different: adapt and

above all don't stand out, that was the message that parents passed on to their children. Consequently, the first *Pasar Malam* was a sort of homecoming for this group of people.

And in fact that is still the case today. Every year in the month of June the *Pasar Malam Besar* (which translates as 'Great Evening Market') draws more than 100,000 visitors – though today these are no longer just Indo-Europeans, but also Dutch people and foreign visitors, most of whom have some link with the Dutch East Indies or Indonesia.

In the period between 1946 and 1964, following Indonesia's declaration of independence in 1945 (see *The Low Countries* 1993-94: 107-110), some 300,000 Indo-Europeans (people of mixed race with European and Indonesian forbears) moved to the Netherlands. They possessed Dutch nationality and had historical and emotional ties with the Netherlands. Formally, they were able to adopt Indonesian citizenship, but for many of them this was not a realistic option in practice. Their ties with the Dutch meant they were seen as enemies, or at the very least as less than full Indonesian citizens.

The Dutch government did everything in its power to enable this group of newcomers to assimilate into Dutch society as quickly as possible. Much of the suffering which had taken place during the War and the turbulent Bersiap period between 1945 and 1949 when Indonesia was struggling for its independence, was suppressed. Indo-Europeans quietly set about building a new existence in what for many was an unknown fatherland. And yet they form the largest group of newcomers in Dutch immigration history; a group, moreover, which for decades has been held up in the literature as successful immigrants.

Against the tide of this idea of assimilation, writer / journalist Tjalie Robinson (pseudonym of Jan Boon) exhorted his fellow Indo-Europeans not to be ashamed of their cultural background, their appearance or their history. He was one of the initiators of the *Pasar Malam* in The Hague. He had spent his youth and part of his journalistic career in the former Dutch East Indies, moving to the Netherlands in 1954 and launching the monthly publication *Tong Tong*, which was sometimes referred to as the voice of Indo-European Holland.

In the former Dutch East Indies, the *pasar malams* were held in the open air. They were festive occasions to which people could look forward, with good food and a big wheel, with merry-go-rounds, with *gamelan* music and *wayang* (shadow puppet theatre) performances. And there was trading, too: the *pasar* was traditionally the place where business was done, deals struck.

This was the atmosphere and the flavour which Tjalie Robinson, together with Ellen Derksen – who was quickly put in overall charge and has since become the person with ultimate responsibility – succeeded in creating at the *Pasar Malam* in the Netherlands.

The fifth anniversary *Pasar Malam Besar* 1963 was held in the Houtrusthallen sports complex in The

A Sumatran *martabak* ('omelette') baker (Photo Stichting Tong Tong).

Hague. In addition to Indonesian music and dance productions, the stage was also open to younger 'Indos', who with their Indorock turned out to be the forerunners of Beat music. Groups such as The Blue Diamonds – who quickly became known as the Dutch Everly Brothers – the Tielman Brothers and The Hot Jumpers played the music of Elvis Presley, Bill Haley and His Comets and Little Richard; with their instrumentals they brought Rock 'n Roll to the Netherlands.

If in the early years the *Pasar Malam Besar* was still a typical Indo-European affair, by the end of the sixties it had taken on a more generally tropical character. Woodcuts from Thailand and India, Surinamese and Dutch musicians on stage, a Vietnamese spring-roll stall squeezed between the Indo-European food stands, and more Dutch visitors with no roots in the East. And there were the younger Indo-Europeans, born in the Netherlands and beginning to add their own colour and flair to the *Pasar Malam*. The second generation expressed itself through literature (e.g. Marion Bloem) and the visual arts, and also wanted to be seen at the *Pasar*. Since the end of the seventies these people, who for years had had to suppress their Indo-European culture, to become as 'Dutch' as possible, have been standing up for their own identity.

The *totoks* – full-blood Dutch people who had spent their youth in the Indies – and the first-generation Indo-Europeans are getting older; they have more time at their disposal and want to return one more time to the land of their youth. At the *Pasar* they rediscover the atmosphere and the smells to set them on their journey. The organisation tries to cater for this demand and provides information stands and lectures on journeying to Indonesia.

The *Pasar Malam Besar* was held in the Houtrusthallen for the last time in 1987. The complex was being redeveloped and there was no longer room for this annual tropical event. The city fathers of The Hague

offered a new hall, but its management left the *Pasar* organisers with no illusions. At the opening of the last *Pasar Malam* held in the Houtrusthallen, Ellen Derksen uttered the following words: *'All that frying and cooking will smear the windows, and what then? It will probably therefore be mandatory for every stall-holder to use an extractor hood. And that, of course, will immediately rob us of those wonderful cooking smells. It is the old story. When Indo-European people first came to the Netherlands, they too were continually assaulted with "your food smells so".'* Ellen Derksen and her staff declined the offer of the new hall and, since 1988, have succeeded each year in setting up tents on the Malieveld site in The Hague.

Tjalie Robinson thought that when 'the old ones' died the Indo-European culture would die with them. His granddaughter Siem Boon runs *De Pasarkrant,* an Indo-European newspaper which appears three times a year and which provides a forum for both young and old. And a look at the 1994 *Pasar Malam Besar* disproves Tjalie's fears. For eleven days, ten marquees provided the setting for a market with tropical wares, small restaurants and an extensive cultural programme, with four stages offering scope for dance and music performances from Indonesia, interviews with authors, films, accounts of journeys in Indonesia and workshops in Balinese dance for children.

For eleven days the Malieveld site was filled with the smells of the tropics, the scent of fresh fruit, of the charcoal fires for the *saté* and other delicious foods, and of *kretek,* the Indonesian clove cigarette. Memories for the older generation and recognition for the younger generation, which wishes to preserve and pass on its Indo-European culture, in the form of symposia, exhibitions and lectures. It is an event which has its origins in the former Dutch East Indies and to which Indonesia makes a worthwhile contribution.

TANNEKE DE GROOT
Translated by Julian Ross.

FURTHER INFORMATION
Tong Tong Foundation
Celebesstraat 62 / 2585 TM The Hague / The Netherlands
tel. +31 70 355 77 77 / fax +31 70 350 44 97

Visual Arts

Poetry in Furniture Design The Work of Emiel Veranneman

On 21 September 1994 the furniture designer Emiel Veranneman (1924-) celebrated his seventieth birthday. This prompted the Museum of Decorative Arts in Ghent to mount a retrospective exhibition of his work in the summer of 1994, entitled *Fifty Years of Furniture Design by Emiel Veranneman*. It was a fitting tribute to the only Fleming to make an international name for himself as a furniture designer during the postwar years. Another recent exhibition of Veranneman's work was held at the Marlborough Gallery in New York (16 June - 7 July 1995).

Emiel Veranneman turned out to be a successful designer; he not only designed interiors for various world-famous artist friends, but was also much in demand in financial and political circles from Tokyo to New York. Even so, you will not find a great deal of space devoted to him in the reference works on the evolution of furniture. Veranneman is not a theoretician who sets to work using innovative concepts and comes up with designs which are revolutionary in form. His work is closer to the traditional view of furniture. In contrast to someone like Gerrit Rietveld (see *The Low Countries* 1993-1994: 264-265), who, in the period between the wars, sought a spatially transparent, skeletal construction, Veranneman considered pieces of furniture to be objects with an emphatic presence in the room.

At the start of his career, Emiel Veranneman did, to some extent, go along with the international endeavour to create furniture for a broad social base. Designers believed that with new materials and production techniques it should be possible to put high-quality products within reach of the mass consumer. This democratic aspiration was already long established when the 20-year-old Veranneman took up his studies at the National Higher Institute for Architecture and the Decorative Arts in La Cambre (Brussels) in 1944. Although Henry van de Velde (see *The Low Countries* 1994-95: 244-250) was no longer actively involved in teaching, it was his spirit that still determined the prevailing climate, which stemmed from the Arts and Crafts Movement. As a student Veranneman was regarded favourably by Herman Teirlinck, the director, and by Henry van de Velde, who still often came to cast an eye over 'his' school. The influence of Van de Velde was very clear to see in Emiel Veranneman's initial pieces.

The pieces of furniture from this initial period are sturdy, unornamented constructions with a pure line. You can see in them the logical conception of the architect seeking to create a functional object. This should come as no surprise: Veranneman had already studied architecture in Ghent before he went to La Cambre. While the taste for Scandinavian pinewood furniture pervaded Flanders like everywhere else, Veranneman held on to solid oak and cherry. This gave his furniture a 'Flemish' solidity. However, this should not create the impression that Veranneman's early furniture looked unwieldy. The component parts may not be delicate, but the precise relationship between them gives the whole a certain lightness. The start of Veranneman's career coincided with Belgium's reconstruction after the Second World War. The Marshall Plan provided the boost needed for the development of a modern consumer society, which was to present designers with new challenges. The furniture industry was looking for designs suitable for standardisation and mass production. Competitions were organised to stimulate new talent and Emiel Veranneman carried off several prizes.

But in Veranneman's case, the belief that the furniture industry was looking out for designers to produce affordable modern furniture for the mass market was soon seriously dented. As early as 1952 he was already expressing his criticism of the conservatism of furniture manufacturers.

Veranneman gradually evolved a style of his own. He had steeped himself in Zen philosophy and studied the Chinese Ming dynasty for five years, and this had a subtle influence on his style. But the Oriental element in his work was undoubtedly due in part to the sports centres he fitted out in various places in Europe in 1958, under commission from the Japanese Zen master Oshawa.

After ten years, his work began to make its mark on the international scene. The culmination of this recognition was an exhibition in the Palace of Fine Arts in Brussels in 1958, where his work was displayed alongside paintings by his friend Octave Landuyt. As well as his earlier, more sober and solid furniture, there were also pieces that showed the influence of his interest in the East. His bucket seats upholstered in antelope skin – with a clear debt to the American designer Charles Eames – also appeared there for the first time. He was later to design many variations on this concept. Several enamel-painted pieces (for a child's room) were also displayed. Veranneman had only just begun to use enamel paint.

From the sixties on, Emiel Veranneman distanced himself permanently from the Belgian furniture industry. At that time his designs were in a much more personal style, and he preferred furnishing interiors for individual clients to the mass-production of furniture. The Osaka chair, designed for the Belgian pavilion at the 1970 World Fair in Osaka was undoubtedly one of the high points of his career. Veranneman worked for years on the development of this dark-brown mahogany chair, which is conspicuous for its monumentality, in

Emiel Veranneman,
Cupboard. 1993.
210 x 120 x 36 cm.

contrast to the rest of European design at the time. The international design world, which in the sixties was experimenting with garish plastic, under the influence of Pop Art, underwent a crisis in the seventies. It was the Italians in particular, led by Allessandro Mendini and Ettore Sottsass, who resisted the strict formalism of the modernists. They reclaimed the freedom to fill their designs with fantasy and copious decoration. Veranneman's furniture also became freer in the seventies. He opted determinedly for colour, treating the furniture with multiple coats of paint to make it as shiny as a mirror. Nor did the ornamentation restrict itself, as it previously had, to constructional elements such as handles. Despite the sometimes glaring and highly contrasting use of colours – white, black, turquoise, blue, lemon yellow – we are here talking about monumental objects, not frivolous diversions. He plays a disciplined game with areas of colour, which are in their turn punctuated by decorative geometric elements. Veranneman did not embellish his pieces of furniture: they *are* art objects.

The evolution of Emiel Veranneman's work, in which pieces of furniture increasingly emerge as works of art, is probably not unconnected with his continued interest in the visual arts. Indeed, since 1953 he has been a gallery owner as well as a furniture-maker. His oeuvre towers above everything else designed in post-war Belgium. He himself would hardly consider this a compliment. After all, in an interview in 1982 he described the situation like this: *'In my view, our furniture design doesn't have the slightest international significance. In comparison with foreign examples I would even venture to refer to it as a low point: so low that it even reaches freezing.'*

ERIC BRACKE
Translated by Gregory Ball.

FURTHER READING
Emiel Veranneman, 50 jaar meubelcreaties. Brussels / Ghent, 1994.

'Who Described the Art of Painting in so Edifying and Instructive a Manner'

Karel van Mander's *Book on Painting* (Schilder-boeck) was published in Haarlem in 1604. Van Mander (1548-1606), renowned as *'Painter and Poet'*, was born in Meulebeke in West Flanders. However, the unsettled political situation in the South and his own Baptist beliefs had prompted the 35-year-old Van Mander to settle first in Haarlem and later in Amsterdam. The structure of the *Book on Painting* – an extensive work, the three parts of which run to more than 800 closely printed pages – was exceptionally ambitious. The first part presents 'The Foundations of the Noble and True Art of Painting ('Den Grondt der Edel vry Schilder-const'), a didactic poem on the *'ghestalt, aerdt ende wesen'* ('form, nature and essence') of the *ars pictoria*. The poem was long considered to be a solid and carefully constructed handbook for novice painters, *'the rising generation of Painters'* to whom the poem seems, at first sight, to be addressed. However, this allegorical and moralising poem, full of philosophical, ethical and also astro-psychological references, could never have functioned in this way. 'The Foundations' is rather a mnemonic device imbued with ethical content and intended for the experienced artist and connoisseur. The second part of the collection is the most extensive. It is an example of the classical genre of artist biography and contains the lives of *'the ancient Classical Painters'* (principally based on Pliny's *Natural History),* the *'Italian Painters'* (for which Vasari was the principal source) and finally the *'Netherlandish and German Painters'* (after an idea of Van Mander's Ghent teacher, the artist / poet Lucas d'Heere). With their strict rhetorical structure, these artists' biographies had a multiple effect. The exemplary structure had a moral-pedagogical aim while the lives described ensured a reassessment of the painter as artist. Moreover, the final series on Dutch painters was a conscious contribution to the glory of the Netherlands in general and Haarlem in particular. Finally, part II of the *Book on Painting* had a different structure and was in two parts: the 'Rendering of Figures' ('Wtbeeldinghe der figueren'), a concise iconological handbook, preceded by a lengthy commentary on Ovid's *Metamorphoses,* in which the various tales were metaphorically interpreted and explained in ethical terms. The intended public was primarily poets and painters, and consequently, this part of the *Book on Painting* was the most popular in the seventeenth century – as can be seen from the several reprints.

In art-historical circles it is the lives *'of the illustrious Netherlandish and German Painters'* in particular which have attracted attention. Indeed, the image that we now have of art in the fifteenth and sixteenth centuries seems to have been largely shaped by Van Mander. It is all the more surprising, therefore, that up to now only inadequate modern paraphrases in French, German, English and Dutch have been available for this part of the *Book on Painting* and that only partial editions (by R. Vos and W. Waterschoot) are available to meet the requirements of modern scholarship. As a result, many modern studies suffer from a mistaken understanding of Van Mander's jargon and this can lead to mistranslations, as in the case of W.S. Melion's book *Shaping the Netherlandish Canon* (See the reviews in *Dutch Crossing* (1992): 99-102 and *Oud-Holland* (1993): 152-159).

The project begun by the Utrecht art historian Hessel Miedema therefore meets a clear need. The aim is to produce a complete edition of the *Lives,* together with a scholarly English translation and a modern commentary with reproductions of the paintings discussed by Van Mander. In this way, the text will be opened up as a source for art and literary history and made accessible for the history of ideas and thought. The enterprise is taking place in auspicious circumstances. No one is more at home in Van Mander's literary oeuvre and his sometimes difficult jargon than Miedema. This

Jacob de Gheyn, *Karel van Mander on his Deathbed.* 1606.

Drawing, 14.2 x 17.7 cm. Städelsches Kunstinstitut, Frankfurt.

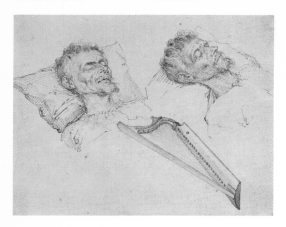

is demonstrated not only by his well-received study with translation and commentary of 'The Foundations' (1973) but also from the reasoned survey of Van Mander's ideas on art, the artist and the work of art (1981) and the detailed analyses of the terms *'fraey'* ('nice'), *'aerdigh'* ('representing the essence'), *'schoon'* ('beautiful') and *'moy'* ('lovely') (1984) and recently of the concept of *'inventy'* ('invention') in Van Mander's *Book on Painting* (1993). These are part of the various preparatory phases of the current enterprise.

The first volume in the series, which will ultimately comprise six substantial volumes, contains Van Mander's biography and *Lives* of Netherlandish and German painters. The modern English translation is given in parallel with the facsimile pages of Van Mander's text. An index of names concludes the volume. The subsequent volumes will contain the commentary, the photographic material and an extensive concluding index. A demonstration of the method Miedema plans to employ in the current undertaking can be found in the collection *Goltzius-studies* (Nederlands kunsthistorisch jaarboek 1991-92) where Miedema has edited Van Mander's biography of Goltzius, and added a commentary.

MARC VAN VAECK
Translated by Lesley Gilbert.

Karel van Mander, *The Lives of the Illustrious Netherlandish and German Painters, from the first edition of the 'Schilder-boeck' (1603-1604). Preceded by The Lineage, Circumstances and Place of Birth, Life and Works of Karel van Mander, Painter and Poet and likewise his Death and Burial, from the second edition of the 'Schilder-boeck' (1616-1618).* With an Introduction and Translation (Michael Hoyle, Jacqueline Pennial-Boer and Charles Ford), edited by Hessel Miedema. Volume I: the Text. Doornspijk: Davaco Publishers, 1994; VIII + 510 pp. ISBN 90-70288-85-0.

Sanctuaries for New Art De Appel and Witte de With

De Appel Foundation in Amsterdam, set up in 1975, is one of the oldest and best-known of Dutch art sanctuaries. Since 1990, Rotterdam has had a similar internationally renowned institute, Witte de With. Both institutions aim at challenging the art establishment. They're laboratories for new art.

According to its autumn 1983 bulletin, *'De Appel has a personality all its own'*. De Appel was the only arts centre in the Netherlands to welcome body art and performance art. Foreign performers came to Amsterdam, Americans in particular: James Lee Byars, Chris Burden and Laurie Anderson. Since its founding by Wies Smals, De Appel has been a centre where new art forms such as installations or multi-media projects are presented and documented.

After the tragic death of Wies Smals when the private plane in which he was flying crashed into a mountain in Switzerland, Saskia Bos became the director of De Appel. The accent gradually shifted from the exclusive presentation of art to the stimulation and organisation of various projects. According to Bos, it is important that art should not only take place *'within the frame'* but should involve the public as well. She finds many museums and galleries boring because of their contrived *'clinical visual experience'*: it's all too easy to overlook the works of art. In De Appel, the focus is on direct and all-encompassing, even physical experiences.

Since 1994, De Appel has had new lodgings in the centre of Amsterdam. The foundation's objective is to keep up with current art that is not market-oriented and is difficult to contain in a collection. The image that De Appel projects is that of an institution with a strong social involvement. It's a platform for political-social issues.

The manner of presentation in De Appel is always being examined, and therefore a spatial intervention (raising a brick wall in the gallery, painting the walls) is often an integral element of the art being displayed. Work is always underway at the site itself.

De Appel has outgrown its early experimental phase. Now it's a reputable clearing house for foreign artists in particular, because in Bos' opinion art only becomes fascinating *'when it crosses those confining borders'*. Still, it remains an institute for experiment and reflection. De Appel, like Witte de With, hopes to stimulate theoretical debate on art.

The Rotterdam art institute Witte de With is housed two stories up with a view of a dozen tower blocks. The path to the centre was smoothed by the Rotterdam Art Foundation's previous avant-garde gallery, 't Venster. For fifteen years, Gosse Oosterhof exhibited artists there who have since become leaders in the art world: Kiefer, Penone, Dokoupil, Holzer and Haring.

The centre, says the Belgian director Chris Dercon, is a *'homeopathic vaccine'* for other exhibitors. In Witte de With, the accent is not on presentation but on simply showing and thinking about what is seen. Since the opening of the institute, Dercon has not made it easy for himself. Witte de With's programme style is not a fashionable one. The Centre for Contemporary Art, like

De Appel in Amsterdam, wants to be a bit challenging.

Witte de With has not published an exhibition catalogue since 1994; instead it issues workbooks, magazines in which debates about art are conducted. For each exhibition in Witte de With, a discussion is organised with the artist or critics. The centre is a school for seeing, something that Dercon calls *'art education'* – not cavilling, but a kind of provocative training programme for formulating one's own opinions.

According to Chris Dercon, who will be taking over as director of the Boymans-Van Beuningen Museum in Rotterdam in 1996, *'the curator or museum director is not a star'*. He prefers to call himself *'a manager who makes things possible'*.

Dercon has often made decisions about the way in which works of art will be displayed, about the exhibition effect. More and more, an exhibition is an uninterrupted collage: *'What interests the visitor most is not one or more works in particular, but their organisation or arrangement (which is often purely accidental).'* At Witte de With he shows that the main focus is on the programme, with less stress on the spectacle, the museum building or even the exhibitor. *'The art world should not imitate the mass media'*, says Dercon. *'In fact, it should offer an antidote.'* People are talking about Witte de With and Amsterdam's De Appel just because everything there is in a state of continual flux.

PAUL DEPONDT
Translated by Nancy Forest-Flier.

Tiong Ang, *Portrait of a Young Woman (Imitation).* 1991. 130 x 190 x 13 cm. Collection P.H. Polak Schoute. Amsterdam. This work was part of *The Spine,* the exhibition which inaugurated the new De Appel premises in 1994.

The Witte de With premises in Rotterdam (Photo by Bob Goedewaagen).

ADDRESSES
De Appel
Nieuwe Spiegelstraat 10 / 1017 DE Amsterdam / The Netherlands
tel. +31 20 625 56 51 / fax +31 20 622 52 15
Witte de With
Witte de Withstraat 50 / 3012 BR Rotterdam / The Netherlands
tel. +31 10 411 01 44 / fax +31 10 411 79 24

A Rehabilitation of Belgian Art

From Ensor to Magritte: Belgian Art 1880-1940 (1994), by the British author Michael Palmer, is a kind of rehabilitation. Palmer contends that Belgian art is much less tributary to the various artistic revolutions that took place in Paris during the previous century than has been thought until now. On the contrary, Belgian artists put their own stamp on the Modernist adventure. They helped determine its course.

The book coincides with an increasing international interest in Belgian Modernism, especially in its first period. The study of the avant-garde artists belonging to Les XX (Le Cercle des vingts) is today mainly an American endeavour. Henry van de Velde is the domain of German specialists, Georges Vantongerloo has been claimed by Swiss specialists, and Jules Schmalzigaug was canonised as an authentic Futurist in Italy not so long ago. James Ensor, René Margritte and Paul Delvaux have obviously been objects of international study for much longer.

It is the special merit of Palmer's book to synthesise this growing revaluation. This synthesis is achieved on the basis of impressive background reading, with an eye for the international artistic context, for social influences, and for what is happening in the other arts. This global vision leads Palmer to various new insights, the most controversial of these being that French influence on the development of Belgian art has been overestimated. Palmer sees the reason for this in the wholesale take-over of French labels for artistic currents in other countries. These labels are very often used in the wrong way. A prime example is 'Brabant Fauvism'; according to the author, the group that bears that name counted at most one Fauvist, in the French sense of the word, among its members. All the other members were *'consciously modern painters, but (...) not fauves'*. They were more influenced by Cézanne, Ensor, Bonnard and Vuillard than by Derain or Matisse. It is hard to find fault with Palmer's position. But when he proposes to replace the misleading name 'Brabant Fauvists' by 'Brabant Painters', he runs the risk of merely increasing the confusion. Regional stylistic differences do constitute a useful criterion for subdividing modern art in Belgium, but there is a certain hesitancy in applying that criterion consistently. That hesitancy is shared by Palmer. As a result, opportunities of going to the very heart of those differences are missed. For instance, in his analysis of the first and second Latem groups (see *The Low Countries* 1994-

307

95: 148-155), Palmer does point out the differences between what he calls the Symbolists of the first Latem school and the Expressionists of the second school, but he fails to notice that both schools consisted of painters who came exclusively from East and West Flanders, and that both schools refer to Ghent as the artistic centre. The Impressionist Leie painters around Emile Claus behaved in exactly the same way. To stress the local roots of the different traditions in Belgium may at first sight seem to be a return to regionalism, but the fact remains that cities like Ghent, Brussels, Antwerp and, later, with the rise of Surrealism, even La Louvière each had their very own atmosphere and sensibility.

Though interesting, Palmer's suggestion to refer simply to the 'Brabant Painters' from now on has not been carried out consistently in his own book.

The radical iconoclasm propagated by Dadaist artists proves not to be the author's strongest point. His survey of this generation of idol-smashers does not

René Magritte,
The Meaning of Night.
1927. Canvas, 139 x 105 cm. The Menil Collection, Houston.

James Ensor,
The Gendarmes. 1892.
Canvas, 45 x 55 cm.
Museum voor Schone
Kunsten, Ostend.

Léon Spilliaert, *Seascape.*
1919. Pastel, 51 x 69 cm.
Private Collection.

exhibit any major oversights, but he does not seem aware of all the finer points. Palmer writes: *'(…) dada in Belgium was but an antechamber through which Magritte and some other artists passed quickly on their way to Surrealism.'* This is quite a radical statement. Belgian Dadaism had an important and acknowledged impact on its French counterpart. In fact, the French movement disintegrated because of the Belgian artist Clément Pansaers. Add to this that both René Magritte and E.L.T. Mesens started out as Dadaists, and that Dadaist sarcasm continued to be a characteristic feature in the work of both painters.

In his conclusion the author names realism, closeness to nature, sensitivity to the light of the North and a maritime atmosphere as the fundamental characteristics of Belgian art. It is striking that all these are merely formal characteristics. From Ensor to Magritte an attitude of detached relativism, irony, and a conscious sense of independence represent constant features of at least equal importance. Palmer himself admits as much, albeit indirectly: *'Belgian art is less conceptual, more earthy than French, less literal than most Dutch painting and in abstraction less dogmatic, less anecdotic than British painting though sharing with the English a fascination for atmospheric effects.'* Palmer does not deny that Belgian artists were influenced by artistic currents from these countries, but he maintains that Belgian art was strong enough to exert its own influence on its neighbours, and he singles out Ensor, Minne, Van de Velde, Vantongerloo, Evenepoel and Magritte in this context. The author concludes that this is enough evidence to speak of the rebirth of a tradition that has been in existence since the Renaissance. Finally, Palmer regrets that Léon Spilliaert and Rik Wouters still have to wait for the international recognition that is their due as great artists.

From Ensor to Magritte is an impassioned plea for the rediscovery of a territory that has remained relatively unknown in European art. But love never blinds the author. That is apparent when, for instance, he weighs Floris Jespers in the balance and finds his work too light: *'he sought Modernism, but the Modernism he found was only too often not his own.'*

JEF LAMBRECHT
Translated by André Lefevere.

Michael Palmer, *From Ensor to Magritte: Belgian Art 1880-1940.* Brussels: Editions Racine, 1994; 230 pp. ISBN 2-87386-025-1.

What I Like about Vermeer

The phenomenally high artistic quality of Vermeer's paintings has been an accepted truth ever since Théophile Thoré's 'rediscovery' of Vermeer in the mid-nineteenth century. And judging by Goethe's laconic annotation in his copy of a guide to the Dresden Gallery (*'No. 229: A young courtesan with a young man – Vermeer. Good.'*), this quality had been obvious to some viewers long before Thoré's masterly definition of Vermeer's oeuvre as different from all others.

Jean Cocteau's reaction to Vermeer's *Procuress* may serve as an example of a very personal response, a response, moreover, that is not based so much on issues of taste as on an artist's extraordinary encounter with art, a kind of instant recognition, articulated here in Cocteau's discussion with Louis Aragon (1956): *'At the sight of this astonishing painting by Vermeer one stands as if confronted by a postcard sent by someone who has died from a better world, or sent into the world of the waking from out of the abyss of sleep. Here something incredible is happening.'*

Asked to write an essay on why I like Vermeer, I cannot answer the question without first putting it in a biographical and, in this sense only, a historical perspective. Once upon a time I was an art pilgrim – by bicycle: from Bonn to Delft, The Hague and Amsterdam, to see the beautiful Vermeers. I was with a friend and this meant that equal amounts of time were spent in museums and in second-hand record stores in search of rare performances of Jazz and Blues. This dual pursuit of the rare and the beautiful framed the wish of writing, some day, something meaningful about Vermeer. Years later I had become an art historian – now travelling by plane and by train: to Berlin, Dresden, Braunschweig, Frankfurt, London, Vienna, Boston, New York and Washington, to see the beautiful but difficult Vermeers; and to other places, as different as Wolfenbüttel and San Antonio, to speak about Vermeer and the complex questions of interpretation his art raises.

More recently, however, I have begun to read and listen and look at how other, non-academic beholders respond to Vermeer, particularly artists. Liking Vermeer now also means trying to understand how and why, outside of sophisticated academic discourses, Vermeer's paintings continue to be so powerful. Why do they challenge the individual, as if they were contemporary works of art, works in which, *now, 'something incredible is happening'?* What follows here is a selection of such artistic responses and reflections on these. The different voices convey something about the actuality of Vermeer, and I will let them speak here for themselves and to each other. My selection begins with Marcel Proust and the famous interpretation of Vermeer's *View of Delft* by the novelist Bergotte, a character in *Remembrance of Things Past* (A la recherche du temps perdu): *'At last he came to the Vermeer which he remembered as more striking, more different from anything else he knew, but in which, thanks to the critic's article, he noticed for the first time some small figures in blue, that the bank was pink, and, finally, the precious substance of the tiny patch of yellow wall. His dizziness increased; he fixed his gaze, like a child upon a yellow butterfly that it wants to catch, on the precious little patch of wall. "That's how I ought to have written," he said. "My last books are too dry, I ought to have gone over them with a few layers of colour, made my language precious in itself, like this little patch of yellow wall." Meanwhile he was not unconscious of the gravity of his condition. In a celestial pair of scales there appeared to him, weighing down one of the pans, his own life, while the other contained the little patch of wall so beautifully painted in yellow. He felt that he had rashly sacrificed the former for the latter. "All the same," he said to himself, "I shouldn't like to be the headline news of this exhibition for the evening papers."'*

Contrary to Bergotte's wish, his death and final insight into Vermeer's true art become famous. The filmmaker Jon Jost responds to both in his film of 1991: *'One other item: the French text referred to in "All the Vermeers in New York" is a passage from Proust's "Remembrance of Things Past". In it, an old man goes to visit an exhibit of Vermeer's paintings, seeking to see a little brushstroke fleck of yellow paint, as he thinks he remembers it, on a wall in one of the paintings. While there he has a gastrointestinal attack and sits down to recover. He then keels over dead. In "All the Vermeers", half this passage is read in French ...; the final part is the voiceover, in English, at the very end of the film, in which the striving of the artist to find a perfection is cast in doubt, as the voice notes that we scarcely know a thing about the painter, except for his name, "Vermeer".'*

Proust's scene of an existential encounter with Vermeer appears to be the foil of this gallery review of William Wilson's work, in 1992: *'In "Gathering: After Vermeer" (1991), Wilson takes as his subject one of Vermeer's paintings of women reading or writing letters. (...) Behind the seated woman hangs a body swaddled in a shroud, bound with ropes, and covered with monarch butterflies. (...) Wilson pumps male subjectivity back into the painting. Enunciating the heretofore secret content of Vermeer's serene and mysterious letter writer, he transforms her into a cunning murderess, evoking a mental state verging on male hysteria.'*

Exactly how Vermeer's compositions and painting techniques suggest such existential experiences is a question that has occupied earlier modern artists as well. Here is Walter Richard Sickert's 'advice to young artists' (*The Daily Telegraph*, 4 October 1932): *'I have made a special study of Vermeer under, in the beginning, my father's influence, for just seventy years, in England, Holland, France and Germany, and elsewhere, and I came to the following conclusion: That Vermeer, like Canaletto, worked on the basis of the camera (my friend Clara Montalba told me she had seen "camera lucida" drawings of Canaletto). No models were ever so still as Vermeer's. The very curtains, and even the musical instruments, are asleep. The clearcut divisions between the mathematical ranges of tones are inconsistent with painting from what is called nature …'*

Finally, the Proustian notion of a demanding dialogue between artists across time takes a very concrete shape in the work of George Deem, who wrote when working on one of his Vermeers, *Home* of 1977: *'"Home", the picture I used to think of as "The House of Vermeer", is coming together again. There are times when a painting cannot tell me anything. "The House of Vermeer" had been so silent I decided it was not here and I began to tell it what to do, and now it is telling me what should be done: "Blue top and Red bottom".TODAY.'*

These encounters with Vermeer, I believe, suggest that his art is at once quite specific and general; that it is historical and yet transcends history, speaking across centuries and renewing its presence and actuality in modern as well as postmodern times. This appears to mean less 'to invent' something entirely new and original than to search for one's (artistic) identity, to find one's specific way of transforming the familiar world into something 'incredible', 'hallucinatory', 'mysterious', 'extraordinary', etc. This is true as much for the moderns, like Proust and Sickert, as for the postmoderns, like Wilson and Jost, who in their 'citations' and 'appropriations' – or, as one might say less respectfully, their 'knock-offs' – of Vermeer's paintings take up the challenge to determine themselves. This, then, is something I have come to like about Vermeer; and again no one has given it a more poignant expression than Proust, towards the end of his novel: *'Thanks to art, instead of seeing one world only, our own, we see that world multiply itself and we have at our disposal as many worlds as there are original artists, worlds more different one from the other than those which revolve in infinite space, worlds which, centuries after the extinction of the fire from which their light first emanated, whether it is called Rembrandt or Vermeer, send us still each one its special radiance.'*

CHRISTIANE HERTEL

The first monographic exhibition of Vermeer's work will be held at the National Gallery of Art (Washington DC) from 12 November to 11 February 1995. The same exhibition can be seen at the Mauritshuis (The Hague) from 1 March to 2 June 1996.

Johannes Vermeer, *The Little Street*, c.1658. Canvas, 54.3 x 44 cm. Rijksmuseum, Amsterdam.

George Deem, *Home*. 1977. Oil on canvas, 92 x 72 cm. Collection Gerarda De Orleans-Borbon, New York.

Bibliography

of Dutch-Language Publications translated into English (traced in 1994)

Akkerman, Dinie
To catch the moon / text by Paul van Loon; concept and ill. by Dinie Akkerman. London: Hamilton, 1993. [23] p. Also ed.: Happauge: Barron's, cop. 1993. Transl. of: Maantjelief. 1993.

Allen, Michael
Gatso, the never ending race / Michael Allen; with Maurice Gatsonides. Overveen: Gatsometer, [1993]. 239 p. Transl. of: Gatso: race zonder finish. 1990.

Arts, Herwig
Faith and unbelief: uncertainty and atheism / Herwig Arts. Collegeville: Liturgical Press, cop. 1992. 187 p. (A Michael Glazier book). Transl. of: Het ongeloof gewogen: over onzekerheid en atheïsme. 1982.

Arts, Herwig
God, the Christian, and human suffering / Herwig Arts; transl. by Helen Rolfson. Collegeville: Liturgical Press, 1993. Transl. of: Waarom moeten mensen lijden? 1985.

Baantjer, A.C.
DeKok and murder in ecstasy / by Baantjer; transl. by H.G. Smittenaar. 1st ed. Fairfax Station: Intercontinental Publishing, 1994. 240 p. Transl. of: De Cock en de moord in extase. 1982.

Baantjer, A.C.
DeKok and murder in seance / by Baantjer; transl. by H.G. Smittenaar. 1st ed. Fairfax Station: Intercontinental Publishing, 1994. 240 p. Transl. of: De Cock en de moord in seance. 1981.

Baantjer, A.C.
DeKok and murder on the menu / by Baantjer; transl. by H.G. Smittenaar. 1st ed. Virginia: New Amsterdam, 1992. 180 p. Transl. of: De Cock en moord à la carte. 1990.

Baantjer, A.C.
DeKok and the begging death / by Baantjer; transl. by H.G. Smittenaar. 1st ed. Fairfax Station: Intercontinental Publishing, 1994. 240 p. Transl. of: De Cock en de smekende dood. 1982.

Baantjer, A.C.
DeKok and the brothers of the easy death / by Baantjer; transl. by H.G. Smittenaar. 1st ed. Fairfax Station: Intercontinental Publishing, 1994. 240 p. Transl. of: De Cock en de broeders van de zachte dood. 1979.

Baantjer, A.C.
DeKok and the careful killer / by Baantjer; transl. by H.G. Smittenaar. Fairfax: Intercontinental Publishing, cop. 1993. 245 p. Transl. of: De Cock en de zorgvuldige moordenaar. 1976.

Baantjer, A.C.
DeKok and the corpse at the church wall / by Baantjer; transl. by H.G. Smittenaar. 1st ed. Fairfax Station: Intercontinental Publishing, 1994. 202 p. Transl. of: De Cock en het lijk aan de kerkmuur. 1976.

Baantjer, A.C.
DeKok and the dancing death / by Baantjer; transl. by H.G. Smittenaar. 1st ed. Fairfax Station: Intercontinental Publishing, 1994. 217 p. Transl. of: De Cock en de dansende dood. 1975

Baantjer, A.C.
DeKok and the dead harlequin / by Baantjer; transl. by H.G. Smittenaar. 1st ed. Fairfax Station: Intercontinental Publishing, 1993. 226 p. Transl. of: De Cock en de dode harlekijn. 1974.

Baantjer, A.C.
DeKok and the deadly accord / by Baantjer; transl. by H.G. Smittenaar. 1st ed. Fairfax Station: Intercontinental Publishing, 1994. 240 p. Transl. of: De Cock en het dodelijk akkoord. 1980

Baantjer, A.C.
DeKok and the desillusioned corpse / by Baantjer; transl. by H.G. Smittenaar. 1st ed. Fairfax Station: Intercontinental Publishing, 1993. 246 p. Transl. of: De Cock en de ontgoochelde dode. 1977

Baantjer, A.C.
DeKok and the dying stroller / by Baantjer; transl. by H.G. Smittenaar. 1st ed. Fairfax Station: Intercontinental Publishing, 1994. 199 p. Transl. of: De Cock en de stervende wandelaar. 1975

Baantjer, A.C.
DeKok and the geese of death / by Baantjer; transl. by H.G. Smittenaar. 1st ed. Fairfax Station: Intercontinental Publishing, 1994. 240 p. Transl. of: De Cock en de ganzen van de dood. 1983.

Baantjer, A.C.
DeKok and the naked lady / by Baantjer; transl. by H.G. Smittenaar. 1st ed. Fairfax Station: Intercontinental Publishing, cop. 1994. 205 p. Transl. of: De Cock en de naakte juffer. 1978

Baantjer, A.C.
DeKok and the romantic murder / by Baantjer; transl. by H.G. Smittenaar. 1st ed. Fairfax Station: Intercontinental Publishing, 1994. 199 p. Transl. of: De Cock en de romance in moord. 1977.

Baantjer, A.C.
DeKok and the somber nude / by Baantjer; transl. by H.G. Smittenaar. 1st ed. Fairfax: New Amsterdam, 1992. 232 p. Transl. of: De Cock en het sombere naakt. Originally publ. with: Tien kleine negertjes / Agatha Christie. 1967.

Baantjer, A.C.
DeKok and the sorrowing tomcat / by Baantjer; transl. by H.G. Smittenaar. 1st ed. Fairfax Station: Intercontinental Publishing, 1993. 240 p. Transl. of: De Cock en de treurende kater. 1977

Baantjer, A.C.
DeKok and variations on murder / by Baantjer; transl. by H.G. Smittenaar. 1st ed. Fairfax Station: Intercontinental Publishing, 1995. 240 p. Transl. of: De Cock en een variant op moord. 1984.

Baantjer, A.C.
Murder in Amsterdam: (DeKok and the sunday strangler and DeKok and the corpse on Christmas Eve) / by Baantjer; transl. by H.G. Smittenaar. 1st ed. Fairfax Station: Intercontinental Publishing, 1993. 215 p. Transl. of: De Cock en de wurger op zondag. 1975 (originally publ. in 1965) and: De Cock en het lijk in de kerstnacht. 1975 (originally publ. in 1965).

Baeten, Lieve
The curious witch / Lieve Baeten. [S.l.]: Viking, 1992. [28] p. Transl. of: Nieuwsgierige Lotje. 1992.

Baeten, Lieve
Nicky at the magic house / Lieve Baeten. [Willowdale]: Annick Press, cop. 1993. [30] p. Transl. of: Nieuwsgierige Lotje. 1992.

Beek, Tom van
Degas, the ballet, and me / by Tom van Beek; ill. by Thea Peters; [transl. by John Tilleard]. New York:

Checkerboard Press, cop. 1993. 48 p. Transl. of: Ik houd van het ballet van Degas. 1993.

Berg, Marinus van den
The three birds: a story for children about the loss of a loved one / by Marinus van den Berg; ill. by Sandra Ireland. Milwaukee, Wis: G. Stevens Publ, cop. 1994. Transl. of: De drie vogels. 1990

Berg, Peter v.d.
Waterland: a cycling trip / [text by Peter v.d. Berg & Diny Meijzan; rev. and transl. by Elbert Rijnberg ... et al.]. Limmen: Stichting Landschapsinformatie 1994. 46 p. Transl. of: Waterland: fietstocht. 1988.

Bomans, Godfried
Eric in the land of the insects / Godfried Bomans; transl. by Regina Louise Kornblith; ill. by Mark Richardson. 1st ed. Boston: Houghton Mifflin, 1994. 196 p. Transl. of: Erik, of Het klein insectenboek. 1941.

Boon, Louis Paul
Chapel Road / by Louis Paul Boon; transl. by Adrienne Dixon. New York: Hippocrene; Sawtry: Dedalus, 1991. [338] p. 1st English ed.: New York: Twayne, 1972. Transl. of: De Kapellekensbaan. 1953.

Bosmans, Phil
Whispering hope / Phil Bosmans; [transl. from the German by Dinah Livingstone]. Slough: St Paul Publ., 1990. 125 p. Transl. of: Worte zum Menschsein. 1986. Original published in Dutch as: Zomaar voor jou: vrede en alle goeds. 1986.

Breebaart, Joeri
When I die, will I get better? / Joeri and Piet Breebaart; [transl.; pref. by Harold Kushner]. 1st ed., [2nd impr.]. New York: Peter Bedrick Books, cop. 1993. 29 p. Transl. of:

Als je dood bent, word je dan nooit meer beter? 1993.

Bruna, Dick
Miffy's bicycle / Dick Bruna. Repr. London: Little Mammoth, 1993. [32] p. 1st English ed.: London: Methuen Children's Books, 1984. Drawings originally publ. in: Nijntje op de fiets. 1982.

Children's
A children's view of the Netherlands / [comp.:] Marie Wijk; [transl.: Jacky Meijer; rev. by: Ron Rishworth; drawings by Dutch children]. 1st ed. Meppel: Edu'Actief, cop. 1993. 93 p. (Kinderogen; 2). Publ. in cooperation with Unesco Centrum Nederland, on the initiative of Stichting Interculturele Kinderboeken (s.i.k.). Transl. of: Nederland, gezien door kinderogen. 1991.

Claus, Hugo
Four works for the theatre / by Hugo Claus; ed. with an introd. by David Willinger; transl. by David Willinger, Luk Truyts and Luc Deneulin. New York: CASTA, cop. 1990. XIX, 198 p. (CASTA plays in translation. Belgian series). Originally publ. in Dutch.

Claus, Hugo
Friday / Hugo Claus; transl. by David Willinger & Lucas Truyts. Amsterdam: International Theatre & Film Books, 1993. 156 p. (Theatre in translation). Transl. of: Vrijdag: toneelstuk in 5 scènes. 1969.

Claus, Hugo
The sorrow of Belgium / Hugo Claus; transl. by Arnold J. Pomerans. [New ed.]. London: Penguin, [1994]. 608 p. (Penguin twentieth-century classics). 1st English ed.: London [etc.]: Viking, 1990 Transl. of: Het verdriet van België. 1983

Crum, Gert
The Moldovan wine

adventure / Gert Crum; [photogr.: Jan den Hengst; transl.: Babel]. Wormer: Inmerc, cop. 1993. 128 p. Transl. of: De wijnen van Moldova. 1993.

Dedalus
Dedalus Book of Belgian fantasy / ed. by Richard Huijing. Sawtry: Dedalus, 1994. [400] p. Contains Dutch-language and French-language Belgian literature in transl.

Dedalus
The Dedalus book of Dutch fantasy / ed. and transl. by Richard Huijing. Sawtry: Dedalus, cop. 1993. 377 p. Contains Dutch literature in transl.

Deddens, K.
Where everything points to Him / by K. Deddens. Neerlandia; Caledonia: Inheritance Publications, 1993. Transl. of: Waar alles van Hem spreekt: bezinning op de eredienst. 1981.

Dekkers, Midas
Dearest pet: on bestiality / Midas Dekkers; transl.: P. Vincent. [S.l.]: Verso, 1994. [276] p. Transl. of: Lief dier: over bestialiteit. 1992.

Dendermonde, Max
228 seconds of silence: an Arnhem story / Max Dendermonde; transl. by David Colmer. Baarn: De Prom, 1994. 178 p. Transl. of: 228 seconden van stilte: een Arnhemverhaal. 1994.

DNA-makers
DNA-makers: architects of life / Huub Schellekens a.o.; ed. and transl. H. Schellekens; final ed.: T. Kortbeek; drawings: D. Gorissen ... et al.]. Maastricht [etc.]: Natuur & Techniek, cop. 1993. 253 p. Transl. of: De DNA-makers: architecten van het leven. 1993.

Doel, Hans van den
Democracy and welfare economics / Hans van den

Doel and Ben van Velthoven. 2nd ed. Cambridge [etc.]: Cambridge University Press, 1993. XII, 212 p. 1st English ed.: 1978. Transl. of: Democratie en welvaartstheorie. 3rd rev. ed. 1990. Original published in Dutch as: Demokratie en welvaartstheorie: een inleiding in nieuwe politieke ekonomie. 1975.

Dorrestein, Renate
Unnatural mothers: a novel / by Renate Dorrestein; transl. by Wanda Boeke. Seattle: Women in Translation, 1994. Transl. of: Ontaarde moeders. 1992.

Douven, Karel
Christianity on the way to the 21st century: from Christ-confession to Christ-experience / Karel Douven; [transl.: Jan van den Driesschen]. Soest: Correspondence Course 'A Search for Spiritual Growth', [1993]. 255 p. Transl. of: Het christendom op weg naar de 21e eeuw: van Christusbelijdenis tot Christuservaring. 1988.

Duister, Frans
Ru van Rossem / [text] Frans Duister; [transl.: B. Ruijsenaars; slides: Richard van Rossem; photos: Will Dusseldorp]. Venlo [etc.]: Van Spijk, cop. 1994. 120 p. 1st ed.: 1984. Bilingual ed. in Dutch and English.

Dunning, A.J.
Extremes: reflections on human behavior / A.J. Dunning; transl. by Johan Theron. London: Secker & Warburg, 1993. 206 p. 1st English ed.: New York: Harcourt Brace Jovanovich, 1992. Transl. of: Uitersten: beschouwingen over menselijk gedrag. 1990.

Dutch
The Dutch revolt / ed. and transl. by Martin van Gelderen. Cambridge [etc.]: Cambridge University Press, 1993. XLVIII, 250 p.

(Cambridge texts in the history of political thought). Contains a transl. of: Vertoogh ende openinghe om een goede, salighe ende generale vrede te maken in dese Nederlanden, ende deselven onder de ghehoorsaemheyt des Conincx, in haere oude voorspoedicheyt, fleur ende welvaert te brenghen: by maniere van supplicatie. 1576, p. [79]-122, Politicq onderwijs. 1582 p. [123]-164, and: Corte vertoninghe van het recht byden ridderschap, eedelen ende steden van Hollandt ende Westvrieslant van allen ouden tijden in den voorschreven lande gebruyckt tot behoudenisse vande vryheden, gherechticheden, privilegien ende loffelicke ghebruycken vanden selve lande. 1587. p. [227]-238.

Elsinck (pseud. of: Henk Elsink)
Confession of a hired killer / Elsinck; transl. by H.G. Smittenaar. 1st ed. Fairfax Station: Intercontinental Publishing, 1993. 273 p. Transl. of: Biecht van een huurmoordenaar. 1992.

Elsinck (pseud. of: Henk Elsink)
Murder by fax / by Elsinck; transl. by H.G. Smittenaar. 1st ed. Fairfax: New Amsterdam Publishing, 1992. 242 p. Transl. of: Moord per fax. 1991.

Elsschot, Willem (pseud. of Alphonsus Josephus de Ridder)
Villa des roses / Willem Elsschot; transl. with an introd. and notes by Paul Vincent. London [etc.]: Penguin Books, 1992. 140 p. (Penguin twentieth-century classics). Transl. of: Villa des roses. 1913.

Europe
Europe and women in the South: European trade and aid policies and their impact upon women in developing countries / Annet Tesselaar

(red.); [text: Carmen Brandon ... et al.; ed. by: Udo Sprang; transl.: Bram Posthumus]. Amsterdam: InZet, Association for North-South campains, 1994. 51 p. Transl. of: Europa en vrouwen in het zuiden: de gevolgen van het Europese hulp- en handelsbeleid voor vrouwen in ontwikkelingslanden. 1993.

Faverey, Hans
Against the forgetting: selected poems / Hans Faverey; transl. by Francis R. Jones. London: Anvil Press Poetry, 1994. 255 p. Transl. of: Tegen het vergeten. 1988.

Ferwerda, Tineke
Sister Philothea: Relationships between women and Roman Catholic priests / Tineke Ferwerda; [transl.: John Bowden]. [London]: SCMP, 1993. [224] p. Transl. of: Zuster Philothea, ziet gij nog niets komen...?: hoe vrouwen een relatie met een priester beleven. 1989.

Fransen Imbens, Annie
Christianity and incest / Annie Fransen Imbens and Ineke de Putter Jonker; transl. by Patricia McVay; forew. by Marie Fortune. 1st ed. Minneapolis: Fortress Press, 1992. 298 p. Also ed.: Turnbridge Wells: Burns & Oates, 1992. Transl. of: Godsdienst en incest. 1985.

Friedman, Carl
Nightfather: a novel / Carl Friedman; transl. by Arnold and Erica Pomerans. New York: Persea Books, 1994. Transl. of: Tralievader. 1991.

Goes, Benedict
The intriguing design of tobacco pipes / Benedict Goes; [photogr.: Benedict Goes; transl.: Lysbeth Croiset van Uchelen-Brouwer]. Leiden: Pijpenkabinet, [1993]. 79 p. Transl. of: 25 eeuwen roken, de verwonderlijke

vormgeving van de pijp. 1993.

Gomes, Paula
Let it be / Paula Gomes; transl. by Margaret M. Alibasah. Kuala Lumpur; Oxford: Oxford University Press, 1993. VII, 102 p. Transl. of: Sudah, laat maar. 1975.

Goudzwaard, Bob
Beyond poverty and affluence: toward an economy of care, with a twelve-step program for economic recovery / by Bob Goudzwaard and Harry de Lange; with a foreword by Maurice F. Strong; transl. and ed. by Mark Vander Vennen. Grand Rapids: W.B. Eerdmans Pub. Co, 1994. Transl. of: Genoeg van te veel, genoeg van te weinig: wissels omzetten in de economie. 1986.

Griend, Pieter van de
The wee light house knot / Pieter van de Griend; ill. by the author. Århus: Pieter van de Griend; Ipswich: sole distributor: Footrope Knots, 1993. 22 p. Transl. of: Het vuurtoren knoopje. 1993.

Haasse, Hella S.
The scarlet city: a novel of 16th-century Italy / Hella S. Haasse; transl. by Anita Miller. 1st paperback ed. Chicago: Academy Chicago Publishers, 1992. 367 p. 1st English ed.: London: McGraw-Hill, [1954]. Transl. of: De scharlaken stad: roman. 1952.

Haasse, Hella S.
Threshold of fire: a novel of fifth century Rome / Hella S. Haasse; transl. by Anita Miller and Nini Blinstrub. 1st ed. Chicago: Academy Chicago Publishers, 1993. 255 p. Transl. of: Een nieuwer testament. 1966.

Haeringen, H. van
Super chess and monarch: the laws / H. van Haeringen. Leiden:

Coulomb Press Leyden, 1993. 32 p. Transl. of: Superschaak en monarch: de spelregels. 1993.

Hagenaars, Albert
Linguisticum / Nederlands Albert Hagenaars; [transl.] Deutsch Michel Malm ... [et al.; ill.: Mart Franken]. Luxembourg: Double You, 1994. 67 p. Dutch poems with transl. in: German, French and English. Previous publ. in English in: I.E.-magazine. 1993. Orig. publ. in: Op komst. 1983 and: Intriges. 1986

Hamaker-Zondag, Karen
The house connection: how to read the houses in an astrological chart / by Karen Hamaker-Zondag; [transl. by Transcript]. York Beach: Weiser, 1994. Transl. of: Huisheren en huizenverbanden. 1984.

Hartog, Jan de
The outer boy: a story of the ultimate voyage / Jan de Hartog. New York: Pantheon Books, 1994. (A Cornelia & Michael Bessie book). Transl. of: De buitenboei: roman. 1994.

Haspels, Jan Jaap
Musical automata: catalogue of automatic musical instruments in the National Museum 'From Musical Clock to Street Organ' / [text: Jan Jaap Haspels; photogr.: Dea Rijper ... et al.; transl. from the Dutch]. Utrecht: National Museum 'From Musical Clock to Street Organ', 1994. 256 p. Transl. of: Automatische muziekinstrumenten. 1994.

Helman, Albert
Chieftains of the Oayapok!: novel / Albert Helman; transl. by Scott Rollins. Amsterdam: In de Knipscheer, cop. 1993/4. 74 p. Transl. of: Hoofden van de Oayapok!: roman in vijf redevoeringen. 1984.

Hertzsprung-Kapteyn, Henrietta

The life and works of J.C. Kapteyn / Henrietta Hertzsprung-Kapteyn; an annotated transl. with pref. and introd. by E. Robert Paul. Dordrecht [etc.]: Kluwer Academic Publishers, cop. 1993. XIX, 92 p. Originally publ. in: Space science reviews. Vol 64, nos. 1-2, 1993. Transl. of: J.C. Kapteyn: zijn leven en werken. 1928.

Herzberg, Judith
Scratch / Judith Herzberg; vert. John Rudge. Amsterdam: International Theatre & Film Books, 1993. (Theatre in translation). Transl. of: Kras. 1989.

Hillesum, Etty
Interrupted life / Etty Hillesum. New York: Pocket Books, 1991. Transl. of: Het verstoorde leven: dagboek van Etty Hillesum 1941-1943. 1981.

Hin, Floris
This is knotting and splicing / Floris Hin. Rev. ed. New York: Hearst Marine Books, 1993. Transl. of: Dit is knopen en splitsen. 1982.

Hol, Coby
Niki's little donkey / by Coby Hol; transl by J. Alison James. New York: North-South Books; Gossau ZH: Nord-Süd Verlag, 1993. [26] p. Transl. of: Niki's ezeltje. 1993.

Honderd
Honderd hoogtepunten uit de Koninklijke Bibliotheek = A hundred highlights from the Koninklijke Bibliotheek / [red.: Wim van Drimmelen ... et al.; English transl.: Lysbeth Croiset van Uchelen-Brouwer; contributors: Paul van den Brink ... et al.]. Zwolle: Waanders, cop. 1994. 223 p. Publ. in cooperation with: Koninklijke Bibliotheek, The Hague on the occasion of the exposition: 'Honderd Hoogtepunten uit de

Koninklijke Bibliotheek' in the Rijksmuseum Meermanno-Westreenianum/Museum van het Boek. Bilingual ed. in Dutch and English.

Hondius, Dienke
Anne Frank in the world: 1929-1945 / [photo research and text Dienke Hondius, Joke Kniesmeijer and Bauco T. van der Wal; English language text provided by Steven Arthur Cohen = Le monde de Anne Frank: 1929-1945 / recherche iconographique, textes et réd.: Dienke Hondius, Joke Kniesmeijer et Bauco T. van der Wal; texte français: Guy Geuens et César Heukeshoven. Amsterdam: Anne Frank Stichting, cop. 1993. 144 p. 5th rev. English ed.: 1993. 1st English ed.: 1985. 1st bilingual ed. in English and French. Exhibition Catalogue. Transl. of: Anne Frank in the world: 1929-1945 = De wereld van Anne Frank: 1929-1945, 1985. Other bilingual ed. in: Arabic, Hebrew, Italian, Polish, Portuguese and Spanish.

Hurk, Nicolle van den
Where is Skipper? / Nicolle van der Hurk (ill.); Ivo de Wijs (text); Tjaart Theron (transl.). New York: Barron's, cop. 1993. [26] p. Transl. of: Waar is Springer, waar is Twikkie? 1994.

Jansen, A.C.M.
Cannabis in Amsterdam: a geography of hashish and marihuana / A.C.M. Jansen; [art work: N.A.M. de Winter; transl.: N.J. Williams]. Muiderberg: Coutinho, 1991. 178 p. Transl. of: Cannabis in Amsterdam: een geografie van hashish en marijuana. 1989.

Jansen, Eva Rudy
The book of Hindu imagery: gods, manifestations and their meaning / comp. by: Eva Rudy

Jansen; [ill.: Harm Kuiper... et al.; transl.: Tony Langham].
Diever: Binkey Kok, cop. 1993. X, 150 p.
Transl. of: De beeldentaal van het hindoeïsme: goden, verschijningsvormen en hun betekenis. 1993.

Julius, Frits Hendrik
Imagery of the Zodiac / Frits H. Julius; transl. T. Langham and P. Peters. [S.l.]: Floris Books., 1993. [192] p.
Transl. of: De beeldentaal van de dierenriem en de opbouw van een nieuwe samenleving. 1966.

Kaai, Anneke
Apocalypse: meditations on the Revelation of John in world and picture. Carlisle: Paternoster, 1992. 56 p, Transl. of: Openbaring in beeld. [1990].

Kamst, J.
What is ASR-therapy? / [text and ill.:] J. Kamst; [transl.: J. Draaisma]. Hengelo (Ov.): TCT, cop. 1993. 24 p. Transl. of: Wat is ASR-therapie?. 2d rev. ed. 1983.

Kossmann-Putto, J.A.
The Low Countries: history and language / J.A. Kossmann-Putto, E.H. Kossmann, O. Vandeputte; [transl. and adapt. by] P. Vincent, T. Hermans. Rekkem: Stichting Ons Erfdeel, 1993. 128 p. Publ. on the occasion of the 45th Frankfurter Buchmesse. Transl. of: De Lage Landen: geschiedenis en taal. 1993.

Krabbé, Tim
The vanishing / by Tim Krabbé; [transl. by Claire Nicolas White]. Harmondsworth: Penguin Books, 1993. Transl. of: Het gouden ei. Amsterdam: Bakker, 1984.

Krogt, Peter van der.
Globi Neerlandici: the production of globes in the Low Countries / Peter van

der Krogt; [transl. by Elizabeth Daverman]. Utrecht: HES, cop. 1993. 647 p, XVI p. pl. Enlarged transl. of: Globi Neerlandici: de globeproduktie in de Nederlanden. Thesis Utrecht, 1989.

Langenus, Ron
Merlin's return / Ron Langenus; [transl. N.H. Delmonte]. [Dublin]: Wolfhound, cop. 1993. [128] p. Transl. of: Weg van weggeweest. 1989.

Leeuw, Ronald de
Van Gogh at the Van Gogh Museum / Ronald de Leeuw; [transl. by Andrew McCormick]. Zwolle: Waanders, cop. 1994. 166 p. Transl. of: Van Gogh in het Van Gogh Museum. 1994.

Leeuwen, Boeli van
Shields of clay / Boeli van Leeuwen; transl. by Richard Huijing. Amsterdam: In de Knipscheer, cop. 1994. 156 p. Transl. of: Schilden van leem. 1985.

Leeuwen, Boeli van
The sign of Jonah / Boeli van Leeuwen; transl. by André Lefevere. Amsterdam: In de Knipscheer, cop. [1993]. 182 p. Transl. of: Het teken van Jona: roman. 1988.

Lieshout, Ted van
The dearest boy in all the world / Ted van Lieshout; transl. by Lance Salway. London [etc.]: Penguin, 1993. 76 p. 1st English ed.: Woodchester [etc.]: Turton & Chambers, 1990. Transl. of: De allerliefste jongen van de hele wereld. 1988.

Living
Living rivers: study commissioned by the World Wide Fund for Nature / [compilation W. Helmer ... et. al; pictures Wouter Helmer ... et al.; drawings Jeroen Helmer; transl. by Invitaal Wageningen/ M.A.G. Wennekers]. Zeist: World Wide Fund for

Nature, 1993. 28 p.
Transl. of: Levende rivieren. 1992.

Los, D.
Thou holdest my right hand: on pastoral care of the dying / by D. Los; transl. by Theodore Plantinga. Neerlandia; Caledonia: Inheritance Publ., 1993. (Pastoral perspectives; 2).
Transl. of: Gij hebt mijn rechterhand gevat: pastorale hulp aan terminale patiënten. 1988.

Maastricht
Maastricht: 'portrait of a city' / [ed.: Jaap van Term; together with Hans Kamphoven ... et al.; text: Jaap van Term; photogr.: Guy van Grinsven ... et al.; transl. by Guy van Grinsven ... et al.]. Maastricht: CommunicationLINE, [1994]. 128 p.
Transl. of: Maastricht: 'een beeld van een stad'. 1993.

Man, Hanneke de
Boymans-Van Beuningen Museum / Hanneke de Man. [S.l.]: Scala Publ, 1992. [128] p.
Transl. of: Museum Boymans-van Beuningen. 1993.

Manen Pieters, Jos van
The discerning heart / Jos van Manen Pieters; [transl. by J.W. Medendorp].
Grand Rapids: Revell. 1992. 304 p.
(Warbler Cottage romances; book 1).
Transl. of: En de tuinfluiter zingt. 1955.

Manen Pieters, Jos van
A gleam of dawn / Jos van Manen Pieters; [transl. by J.W. Medendorp]. Grand Rapids: Revell. 1992. 192 p.
(Warbler Cottage romances; book 3).
Transl. of: Als de tuinfluiter zwijgt... 1964.

Manen Pieters, Jos van
A longing fulfilled / Jos van Manen Pieters; [transl. by J.W. Medendorp].
Grand Rapids: Revell. 1992. 256 p.
(Warbler Cottage romances; book 2). Transl. of:
Een nest vol tuinfluiters: het verhaal van een gelukkige familie. 1961.

Mariken
Mariken van Nieumeghen: a bilingual edition / ed., transl., and with an introd. by Therese Decker, Martin W. Walsh. Columbia, S.C.: Camden House, cop. 1994. 144 p. (Studies in German literature, linguistics, and culture. Medieval texts and translations).
Bilingual ed. in Middle Dutch and English.

Mastenbroek, Willem F.G.
Conflict management and organization development / Willem F.G. Mastenbroek. Expanded ed. Chichester [etc.]: John Wiley, cop. 1993. [XI], 184 p.
1st English ed.: 1987.
Transl. of: Conflicthantering en organisatie-ontwikkeling.
1981. Thesis Leiden.

Minco, Marga
The other side / Marga Minco; transl. by Ruth Levitt. London: Peter Owen; Paris: UNESCO Publishing, 1994. 118 p.
Transl. of: De andere kant: verhalen. 1959.

Minnaert, Marcel
Light and color in the outdoors / Marcel Minnaert; transl. and rev. by Len Seymour. New York; Berlin [etc.]: Springer, cop. 1993. XVI, 417 p.
Originally publ. as: Licht en kleur in het landschap. 1937.

Mondrian, Piet
New art, the new life: collected writings of Piet Mondrian / Piet Mondrian; edited and transl. by Harry Holtzman and Martin S. James. New ed.
New York: Da Capo, 1993. [XXV, 414] p.
(Documents of twentieth century art series)

1st English ed.: Boston: Hall, cop. 1986. (The documents of twentieth century art).

Moolenburgh, H.C.
Meetings with angels: a hundred and one real-life encounters / H.C. Moolenburgh; transl. T. Langham and P. Peters. Saffron Walden: C.W. Daniel, 1992. XIV, 210 p.
Transl. of: Een engel op je pad: honderd en één engelenervaringen. 1991.

Moor, Margriet de
First grey, then white, then blue / Margriet de Moor; transl. by Paul Vincent. London [etc.]: Picador, 1994. 218 p.
Transl. of: Eerst grijs dan wit dan blauw: roman. 1991.

Nice
Nice people: a collection of Dutch short stories / Ed. by Gerrit Bussink; [transl. by Guernica ed. and the translators]. Montreal: Guernica, 1992. 233 p. (Prose series; 23). Contains short stories from: Renate Dorrestein, Ad van Iterson, Jan Siebelink, Lévi Weemoedt, Simon Carmiggelt, W.F. Hermans, Anton Koolhaas, Hannes Meinkema, Armando, Fleur Bourgonje, Maarten Biesheuvel, Margaretha Ferguson, Remco Campert, Margriet de Moor, Tim Krabbé and L.H. Wiener.

Nooteboom, Cees
The following story / Cees Nooteboom; transl. by Ina Rilke. 1st ed. New York: Harcourt Brace, 1994. (A Helen and Kurt Wolff book). 1st English ed.: London: Harvill, cop. 1993.
Transl. of: Het volgende verhaal. 1991.

Oordt, Karel R. van
A part of Israel: Samaria-Judea / Karel R. van Oordt; Pee Koelewijn photos. Kampen: Kok Voorhoeve, cop. 1994. 126 p.
Publ. in cooperation with Christenen voor Israel.

Transl. of: Ook dit is Israël. 1994.

Oostrom, Frits Pieter van
Court and culture: Dutch literature, 1350-1450 / Frits Pieter van Oostrom; transl. by Arnold J. Pomerans; forew. by James H. Marrow. Berkeley [etc.]: University of California Press, cop. 1992. XVI, 373 p.
Transl. of: Het woord van eer. 1987.

Palmen, Connie
The laws / Connie Palmen; transl. by Richard Huijing. 1st ed. New York: Braziller, 1993. 196 p.
1st English ed.: [S.l.]: Secker & Warburg, 1992.
Transl. of: De wetten: roman. 1991.

Pelgrom, Els
The acorn eaters / Els Pelgrom; [transl.: Johanna H. Prins and Johanna W. Prins]. New York: Farrar, Straus & Giroux, 1994.
Transl. of: De eikelvreters. 1989.

Penninc
Roman van Walewein / Penninc and Pieter Vostaert; ed. and transl. by David F. Johnson. New York [etc.]: Garland, 1992. LVII, 575 p. (The Garland library of medieval literature; 81. Series A, Texts and translations).
Bilingual ed. in Middle Dutch and English.

Polzer, H.H.
Lyriana: poems and songs in English = poèmes et chansons en français = Gedichte und Lieder auf Deutsch / H.H. Polzer; introd. by Cees van der Pluijm; [comp. by Kees van den Heuvel ... et al.; introd. transl. by Kees van den Heuvel ... et al.]. Nijmegen: De Stiel, 1993. 211 p.

Poortvliet, Rien
The complete book of the gnomes / by Rien Poortvliet and Wil Huygen. New York: H.N. Abrams, 1994.
Transl. of: Leven en werken van de kabouter. 1976 and:

De oproep der kabouters. 1981.

Poortvliet, Rien
Farm book / Rien Poortvliet; New York: Abrams, 1994. Transl. of: Te hooi en te gras. 1975.

Poortvliet, Rien
Journey to the Ice Age: mammoths and other animals of the wild / by Rien Poortvliet; transl. by Karin H. Ford. New York: Abrams, 1994. Transl. of: Aanloop. 1993.

Pronk, Pieter
Against nature?: types of moral argumentation regarding homosexuality / Pim Pronk; transl. by John Vriend. Grand Rapids: Eerdmans, cop. 1993. Transl. of: Tegennatuurlijk?: typen van morele argumentatie inzake homosexualiteit. 1989.

Rijckenborgh, J. van
(pseud. of Jan Leene)
The alchemical wedding of Christian Rosycross: esoteric analysis of the chymische Hochzeit Christiani Rosencreutz anno 1459 / by J. van Rijckenborgh; [transl.; ill. Johfra]. Haarlem: Rozekruis Pers, 1991-1992. 2 vols. (The secrets of the Brotherhood of the Rosycross; 3). Originally publ. as: De alchemische bruiloft van Christiaan Rozenkruis: esoterische analyse van de Chymische Hochzeit Christiani Rosencreutz Anno 1459. 1967.

Rijckenborgh, J. van
(pseud. of Jan Leene)
The Egyptian Arch-gnosis and its call in the eternal present / newly proclaimed and explained from the Tabula Smaragdina and Corpus Hermeticum of Hermes Trismegistus by J. van Rijckenborgh. 1st ed. Haarlem: Rozekruis Pers, 1994. 252 p. Pt. 3. Transl. of: De Egyptische Oergnosis en haar roep in het eeuwige nu. Dl. 3. 2e rev. ed. 1985.

Rijckenborgh, Jan van
(pseud. of Jan Leene)
The mystery of life and death / by Jan van Rijckenborgh. Haarlem: Rozekruis Pers, 1993. 67 p. Transl. of: Het mysterie van leven en dood.

Roemer, Astrid
The order of the day: a novella / Astrid Roemer; transl. by Rita Gircour; [with an introduction by Michiel van Kempen]. Amsterdam: In de Knipscheer, 1994. 45 p. Originally publ. as: De orde van de dag. 1988.

Roos, Betty
No can do is dead: a Dutch girl in a Japanese POW camp: novel / Betty Roos; transl. by Robert Hersee. Amsterdam: In de Knipscheer Publishers, 1994. 132 p. Transl. of: Kan-niet is dood: kinderjaren in een Jappenkamp. 1989.

Ros, Martin
Night of fire: the black Napoleon and the battle for Haiti / by Martin Ros; transl. by Karin Ford-Streep. New York: Sarpedon, cop. 1994. 224 p. Transl. of: Vuurnacht: Toussaint Louverture en de slavenopstand op Haïti. 1991.

Ruusbroec, Jan van
Adornment of a spiritual marriage; Sparkling stone: the book of supreme truth / Jan Van Ruusbroec; ed. by E. Underhill; transl. C.A. Wynschenk. facsim. of 1916 ed. [S.l.]: Llanerch Publishers, 1994. [320] p. Originally publ. as: Die chierheit der gheesteliker brulocht, and: Van den blinckenden steen.

Ruusbroec, Jan van
Flowers of a mystic garden/ from the works of John Ruysbroeck; transl. from the French of Ernest Hello by C.E.S. Felinfach: Llanerch Publishers, 1994. 139 p. Originally publ. in Middle Dutch.

Schalkwijk, Frans
Music and people with developmental disabilities: music therapy, remedial music making and musical activities / Frans Schalkwijk; transl. by Andrew James. London [etc.]: Kingsley, 1994. XII, 112 p. Transl. of: Muziek in de hulpverlening aan geestelijk gehandicapten. 1988.

Scheerens, Jaap
Effective schooling: research, theory and practice / Jaap Scheerens. London [etc.]: Cassell, 1992. VIII, 168 p. (School development series). Transl. of: Wat maakt scholen effectief?: samenvatting en analyse van onderzoeksresultaten. 1989.

Schmidt, Annie M.G.
Minnie / Annie M. G. Schmidt; transl. L. Salway. Minneapolis: Milkweed Editions, 1994. 1st English ed.: Woodchester, Stroud, Glos.: Turnton & Chambers, 1992. Transl. of: Minoes. 1970.

Spier, Peter
Father, may I come? / Peter Spier. New York: Doubleday Book for Young Readers, 1993. Transl. of: Vader, mag ik mee? 1992.

Stork
Stork: 120 years of industrial dynamism. Utrecht: Matrijs, cop. 1990. 148 p. Transl. of: Stork: 120 jaar industriële dynamiek. 1989.

Straaten, Peter van
Have you got it on yet? / Peter van Straaten; [transl. by Jan Michael]. London: Fourth Estate, 1993. [96] p. Transl. of: Zo beter? 1992.

Straaten, Peter van
How was it for you? / Peter van Straaten; [transl. by Jan Michael ... et. al.]. Repr. London: Fourth Estate, 1993. [96] p. Transl. of: Doe ik het goed? 1990.

Straaten, Werenfried van
They call me the bacon

priest: the story of the world-wide pastoral relief organisation founded by the author / Werenfried van Straaten; [transl. from the German]. Rev. ed. San Francisco: Ignatius Press, 1991. 241 p. Previous American ed.: New York: New City Press, 1965. Transl. of: Sie nennen mich Speckpater. 1961. Original Dutch text publ. as: Ze noemen mij Spekpater. 1962.

Straten, Roelof van
An introduction to iconography / Roelof van Straten; transl. from the German by Patricia de Man. Rev. English ed. Yverdon [etc.]: Gordon and Breach, cop. 1993. XV, 151 p. (Documenting the image; vol. 1). Transl. of: Einführung in die Ikonographie. 1989. Originally publ. as: Een inleiding in de iconografie: enige theoretische en praktische kennis. 1985.

Style
Style: standard and signature in Dutch architecture in the nineteenth and twentieth centuries / Bernard Colenbrander (ed.); [transl.: John Kirkpatrick ... et al.]. Rotterdam: NAI Publishers, cop. 1993. 359 p. Publ. on the occasion of the exhibition in the Nederlands Architectuurinstituut, October 29th, 1993 - January 30th, 1994. Transl. of: Stijl: norm en handschrift in de Nederlandse architectuur in de negentiende en twintigste eeuw. 1993.

Suurmond, Jean-Jacques
Word and Spirit at play: towards a charismatic theology / Jean-Jacques Suurmond; [transl. by John Bowden]. London: S.C.M.P., 1994. [224] p. Transl. of: Het spel van woord en geest: aanzet tot een charismatische theologie. 1994.

Szulc-Krzyzanowski, Michel
Deep-rooted words / Michel

Szulc-Krzyzanowski photogr.; Michiel van Kempen text; transl. by Sam Garrett; [photo ed. Adriaan Monshouwer]. Amsterdam: Voetnoot, cop. 1992. 239 p. Transl. of: Woorden die diep wortelen. 1992.

Tellegen-Couperus, Olga
A short history of roman law / Olga Tellegen-Couperus. London [etc.]: Routledge, 1993. XII, 174 p. Transl. of: Korte geschiedenis van het Romeinse recht. 1990.

Twelve
Twelve Jews discover Messiah / [interviews by] Ben Hoekendijk. Repr. [S.l.]: Kingsway Publications, 1993. [192] p.; 18 cm. Transl. of: Twaalf Joden vinden de Messias. 1991.

Uyl, Marion den
Invisible barriers: gender, caste and kinship in a southern Indian village / Marion den Uyl; [transl. by Aileen Stronge]. Utrecht: International Books, 1994. Transl. of: Onzichtbare muren: over het verinnerlijken van seksuele grenzen; een onderzoek in een dorp in Zuid-India. 1992. Thesis Universiteit van Amsterdam.

Vallensis, Lepusculus (pseud. of Tamme Jan Albert Delhaas)
The Belgic Confession and its biblical basis / Lepusculus Vallensis; transl. by Rene Vermeulen. Neerlandia, [etc.]: Inheritance Publ., cop. 1993. 262 p. Transl. of: Belijden naar het Woord. Dl. 1. 2nd ed. 1952.

Vanhuysse, T.
The gift of grace: Roman Catholic teaching in the light of the Bible. [S.L.]: Evangelical Press, 1992. 109 p. Transl. of: Wat Rome leert aan de Bijbel getoetst. 1988.

Velthuijs, Max
Frog is frightened / Max

Velthuijs. London: Andersen Press, cop. 1994. [24] p. Simultaneous publ. in Dutch as: Kikker is bang. 1994.

Verdeyen, Paul
Ruusbroec and his mysticism / Paul Verdeyen; transl. by André Lefevere. Collegeville: Liturgical Press, 1994. (Way of the Christian mystics; vol. 11). (A Michael Glazier book). Transl. of: Ruusbroec en zijn mystiek. 1981.

Vestdijk, Simon
The garden where the brass band played: (fragment) / Simon Vestdijk; [transl. by: Ydwine Schneider ... [e.a.]. [S.l.]: Foundation Simon Vestdijk, 1994. 50 numbered copies for the Friends of the Stichting Administratiekantoor Auteursrechten Simon Vestdijk. Transl. in German, English and French.

Victorian
Victorian inventions / Leonard de Vries; comp. in collab. with Ilonka van Amstel; [transl. by Barthold Suermondt]. Repr. London: J. Murray, 1993. 192 p. 1st English ed.: 1971. Composed of articles publ. between 1865 and 1900 in the periodicals: Scientific American, La nature, and: De natuur.

Vink, Willem de
Jesus Messiah / text and ill.: Willem de Vink. Amerongen: Proclama, 1993. 64 p.: Transl. of: Jezus Messias. 1993.

Visser, Carolijn
Voices & visions; a journey through Vietnam today / Carolijn Visser; [transl. by Susan Massotty]. Boulder: Sycamore Island Books, 1994. Transl. of: Hoge bomen in Hanoi. cop. 1993.

Vos, Ida
Anna is still here / Ida Vos; transl. by Terese Edelstein and Inez Smidt. 1st ed. Boston: Houghton Mifflin,

1993. 139 p. Transl. of: Anna is er nog. 1986.

Vos, Reinout
Gentle Janus, merchant prince: the VOC and the tightrope of diplomacy in the Malay world, 1740-1800 / Reinout Vos; transl. by Beverley Jackson. Leiden: KITLV Press, 1993. VI, 252 p. (Verhandelingen van het Koninklijk Instituut voor Taal-, Land- en Volkenkunde; 157). Transl. of: Koopman en koning: de VOC en de Maleise tinhandel, 1740-1800. 1990. Thesis Utrecht.

Vries, Peter de
John Bunyan on the order of salvation / Peter de Vries. New York: P. Lang, 1994. (American university studies; vol. 176). Transl. of: De orde van het heil bij John Bunyan. 1989.

Vroman, Leo
Love, greatly enlarged / Leo Vroman; forew. by Claire Nicolas White. Merrick: Cross Cultural Communications, 1992. 135 p. (Cross-cultural review. International writers; 1). In cooperation with Querido. Bilingual ed. in English and Dutch. Transl. of: Liefde, sterk vergroot. 1981.

Water
Water quality control at ship locks: prevention of salt- and fresh water exchange / J. Kerstma ... [et al.]. Rotterdam [etc.]: Balkema, 1994. XI, 92 p. Transl. of: Zout-zoetscheiding bij schutsluizen. 1991.

Weeber, Frans
Going to school in the Netherlands / Ministry of Education and Science; [author: Frans Weeber; ed. Peter van Loon; transl. Vertaalcircuit Bussum]. Leeuwarden: LDC; Zoetermeer: Ministerie van Onderwijs en Wetenschappen, Directie Voorlichting, Bibliotheek en Internationale

Betrekkingen, 1992. 48 p. Transl. of: Naar school in Nederland.

Wetering, JanWillem van de
Just a corpse at twilight / JanWillem van de Wetering. New York, NY: Soho, 1994. Transl. of: Drijflijk. 1993.

Winter, Leon de
La Place de la Bastille: novella / Leon de Winter; transl. by Scott Rollins. Haarlem: In de Knipscheer, cop. [1993]. Transl. of: La Place de la Bastille: vertelling. 1981.

Wolf, Alex de
What about me? / Alex de Wolf; [text Martine Schaap]. London: Mammoth, 1994. [32] p. Transl. of: En ik dan? 1993.

Zwart, Frank de
The bureaucratic merry-go-round: manipulating the transfer of Indian civil servants / Frank de Zwart; transl. by Gregor Benton. [Amsterdam]: Amsterdam University Press, cop. 1994. VIII, 145 p. Transl. of: Mobiele bureaucratie: manipulaties met overplaatsingen van ambtenaren in India. Originally Thesis Universiteit van Amsterdam, 1992.

Editor:
Dutch-Language Books in Translation
Koninklijke Bibliotheek,
The Hague
The Netherlands

Ludo Abicht (1936-)
Lecturer in Philosophy
(PHITC, Antwerp) / Guest
lecturer in Philosophy
(University Institute
Antwerp)
Mechelsesteenweg 212,
2018 Antwerp, Belgium

Fons Asselbergs (1940-)
Director of the Dept. for the
Protection of Monuments
and Historic Buildings
Regentesselaan 15,
3818 HH Amersfoort,
The Netherlands

Fred G.H. Bachrach (1914-)
Emeritus Professor of
English Literature
(University of Leiden)
55 Cole Park Road,
Twickenham TW1 1HT,
United Kingdom

Geert Bekaert (1928-)
Chief Editor (Archis)
Koepoortbrug 4,
2000 Antwerp, Belgium

Rob Berends (1957-)
Staff member of the
Ministry of Health, Welfare
and Sport / Journalist
Zeekant 95j, 2586 JC
The Hague, The Netherlands

**Joop Th. J. van den Berg
(1941-)**
Professor of Dutch Political
and Parliamentary History
(University of Leiden) / MP
(First Chamber of the States
General) PvdA
W.M. Offringalaan 6,
2406 JB Alphen aan den
Rijn, The Netherlands

Jan Berkouwer (1947-)
Professor of Economics
(University of Stettin) /
Lecturer in Economics and
Law (Holland College,
Diemen)
Kerkweg 83,
2825 NA Berkenwoude,
The Netherlands

Franz Bingen (1932-)
Professor of Mathematics
(VUB; Free University of
Brussels)
Dageraadlaan 31,
1652 Alsemberg, Belgium

Jos Borré (1948-)
Teacher / Critic
Vredelaan 8, 2500 Lier,
Belgium

Frans Bosman (1950-)
Journalist (Het Parool)
Zeeburgerkade 346,
1019 HN Amsterdam,
The Netherlands

Eric Bracke (1960-)
Journalist (De Morgen)
Wegvoeringstraat 115,
9230 Wetteren, Belgium

Hugo Brems (1944-)
Professor of Modern Dutch
Literature (Catholic
University of Leuven)
Huttelaan 263,
3001 Leuven, Belgium

James Brockway (1916-)
Poet / Writer / Translator
Riouwstraat 114,
2585 HH The Hague,
The Netherlands

Jean van Cleven (1953-)
Assistant lecturer
(University of Ghent)
Dept. of Art History,
Musicology and
Dramaturgy, Sint-Hubertus-
straat 2, 9000 Ghent,
Belgium

Huib Dejonghe (1931-)
Journalist (De Standaard)
Kerkstraat 48,
2640 Mortsel, Belgium

Paul Demets (1966-)
Teacher / Theatre critic
Kasteelstraat 56,
9870 Olsene, Belgium

Paul Depondt (1953-)
Journalist (de Volkskrant)
Korenmarkt 25,
9000 Ghent, Belgium

Leen van Dijck (1953-)
Deputy Curator AMVC /
Antwerp Municipal Library
Schulstraat 9,
2018 Antwerp, Belgium

Joris Duytschaever (1944-)
Professor of English
Literature (University
Institute Antwerp)
E. Casteleinstraat 28,
2020 Antwerp, Belgium

Kurt van Es (1949-)
Journalist (Het Parool)
Hofmark 128,
1355 HK Almere,
The Netherlands

Charles Ford (1952-)
Lecturer in History of Art
(University of London)
University College London,
Gower Street, London
WC1E 6BT, United
Kingdom

Jaap Goedegebuure (1947-)
Professor of Literary
Theory and Literary History
(Catholic University of
Brabant)
Antoniusstraat 5,
2382 BD Zoeterwoude-
Rijndijk, The Netherlands

S. Groenveld (1941-)
Professor of the History and
Culture of the Dutch
Republic (University of
Leiden)
Vrijbuiterhof 25,
2312 TM Hoofddorp,
The Netherlands

Tanneke de Groot (1964-)
Programme maker
(VPRO Radio)
Swammerdamstraat 55hs,
1091 RS Amsterdam,
The Netherlands

Christiane Hertel (1958-)
Assistant Professor of
History of Art (Bryn Mawr
College)
Dept. of History of Art,
101 North Merion Avenue,
Bryn Mawr, PA 19010, USA

Erwin Jans (1963-)
Dramaturgist (KVS, Brussels)
Poststraat 10,
1250 Brussels, Belgium

Lisa Jardine
Professor of English
(University of London)
Queen Mary and Westfield
College, Mile End Road,
London E1 4NS, United
Kingdom

Jan Kerkhofs SJ (1924-)
Emeritus professor of
Theology (Catholic
University of Leuven)
Waversebaan 220,
3001 Leuven, Belgium

Johan Kolsteeg (1963-)
Editor (Mens & Melodie /
Keynotes) / Music critic
Javastraat 77,
1094 HB Amsterdam,
The Netherlands

Anton Korteweg (1944-)
Director of the Netherlands
Literature Museum and
Documentation Centre
(The Hague) / Poet
Wasstraat 23, 2313 JG
Leiden, The Netherlands

Jef Lambrecht (1948-)
Journalist (BRTN Radio)
Kattenberg 45,
2140 Borgerhout, Belgium

Pascal Lefèvre (1963-)
Editor (BRTN Television)
Eikkapellaan 19,
3400 Landen, Belgium

Jo Lernout (1948-)
President of Lernout &
Hauspie
Sint-Krispijnstraat 7,
8900 Ypres, Belgium

Joke Linders (1943-)
Children's literature critic
(Algemeen Dagblad) /
Lecturer in Children's and
Adolescent Literature
(Colofon / Script Plus)
Schaepmanlaan 14,
2081 EZ Santpoort-Zuid,
The Netherlands

Gerdin Linthorst (1946-)
Film critic
Admiraal de Ruyterweg
274, 1055 MR Amsterdam,
The Netherlands

Yann Lovelock (1939-)
Writer / Translator
80 Doris Road,
Birmingham, B11 4NF,
United Kingdom

Filip Matthijs (1966-)
Editorial secretary
(The Low Countries)
Murissonstraat 260,
8931 Rekkem, Belgium

Henk van Nierop (1949-)
Lecturer in History
(University of Amsterdam)
Spuistraat 134,
1012 VB Amsterdam,
The Netherlands

Frits Niessen (1936-)
Deputy Editor
(The Low Countries)
Rijvoortshoef 265,
4941 VJ Raamsdonksveer,
The Netherlands

Jos Nijhof (1952-)
Teacher / Theatre critic
Berkenkade 14,
2351 NB Leiderdorp,
The Netherlands

Geert Opsomer (1957-)
Lecturer in Dramaturgy
(Catholic University of
Leuven) / Staff member VTI
Ankerlaan 14,
9050 Gentbrugge, Belgium

Herman Pleij (1943-)
Professor of Medieval
Dutch Literature
(University of Amsterdam)
Van Ostadelaan 40,
1412 JK Naarden,
The Netherlands

Kees Polling (1956-)
Journalist
Utrechtseweg 7,
1213 TK Hilversum,
The Netherlands

Wim de Poorter (1939-)
Teacher / Film critic
Rijselstraat 280B,
8200 Bruges, Belgium

Ine Rietstap (1929-)
Dance critic
(NRC-Handelsblad)
Prinsengracht 755,
1017 JX Amsterdam,
The Netherlands

Dan Roodt (1957-)
Writer / Critic
Elgin 77, The Willows,
Kelland 2194, South Africa

Jan Rubinstein (1931-)
PR advisor / Music critic
Minervalaan 31,
1077 NL Amsterdam,
The Netherlands

Marc Ruyters (1952-)
Journalist / Scriptwriter
Drie Eikenstraat 282/4,
2650 Edegem, Belgium

Reinier Salverda (1948-)
Professor of Dutch
Language and Literature
(University of London)
69 St James's Lane,
Muswell Hill,
London N10 3QY,
United Kingdom

Govert Schilling (1956-)
Science journalist /
Programme director of the
Artis Planetarium
Dr. H. Th. 's Jacoblaan 36,
3571 BM Utrecht,
The Netherlands

Maurits Smeyers (1937-)
Professor of Medieval
Studies (Catholic
University of Leuven)
Bruineveld 96,
3010 Leuven, Belgium

Kees Snoek (1952-)
Lecturer in Dutch
(University of Auckland)
31 Halesowen Avenue,
Sandringham 1003,
Auckland, New Zealand

A.L. Sötemann (1920-)
Emeritus Professor of
Modern Dutch Literature
(University of Utrecht)
P. Saenredamstraat 5,
3583 TA Utrecht,
The Netherlands

Eddy Stols (1938-)
Professor of History
(Catholic University of
Leuven)
Toverbergstraat 5/5,
3020 Veltem-Beisem,
Belgium

C.L. Temminck Groll
(1925-)
Emeritus Professor (Delft
Polytechnic) / Restoration
architect / Associate profes-
sor of Restoration and
Conservation Studies
(University of Amsterdam)
Hoofdstraat 43,
3971 KB Driebergen,
The Netherlands

Herwig Todts (1958-)
Staff member of the
Antwerp Royal Museum of
Fine Arts
Bredabaan 635,
2930 Brasschaat, Belgium

Marc van Vaeck (1959-)
Lecturer in Dutch
Renaissance Literature
(Catholic University of
Leuven)
Opvoedingsstraat 24,
3010 Kessel-Lo, Belgium

Hans Vanacker (1960-)
Editorial secretary
(Septentrion)
Murissonstraat 260,
8931 Rekkem, Belgium

Sabine Vanacker (1962-)
Lecturer in Dutch
(University of Hull)
Dept. of Dutch Studies,
Cottingham Road,
Hull HU6 7RX,
United Kingdom

Paul van Velthoven (1947-)
Journalist (Het Binnenhof)
Geestbrugweg 68,
2281 CP Rijswijk,
The Netherlands

Katie Verstockt (1953-)
Dance critic
Leopold de Waelplaats 8,
2000 Antwerp, Belgium

Marina de Vries (1958-)
Journalist (Het Parool)
P. Aertszstraat 69
(2nd floor), 1073 SK
Amsterdam,
The Netherlands

Leo Vroman (1916-)
Biologist / Writer / Poet
2365 East 13th Street,
Apt. 6U, Brooklyn,
NY 11229, USA

Jeroen Vullings (1962-)
Teacher / Literary critic
Madelievenstraat 25,
1015 NV Amsterdam,
The Netherlands

Christopher White (1930-)
Director of the Ashmolean
Museum (Oxford)
Beaumont Street, Oxford
OX1 2PH, United Kingdom

Hendrik Willaert (1948-)
Music teacher
Krommekeerstraat 5,
8755 Ruiselede, Belgium

Manfred Wolf (1935-)
Professor of English
(San Francisco State
University)
2531 - 21st Avenue,
San Francisco, CA 94116,
USA

As well as the yearbook *The Low Countries*, the Flemish-Netherlands foundation 'Stichting Ons Erfdeel' publishes the following booklets covering various aspects of the culture of the Netherlands and Flanders:

O. Vandeputte / P. Vincent /
T. Hermans
Dutch. The Language of Twenty Million Dutch and Flemish People.
Illustrated; 64 pp.

J.A. Kossmann-Putto &
E.H. Kossmann
The Low Countries. History of the Northern and Southern Netherlands.
Illustrated; 64 pp.

Jaap Goedegebuure &
Anne Marie Musschoot
Contemporary Fiction of the Low Countries.
Illustrated and with translated extracts from 15 novels; 128 pp.

Hugo Brems &
Ad Zuiderent
Contemporary Poetry of the Low Countries.
With 52 translated poems; 112 pp.